1991

Teaching Mathematics
to Children

Teaching Mathematics to Children

Robert J. Sovchik

The University of Akron

1817

HARPER & ROW, PUBLISHERS, New York
Cambridge, Philadelphia, San Francisco, London,
Mexico City, São Paulo, Singapore, Sydney

Sponsoring Editor: Alan McClare
Project Editor: Vivian Koenig
Text Design: Laura Ferguson
Cover Design: Jean Wycoff Tock
Text Art: ComCom Division of Haddon Craftsmen, Inc., and Fineline
  Illustrations Inc.
Production Manager: Jeanie Berke
Production Assistant: Beth Maglione
Compositor: ComCom Division of Haddon Craftsmen, Inc.
Printer and Binder: R. R. Donnelley & Sons Co.
Cover Printer: Lehigh Press

TEACHING MATHEMATICS TO CHILDREN

Library of Congress Cataloging-in-Publication Data

Sovchik, Robert.
  Teaching mathematics to children.

  Includes bibliographies and index.
  1. Mathematics—Study and teaching (Elementary)
I. Title.
QA135.5.S577 1989   372.7'2044   88-24278
ISBN 0-06-046385-6

88 89 90 91 9 8 7 6 5 4 3 2 1

This book is dedicated to Jim Sovchik.

Brief Contents

Detailed Contents   *ix*

1. Trends in Elementary School Mathematics Instruction   *1*
2. Managing the Elementary School Mathematics Classroom   *29*
3. Foundations for Beginning Mathematics   *57*
4. Numeration and Place-Value Concepts   *85*
5. Mathematics Anxiety   *111*
6. Teaching Mathematics to Exceptional Children in the Regular Classroom   *127*
7. Hand Calculators and Computers in Elementary School   *165*
8. Introducing Addition and Subtraction of Whole Numbers   *195*
9. Addition and Subtraction Algorithms   *229*
10. Teaching Problem-Solving Strategies   *255*
11. Introducing Multiplication and Division of Whole Numbers   *287*
12. Developing Understanding of Algorithms for Multiplication and Division   *315*
13. Fractions   *339*
14. Decimal Numeration and Operations   *369*
15. Ratio, Proportion, and Percent   *399*
16. Special Topics: Integers and Number Theory   *415*
17. Probability, Statistics, and Graphs   *433*
18. Measurement   *457*
19. Geometry   *487*
   Appendix A: Mathematics Exams   *515*
   Appendix B: Mathematics Material Suppliers   *519*
   Appendix C: Computer Software Publishers and Distributors   *523*
   Appendix D: Sample Children's Books   *531*

Index   *533*

Detailed Contents

Preface   *xxvii*

Chapter 1. **Trends in Elementary School Mathematics Instruction**   *1*

Mathematics Teaching Effectiveness   *2*
   Activity 1.1: Experiences with Math Teachers   3
Historical Trends in Elementary School Mathematics   *3*
Mathematics from 1955 to 1975   *6*
Mathematics from 1975 to the Present   *6*
   Activity 1.2: Basic Skills   8
Current Trends   *8*
   Problem Solving   *8*
   Activity 1.3: Nontraditional Problem Solving   9
   Activity 1.4: Planning to Solve a Problem   9
   Developing Mathematics from the Concrete Level to the
      Abstract Level   *9*
   Active Learning   *10*
   Hand Calculators   *10*
   Microcomputers and Estimation   *11*
   Activity 1.5: Estimating   12
   Activity 1.6: Microcomputer Decimal Equivalents   12
   Diagnosis and Corrective Teaching   *13*
   Activity 1.7: Diagnosing a Solution Strategy   13
   Geometry   *13*
   Activity 1.8: Symmetry   14
   Mathematics Attitudes and Equity   *14*

Activity 1.9: Improving Attitude   14

Activity 1.10: Hidden Assumptions   15

Mathematics Structure   *15*

Evaluation of Mathematics Programs   *15*

The Gifted Mathematics Student   *16*

Activity 1.11: Brain Teasers   16

Mainstreaming   *17*

Contemporary Learning Theories for Elementary School
  Mathematics   *17*

Preoperational Stage   *18*

Concrete Operations Stage   *19*

Formal Operations Stage   *19*

The Development of Concrete Operational Thinking   *19*

Activity 1.12: Conservation of Length   20

Activity 1.13: Reversing an Attribute of Time   21

Jerome Bruner   *21*

Activity 1.14: Classification   22

Activity 1.15: Retaining Information   22

Robert Gagne   *23*

B. F. Skinner   *24*

An Integration of Developmental and Learning Theorists   *24*

Summary   25

Discussion Questions   25

References   26

**Chapter 2.   Managing the Elementary School Mathematics
            Classroom**   *29*

Planning for Successful Management   *31*

Daily Lesson Plans   *32*

Objectives   *35*

Activity 2.1: Writing an Objective   35

Materials   *36*

Procedures   *36*

Activity 2.2: "Guess My Number"   36

Activity 2.3: Word Values   38

Evaluation   *38*

Sample Lesson Plan   *39*

Lesson Plan: Grade 1   *39*

Additional Classroom Management Strategies   *40*

Start Early to Manage Your Classroom   *40*

Utilize Bulletin Boards   *40*

Use a Microcomputer   *41*

Plan "Bell Work" Activities   *41*

Activity 2.4: Setting the Motivational Tone   41
Establish "Problems of the Week"   *41*
Activity 2.5: Problem of the Week   41
Use Praise Effectively   *42*
Hold a Recreational Mathematics Day   *42*
Contact Resource People   *42*
Modify Classroom Procedures   *43*
Involve Parents   *43*
Balance Group and Individual Management Strategies   *43*
Evaluation in the Mathematics Classroom   *45*
General Considerations   *45*
Informal Assessment Procedures   *47*
Daily Lessons   *47*
Interviews   *47*
Checklists   *48*
Teacher-Made Achievement Tests   *49*
Constructing Diagnostic Tests   *50*
Activity 2.6: Using Diagnostic Tests   51
Standardized Tests   *52*
Attitudes Toward Mathematics   *52*
Sentence Completion   52
Attitude Questionnaires   53

Summary   53
Discussion Questions   54
References   54

Chapter 3.   Foundations for Beginning Mathematics   *57*

Introduction   *58*
Expectations   *58*
Preformal Mathematics   *59*
Classification   *60*
Activity 3.1: Classification Skill   61
Activity 3.2: Classification by Shape   61
Activity 3.3: Classification by Attribute   62
Seriation   *62*
Patterns   *63*
Vocabulary   *63*
Summary   *64*
Numbers and Counting   *64*
Activity 3.4: One-to-One Correspondence   65
Activity 3.5: Number Comprehension   65
Activity 3.6: Auditory Counting   66
Activity 3.7: Pocket Chart   66

Order Relations   67
    Activity 3.8: Practicing Counting   69
    Activity 3.9: Practicing at the Semiconcrete Level   69
Numeral Formation   69
    Activity 3.10: Dominance Tests   70
Ordinal Numbers   70
    Activity 3.11: Ordinal Numbers   71
Time   71
    Activity 3.12: Relativity of Time   72
Money   73
Measurement   74
    Length   75
    Activity 3.13: Linear Measurement   76
    Activity 3.14: Arbitrary Measurement Units   76
    Weight (Mass)   76
    Capacity and Volume   77
    Activity 3.15: A Cooking Application of Measurement   78
    Temperature   78
Geometry   78
    Activity 3.16: Topological Concepts   79
Microcomputers   81
    Activity 3.17: Computer Usage   81

Summary   81
Discussion Questions   82
References   83

Chapter 4.   Numeration and Place-Value Concepts   *85*

Refinements of Counting   86
A Brief History of Numeration   87
    Hindu-Arabic Numeration   91
    Contemporary Place-Value Numeration   91
Strategies for Teaching Place-Value Concepts and Numeration   93
Initial Experiences   93
    Activity 4.1: The Banker's Game   94
Teaching Base-10 Place-Value Concepts   95
Developing Place-Value Concepts with Nonproportional
   Materials   98
Extending Numeration   99
    Activity 4.2: Place-Value Card Game   101
    Activity 4.3: Number Accordions   101
    Activity 4.4: Lunch Bag Pocket Charts   102
    Activity 4.5: Number Sequencing   102

Refinements of Place Value and Numeration   *103*
  Activity 4.6: Graph Paper Models   104
  Activity 4.7: Estimating and Grouping   105
  Activity 4.8: Estimation Strategies   105
  Activity 4.9: Estimating Strategies for Large Numbers   105
  Activity 4.10: Estimate the Price   106
  Activity 4.11: Great Numbers   107
  *Activity 4.12: Using a Thermometer to Show Greater-Valued
    Numbers   108*
  Activity 4.13: Diagnosing Place-Value Errors   108

Summary   108
Discussion Questions   109
References   109

Chapter 5.   Mathematics Anxiety   *111*

Introduction   *112*
Equity in Elementary School Mathematics   *112*
Measuring Mathematics Anxiety   *113*
  Activity 5.1: Assessment of Feelings About Mathematics   114
  Activity 5.2: Teacher's Level of Mathematics Anxiety   115
Characteristics of Mathematics Anxiety   *115*
Strategies for Coping with Mathematics Anxiety   *119*
  Activity 5.3: Alternative Solutions   120
  Activity 5.4: Organizing a Party's Budget   120
  Activity 5.5: Creative Responses   120
  Activity 5.6: Natural Breathing   120
  Activity 5.7: Progressive Relaxation   121
  Activity 5.8: Creative Imagery   121
  Activity 5.9: Solving Riddles   122
  Activity 5.10: Television Quiz   122
  Activity 5.11: Humorous Assumptions   123
  Activity 5.12: Estimating Movement   123

Summary   124
Discussion Questions   124
References   125

**Chapter 6.   Teaching Mathematics to Exceptional Children in the
    Regular Classroom   *127***

Teaching the Mildly Handicapped Student   *128*
  Specific Learning Disabilities (SLDs)   *129*
  Mild Mental Retardation   *130*

Activity 6.1: Standards for Special Education   *130*
Distractibility   *130*
Short Attention Span   *132*
Hyperactivity   *133*
Activity 6.2: Using Physical Exercise   *135*
Impulsivity   *135*
Auditory Perception   *136*
Visual Perception   *137*
Activity 6.3: Follow the Maze   *137*
Fine Motor Problems   *138*
Activity 6.4: Creative Worksheets   *139*
Reading Problems   *139*
Resistance to Change   *140*
Conceptual Difficulties   *140*
General Comments   *141*
Teaching the Gifted Mathematics Student   *142*
Characteristics of Gifted Mathematics Students   *143*
Activity 6.5: Measuring Creativity   *146*
Activity 6.6: Spatial Relationships   *147*
Activity 6.7: Similarities   *147*
Activity 6.8: More Spatial Relationships   *147*
Activity 6.9: Developing Creativity   *148*
Selection of Gifted Students   *148*
Teacher Attitudes   *149*
Program Options for Teaching the Gifted Mathematics
    Student   *151*
Strategies for Teaching the Gifted Mathematics
    Student   *153*
Activities for Teaching the Gifted Primary-grade
    Student (K–3)   *154*
Activity 6.10: Number Tricks   *156*
Activity 6.11: Hand Calculators   *156*
Activities for Teaching the Gifted Intermediate-grade Student
    (4–6)   *156*
Activity 6.12: Mathematical Patterns   *159*
Microcomputer Experiences for Gifted Mathematics
    Students   *159*
*Activity 6.13: Locating Suitable Software
    Programs*   *162*

Summary   162
Discussion Questions   162
References   163

Chapter 7.   Hand Calculators and Computers in Elementary School
         Mathematics   *165*

  Hand Calculators in Elementary School Mathematics
   Classrooms   *166*
  Pros and Cons of Hand Calculator Usage   *166*
  Criteria for Selecting a Hand Calculator   *168*
  Instructional Strategies for Using Hand Calculators   *169*
   Develop Understanding of Computational Algorithms
    and Mathematics Concepts   *169*
   Activity 7.1: Patterns in Decimal Multiplication   *169*
   Activity 7.2: Using a Calculator to Introduce Subtraction
    and Division   *169*
   Activity 7.3: Repeated-Addition Technique   *170*
   Formulate Generalizations from Number
    Patterns   *170*
   Activity 7.4: Patterns in Multiplication   *170*
   Activity 7.5: A Number Trick   *171*
   Activity 7.6: More Patterns in Multiplication   *171*
   Develop Problem-Solving Skills   *172*
   Activity 7.7: Number Operation   *172*
   Activity 7.8: Numbers That Resemble Words   *172*
   Activity 7.9: Collect and Interpret Data   *173*
   Activity 7.10: Strategies for Winning   *174*
   Reinforce Computational Practice   *174*
   Activity 7.11: Computational Practice   *174*
   Develop Estimation Skills   *175*
   Activity 7.12: Estimating Products and Quotients   *175*
   Activity 7.13: Estimating Percentages   *176*
   Activity 7.14: Estimating Area Size   *176*
   Solve Practical and Consumer-related Problems   *176*
   Activity 7.15: Averaging Test Scores   *176*
   Activity 7.16: Balancing a Checkbook   *176*
   Motivate Mathematical Curiosity   *176*
   Activity 7.17: Motivating Mathematical Curiosity   *177*
   Activity 7.18: Magic Squares   *178*
   Activity 7.19: Palindromes   *179*
  Microcomputers in Elementary School Mathematics
   Classrooms   *179*
  A Brief History and Examples of Social Uses of
   Computers   *180*
  Microcomputer Terminology   *181*
   Activity 7.20: Scrambled Computer Terms   *183*

Strategies for Using Microcomputers with Elementary School
    Children   *183*
        Drill and Practice Programs   *184*
        Tutorial Programs   *184*
        Problem-Solving Simulation   *184*
    Evaluation of Software   *185*
        Activity 7.21: Evaluating Microcomputer Software   188
    Sample BASIC Programs   *188*
    LOGO Experiences   *189*
        Activity 7.22: Collecting Microcomputer Materials   191

    Summary   191
    Discussion Questions   192
    References   192

**Chapter 8.   Introducing Addition and Subtraction of Whole
                Numbers**   *195*

    Introduction   *196*
    Preliminary Considerations   *197*
    Introducing Addition of Whole Numbers   *199*
        Materials and Strategies for Beginning Addition   *200*
        Activity 8.1: Envelope Computer Game   203
        Activity 8.2: Magic Squares   203
    Introducing Subtraction of Whole Numbers   *205*
        Materials and Strategies for Beginning Subtraction   *207*
        Activity 8.3: Deliver the Mail   209
        Activity 8.4: Introducing the Calculator   210
        Activity 8.5: Addition and Subtraction Envelopes   210
        Activity 8.6: Sunshine Subtraction   211
    Addition and Subtraction as Inverse Operations   *211*
    Vertical Format for Addition and Subtraction   *212*
    Basic Properties for Operations   *212*
    Organizing and Memorizing the Basic Facts of Addition and
        Subtraction   *214*
        Activity 8.7: How Children Think   215
        Estimation Strategies   *219*
        General Comments   *220*
        Activity 8.8: Computer-Assisted Memorization   221
        Activity 8.9: Matching Domino Cards   222
        Activity 8.10: Concentration   223
        Activity 8.11: Math Match   224
        Activity 8.12: Less Is More   224
        Activity 8.13: Matho   225
        Activity 8.14: Number Cards   225

Summary   226
Discussion Questions   226
References   227

Chapter 9.   Addition and Subtraction Algorithms   *229*

Introduction   *230*
Developing Addition Algorithms   *230*
Sample Sequence for Addition   *230*
Developing Non-Regrouping Addition Examples   *231*
Activity 9.1: Find the Number Pattern   233
Activity 9.2: Bottle Cap Math Practice   234
Activity 9.3: Teacher's Assessments   234
Developing Regrouping Addition Examples   *235*
Activity 9.4: Teacher–Child Interaction   237
Activity 9.5: Search for Palindromes   238
Activity 9.6: Identify Patterns in the Calendar   238
Activity 9.7: Greater Sum Game   239
Estimation Strategies for Addition   *239*
Activity 9.8: Compensation Strategies   240
Developing Subtraction Algorithms   *241*
Sample Sequence for Subtraction   *241*
The Methods of Decomposition and Equal Addition   *242*
Developing Non-Regrouping Subtraction Examples   *243*
Developing Regrouping Subtraction Examples   *244*
Activity 9.9: Diffy Board   246
Activity 9.10: Diagnosing Subtraction Errors   248
Activity 9.11: Concrete Modeling of Subtraction   248
Activity 9.12: Hangman   248
Estimation Strategies for Subtraction   *249*
Activity 9.13: Equation Loop   250
Activity 9.14: How Much Is the Check?   251
Activity 9.15: Calculator Estimation   251
Activity 9.16: Find More Patterns   252

Summary   252
Discussion Questions   253
References   253

Chapter 10.   Teaching Problem-Solving Strategies   *255*

Introduction   *256*
Developing a Classroom Environment for Problem Solving   *257*

Characteristics of Good Problem Solvers *258*
A Model for Solving Problems *259*
    Problem-Solving Strategies and Sample Problems *261*
    Activity 10.1: Make a Graph 263
    Activity 10.2: Make a Table 264
    Activity 10.3: Patterns with a Hand Calculator 266
    Activity 10.4: Make a Diagram 267
    Activity 10.5: Guess and Check 272
    Activity 10.6: Work Backward 274
    Activity 10.7: Find Another Solution 276
    Activity 10.8: Think of Imaginative Solutions 277
    Activity 10.9: Identify Given and Wanted Information 278
    Activity 10.10: Estimate the Discounted Price 279
    Supplementary Strategies for Standard Textbook
        Problems *279*
    Activity 10.11: Tic-Tac-Toe 282
    Activity 10.12: Invent a Word Problem 283

Summary 283
Discussion Questions 284
References 285

**Chapter 11. Introducing Multiplication and Division of Whole
                Numbers**   *287*

Introduction *288*
Introducing Multiplication of Whole Numbers *289*
    Set Model *289*
    Array Model *290*
    Repeated Addition *290*
    Number Line *290*
    Number Balance *290*
    Situation Cards *291*
    Activity 11.1: Using Concrete Materials 292
    Activity 11.2: Finger Multiplication 293
    Vocabulary and Symbolism *293*
    Activity 11.3: Trace a Path of Multiples 294
Properties of Multiplication *295*
    Commutative Property of Multiplication *295*
    Associative Property of Multiplication *295*
    Identity Element *295*
Introducing Division of Whole Numbers *295*
Measurement and Partitive Division *296*
    Activity 11.4: Role Playing 297
    Relating Division to Multiplication *297*

Activity 11.5: Cuisenaire Rods   *298*
Repeated Subtraction   *299*
Number Line   *299*
Terminology and Symbolism   *299*
Basic Multiplication Facts   *301*
Activity 11.6: Array Game   *302*
Activity 11.7: Math Bingo   *303*
Activity 11.8: Review of Basic Facts Game   *303*
Activity 11.9: Punch and Check   *305*
Activity 11.10: Tic-Tac-Toe   *306*
Basic Division Facts   *306*
Activity 11.11: Board Games   *308*
Activity 11.12: Division Squares   *308*
Activity 11.13: Math Marks   *309*
Activity 11.14: Computer-Assisted Division   *309*
Activity 11.15: Division Track   *310*
Checking Division by Multiplication   *310*

Summary   311
Discussion Questions   311
References   312

Chapter 12.   Developing Understanding of Algorithms for
              Multiplication and Division   *315*

Introduction   *316*
Developing Multiplication Algorithms   *316*
Activity 12.1: Russian Peasant Multiplication   *316*
Multiplying 1- and 2-Place Numbers   *318*
Multiplying Two 2-Place Numbers   *322*
*Activity 12.2: An Application of Multiplication and
    Division*   *324*
Activity 12.3: Lattice Method of Multiplication   *325*
Estimation Strategies for Multiplication   *326*
Activity 12.4: Estimation of Products   *327*
Developing Division Algorithms   *327*
Modeling Division Examples   *328*
*Activity 12.5: Analyzing and Correcting Students'
    Errors*   *333*
*Activity 12.6: More Ways to Diagnose and Correct Students'
    Errors*   *334*
Division with Remainders   *334*
Estimation Strategies for Division   *335*
Activity 12.7: Creating a Lesson Plan   *335*
Activity 12.8: Computer Factors   *336*

Summary   336
Discussion Questions   336
References   337

Chapter 13.   Fractions   *339*

Introduction   *340*
Beginning Activities and Concepts   *340*
  Fraction Models   *340*
  Activity 13.1: Tic-Tac-Toe Fractions   342
  The Concept of Order   *343*
  Equivalent Fractions   *344*
  Activity 13.2: Trace the Maze   346
  Activity 13.3: Match the Squares   347
  Activity 13.4: Match the Popsicle Sticks   347
  Activity 13.5: Make a Whole   348
  Simplifying Fractions   *351*
  From Concrete to Abstract Experiences   *352*
  Transforming Mixed Numerals to Improper Fractions   *353*
Introducing Addition and Subtraction of Fractions   *354*
  Activity 13.6: Fraction Baseball   358
  Activity 13.7: Fraction Addition   359
  Activity 13.8: Diagnosing Errors   360
Introducing Multiplication of Fractions   *360*
  Activity 13.9: Fractional Magic Square   362
Introducing Division of Fractions   *362*
  Activity 13.10: Using 4 Threes   365
  Activity 13.11: Fractional Time   366

Summary   366
Discussion Questions   366
References   367

Chapter 14.   Decimal Numeration and Operations   *369*

Introduction   *370*
Beginning Decimal Concepts   *370*
  Ordering Decimals   *372*
  Activity 14.1: Trace a Path of Decimals   373
  Activity 14.2: Number Accordion   373
  Equivalent Decimals   *374*
  Activity 14.3: Creative Decimal Models   375
  Activity 14.4: Tic-Tac-Toe Decimals   375
  Reading Decimals   *375*

Activity 14.5: Reading Decimals with a Calculator   *376*
Transforming Decimal Numbers to Common Fractions   *377*
Transforming Fractions to Decimals   *377*
Addition and Subtraction of Decimal Numbers   *380*
Activity 14.6: Magic Square   *384*
Activity 14.7: Trace a Path   *385*
Multiplication of Decimal Numbers   *385*
Activity 14.8: Spinning Decimals   *388*
Division of Decimal Numbers   *389*
Activity 14.9: Math Rummy   *393*
Estimating Decimal Quotients   *394*
Activity 14.10: Calculator-Assisted Estimation   *394*
Activity 14.11: Estimating to Find the Problem   *395*
Exponential and Scientific Notation   *395*

Summary   397
Discussion Questions   397
References   398

Chapter 15.   Ratio, Proportion, and Percent   *399*

Introduction   *400*
Introducing the Concepts of Ratio and Proportion   *400*
Introducing the Concept of Percent   *402*
Activity 15.1: Misleading Uses of Percents   *404*
Using Ratios to Solve Percent Problems   *405*
Activity 15.2: Percent by Ratio and Proportion   *408*
Activity 15.3: An Application of Percent   *408*
Activity 15.4: Another Application of Percent   *408*
Applications of Percent—Estimation Strategies   *408*
Activity 15.5: Calculator Percents   *409*
Activity 15.6: Rummy Card Game   *409*
Relationships Among Fractions, Decimals, and Percents   *410*
Activity 15.7: Concentration   *410*
Activity 15.8: Computer-Assisted Percent Calculation   *410*

Summary   411
Discussion Questions   411
References   412

Chapter 16.   Special Topics: Integers and Number Theory   *415*

Introduction   *416*
Integers   *416*
Properties of Integers   *416*
Addition and Subtraction of Integers   *417*

Activity 16.1: Integer Nomograph   417
Activity 16.2: Name Positive 4   418
Multiplication and Division of Integers   *421*
Activity 16.3: Story Problems   423
Number Theory   *423*
  Prime and Composite Numbers   *423*
  Activity 16.4: Factoring Composite Numbers   425
  Activity 16.5: Problem Solving   426
  Finding the Greatest Common Factor by Using Prime
    Numbers   *427*
  Finding the Least Common Multiple by Prime
    Factorization   *427*
  Activity 16.6: Goldbach's Conjecture   428
  Activity 16.7: Triangular Numbers   428
  Activity 16.8: Number Curiosities   429
  Activity 16.9: Number Tricks   429
  Tests of Divisibility   *429*

Summary   430
Discussion Questions   431
References   431

Chapter 17.   Probability, Statistics, and Graphs   *433*

Introduction   *434*
Probability   *434*
  Primary-Grade Instruction   *434*
  Intermediate-Grade Instruction   *435*
  Activity 17.1: Find the Most Common Letter   438
  Activity 17.2: Favorite Numbers   438
  Activity 17.3: Computer-Assisted Probability Calculations   439
  Pascal's Triangle   *439*
  Activity 17.4: Simulation Game   441
Statistics   *442*
  Activity 17.5: Predicting Proportions   447
  Activity 17.6: Collecting Data   448
  Activity 17.7: Statistical Mistakes   448
  Activity 17.8: Computer-Assisted Statistical Calculations   448
Graphs   *449*
  Bar Graphs   *449*
  Line Graphs   *450*
  Circle Graphs   *451*
  Coordinate Graphs   *451*
  Activity 17.9: Monte Carlo Simulation   452

Activity 17.10: Graphing Stock Market Fluctuations   453
Activity 17.11: Find the Graph's Message   454

Summary   454
Discussion Questions   455
References   455

Chapter 18.   Measurement   *457*

Introduction   *458*
A Brief History of Measurement   *459*
    Development of the Metric System   *461*
    Activity 18.1: Metric Proverbs   464
Guidelines for Teaching Measurement to Children   *465*
Metric Measurement Experiences   *465*
    Primary-Grade Students (K–3)   *465*
    Activity 18.2: Outdoor Mathematics   467
    Activity 18.3: Spin a Meter   467
    Intermediate-Grade Students (4–8)   *468*
    Activity 18.4: Metric Weights of Common Items   469
    Activity 18.5: Metric Volumes of Common Items   470
    Activity 18.6: Metric Measurements of Height   470
    Activity 18.7: Metric Measurements of Weight   471
Conversions Within the Metric System   *471*
    Perimeter   *473*
    Area   *473*
    *Activity 18.8: Estimating the Area of Irregularly Shaped
        Objects*   474
    Volume   *474*
Customary Units of Measurement   *475*
    Length   *475*
    Activity 18.9: Measurement Scavenger Hunt   475
    Activity 18.10: Personal Data—Customary Units   476
    Units of Capacity   *477*
    *Activity 18.11: Estimating Liquid Capacities of Common
        Objects*   478
    Weight   *479*
    *Activity 18.12: Estimating the Weight of Common
        Objects*   479
    Activity 18.13: Personal Data   480
    Activity 18.14: Concentration   480
    Temperature   *481*
    Activity 18.15: Measurement Stories   481
    Perimeter, Area, and Volume   *482*

Activity 18.16: BASIC Program for Finding the Perimeter and
    Area of a Rectangle   483
Sample Lesson Plan   *483*

Summary   484
Discussion Questions   485
References   485

Chapter 19.   Geometry   ***487***

Introduction   *488*
Early Geometric Experiences   *488*
    Activity 19.1: Constructing Geometric Shapes   489
    Activity 19.2: Exploring Symmetric Designs   490
Introducing Geometric Concepts   *490*
    Points, Lines, and Planes   *490*
    Activity 19.3: Geometric Problem Solving   491
    Angles   *492*
    Activity 19.4: Identifying Angles and Lines   493
    Activity 19.5: Make a Clinometer   493
    Open and Closed Curves   *494*
    Polygons   *495*
    Activity 19.6: Sum of the Angles of a Triangle   497
    Activity 19.7: A Hands-on Method for Showing That a Triangle
     Has 180°   497
    Circles   *497*
    Activity 19.8: A Circle Problem   498
    Further Study of Solids   *499*
    Activity 19.9: Discover Euler's Formula   500
Introducing the Concept of Congruence   *500*
    Angles   *501*
    Line Segments   *501*
    Polygons   *501*
    Activity 19.10: Symmetrical Lines   503
    Activity 19.11: Tangrams   503
    Activity 19.12: Geometric Shadows   504
The Development of Perimeter and Area   *504*
    Perimeter   *505*
    Activity 19.13: Perimeter Problems   506
    Area of Squares and Rectangles   *506*
    Area of Parallelograms   *507*
    Area of Triangles   *508*
    Area of Circles   *508*
    Surface Areas   *509*

Activity 19.14: Geometric Visualizations *510*
Volume of Solids *510*
Activity 19.15: Spatial Relationships *511*
Activity 19.16: Computer Graphics *511*

Summary 512
Discussion Questions 512
References 513

Appendix A.   Mathematics Exams   *515*

Appendix B.   Mathematics Material Suppliers   *519*

Appendix C.   Computer Software Publishers and Distributors   *523*

Appendix D.   Sample Children's Books   *531*

Index   *533*

Preface

With the advanced technology and service economy of the postindustrial era, drill and repetitive computations can no longer serve as the foundation of mathematical education. Today, children need to learn to think critically, to examine and experiment, and to have meaning emphasized in their mathematics study. This book exists to help pre-service and in-service elementary school teachers do these in their classes.

Contemporary children are vastly different from their predecessors: They are more influenced by the media, particularly television, and they have a variety of emotional needs because of changing family structures. Mathematics teachers are therefore challenged to provide more emotional support and guidance than their counterparts of a decade ago.

To meet the needs of children from a multitude of backgrounds, this book takes an eclectic approach to theory and combines it with practice. Emphasis is placed on developing a variety of methods to meet the demands of diverse groups of children and school situations.

Changes in technology have caused educators to rethink the elements that comprise an effective elementary school mathematics curriculum. Topics such as estimation and problem solving are increasingly important aspects of the elementary mathematics curriculum. This book has been developed with these developments in mind. Topics in this book are consistent with recommendations of the National Council of Teachers of Mathematics in *An Agenda for Action* as well as the more recent proposed *Standards for Mathematics Education*.

This book offers a wealth of unique features. It includes a chapter on managing the elementary school classroom, because before children can learn mathematics a positive climate of expectations, both personal and environmental, must be established. Suggestions for maintaining a positive classroom climate and preventing discipline problems are offered in this chapter. There is also a chapter on mathematics anxiety. Numerous psychological studies were examined so that a valuable affective dimension of instruction is emphasized. Further, the increasing examples of mainstreaming in public schools and emphasis on gifted education demanded a chapter that highlights the teaching strategies for these special students.

Technology has been emphasized with a chapter on hand calculators and computers. Throughout the book, sample programs in the BASIC language are provided so that teacher education students have the option of collecting and preserving these programs on a disk to use later with elementary students. Finally, an extended problem-solving chapter emphasizes "process" problems and strategies as well as traditional verbal problems.

The text is organized to emphasize student involvement. Each chapter begins with a list of objectives that focuses the main themes of the chapter and ends with discussion questions that extend and amplify these themes. Interspersed throughout the chapters are historical notes that point out pertinent historical facts about selected chapter topics. Also, each chapter contains activities that review, reinforce, or apply the methodology considered in the chapter. These activities can be used by college students to help them master the material in the chapter, and they can be easily adapted for use by elementary school students. In this way they can become part of the college student's file of activities for later use.

This book is designed to help pre-service and in-service teachers teach meaningful mathematics to today's elementary students. However, the ultimate litmus test of any methods text is the degree to which it serves as a stimulus for college students and professors to interact as they investigate children's development of mathematical thinking.

The process of writing this text involved revising and editing the material with the aid of reviewers who offered constructive and insightful observations. Many of their suggestions were incorporated into the final work. I am grateful for the contributions made by the following mathematics educators: Charles Allen, University of Pittsburgh; Catherine Brown, Virginia Polytechnic Institute; Jon Engelhardt, Arizona State University; Virginia Harvin, Indiana University; Carol Larson, University of Arizona; and Walter Secada, University of Wisconsin.

Also, I wish to thank the following people for their personal or professional contributions to the creation of this book: Mary Sartoris, John Sovchik, Katherine Sovchik, Alice Christie, and Roberta Owen Reese. In particular, Dr. Christie made valuable contributions to the section concerned with teaching the mildly handicapped student.

ROBERT J. SOVCHIK

Teaching Mathematics
to Children

CHAPTER 1

Trends in Elementary School Mathematics Instruction

Objectives

After reading this chapter you will be able to:

1. Describe several procedures and interaction styles of effective mathematics teachers.

2. List several current trends in elementary school mathematics.

3. Explain the contributions that several learning theorists have made to the study of elementary school mathematics.

4. Compare and contrast several historical trends in elementary school mathematics instruction.

5. Identify several basic skills that are relevant to the contemporary teaching of elementary school mathematics.

Mathematics Teaching Effectiveness

Teaching mathematics is an important contribution to our world. The effort and creative challenge of teaching children in an age of rapid technological and social change is, indeed, a noble activity. Mathematics is seen in all walks of life, from the scientific advances in space flight to the computerized checkout counter at the neighborhood supermarket. It is important to view mathematics as a significant part of our culture, not only for its valuable scientific applications but also for its enrichment of our cultural life. We use mathematical thinking when we play bridge, determine batting averages, estimate budgets, and design clothing styles. This book will equip you with skills and values for effectively teaching mathematics to elementary school children.

As one prepares to teach elementary school mathematics, it can be valuable to reflect upon one's personal experience as a mathematics student. We can all, hopefully, remember creative, spontaneously exciting mathematics classes. On the other hand, we might also remember mathematics classes which seemed dull and meaningless. Rote computational procedures with little meaningful teaching seem to characterize these negative experiences. To a great extent, our images of mathematics classes, based on our personal experience, has a strong influence on our future mathematics teaching style.

There are several characteristics of the instructional procedures and interaction styles that good teachers use. Hamacheck (1975) has compiled a research summary of these strategies. Good teachers tend to be flexible, to have a willingness to experiment, to display knowledge of subject matter, and to be able to reflect an appreciative attitude to their students in the form of nods, smiles, and positive comments. They can see the world from their students' point of view, and they perceive themselves as identified with people rather than withdrawn or alienated from others.

A complete list of these characteristics is presented below.

1. Willingness to be flexible, to be direct or indirect as the students demand

2. Ability to perceive the world from the students' point of view

3. Ability to personalize their teaching

4. Willingness to experiment

5. Skill in asking questions

6. Knowledge of subject matter and related areas

7. Provision of well-established examination procedures

8. Provision of definite study help

9. Reflection of an appreciative attitude (nods, smiles, comments)

10. Use of conversational matter in teaching—informal, easy style

Recalling your own mathematics instruction experiences is important because it can yield a general guideline for change (see Activity 1.1). If your history of mathematics instruction has been favorable, then you can build new skills and content to enrich the solid base. However, even if you had negative experiences, you can resolve to avoid these erroneous styles of teaching and interacting. That alone can be corrective, but if, in addition, new learning of mathematics can be undertaken, the result will be more positive.

ACTIVITY 1.1   Experiences with Math Teachers

This activity is designed to help you clarify your experiences with mathematics teachers.

Use the list of good teacher characteristics to recall five experiences you had in mathematics classes that helped you to learn mathematics. Also, think of five experiences that negatively influenced your mathematics learning. Share these with a friend. Use your lists to develop an image of the kind of elementary school mathematics teacher that you would like to be.

Historical Trends in Elementary School Mathematics

Elementary mathematics instruction has undergone great change over the last 200 years. An example of this is found by considering the content of a once popular book, first published in 1788, by Nicholas Pike. Entitled *A New and Complete System of Arithmetic,* Pike's textbook had as its major goal the mastery of long, laborious computational rules. For example, students were taught to add up to twelve 10-digit numbers but developed no understanding of the process; they learned only the blind repetition of rules of calculation.

For the most part, the major goal of elementary school mathematics instruction in the first half of the nineteenth century was computation—computation involving large numbers and repetitious rules (NCTM, 1973). Perhaps a notable exception to this was the elementary mathematics textbook by Warren Colburn which was published in 1821. Colburn's book, entitled *First Lessons in Arithmetic,* attempted to provide physical experiences for the learner instead of a rote repetition of rules. Tactile, concrete experience with objects was emphasized as a means for developing mathematics concepts. In fact, Colburn advocated what might be called a *diagnostic approach* to teaching mathematics, shifting the emphasis from rules to be memorized to the learner's methods of solution.

=== *MATH HISTORY 1.1* ===

The first appearance in print of our present plus (+) and minus (−) signs was in an arithmetic, published in Leipzig in 1489 by Johannes Widman. The symbols did not refer to operations, but indicated excess and deficiency.

Although much mathematics instruction toward the end of the nineteenth century remained rule centered and computationally oriented, often called a *mental-discipline approach,* influences began to be heard which reinforced the teaching ideas of Colburn. G. Stanley Hall, one of the first child psychologists, began advocating a child-centered curriculum in the elementary school. William James (1905), another early psychologist, also favored a teaching approach that viewed the child's interests, needs, and experiences as important considerations for the elementary teacher.

Here are some examples of James's teaching suggestions:

> Begin with the line of his native interests, and offer him objects that have some immediate connection with these. . . . Next, step by step, connect with these first objects and experiences the latter objects and ideas which you wish to instill. Associate the new with the old in some natural and telling way, so that the interest being shed along from point to point, finally suffuses the entire system of objects of thought.

Thus, the emerging twentieth century brought with it the gradual acceptance of the child as an important part of the learning process. Exerting a force on the teaching of mathematics in the first quarter of the century was the *connectionism theory* of E. L. Thorndike. Thorndike placed great emphasis on speed, accuracy, and memorization in order to ensure that basic facts such as 8×9 would be recalled. Understanding these facts did not rate a very high priority in Thorndike's early connectionism theory. Drill became an important component of elementary school mathematics instruction.

Opposing Thorndike's connectionism theory was the mathematics instruction approach of William Brownell. In a major article written in 1947, Brownell summarized his 20-year-long position advocating meaning and understanding in elementary school mathematics:

The chief reason for our vital interest in arithmetical meanings is to be found, I think, in the demonstrated failure of relatively meaningless programs. The latter programs have not produced the kind of arithmetic competence required for intelligent adjustment to our culture. Evidence of this failure has been accumulating from several sources. (p. 259)

Brownell felt that meaningful mathematics instruction would help children retain mathematical ideas and avoid making absurd statements like

$$
\begin{array}{r}
24 \\
+7 \\
\hline
211
\end{array} \; .
$$

Brownell wanted children to understand that 24 could be named as 2 tens and 4 ones and that a regrouping was occurring from the ones to the tens place. In short, he wanted children to explain verbally what they were doing with mathematics.

====================== *MATH HISTORY 1.2** ======================

A 1915 school department manual contained these rules:

1. Do not get married.
2. Do not keep company with men.
3. Be home between 8 P.M. and 6 A.M. unless attending a school function.
4. Do not loiter downtown in ice cream stores.
5. Do not leave town at any time without permission of the school board.
6. Do not smoke.
7. Do not get into a carriage with any man except your father or brother.
8. Do not dye your hair.
9. Do not dress in bright colors.
10. Do not wear any dress more than two inches above the ankle.
11. Always wear at least two petticoats.
12. Keep the school room neat and clean. Sweep the floor at least once daily. Scrub the floor at least once weekly. Clean the blackboards once a day, and start a good fire at 7 A.M. daily.

*Source: Instructor, Aug./Sept. 1973, p. 54. Used with permission of The Instructor Publications, Inc.

Mathematics from 1955 to 1975

Many people characterize the period from about 1955 to 1975 as the era of "new math" (estimates of these years may vary). Prior to the Soviet Union's launching of *Sputnik* in 1957, some experimental mathematics curriculum programs were in existence in the United States. For example, Dr. Max Beberman formed the University of Illinois Committee on School Mathematics in 1951. However, the launching of Sputnik tended to unite public opinion on the need to establish strong mathematics and science programs at all grade levels.

During the 1950s and 1960s, many experimental elementary school mathematics curricula were developed. Many of these originated at universities and gradually affected the content of elementary school mathematics textbooks. The general public began to call the developments in elementary school mathematics the "new math."

Just what was this new math? For one thing, the mathematical content appearing in elementary mathematics textbooks was modified. The study of sets was emphasized, but the idea had been around since the late 1800s. Stress was placed on the term "mathematics structure," which emphasized number systems, such as the whole numbers $\{0, 1, 2, 3, 4, . . .\}$ and related properties of operations, such as the commutative property of addition. Other number bases such as base 8 and base 6 were taught. Even in the primary grades children were taught to be more conscious of number sentences written in the form $2 + \square = 8$. Although the mathematical content appearing in elementary school textbooks was well known by mathematicians, there was a decidedly different elementary school textbook design in the 1960s as opposed to that in previous decades of the twentieth century. There was also a view of instruction that placed great emphasis on guided discovery instead of lecturing. Children were urged to discover mathematical patterns and relationships.

There is some suggestion that even though elementary school textbooks emphasized these "new" topics, the teaching style of these topics left much to be desired. The new approaches to mathematics materials were sometimes criticized as being more formal, more difficult to read, and more concerned with mathematical terms than children's developmental stages warranted (NACOME, 1975).

Mathematics from 1975 to the Present

By the mid-1970s a public reaction to innovative programs in education had set in. "Back to basics" became a rallying cry among many critics of education. In mathematics, concern was raised about children's performance on tests. At the high school level there was much discussion about declining SAT scores for the period 1963–1975.

A back-to-basics movement which seemed to emphasize computational skill, teacher lectures, and strict discipline was advocated by some conservative groups. However, it was never very clear just what basic education consisted of. Should mathematics in the elementary school be taught as it was in 1850? What should the role be of hand calculators, computers, problem solving, and geometry in a basic skills program? Since technological change had occurred so rapidly, it seemed unfair to educate children as they had been educated in 1850. In fact, omitting current topics and just teaching computational skills could be a step backward and an avoidance of social responsibility to the next generation.

John Naisbitt, in *Megatrends* (1982), has stated that approximately 600,000 new companies are created each year. The skills needed for jobs with these firms require thoughtful workers oriented to problem solving. There are few jobs being created which require that an applicant perform rapid numerical computation as a prerequisite to being hired. Most hiring seems to be in the burgeoning information processing industry, with less being done in traditional manufacturing. Thus, mathematical problem solving, applications, and the ability to use critical thinking skills become very important.

Responding to the concerns of citizen groups, in 1977 the National Council of Supervisors of Mathematics (NCSM) developed an expanded list of basic skills which seemed relevant to the later stages of the twentieth century. These ten basic skills are listed below:

1. Problem solving
2. Applying mathematics to everyday situations
3. Alertness to the reasonableness of results
4. Estimation and approximation
5. Appropriate computational skills
6. Geometry
7. Measurement
8. Reading, interpreting, and constructing tables, charts, and graphs
9. Using mathematics to make predictions
10. Computer literacy

The mathematics supervisors went further, describing methods of instruction as follows:

> Certainly drill and practice is a viable option, but it is only one of many possible ways to bring about learning and to create interest and motivation in students. Learning centers, contracts, tutorial sessions, individual and small group projects, games, simulations and community-based activities are some of the other options that can

provide the opportunity to learn basic skills. Furthermore, to help students fully understand basic mathematical concepts, teachers should utilize the full range of activities and materials available, including objects the student can actually handle. (NCSM, 1977, pp. 21–22)

In summary, a broadened interpretation of basic skills in mathematics provides a plan for elementary school mathematics programs that enables children to acquire understanding and skill for living in the last quarter of the twentieth century (see Activity 1.2).

ACTIVITY 1.2   Basic Skills

This activity is designed to broaden your concept of what basic skills in mathematics mean.

Take a few minutes and list what you think are some of the basic skills in elementary school mathematics. Compare your list to the list compiled by the National Council of Supervisors of Mathematics. How many categories do your skills consider? What areas are you omitting?

Current Trends

The 1980s have witnessed a new revolution in elementary school mathematics. Technological change in the form of hand calculators and microcomputers has greatly changed the elementary school mathematics curriculum. These major trends are described in the next sections.

Problem Solving

In its *Agenda for Action* (1980a) the National Council of Teachers of Mathematics (NCTM) recommended that problem solving be the focus of school mathematics throughout the decade. The approach to problem solving involves applying mathematics to the real world but also emphasizes the future. A wide range of knowledge, skills, and unifying relationships is the goal of this priority. Students need to learn strategies that will help them do the following:

1. Formulate key questions
2. Analyze and conceptualize problems
3. Define the problem and the goal
4. Discover patterns and similarities

5. Seek out appropriate data

6. Experiment

7. Transfer skills and strategies to new situations

8. Draw on background knowledge to apply mathematics. (NCTM, 1980a)

Problem solving is viewed more broadly than traditional "story" problems. Puzzles, geometric problems, and games may be vehicles for nontraditional problems (see Activities 1.3 and 1.4). Since hand calculators and microcomputers are reducing the need for long paper-and-pencil computations, problem solving is seen as a means of coping with future change.

ACTIVITY 1.3   Nontraditional Problem Solving

This activity represents an example of a nontraditional problem-solving experience.

Move exactly three chips so that the triangular shape is pointed downward.

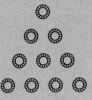

ACTIVITY 1.4   Planning to Solve a Problem

Here is another problem-solving activity which emphasizes planning.

Develop a plan for determining how much $2 million weighs.

Developing Mathematics from the Concrete Level to the Abstract Level

Although it is not a new trend, most elementary school textbook writers advocate teaching mathematics concepts in the elementary school through three stages: (1) a concrete level, (2) a semiconcrete level, and (3) an abstract level. For example, let us consider $3 + 2 = 5$.

Initially you could use an overhead projector to show a set of three chips and a set of two chips.

Now join these two groups. The result is five.

Children should have chips at their desks so that they can manipulate objects representing various beginning addition sentences. After many experiences manipulating objects at the concrete level, children are ready for the semiconcrete stage of concept development.

At the semiconcrete level, pictures of objects are presented and associated with sentences such as $3 + 2 = 5$. Finally, at the abstract level, students are expected to read and write $3 + 2 = 5$. Practice activities for memorizing these facts are then performed.

Whenever possible, this approach to mathematics instruction at the elementary school level is advocated to help children understand concepts and then develop skill with operations.

Active Learning

The research of Piaget and others has emphasized that from a developmental standpoint children need to be active participants in the learning process. Lectures and examples are important, but a greater proportion of time in elementary school mathematics classes needs to be allocated for concrete manipulation of objects, experimenting and collecting data, forming questions, and verifying results. Children at the elementary school level simply cannot sit for 30 minutes and pay attention to a teacher talking (research also finds that adults have a hard time paying attention to a 30-minute lecture). For example, McLeish (1968) reported that adults retained 40 percent of the information presented during the first 15 minutes of a lecture. Those who listened to 30 and 45 minutes of the same presentation were able to retain only 20 percent of the material.

Hand Calculators

The widespread availability of hand calculators makes it fundamental to utilize the hand calculator in elementary school mathematics classes. Hand calculators are useful for more than checking computations. Creative uses of the hand calculator to enhance problem solving, real-world applications, and number patterns need to be developed. Specific techniques for using a hand calculator to foster these skills will be discussed later in this book. Also, at various points in this text, hand calculator activities are included to show how the hand calculator can be used to enhance the learning of mathematics concepts.

Microcomputers and Estimation

The development of microcomputers has dramatically influenced the elementary school mathematics program. Morsund (1982) reported that over 90 percent of the school districts in the United States made some educational use of computers. The same report claimed that 100,000 computers were in elementary schools as of October 1982. More recently, the NCTM's Commission on Standards for School Mathematics (1987) made recommendations for elementary school mathematics which assumed that every elementary school student could have access to a microcomputer for individual work.

Schools are attempting to develop computer literacy courses for students; some of these are aimed at the primary school level. At this point, there is no universal agreement on what should be taught in these programs. Some courses teach children how to write programs; others emphasize the use of commercial software which requires minimal knowledge of computer operation. Still other courses emphasize the historical, cultural, and industrial aspects of the microcomputer.

One generalization seems quite clear: The day and age when long, laborious paper-and-pencil computations were necessary is over. Surely elementary students *need to memorize basic facts* and perform *routine* calculations with paper and pencil. However, the National Council of Teachers of Mathematics (1980a) has questioned the value of having children practice paper-and-pencil calculations with examples such as 3841 × 937.

The influence of computers and hand calculators on mathematics seems to require that more classroom time be spent on estimation and problem-solving activities. In other words, the answer to our previous example of 3841 × 937 is *about* 3,600,000. Now students will be able to tell whether their hand calculator or microcomputer is malfunctioning, but they are freed from the drudgery of long computations (see Activity 1.5).

Also, problem-solving activities can now be stressed. Students can collect and organize data, interpret information, and use charts and diagrams to display results. These and other problem-solving strategies and activities will be developed in the chapter on problem solving.

In many of the chapters of this text, a sample microcomputer program is provided to show how such programs can be integrated into the elementary school mathematics curriculum (see Activity 1.6). Interested readers may choose to copy some of these programs onto a disk and thus record a sample of microcomputer programs for teaching elementary school mathematics.

=========================== *MATH HISTORY 1.3* ===========================

One of the first computers was built by Howard H. Aiken of Harvard University in 1939. The computer consisted of a panel 51 feet long and 8 feet high on which were mounted the tape readers, relays, and rotary systems that controlled the machine.

ACTIVITY 1.5   Estimating

Estimation is an important daily life skill. Try this activity, which is designed for use with elementary school pupils.

Estimate the total of this grocery bill:

Meat	$ 2.89	
Meat	1.99	
Grocery	.79	Don't add—*estimate*
Grocery	2.09	
Produce	.84	
Produce	1.01	
TAX	.48	

ACTIVITY 1.6   Microcomputer Decimal Equivalents

This sample program prints out decimal equivalents for simple fractions. It is written in the BASIC computer language. A program such as this can be an alternative vehicle for reviewing fraction and decimal equivalents.

```
 5    REM DECIMAL EQUIVALENT
10    PRINT: ''THIS PROGRAM PRINTS OUT DECIMAL EQUIVALENTS
      FOR SIMPLE FRACTIONS''
20    PRINT: PRINT
30    PRINT: ''DENOMINATOR?''
```

```
40    INPUT D
50    FOR X = I TO D
60    PRINT X; ''/''; D; ''=''; X/D
70    NEXT X
80    PRINT: PRINT
90    END
```

Diagnosis and Corrective Teaching

Diagnosis and corrective teaching is not really a new trend, but it has been reemphasized in recent years. Attempting to locate the learner's solution strategies for mathematics exercises and problems and then using a variety of techniques and materials to correct the strategies are the cornerstone of this approach. It is important to look at the student's work and examine the processes the student uses, rather than focusing on a narrow result (see Activity 1.7). Simply grading a student's paper as correct or incorrect does not allow the diagnostician to prescribe corrective teaching techniques. Examples of diagnostic teaching strategies will be found as you work through this book.

ACTIVITY 1.7 ## Diagnosing a Solution Strategy

Teachers need to diagnose and remediate children's work every day. See if you can identify this student's solution strategy.

24	81	32	53
-7	-9	-7	-4
3	8	5	1
20	80	30	50
17	72	25	49

What would you ask the student who had done this work?

Geometry

Geometry has assumed an important place in elementary school mathematics. Children have much experience with geometric shapes, especially when playing with balls, bikes, and other objects. It is necessary that children at the primary level have much experience filling and emptying various containers and experimenting with objects of different shapes and sizes. Much of what is taught in elementary school geometry needs to be taught from a visual- and spatial-awareness point of view (see Activity 1.8). This is not a place for deductive proofs or wordy explanations.

ACTIVITY 1.8   Symmetry

This geometry activity emphasizes the concept of symmetry.

Some words have line symmetry. Letters in the word ~~"BOB"~~ could be folded downward along the dotted line to fit together perfectly. "MØM" could be folded together along the vertical dotted line. Find some other words that have line symmetry.

~~-DEED-~~   OTTO   TOT

Mathematics Attitudes and Equity

Concern with feelings and attitudes toward mathematics has been growing. The term "mathematics anxiety," defined as an avoidance or fear of mathematics, has been widely discussed. A chapter discussing the characteristics of and therapies for this state of being is presented later in this book.

A trend that is perhaps related to the concern for feelings and attitudes toward mathematics is the issue of equity or fairness in mathematics instruction. Minorities, including women, need to be apprised of the value of studying mathematics for future careers (see Activity 1.9). The report of the NCTM task force on the mathematical education of girls and young women (1980b) has shown that females will continue to study mathematics when encouraged. It is estimated that there are more women in college and graduate school than there are men, and predictions are that by 1990 the number of women earning business degrees will be eight times that of the 1960s.

ACTIVITY 1.9   Improving Attitude

Suppose a sixth-grade female math student is sullen and inattentive in your math class. When questioned, the student replies that mathematics is boring. List some strategies that you would use to help the student develop a better attitude toward mathematics.

===== MATH HISTORY 1.4 =====

The first woman mathematician was Hypatia, a Greek. She was distinguished in mathematics, medicine, and philosophy. She died in 415 A.D.

Since mathematics is so important for future careers, it is important for elementary school mathematics teachers to encourage females to study and gain confidence with mathematics. Sexual stereotyping of math as a male area of study cannot be tolerated.

ACTIVITY 1.10   Hidden Assumptions

A man and his son were involved in an automobile accident and taken to a hospital. The surgeon, upon seeing the injured boy on the operating table, exclaimed, "I can't operate on this boy. He is my son!" How can this be? Discuss your answers in class. How does this exercise cause us to evaluate our hidden assumptions?

Mathematics Structure

Mathematics structure consists of number systems, operations on those number systems, and related properties of those operations. For example, the set of whole numbers {0, 1, 2, 3, 4, 5, 6, 7, 8, . . .} under the operation of addition exhibits a commutative property. That is, for any two whole numbers, the order in which they are added does not change the sum ($2 + 3 = 3 + 2 = 5$). A later chapter in this book contains an in-depth discussion of mathematics structure. Although the emphasis on mathematical structure is less today than it was in the late 1960s, the inherent importance of relating numbers and basic properties is necessary for a meaningful mathematics program. Care must be taken that the developmental needs of children are considered when developing structural properties. Concrete and semiconcrete experiences are extremely important.

Evaluation of Mathematics Programs

Many states are requiring that competency tests be administered to children at various points in elementary school, junior high school, and high school. Also, increased attention to measuring educational achievement has led to the National Assessment of Educational Progress (NAEP), which measures achievement of 9-, 13-, and 17-year-olds in several curricular areas. The purpose of the national assessment is to provide information on changes in achievement; the mathematics area has been reported on since 1972. The ongoing analysis of mathematics achievement is considered helpful in determining major trends in mathematics education and locating areas that may require additional emphasis. Here is an example of the item reporting style of the National Assessment in Mathematics:

**Division Exercises, Age 13,
Third Assessment. Source:
Lindquist et al. (1983).**

Exercise	Percent Correct
a. $3\overline{)304}$	77
b. $5\overline{)150}$	91
c. $12\overline{)2496}$	57

This way of reporting items allows for easy reading; however, value judgments regarding the level of achievement must await comparisons with items from other test administrations. Thus, in the above example, is "77 percent correct" an indication of high achievement for 13-year-olds on the item $3\overline{)304}$? This decision must come from local- and state-level organizations of teachers, administrators, and parents.

The Gifted Mathematics Student

Recently, elementary school mathematics teachers have been attempting to identify and provide suitable mathematics activities for the gifted mathematics student (see Activity 1.11). Programs ranging from math olympiads to independent study have been established by school districts.

ACTIVITY 1.11   Brain Teasers

Here are some examples of problems that gifted elementary mathematics students can enjoy.

How much dirt is in a hole with a diameter of 3 meters?
What is the next number in the sequence below?

61, 52, 63, 94, 46, _____

Locate some more "brain teaser" types of problems to use with gifted elementary school students.

The unique characteristics and needs of the gifted mathematics student can be serviced by regular classroom teachers—teachers who are not themselves gifted in mathematics. However, it is important for elementary teachers to be aware of strategies and activities that can provide enrichment experiences in mathematics. The identification and teaching of gifted mathematics students will be treated in Chapter 6.

Mainstreaming

For the most part, children with handicaps were excluded from schools until the 1850s. Edouard Seguin began to establish residential schools for the handicapped, but public schools offered very few educational opportunities for these children. During the 1890s, in somewhat rare cases, public schools began to admit handicapped students, often separating them and placing them in special classes. This trend continued until 1975, when Public Law 94-142 was passed. This law stipulates that the education of handicapped children be performed in the "least restrictive environment." Specifically, the law mandates a policy popularly known as *mainstreaming*: If a child is to benefit from instruction in the regular classroom, then the child must be placed in the regular classroom, not segregated in a special education classroom.

In many cases, mathematics teachers will have certain high-incidence handicapped children placed in their classrooms. Mildly mentally retarded and learning disabled children who have auditory or visual perception problems are the most likely to be mainstreamed. Supportive assistance from special education personnel is important to ensure that this procedure is effective.

Guidelines for teaching mathematics to children who have handicaps will be developed at various points in this book.

In summary, current trends in elementary school mathematics represent a somewhat eclectic approach. Borrowing the best from the past and unifying this with current research and technology, mathematics teachers hope to provide maximal learning opportunities for their pupils. The emphasis is on mathematical thinking rather than rote, mechanical computations.

Contemporary Learning Theories for Elementary School Mathematics

There are several learning theorists who have influenced mathematics teaching at the elementary school level. Jean Piaget, a student of intellectual development, was not strictly a learning theorist, but he greatly influenced elementary school mathematics instruction with his concepts regarding child development. It should be noted that Piaget's theories do have critics. In particular, Kagan (1984) criticized Piaget's theory. Among his criticisms was the concern that Piaget placed too much emphasis on knowledge as a result of action. Even so, Piaget's study of children, including his own, affected the teaching of elementary school subjects. Mathematics teaching, with increased attention given to the child as an active participant in learning, was particularly motivated by the research of Piaget.

Piaget stated that children's developmental stages can be described by the following four stages:

1. Sensory motor (about birth to 2 years)
2. Preoperational (about 2 to 6 or 7 years)
3. Concrete operational (about 6 or 7 to 11 or 12 years)
4. Formal, or logical, operations (begins at 11 or 12 years)

According to Piaget, children always pass through these developmental stages but the rates at which they move through the stages vary from child to child. Because of the age level, we will omit the sensory-motor stage and focus discussion on the stages that are most relevant to the elementary school teacher.

Preoperational Stage

The preoperational stage (from 2 to 6 or 7 years of age) is characterized by an egocentric manner of thinking. The child can see things only from his or her personal point of view. However, the child is very good at imitating adults. The child lacks logical thought, is unable to abstract the idea of addition or subtraction, and has difficulty ordering objects and performing step-by-step activities. Also, the child exhibits *centration,* which is focusing on only one attribute at a time. For example, if a ball of clay is stretched into a sausage shape, the child may think the latter shape is larger. The child, unable to compensate for the narrowing of the diameter, focuses only on the length.

Finally, a child at the preoperational stage is unable to reverse the thinking process. Consider the chips in the diagrams at the left.

When spaced this way, the child thinks the two rows contain the same number of chips.

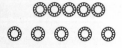

Either you or the child stretches out the chips on the lower row.

The child is unable to reverse the process and slide the chips back to their original position. Thinking that the bottom row is longer and has more chips, the child focuses on one attribute at a time and is unable to conserve number.

The child, very much influenced by the visual information, is initially content to state that the rows have the same number of elements and then, a moment later, to contradict the statement. Again, the process of reversibility is extremely important in assessing the passage from the preoperational stage to the concrete operations stage.

Concrete Operations Stage

At the concrete operations stage (from 6 or 7 to 11 or 12 years of age) the child begins to think logically but at a concrete level. Children can set up one-to-one correspondences, reverse thought processes, and order objects according to one attribute such as height. Children begin to understand space and time. Also, the operations of addition, subtraction, multiplication, and division can be understood, especially if a concrete introduction is established. Much of the elementary mathematics curriculum is based upon children who are at Piaget's concrete operations stage. Teaching mathematics to children at this stage requires that the teacher set up many experiences in which the child can actively experiment with concrete materials.

Formal Operations Stage

This stage (beginning at 11 or 12 years of age) is characterized by abstract thinking, deductive thought processes, and the ability to formulate possible tests and outcomes. An example of the type of thinking that the formal operations stage entails is the study of high school geometry. The linking together of a sequence of logical steps to arrive at a conclusion in a geometry proof is a good example of formal operations. A key element in the formal operations stage is the abstract nature of the thinking. It must be questioned, however, whether students at age 12 are ready for the formal operations stage. Many students doing proofs in high school geometry might argue with the fact that they are placed at a formal operations stage!

The Development of Concrete Operational Thinking

As a child moves from the preoperational stage to the concrete operations stage, the child begins to conserve quantity. *Conservation* means that a quantity stays the same even if the shape, arrangement, position, direction, or container of the quantity is changed. For example, a child is said to have conserved number when able to realize that stretching out a row of chips without adding any new chips yields the original number of chips.

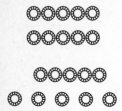

Position the chips as shown to the left. Then ask the child if the two amounts are the same.

Next, spread the chips as shown to the left. Now ask if the amounts are still the same.

Notice again the important element of reversibility. A child can conserve number when the recognition occurs that the chips can be moved back to their original places. There are numerous other conservation activities, such as conservation of length, area, volume, and mass (see Activities 1.12 and 1.13). The interested reader is referred to the works of Richard Copeland, whose book *How Children Learn Mathematics* contains excellent source material for Piagetian questions.

In general, Piaget feels that logico-mathematical thought requires many physical experiences in order to develop necessary generalizations such as the concept of number. Maturation also helps children develop through the stages; however, some children mature quickly and, thus, will pass through these stages at a faster rate than children who take more time to develop concepts. In conclusion, Piaget has presented many interesting questions about the mathematical development of children.

ACTIVITY 1.12   Conservation of Length

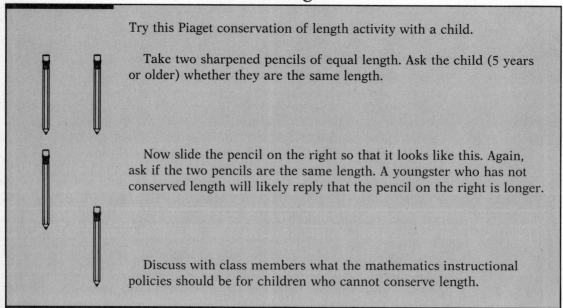

Try this Piaget conservation of length activity with a child.

Take two sharpened pencils of equal length. Ask the child (5 years or older) whether they are the same length.

Now slide the pencil on the right so that it looks like this. Again, ask if the two pencils are the same length. A youngster who has not conserved length will likely reply that the pencil on the right is longer.

Discuss with class members what the mathematics instructional policies should be for children who cannot conserve length.

ACTIVITY 1.13 Reversing an Attribute of Time

This activity illustrates a child's ability to reverse an attribute of the concept of time.

Ask a 5-year-old how old Grandma was when she was the same age as the child. The child may reply that Grandma was always old. Share your results.

=========================== *MATH JOKE* ===========================

$$\frac{0}{\text{Ph.D.}}$$
M.A.   3 degrees
B.S.   below zero

Jerome Bruner

Bruner (1966) in his studies of how people think, describes three methods by which individuals represent knowledge: enactive, iconic, and symbolic. At the enactive level, knowing is at the motor stage. A child may know how to ride a bike or walk but be unable to use language to explain this level of knowledge. Similarly, a child at this stage can bring four blocks and three blocks together to form a set of seven blocks but can't explain the process or give an answer to the symbolic sentence $4 + 3 = 7$.

At the iconic level, mental images of concrete objects are established. A child can picture in his or her mind that four blocks and three blocks make up a group of seven blocks. Visual memory is an important feature of this level.

The symbolic level is characterized by language and symbol use. For example, at the symbolic level a person can read the following problem: "Mary had four candies and gave two to her friends. How many candies does Mary have now?" A child who can read and write a number sentence solution to an example like $4 - 2 = \square$ is said to be at the symbolic level of knowing.

In summary, Bruner's levels of knowing correspond to the strategy of teaching mathematics at the concrete, semiconcrete, and abstract stages. Also, Bruner advocates a guided-discovery, process-oriented approach to concept development. This means that experimentation, meaning, and intuition (hunches) are emphasized so that children are guided to discover generalizations (see Activity 1.14). Thus, the elementary mathematics teacher needs to begin teaching concepts at an informal, intuitive level and gradually increase the sophistication until the child is at the symbolic level (see Activity 1.15).

ACTIVITY 1.14   Classification

This activity can be a useful classification experience for children. For many kindergarten children, it would be an example of problem solving.

Observe these figures. Use the clues to determine the distinguishing characteristics of each type of figure.
These are Berons.

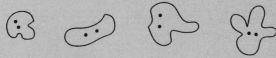

These are not Berons.

Which of these are Berons?

Make up some classificatory examples of your own and see if a classmate or elementary school pupil can solve them.

ACTIVITY 1.15   Retaining Information

Here is an example of how a meaningful presentation of information can aid the development of understanding.

Pair yourself off with a neighbor. Have your partner look at this set of numbers for about six seconds:

1 2 4 8 1 6 3 2 6 4 1 2 8 2 5 6

See how many your partner can recite to you without looking at the list.

Now try to find a pattern to the numbers by rearranging them slightly:

1, 2, 4, 8, 16, 32, 64, 128, 256, _____

Each succeeding number is found by doubling its predecessor.

Show your friend this rule and let him or her try again to duplicate the list. Which method is the easier method for retaining information?

Robert Gagne

Robert Gagne, in his book *The Conditions of Learning* (1965), suggests emphasizing the logical structure of the subject. This means placing an emphasis on the prerequisite subskills necessary for the attainment of a higher-order skill or concept. For example, in order to teach the subtraction example $\frac{24}{-7}$ it is necessary to master many prerequisite skills such as the basic subtraction facts (14 − 7), place value concepts, and reading of the minus (−) sign, among others.

Gagne felt that learning could be described in terms of a hierarchy of eight levels, each level dependent on mastery of the previous levels. These eight learning stages are the following:

1. Signal learning
2. Stimulus-response learning
3. Chaining
4. Verbal association
5. Multiple discrimination learning
6. Concept learning
7. Principle learning
8. Problem solving

Gagne's benefit to elementary mathematics instruction was increased clarification of the sequential nature of mathematics. Clear sequences of mathematics tasks were developed. Finally, Gagne recognized the value of problem solving, an area of curricular emphasis that has been greatly stressed in the 1980s.

─────────────────── *MATH JOKES* ───────────────────

Do they have a Fourth of July in England?
Take two apples from three apples and what do you have?
Some months have 30 days; some 31. How many have 28?

───

B. F. Skinner

The psychologist B. F. Skinner has made contributions to education, and specifically to elementary school mathematics, with his interest in stimulus-response learning. Most behavior, in Skinner's framework, is referred to as *operant behavior.* Examples of operant behavior are walking, talking, working, and playing. A major theme in Skinner's theory is that of positive reinforcement: Shaping or changing behavior can be accomplished using positive reinforcement to reward a given response. Positive reinforcement may be a smile, a word of praise, or, in some cases, tokens or food. The crucial point in Skinner's learning theory is that teachers can change the behavior of students by reinforcing desired behavior. Punishment, according to Skinner, does not have a long-term effect of changing a person's behavior and can have unwanted negative side effects.

In elementary school mathematics classrooms, attention is paid to the memorization of certain basic facts and terms. Skinner would suggest that teachers use positive reinforcement as soon as a desired response is made. The positive reinforcement should initially be given immediately and consistently to develop new skills. After a while, it can be given only intermittently to maintain learned skills. Blaming or punishing should be kept to a minimum. Many elementary school teachers write words of praise on children's papers, or they may draw a smile to indicate correct work. These examples of positive reinforcement are practical applications of Skinner's theory.

An Integration of Developmental and Learning Theorists

In reviewing the contributions of Piaget, Bruner, Gagne, and Skinner, among others, we can develop a theory of instruction for elementary school mathematics. Piaget helps us to understand the cognitive developmental stages of children. As elementary school teachers, we need to be aware of his guidelines regarding the readiness of children for mathematical topics. Furthermore, Bruner and Piaget both seem to agree that tactile, concrete methods along with appropriate semiconcrete approaches are effective means of teaching. Gagne points out the effectiveness of task sequencing, and Skinner is most helpful in managing children's behavior as well as providing positive reinforcement for class lessons.

In short, a synthesis of theoretical positions aims at an active approach to instruction, geared toward the learner's developmental stages. The understanding and meaning of mathematical concepts are developed first, and then skill with concepts and applications is undertaken.

Summary

This chapter has reviewed some of the procedures and interaction styles that effective teachers utilize. Also, historical trends as well as contemporary trends of elementary school mathematics have been discussed. Basic skills, broadened to reflect the needs of postindustrial society, have been described.

Although several different learning theories have been considered, there is common ground for the idea that children need to develop a rich and varied experience with concrete materials as they develop mathematical facts, concepts, and principles. As children actively experiment with mathematical ideas, a foundation is laid for greater levels of abstraction and generalization. In the words of an ancient Chinese philosopher:

> I hear and I forget;
> I see and I remember;
> I do and I understand.

=========== *MATH HISTORY 1-5* ===========

The origin of our word "zero" can be traced to the Hindu word *sunya,* meaning "void" or "empty."

Discussion Questions

1. Investigate several current mathematics textbook series to determine the degree to which microcomputer information is presented in them.

2. Research several elementary school journals such as *The Arithmetic Teacher* and *School Science and Mathematics* in order to develop a list of mathematical questions that require estimation for their solution.

3. What do you think a prospective elementary school teacher should know about microcomputers? Should prospective teachers learn to write programs? Should they learn to operate a microcomputer and evaluate software? Discuss the pros and cons of each goal.

4. Software programs are usually available in three categories: drill and practice; problem-solving simulation; and tutorial, which introduce or aid in mastering a concept. Find some current software catalogs and determine the number of programs produced in each area. Which category seems to have the most programs?

5. Select two of the learning theory positions described in this chapter. Compare and contrast their approach to the teaching of elementary school mathematics.

6. Which of the basic skills presented in this chapter will become more important in the next decade? Can you think of any additional basic mathematical skills that might be added to our list?

7. Read Crosswhite's article on international achievement in mathematics in the October 1986 issue of *The Arithmetic Teacher*. What suggestions from this article can be incorporated into your teaching philosophy?

8. Discuss strategies for encouraging women and other minority groups to increase their achievement in mathematics.

9. Briefly describe the effect that Piaget had on the teaching of elementary school mathematics.

References

Brownell, W. H. (1947). The place of meaning in the teaching of arithmetic. *Elementary School Journal, 47,* pp. 256–265.

Bruner, J. (1966). *Toward a theory of instruction* (p. 27). Cambridge, Mass.: Harvard University Press.

Burton, G. (1985). *Towards a good beginning—Teaching early childhood mathematics.* Menlo Park, Calif.: Addison-Wesley.

Gagne, R. M. (1965). *The conditions of learning.* New York: Holt, Rinehart and Winston.

Hamacheck, D. (1975). Characteristics of good teachers and implications for teacher education. In J. Michael Palardy (ed.), *Teaching today* (pp. 33–42). New York: Macmillan.

Hill, W. F. (1976). *Learning—A survey of psychological interpretations.* Scranton, Pa.: Chandler.

James, W. (1905). *Talks to teachers on psychology: And to students on some of life's ideals* (pp. 95–96). New York: Holt, Rinehart and Winston.

Kagan, J. (1984). *The nature of the child.* New York: Basic Books.

Lechner, G. (1983). *Olympiads for elementary school arithmetic teachers, 32,* pp. 22–24.

Lindquist, M. M., Carpenter, T. P., Silver, E. A., & Matthews, W. (1983). The third national assessment: Results and implications for elementary and middle schools. *Arithmetic Teacher, 31,* pp. 14–19.

McLeish, J. (1968). *The lecture method.* Cambridge, England: Cambridge Institute of Education.

McWhirter, N. (ed.). (1985). *The 1985 Guinness book of world records.* New York: Sterling.

Morsund, D. (1982). *Teacher's guide to computers in the elementary school.* Eugene, Oreg.: University of Oregon Press.

Naisbitt, J. (1982). *Megatrends: Ten new directions for transforming our lives.* New York: Warner Books.

National Advisory Committee on Mathematics Education. (1975). *Overview and analysis of school mathematics, grades k–12.* Washington: Conference Board of the Mathematical Sciences.

National Council of Supervisors of Mathematics. (1977). National Council of Supervisors of Mathematics position paper on basic skills, *Arithmetic Teacher, 24,* pp. 19–22.

National Council of Teachers of Mathematics. (1973). *Instructional aids in mathematics* (34th yearbook). Washington: NCTM.

National Council of Teachers of Mathematics. (1980a). *An agenda for action: Recommendations for school mathematics.* Reston, Va.: NCTM.

National Council of Teachers of Mathematics. (1980b). *Report of the task force on problems in the mathematics education of girls and young women.* Reston, Va.: NCTM.

National Council of Teachers of Mathematics. (1987). *Curriculum and evaluation standards for school mathematics.* Reston, Va.: NCTM.

CHAPTER 2

Managing the Elementary School Mathematics Classroom

Objectives

After reading this chapter you will be able to:

1. Describe several aspects of a well-managed mathematics classroom.

2. Analyze a lesson plan for teaching an elementary school mathematics topic.

3. List supplementary teaching strategies that can enhance the classroom conditions for mathematics learning.

4. Classify several techniques for evaluating performance in an elementary school mathematics classroom.

5. Analyze test questions to determine the efficiency of construction and the suitability of the objectives.

6. Describe procedures for developing diagnostic tests.

Classroom management is considered to be a very important skill of effective teachers. For the past two decades, the Gallup Poll has surveyed the American public's views on education. For a ten-year period, classroom discipline occupied the place of highest educational concern by the general public (Gallup, 1984). Good classroom management affects instruction positively. A well-trained teacher who is an instructional leader for the mathematics class can use effective instructional strategies that can prevent disruptions and interruptions from occurring. Effective classroom management positively influences instruction; likewise, effective instructional practices yield a more harmonious, well-managed classroom.

Let us take an imaginary tour through a fourth-grade mathematics classroom and observe how an effective classroom manager works.

First, we might notice that there is an efficient learning environment for mathematics. The room is organized in such a way that we can easily see a colorful bulletin board, which perhaps has the students' heights displayed in centimeters. In one corner a math center has been set up, consisting of a microcomputer, software, and a box of indexed file folders, each containing a specific mathematics topic of a supplementary nature. These materials are on a flat table behind which is a set of shelves containing Cuisenaire rods and other concrete manipulative objects. We also notice that students are

doing seatwork. Some complete their work early and go to the math center to work with the microcomputer or other materials. The overhead projector displays a transparency showing answers to some seatwork. As we take a seat in the back, we notice that at the front of the room there is a chart displaying the children's names and their solutions for this week's problem of the week. The children seem to be working well; the room has a good traffic flow as children move to either the math center or the teacher's desk.

Our attention now focuses on the teacher. Positioned in a central place in the room, the teacher can monitor the entire class. Eye contact is used when a student seems to be attending to something other than mathematics, but students are permitted to use their "math voice" and talk softly about mathematical work. We note that the teacher has directed the students to come together for a lesson on division of whole numbers. Using the overhead projector, the teacher brings out a bag of small cubes. Six are placed on the overhead projector and then separated into two equally sized groups. Seemingly in a random manner, the teacher calls on students to explain the division sentence. A student says that $6 \div 2 = 3$. Other examples follow with children writing *number sentences, such as $8 \div 2 = 4$, and manipulating concrete objects* to illustrate a division example like $8 \div 2 = 4$.

Now the teacher offers the class a challenge: Smiling, the teacher takes a box out and says that it contains 15 marbles. The teacher will reach into the box several times and take three marbles out each time. Seeming to talk louder, the teacher asks the class how many reaches into the box must be made in order to empty it. The children seem initially puzzled, and the teacher asks them to discuss it. After a moment the children seem to agree that the answer is $15 \div 3 = 5$.

It is now time for us to leave. As we leave, we notice that the teacher has two room messengers collecting materials and returning them to the math center. The teacher briefly tells the students to get ready for their next class, and they do so with little disruption.

Although fictitious, the preceding scenario contains several important points about managing a mathematics classroom. Brophy (1983) has described research findings about effective classroom managers. A major finding is that classroom managers should prevent disruptions rather than react to them. They can nip problems in the bud before they escalate into major disruptions. Also, effective classroom managers are able to do several things at once, not in a chaotic, nervous fashion, but in a calm, deliberate manner. They can help a child with seatwork, and at the same time they can scan the room to be sure that other children are working.

Planning for Successful Management

Effective classroom managers have clear, varied lesson plans. Any materials that are necessary are available. The lesson moves along briskly, with few interruptions for consulting a teacher's manual or backtracking to develop points that should have been covered earlier. The children are given a continuous academic signal. After presenting a new topic, the teacher helps the students review the work at their seats. If an experiment is performed, class members are aware of their roles and are kept active by recording data. For example, if a lesson calls for the students to measure objects in centimeters, the teacher has them write their measurements on paper. Kounin (1970) found that a key to the well-managed classroom is to avoid "downtime," when students have nothing to do and are unsure about their tasks. When playing a group math game, be sure that each child has something to do. If a child has nothing to do for several minutes while waiting for his or her name to be called, a possible interruption to your lesson may be brewing. Even if all remains calm, a child who is waiting for a turn is not doing mathematics. Ensure that students spend time on mathematics tasks.

Planning interesting, well-paced lessons is the foundation of effective teaching. Most school districts and textbook publishers have some form of scope and sequence guide that describes the mathematical topics and the order in which they are taught (see Fig. 2.1). Familiarizing yourself with this can be helpful when developing daily lesson plans for your grade level. In addition to a grade-level scope and sequence, your textbook series will have chapter outlines that furnish a more detailed view of the more immediate mathematical goals. The scope and sequence guide, chapter outlines, and discussions with other teachers will help you allot time as you plan your daily lessons. Discussions with other teachers can also be beneficial in isolating potential trouble spots, places in the mathematics curriculum that need greater emphasis.

Also, as you study these materials and talk with other teachers, you can make some general decisions about grouping strategies. Diagnostic testing, described in a later section of this chapter, can help you make grouping decisions. Grouping strategy will involve a large-group presentation as you introduce new topics. Small-group activities are often useful when you are doing mathematical experiments, solving problems, or having children tutor one another. Individual instruction is most beneficial for you to use with children who need special help. Sometimes more talented students can work on their own while you help children who are having trouble with certain topics. In summary, a general overview of the district's scope and sequence, the mathematics textbook, and discussions with other teachers can help you develop an overall plan for the year's mathematics program.

Daily Lesson Plans

Most lesson plans have four major components: (1) objectives, (2) materials, (3) procedures, and (4) evaluation. Let us consider each of these in detail.

Addition of Whole Numbers

	K	1	2	3	4	5	6	7	8
Meaning									
Basic facts									
Add, no renaming									
Add, 1 renaming									
Add, 3 or more addends									
Add, more than 1 renaming									
Estimating sums									
Properties									

Kindergarten

Meaning, 98-104

Grade 1

Basic facts
- Through six, 24-34, 165-166
- Through twelve, 74-90, 169-170
- Through eighteen, 254-264, 279-280

Related facts, 31-32, 163-164, 167-168, 277-278

Families of facts, 163-164, 167-168, 277-278

Using a number line, 78, 82, 89, 169

Names for numbers, 87

Computation with no renaming, 294-295, 301-302

Renaming, 293-294

Computation with one renaming, 293-294, 305

Three addends, 288-292

Grade 2

Meaning, 3-4

Basic facts
- Through ten, 5-16
- Through eighteen, 35-48

Related facts, 5, 13-14, 35-36, 39-40, 43-44, 103-104, 129-130

Families of facts, 103-104, 129-130

Using a number line, 9, 37, 41, 105

Names for numbers, 16, 42

Computation with no renaming, 196, 200-210, 238, 295-298, 313

Renaming
- Ones to tens, 197-198, 295
- Tens to hundreds, 296

Computation with one renaming
- Two-digit numbers, 199-210, 237-238
- Three-digit numbers, 295-299, 313
- Money as cents, 203-204, 295-296

Three addends, 49-52, 201-210

Subtraction of Whole Numbers

	K	1	2	3	4	5	6	7	8
Meaning									
Basic facts									
Subtract, no renaming									
Subtract, 1 renaming									
Subtract, more than 1 renaming									
Subtract, involving zeros									
Estimating differences									

Kindergarten

Meaning, 105-110

Grade 1

Basic facts
- Through eight, 122-134, 165-166
- Through twelve, 148-160, 169-170
- Through eighteen, 265-276, 279-280

Related facts, 157-158, 163-164, 167-168, 277-278

Families of facts, 163-164, 167-168, 277-278

Using a number line, 132-133, 157, 159, 169

Names for numbers, 151

Computation with no renaming, 299-302

Renaming, 297-298

Computation with one renaming, 297-302, 305

Grade 2

Meaning, 88

Basic facts
- Through ten, 89-106
- Through eighteen, 114-132

Related facts, 91, 97-98, 103-104, 117-118, 121-122, 129-130

Families of facts, 103-104, 129-130

Using a number line, 93-94, 105

Names for numbers, 106, 132

Computation with no renaming, 220, 227-238, 307-310

Renaming
- Tens to ones, 221, 223-226, 305
- Hundreds to tens, 305

Computation with one renaming
- Two-digit numbers, 222, 226-243
- Three-digit numbers, 306-310, 312, 314
- Money as cents, 230, 232

Red type identifies new topics and blue type identifies topics introduced earlier in the program. The page numbers indicate where an idea or skill is presented and/or used.

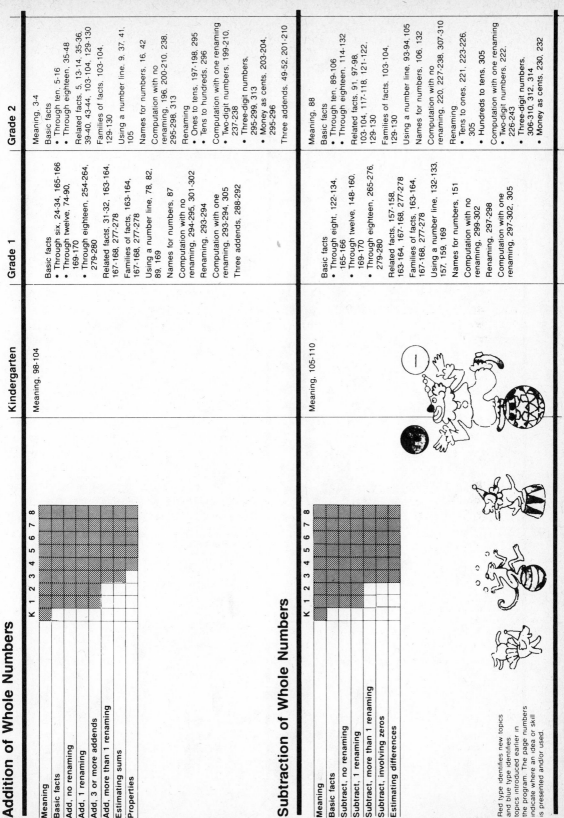

Fig. 2.1 *Source:* Bolster, et al. (1985). *Invitation to mathematics* (pp. 6–7). Glenview, Ill.: Scott, Foresman. Used with permission of publisher.

Scott, Foresman Invitation to Mathematics Scope and Sequence

Grade 3	Grade 4	Grade 5	Grade 6	Grade 7	Grade 8
Meaning. 10-11 Basic facts. 10-15 Families of facts. 22-23 Computation with no renaming. 58-59, 68-69 Renaming. 60-61 Computation with one renaming • Renaming ones. 62-65, 68-69 • Renaming tens. 66-69 • Three or more addends, 70-71, 74-75 • Renaming hundreds. 72-75 • Money. 140-141 Computation with more than one renaming. 76-77, 80-81, 116-117 Estimating sums. 78-79 Missing addends (Challenge). 121	Meaning. 6-7 Basic facts. 6-7, 10-11 Families of facts. 12-13 Renaming. 54-55 Computation • One renaming. 56-57, 62-63, 80 • More than one renaming. 58-59, 62-63, 80 • Three or more addends. 60-62, 80 Estimating sums. 52-53 Missing addends. 18-19	Basic facts. 12-13 Families of facts. 12-13 Computation • One renaming. 16-17 • More than one renaming. 18-19 • Three or more addends. 20-21, 34-35 • Money. 32-33 Estimating sums. 14-15 Missing addends. 36-37 Properties, ordering and grouping (Challenge). 39	Computation. • One renaming. 12-13, 22 • More than one renaming. 14-15, 22 • Three or more addends. 12-15, 22 Estimating sums. 10-11, 22 Missing addends. 24-25 Properties • Commutative. 15 • Associative. 15	Computation. 12-13, 16-17 Estimating sums. 10-11, 16-17 Missing addends. 22-23 Missing minuends. 22-23 Properties • Commutative. 56-57 • Associative. 56-57 • Distributive. 56-57	Computation. 8-9, 18-19 Estimating sums. 6-7 Missing addends. 44-45 Missing minuends. 44-45 Properties. 38-39
Meaning. 16-17 Basic facts. 16-21 Families of facts. 22-23 Computation with no renaming. 90-91, 100-101 Renaming. 92-93 Computation with one renaming • Renaming tens. 94-97, 100-101 • Renaming hundreds. 98-101 • Four-digit numbers. 102-103, 106-107 • Checking. 114-115 Computation with more than one renaming. 104-107, 112-117 Renaming with zeros. 108-109, 112-117 Estimating differences. 110-113 Missing addends (Challenge). 121	Meaning. 8-9 Basic facts. 8-11 Families of facts. 12-13 Renaming. 66-67 Computation • One renaming. 68-69, 74, 80 • More than one renaming. 70-71, 74, 80 • With zeros. 72-74, 80 • Money. 78-79 Estimating differences. 64-65 Missing addends. 18-19	Basic facts. 12-13 Families of facts. 12-13 Computation • One renaming. 24-25 • More than one renaming. 26-27, 34-35 • With zeros. 28-29 • Checking. 24-25 • Money. 32-33 Estimating differences. 22-23 Missing addends. 36-37	Computation • One renaming. 16-17, 22 • More than one renaming. 18-19, 22 • With zeros. 18-19, 22 • Checking. 16-17 Estimating differences. 10-11, 22 Missing addends. 24-25	Computation. 14-17 Estimating differences. 10-11, 16-17 Missing addends. 22-23 Missing minuends. 22-23	Computation. 8-9, 18-19 Estimating differences. 6-7 Missing addends. 44-45 Missing minuends. 44-45 Missing subtrahends. 360-361

Fig. 2.1 (continued)

Objectives

"Clarity" is the key word here. Mathematics objectives need to be clearly stated, measurable, and student centered. Instead of saying that children will learn addition, clarify this further by saying that they will study addition facts with sums up to 10. This makes the objective more specific and provides a basis for assessing student achievement at a later time. Knowledge of your mathematics textbook will help formulate objectives. Also, it is important to have an awareness of the prerequisite skills necessary for mastering your objective. For example, if teaching addition of two-place numbers with one regrouping is covered in your objective, then this implies that children have mastered basic addition facts, place value concepts, counting, and addition of two-place numbers without regrouping (see Activity 2.1).

It is a good idea to use a variety of verbs when you write several objectives. This helps ensure that objectives are not all fact recitations. Some verbs to help in the writing of educational objectives are these:

1. Identify (select, classify, discriminate)
2. Name (label, list, state)
3. Describe (define, explain, analyze)
4. Construct (draw, build, write, apply)
5. Order (sequence)
6. Demonstrate (show the procedure, perform an experiment, translate)

Using a variety of verbs can ensure that objectives reflect problem-solving activities as well as the recall of factual information. Here is a sample objective for teaching recognition of geometric shapes:

> Given tagboard models of squares, rectangles, circles, and triangles, the student will orally identify the correct shapes.

ACTIVITY 2.1 Writing an Objective

Write an objective for teaching children the concept of two-place numbers. Share your objective with a member of your class and compare your objectives.

Materials

Materials for a lesson can be as basic as your textbook or as innovative as a field trip to a local zoo. As you work through this book, you will develop a great number of ideas for materials. Bingo chips, hangers, clothespins, and other household objects are natural materials. There are numerous commercial distributors that are also excellent sources for materials. A list of some mathematics supplies is provided in an appendix of this book. Finally, technological materials, such as an overhead projector, filmstrips and movies, and microcomputers can be extremely useful materials for a mathematics lesson.

Procedures

Procedures for developing your lesson can be classified in three main areas: introduction, development, and practice. An introduction may be to write an exercise or problem on the board which children are to consider as you start the lesson. For primary children it may be an oral question that leads into the lesson. This brief preface to the lesson (perhaps five minutes) can also be a review of an important point from the previous lesson (see Activity 2.2). In short, you want to alert students to the current topic and succinctly review the important prerequisites.

ACTIVITY 2.2   "Guess My Number"

A game to stimulate students' questioning is the "Guess My Number" game. The teacher thinks of a number from 1 to 50 (other variations are possible) and has the class guess the number. Random guesses such as shouting out 45, 50, 2, etc., are disallowed. The class members need to focus on a plan to gradually approach the unknown number with their guesses.

As you move into the main demonstrations of the lesson, the kinds of questions asked are important signposts of the lesson's success. Ask some factual questions, but be sure to emphasize questions that require students to analyze and apply concepts. Even at primary grade levels, this can be done. For example, ask children why they have performed a task a certain way. Just as newspaper reporters use the words "why," "when," "how," "what," and "where," so can mathematics teachers utilize these words to form a broader frame of questions.

Burns (1985) has described some of the questions that she poses to mathematics classes. These are:

1. How did you arrive at your answer?
2. Did someone get the same answer but by a different way of reasoning?
3. Who has a different solution?
4. Can you explain a flaw in someone else's reasoning?
5. Can you convince someone who disagrees with you?
6. Can you change or invent a new problem to ask the class?

Beginning, even experienced, teachers need to have a list of basic questions that they will ask during the lesson. Also, it is important to question as many different students as possible. Alert your students to the fact that they will be called upon. As children answer questions, be sure to praise and encourage their responses. Also, children will raise questions when a supportive classroom climate is developed.

In regard to the development stage of your lesson, a point needs to be made about the examples used to develop student understanding. For example, if a first-grade class is studying recognition of triangles, then several examples of triangles need to be shown in various positions (see Fig. 2.2). However, it is also useful to try a counterexample *after* the children have been given appropriate examples that describe triangles. In other words, show them a circular shape and ask why it is not considered a triangle (round, no points, no line segments—all are appropriate answers).

Fig. 2.2

A practice session on the day's lesson is often useful. Again, everyone in the class should be alerted to the need to do good work. Research on accountability (Good & Grows, 1979) suggests the teacher should let students know their work will be checked and then follow through to check it. Practice work needs to be manageable; a worksheet of 45 multiplication examples is dubious practice. Half of those items, judiciously selected, would serve the purpose. Finally, practice is indeed just that. There should be a reasonably high rate of success. Some researchers state that success rates for practice work should be between 70 and 90 percent (Brophy, 1983).

Also, the timing of the developmental stage of your lesson is extremely important. Estimate approximately 30 minutes at intermediate grade levels but be aware that at first you may be off the mark. Predicting how quickly students will work through a lesson requires experience. Hence, it is a good idea to have a backup activity or two in case a lesson ends earlier. This may be an extra problem, a riddle, or a microcomputer demonstration (see Activity 2.3). Having backup activities enables a teacher to avoid a situation in which students have nothing to do for five minutes, a period of time that is ripe for class disruptions.

ACTIVITY 2.3   Word Values

Use a push button phone for a good backup activity. Using the letter values, find ten words that have a value of 15. For example, "OX" has a total of 15 (6 + 9).

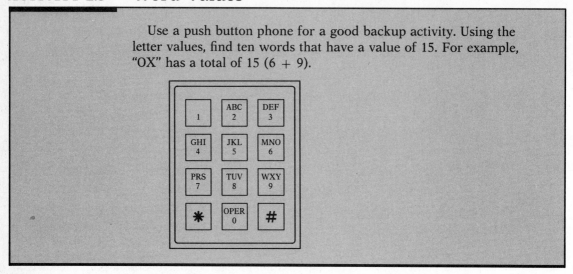

Finally, the conclusion of a lesson should be clearly stated. If an experiment or activity is incomplete, then students should be apprised of what they need to do during the next class period. Also, a brief summary may be necessary. It is important to make a clear, definite transition to the next subject being taught.

Evaluation

A final stage of the lesson plan process is evaluation. Looking back on the lesson allows a teacher to glean information that can be used for modifying future lessons. As a lesson is evaluated, attention needs to be paid to cognitive and affective factors. Some questions to consider are these:

1. Did the students seem to master the topic?

2. Did the lesson move along well? Did students understand their roles in demonstrations, experiments, and individual work?

3. Were the materials adequate? Did any technological materials break down?

4. Did students seem to enjoy learning?

5. How did the teacher perceive the lesson? Did he or she learn anything new that might be incorporated into a new lesson?

6. Were there students who were unusually interested or withdrawn? Why?

A sample lesson plan that illustrates the main components of a plan is presented below.

Sample Lesson Plan

Lesson Plan: Grade 1

Objectives:

1. When given concrete models of addition facts with sums to 10, the student will write the correct mathematical sentence.
2. When given a mathematical sentence describing basic addition facts with sums to 10, the student will display the appropriate concrete model.

Procedure:

1. Motivate the class by telling a story about a child who had three pieces of candy and then got four more pieces of candy. Ask how many the child then had. (two to five minutes)
2. Use an overhead projector to illustrate addition examples like $2 + 3 = 5$ and $5 + 1 = 6$. Children should write these sentences. Also use a clothes hanger with clothespins attached to model addition sentences $4 + 3 = 7$ and $6 + 2 = 8$. Again, children should write these sentences down. (ten minutes)

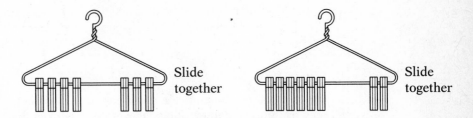

3. Write number sentences such as $4 + 3 = \square$, $7 + 2 = \square$, and $3 + 1 = \square$ on the board. Have children come up and use the hanger and clothespins to solve the addition sentences. Also, have children use chips at their desks to model addition sentences. (five to ten minutes)
4. Practice learning with textbook guide sheets. (five minutes)

Evaluation: Observe how the class solved the examples.

1. Did the students pay attention? Why or why not?
2. Was the class able to translate the concrete models to abstract mathematics at sentences?
3. Was the class able to translate the abstract number sentences to concrete models?
4. What particular students need more help?

Additional Classroom Management Strategies

There are numerous ways to make a mathematics classroom exciting, a place where learning takes place with a spirit of discovery. The following techniques can help you manage the learning environment and prevent student discipline problems.

Start Early to Manage Your Classroom

It is important to set the tone for your mathematics classroom early in the year. Doyle (1979) found that there was some credence in the "old timer's" suggestion to new teachers that they be directive at the beginning of the year. Some rules and guidelines need to be developed at this point. Perhaps five rules, with students providing suggestions, are necessary. Too many rules can cause frustration—to students and teachers alike. But it is much easier to establish policies during the first week of class than in December. Areas to consider are pencil sharpening, working in small groups, working in the mathematics corner with the microcomputer and hand calculator, and moving materials around the room.

Again, students need to be instructed early about classroom policies, but rules need to be brief, flexible, and cooperatively developed by students and teachers.

Utilize Bulletin Boards

Bulletin boards can enhance a mathematics classroom. Interesting topics, such as famous mathematicians or mathematics in daily life, and seasonal topics related to mathematics can serve as source material. Photographs of children doing mathematics, cutouts of various shapes, and samples of children's work can also be used. Bulletin boards may be descriptive or functional.

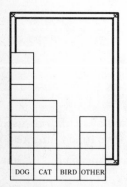

Fig. 2.3

An example of a functional bulletin board may be seen in Fig. 2.3. Children can take tagboard rectangles and place them above the areas that describe their pets. In this way, children participate in the creation of a bulletin board display and at the same time investigate some mathematics.

For further bulletin board ideas, consult the references at the end of this chapter.

Use a Microcomputer

Microcomputers can be useful for individualizing instruction. Children can write programs or work through commercial programs. Commercial software has improved to the point where programs are available for practice, problem solving, and simulations. Elementary mathematics teachers can also use a microcomputer for demonstrations or for small-group work.

Plan "Bell Work" Activities

Bell work is often a problem or exercise that gets the class started and also allows the teacher to set up the lesson, check attendance, or do other routine chores. Bell work may also set the motivational tone for the introductory aspect of the lesson (see Activity 2.4).

ACTIVITY 2.4 Setting the Motivational Tone

Here is an activity that can help motivate the tone of a lesson and introduce a review of fundamental operations.

Take a number. Add 10. Multiply by 2. Divide by 4. Subtract 5. Multiply by 2. Your answer should be your original number.

Establish "Problems of the Week"

These might be nontraditional "extra credit" problems (see Activity 2.5). They could be incorporated with a bulletin board that displays student strategies for solution. Also, students who have attempted the problems might have their names displayed. It is important here to display not only the names of students who have gotten correct answers but the name of *any* student who *attempts* the problem and can show his or her work.

ACTIVITY 2.5 Problem of the Week

Here is a sample problem of the week.

Your sock drawer has 12 brown socks, 14 black socks, and 16 blue socks. If you reach into the drawer while it is dark, how many socks do you need to pull out to be certain that you have a pair that matches?

Use Praise Effectively

Research studies (Gnagey, 1981) indicate that a great deal of student misbehavior may be caused by fear of failure and anxiety. Sometimes disruptive students fear being judged for performance on tests or class recitations. Thus, effective use of praise may alleviate potential trouble. Although verbal praise needs to be a fundamental component of mathematics lessons, there are other ways to make a mathematics class an enjoyable center for learning. Have a "student of the week" award and be sure to pass acclaim along to almost every student as the year unfolds. At certain times during the year, give out awards. Be creative in your titles—Most Valuable Math Student, Most Improved Math Student, Hardest Working Math Student, and Best Math Question are just a few award titles that can be used.

A sample of the kind of award that can be made for children is shown below.

Student of the Week Award in Mathematics

This certifies that

_____

has done outstanding mathematics work this week.
Presented the _____ day of February,
in the year _____.

Hold a Recreational Mathematics Day

Spend a day doing mathematics puzzles or games. Also, going outdoors can be an enjoyable way to apply mathematics concepts and principles. For example, collecting leaves and graphing the frequencies of various leaf arrangements can be part of an outdoor education experience.

Contact Resource People

Park rangers, computer programmers, utility company engineers, and other community sources are helpful adjuncts to the everyday classroom experience. Sometimes companies will have educational materials available without charge. One elementary mathematics teacher obtained a supply of metric system rulers, mathematics activity comic books, and free hamburgers from a national hamburger company chain. As the saying goes, "look in the Yellow Pages" for names and phone numbers of potential human resources.

Modify Classroom Procedures

There are numerous ways to modify your daily lessons. At times, have students write questions on cards and drop them into a hat. Select some at random and use them as a basis for review. Also, on occasion, have students write some of the exam questions and use a few on a test.

Use a "buddy system" sometimes. Allow students to tutor a friend, make some audiovisual materials, and serve as math materials monitor for the mathematics corner. Also, use an overhead projector for displaying answers to homework or seatwork. By doing that, you can circulate around the room and help individual students or groups of students who need more work.

Involve Parents

When possible, use parent volunteers to make materials. Also, sometimes it is a good idea to send home mathematical activities for parent and child involvement. A nice touch for the summer or over holiday periods is a math calendar with activities that can be performed at home (see Fig. 2.4). Furthermore, call individual parents, if possible, to alert them about their child's excessive misbehavior.

Balance Group and Individual Management Strategies

When misbehavior occurs in a mathematics class, it is important that the teacher maintain poise and not overreact. Sometimes punishing a whole class for the misbehavior of a few can lead to alienation of the entire group. Separating students, having a conference with an individual student, using eye contact, and, in some cases, ignoring a minor incident are methods that experienced teachers use to assist the learning of their individual students.

At times, however, there is a need to solidify group identity and pride. Sometimes, at transition times, primary school teachers turn off the lights until children have settled down and focused their attention on the new lesson.

Gnagey (1981) reported on an interesting game designed to reinforce group motivation. The system works like this: Each of five rows of students become a team. A kitchen timer (bell) rings at random during math class. Each time, the teacher looks up to see whether the individuals of each team are "working hard." If each member of a team is working hard, then a point is marked on the chalkboard under the team's name. A team does not receive a point even if only one member is off-task when the bell sounds. But all teams win as long as they score at least five points during a half hour.

Attending to misbehavior in an individual fashion, while building up self-esteem of individual students and the entire class, is an effective classroom management strategy.

In conclusion, this section has developed numerous strategies for

		1 How many books are in your desk?	**2** How many days till school is out?	**3** Count the light bulbs in your house.	**4** Give your dad a hug!	**5** Ride your bike.
6 Read seven comics in the Sunday paper.	**7** Practice writing words for the numbers from 1 to 10.	**8** Help your mother.	**9** Write the ages of your mom and dad.	**10** How many times can you bounce a ball without missing?	**11** Print the days of the week.	**12** Go to the library.
13 Ask your dad and mom four math questions.	**14** What day is the second to the last day of school?	**15** How many hours were you awake today?	**16** Jump rope and count to 50.	**17** Count how many birds you can see.	**18** What is your telephone number?	**19** Watch TV. How many commercials do you count?
20 Sleep late.	**21** Print what season of the year is beginning.	**22** Count how many dishes and glasses are used for dinner.	**23** Help your mother.	**24** Help your father.	**25** Look at the newspaper. How many letters are in the headline?	**26** Go to the library.
27 Count the number of comic strips in the Sunday paper.	**28** Add up the number of toes in your family.	**29** How many numbers can you find on the front page of the newspaper?	**30** Do something nice for everyone in your family.			

Fig. 2.4

managing the elementary school mathematics classroom. The foundation of this approach has been the need for good planning—not only planning lessons well but also planning the classroom environment, anticipating potential disruptions, and defusing them before they escalate. Clear communication and mutual respect are the cornerstones of good management and planning.

Evaluation in the Mathematics Classroom

The evaluation of students' mathematics performance is an important responsibility of an elementary school teacher. Evaluation procedures can be helpful for planning instruction, diagnosing student strengths and weaknesses in mathematics, and measuring achievement for class and individual comparisons. Evaluation, or as it is sometimes called, assessment, involves more than written tests. Daily interaction with students, informal interviews, and observations involving checklists of topics are also valuable forms of information. More formal measures such as teacher-made tests and standardized tests are also a necessary part of the evaluation processes. Attitude checklists and anecdotal records can assist the teacher in planning and evaluating the affective area. Finally, psychomotor tests, although often requiring special training, may prove helpful when educational plans for mainstreamed pupils are being considered. A chapter of this book is devoted to teaching children with special needs such as those who are mainstreamed into the regular classroom.

In conclusion, the proper mix of evaluation techniques must be adjusted to the specific teaching situation. For example, standardized tests are usually used at least once a year in every grade level. However, at the primary level or with children who have been mainstreamed, emphasis might be placed more on observations than on paper-and-pencil test results.

General Considerations

The initial consideration in any evaluation must be the *objectives* of the course. Often these are stated in the textbook or in the school district's scope and sequence. These are usually cognitive objectives, such as "The student will utilize the strategy of making a chart in order to solve a problem." It is helpful to have these objectives sequenced in a manner that allows learning to build from more fundamental topics to more complex topics.

Another consideration when you are using evaluation instruments is to consider the reliability and validity of the testing instrument. In a general sense, *reliability* means consistency. How accurate is our test or checklist?

If we used it tomorrow, would we obtain similar results? If other teachers used our checklist or test, would they obtain similar results? Generally, a test with many well-written items will be more reliable than a test with fewer, poorly written items.

Validity means that the evaluation procedure measures what we want to measure. That is, does the test or evaluation procedure measure objectives that are important for our grade level? Sometimes school districts vary in their expectation of achievement; thus, standardized tests must be closely examined to determine whether the items are appropriate. For example, if a kindergarten class spends a great deal of time sorting objects, classifying objects, and working on similarities and differences, then a standardized test that emphasizes symbol recognition tasks such as $4 + 3 = \square$ might be an invalid measure of achievement.

Continuing, the administration of tests and informal measures such as checklists and observations must be performed carefully. Time must be budgeted, materials made available; most important of all, a proper testing situation must be developed by putting children at ease. A remark such as "Today we are going to get some information to help plan your learning program" is a better statement than "Today we are going to have a tough test." Teachers need to put children at ease in order to gather the most complete and accurate information.

Evaluating children who have been mainstreamed poses special challenges to elementary teachers. Care must be taken so that children are aware of terms like "right" and "left" as well as "top" and "bottom." Also, children with learning difficulties may have short attention spans, so evaluation measures must be administered during short intervals of time. Eye-hand coordination may be poor, so alternatives to writing answers may be necessary, such as having children orally state results. If visual perception problems exist, it may be necessary to design a test with *only one* problem or exercise on a page. A thorough description of strategies for teaching computation to children with learning difficulties is presented by Moyer and Moyer (1978).

Finally, interpreting evaluation results depends on the original purpose of the evaluation. For example, an achievement test used to gather data for marking grades implies that students will be compared. This comparison may be based upon a criterion-referenced test that measures the degree to which children have mastered objectives, or it may be a normative test that compares children to national, local, or classroom standards. In either case, a child's total score is important. On the other hand, total scores are not as important when diagnostic tests are being used. Here, the essential point is to determine what processes children are using so that a teacher can diagnose and then remediate difficulties. A total score does not tell the teacher what specific errors the child is making.

Informal Assessment Procedures

Daily Lessons

Questioning children and observing their work during class can be an informal means of evaluating children's work. The way that children arrive at their answers, the process, is important to observe. For example, a child may use the number line to solve an addition example, as depicted below.

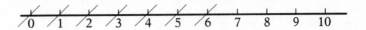

The child counted the number line points and reasoned that $3 + 4 = 6$! Here an immediate method of correction would be to help the child focus on the *distance* between numerals, as indicated below.

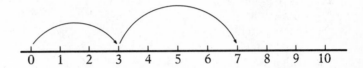

Determining the thought processes that children use, observing their work habits, and understanding their attitudes are all part of an informal evaluation procedure. Briefly describing some of the children's thought processes when you evaluate your lesson can help future planning of lessons.

Interviews

Sometimes interviewing a student during a free period can yield valuable information about the child's mathematical functioning. Although not as objective as written tests, an interview allows the teacher to utilize concrete materials and to probe the understanding that the child exhibits at the concrete and semiconcrete stages of concept development. For example, suppose a child solves a multiplication example such as 2×3 by writing "5" for the answer. An interview easily allows the teacher to utilize two paper cups with three marbles in each as a concrete model for 2×3. By asking whether the child can see any connection between the concrete model and the symbolic statement, the teacher can determine whether more instruction that develops meaning through concrete examples is necessary.

In conclusion, interviews are time-consuming for the classroom teacher; thus, they can be used only with a few children. However, they can yield information about the depth and quality of a child's work that may not be revealed by a paper-and-pencil test. Particularly with children who exhibit learning difficulties and have been mainstreamed, an interview may be exceptionally useful. Interested readers should read Schoen (1979) for further information about interviews.

Checklists

Checklists of mathematics concepts are helpful when primary mathematics objectives are being evaluated or when paper-and-pencil tests seem inappropriate. At the primary level, a sample checklist for each child might be modeled after this one developed by Heddens and Speer (1988):

Relationship

1. Size and Quantity	Introduce	In Process	Mastery
big–little			
long–short			
tall–short			
large–small			
many–few			
high–low			
all–none			
heavy–light			
thick–thin			

Source: From *Today's Mathematics* by James W. Heddens. Copyright © Science Research Associates, Inc. 1988 (with W. Speer), 1984, 1980, 1974, 1971, 1968, 1964. Reprinted by permission of the publisher.

Another checklist, this one emphasizing essential topics of addition, is displayed below. This sequential checklist can be expanded to provide greater clarity, such as stating the number of digits in the computational examples and the number of regroupings to be performed. Also, concrete, semiconcrete, and abstract categories could be included. Children can be evaluated by placing check marks in appropriate columns.

A Sample Checklist for Addition

	Introduce	In Process	Mastery
1. Modeling the operation of addition			
2. Recognizing structural properties such as the commutative property of addition			
3. Developing and memorizing basic addition facts			

4. Developing computational examples beyond the basic facts which involve regrouping

5. Identifying place-value relationships when adding two numbers

6. Estimating sums

7. Developing addition examples involving regrouping

8. Practicing the addition algorithm

9. Applying the operation of addition to problem-solving experiences

Teacher-Made Achievement Tests

Often elementary teachers construct their own tests and quizzes. It is necessary to list a set of objectives for the test and to write careful items. Having a list of objectives as a basis for a test ensures that items can be written which sample the important skills and concepts that you wish to measure.

After a decision has been made on the objectives to be tested, the next step is to write items. Several popular formats for writing items are the following:

1. True-false items

2. Multiple-choice items

3. Essay items

4. Sentence completion items

5. Matching items

Generally, essay items are the most difficult to score objectively, whereas the other formats lend themselves to more objective scoring techniques. There are several guidelines to consider when you are writing test items. Merwin (1961) and McKillip (1979) have produced helpful suggestions for writing good items, and these follow.

1. *Avoid ambiguities and long, involved statements.* For example, consider this test question: "Marian joined a library club that met once a week on Tuesday from 6:00 to 7:00. She read 18 books last year, among them *Jaws* and *Ivanhoe.* On the average, how many books did Marian read each month?" Notice that it is irrelevant to the problem what specific books Marian read. Also, the meeting time for the library club is irrelevant. Keep the information pertinent and clear.

2. *Avoid negatives and double negatives.* For example, "A prime number

can never have more than two factors. Which one of the following is not a prime number? (a) 17; (b) 4; (c) 5; (d) None of the above."

3. *Use diagrams and pictures to evaluate the understanding of mathematics concepts.* For example, you could ask what fraction is suggested by the picture at the left.

4. *Construct a test that students can easily finish within the time allotment of your mathematics class.* Also, be sure to leave enough room on the test for children to show their work. Scoring a test can be made easier if answers are written in a consistent place, say, the right margin of the paper.

5. *Test for understanding, relationships, and problem solving, as well as the recall of factual information.* For example, "Write four mathematical sentences using the numbers 4, 5, and 9."

6. *Keep the reading level low and use words that students understand.* For example, consider the following true-false item in which a word is unfamiliar: "The enclosure of fence around a rectangular shape is called the perimeter." "Enclosure" is a poor word; some students would not know its meaning.

In summary, writing a good test question is difficult. Callahan (1977) has pointed out that even standardized tests can yield items that are difficult for students to interpret. Even so, careful writing of items can help improve teacher-written tests.

Constructing Diagnostic Tests

Diagnostic tests, useful when individualizing instruction, require many of the same item-writing guidelines as achievement tests. However, a diagnostic test for a narrow area such as addition or subtraction of whole numbers, often called an *analytical test,* requires an additional feature. Cox (1975) has reported that after a sequence of content objectives has been developed, at least *three* items for each objective should be written. In this way, mathematical difficulties that might have been disguised are revealed. Diagnostic tests help us evaluate students so that grouping decisions can be made.

Suppose a child solves an exercise like this:

$$\begin{array}{r} 54 \\ -\ 9 \\ \hline 45 \end{array}$$

A teacher might conclude that the child understands this type of subtraction problem. However, suppose the teacher had presented the child with another item and observed this:

$$
\begin{array}{r}
63 \\
-\ 7 \\
\hline
14
\end{array}
$$

The teacher would reach a completely different conclusion! Having three items at each level of a diagnostic sequence ensures that errors such as subtracting the bottom number from each of the top numbers will be revealed (see Activity 2.6). Thus, we can gain more accurate information for constructing remedial instruction programs.

Guidelines for Developing Diagnostic and Remedial Procedures

1. Sequence the topics for a content area, such as multiplication of whole numbers.
2. Write at least three questions for each level in the sequence.
3. Administer the test and interpret the results by focusing on the strategies that children use rather than on whether the answers are correct or incorrect.
4. Prescribe remedial work at the concrete, semiconcrete, and abstract levels.

In conclusion, developing diagnostic tests in mathematics or using standardized diagnostic tests, such as the *Key Math Diagnostic Arithmetic Test,* are only the beginning of the diagnostic remedial process. Remedial devices such as manipulative material, games, and supplementary activities are needed so that the remedial approach supplements the textbook. Also, the diagnosis and remediation process helps us tailor our mathematics instruction for individual differences among children. Some children will need much concrete and manipulative work. Others can benefit from enrichment material. A diagnostic remedial teaching design helps us provide for these differences.

ACTIVITY 2.6   Using Diagnostic Tests

Suppose you constructed the mathematics test questions shown below and discovered that children had answered in the following way:

$$
\begin{array}{llll}
3 + 2 = 5 & \quad 4 & \quad 5 & \quad 8 \\
5 + 8 = 13 & \underline{+\ 7} & \underline{+\ 6} & \underline{+\ 9} \\
4 + 2 = 6 & \quad 47 & \quad 56 & \quad 89
\end{array}
$$

What conclusions might you make? How might you correct this mathematical difficulty? List some of your ideas.

Standardized Tests

Commercial standardized tests, diagnostic as well as achievement, are used in elementary school mathematics classes. These tests have national comparison norms and are usually administered at the beginning or end of the school year. Appendix A lists tests that are commercially produced.

Elementary mathematics teachers need to inform themselves about the particular test being used in their school district. Specifically, care must be taken to ensure that the textbook and school district curriculum objectives match the objectives of the standardized test.

McDonald (1983) has described some of the factors that may influence performance on national standardized tests. For example, a consideration of the language used on the test is important. If the textbook uses the word "regroup" for subtraction exercises while the test uses the word "rename," then children and teachers need to be so informed. Another example of language differences between tests and textbooks is the writing of fractions in "simplest form" or in "lowest terms." Both phrases mean the same thing, but if a test uses "simplest form" and the textbook uses "lowest terms," then some children might not understand that the phrases have the same meaning.

Standardized tests usually require that students mark their answers on a separate answer sheet. Many students need to be taught how to do this. For example, Gregory (1979) analyzed the errors made by a sixth-grade class when the students filled out a computer-scored answer sheet. Over half the errors made on the test occurred when students skipped an item on the test but neglected to skip it on the answer sheet. Some children confused the numerical answer with the choice number on the answer sheet. Children started in the wrong place on the answer sheet, and some even responded on the wrong side of the sheet!

In conclusion, standardized tests are useful for evaluating pupil comparisons. However, elementary mathematics teachers need to familiarize themselves with the objectives of the test and ensure that children are taught necessary objectives, vocabulary, and procedures.

Attitudes Toward Mathematics

Measuring elementary school students' attitudes toward mathematics is an important component of the evaluation process. Two methods of doing this are using the sentence completion technique and administering an attitude questionnaire.

Sentence Completion

Students fill out the remaining parts of incomplete sentences. Ten sentences or so are used with elementary students, with results yielding a profile of the students' attitudes toward mathematics. Some sample items are written below:

When I study mathematics I feel _____.
When we have mathematics class, I _____.
My mother feels that mathematics is _____.
My father feels that mathematics is _____.

Attitude Questionnaires

Attitude questionnaires require that a student respond to statements about mathematics. Students can respond by marking "true" or "false" or by marking the degree to which they agree with a statement. The item below illustrates the latter approach.

	Agree	*Undecided*	*Disagree*
I would take mathematics even if it wasn't required.	_____	_____	_____

For primary age children, Dunlap (1976) has developed an interesting format for attitude assessment. Mathematical topics are listed next to three faces; one is smiling, another is neutral, and a third is frowning. Children are instructed to color in the face that best represents their feeling about the topic. A sample is shown in Fig. 2.5.

4 tens   2 ones

Fig. 2.5 *Source*: Dunlap, W. (1976). An attiudinal device for primary children. *Arithmetic Teacher*, *23*, pp. 29–32. Used with permission of the National Council of Teachers of Mathematics.

Although attitude measurement is often imprecise, particularly with primary children whose moods fluctuate rapidly, an informal assessment of children's attitudes can be extremely helpful when you are planning mathematics lessons.

Summary

This chapter has developed many strategies for managing a mathematics classroom and for evaluating the management results, but these techniques are only the raw material for the creative force of the inspirational teacher.

As Ralph Waldo Emerson said, "The secret of education lies in respecting the pupil." By respecting and caring for students, these techniques can help to create a warm, humane, and effective mathematics learning environment.

Discussion Questions

1. Select any year from grade 1 through grade 6 and list the broad objectives for the study of mathematics. Choose one of these objectives and develop specific objectives to cover one unit.

2. List the desired outcomes of testing students. Are there outcomes that may not be desirable?

3. "An elementary teacher should have a comprehensive view of the entire mathematics program in the elementary school." Explain why you agree or disagree with this statement.

4. Locate and read two articles that deal with classroom discipline. Summarize each and compare the similarities and differences between the approaches.

5. Develop a detailed lesson plan for an outdoor mathematics lesson.

6. Develop four backup activities that can be used by a student who completes assigned work quickly.

7. Read the article by Larson entitled "Organizing for Mathematics Instruction" in the September 1983 issue of *Arithmetic Teacher*. List the advantages for students in a program such as the one explained in this article. What advantages or disadvantages exist for a teacher implementing this type of program?

8. Make a list of possible resource people in your area. Write a letter to at least one requesting educational materials.

9. In your opinion, do formal or informal assessment procedures give you more information about your student? Why? On which type are grades based? Discuss the implications of this for the student.

References

Brophy, J. (1983). Classroom organization and management. In D. C. Smith (ed.), *Essential knowledge for beginning educators* (pp. 22–35). Washington: American Association of Colleges for Teacher Education.

Burns, M. (1985). The role of questioning. *Arithmetic Teacher, 32*, pp. 14–16.

Callahan, Leroy. (1977). Test item tendencies: curiosity and caution. *Arithmetic Teacher, 24,* pp. 10–13.

Cox, L. S. (1975). Diagnosing and remediating systematic errors in addition and subtraction computations. *Arithmetic Teacher, 22,* pp. 151–157.

Doyle, W. (1979). Making managerial decisions in classrooms. In D. L. Duke (ed.), *Classroom management, NSEE yearbook II.* Chicago: University of Chicago Press.

Dunlap, W. P. (1976). An attitudinal device for primary children. *Arithmetic Teacher, 23,* pp. 29–32.

Gallup, G. H. (1984). The 16th annual Gallup poll of the public's attitudes toward education. *Phi Delta Kappan, 66,* pp. 23–28.

Gerber, W. R. (1972). *Educator's treasury of humor for all occasions.* West Nyack, N.Y.: Parker.

Gnagey, W. J. (1981). *Motivating classroom discipline.* New York: Macmillan.

Good, T. L., & Grouws, D. A. (1979). The Missouri mathematical effectiveness project: An experimental study in fourth-grade classrooms. *Journal of Educational Psychology, 71,* pp. 355–362.

Gregory, J. W. (1979). Test failure and mathematics failure: There is a difference. *Arithmetic Teacher, 27,* pp. 50–52.

Heddens, J. W., & Speer, W. (1988). *Today's mathematics.* Chicago: Science Research Associates.

Kounin, J. S. (1970). Observing and delineating techniques of managing behavior in classrooms. *Journal of Research and Development in Education, 4,* pp. 62–72.

McDonald, M. (1983). Factors that may influence performance on standardized tests. In G. Shufelt (ed.), *The agenda in action* (pp. 169–172). Reston, Va.: NCTM.

McKillip, W. D. (1979). Teacher-made tests: Development and use. *Arithmetic Teacher, 27,* pp. 38–44.

Merwin, J. C. (1961). Constructing achievement tests and interpreting scores. In NCTM, *Evaluation in mathematics: Twenty-sixth yearbook of the National Council of Teachers of Mathematics* (pp. 43–69). Washington: NCTM.

Molyneux, L. (1981). *Beating the bulletin board blues.* Dansville, N.Y.: Instructor.

Moyer, J. C., & Moyer, M. (1978). Computation: Implications for learning disabled children. In M. Suydam (ed.), *Developing computational skills* (pp. 78–95). Reston, Va.: NCTM.

Schoen, H. L. (1979). Using the interview to assess mathematics learning. *Arithmetic Teacher, 27,* pp. 34–37.

CHAPTER 3

Foundations for Beginning Mathematics

Objectives

After reading this chapter you will be able to:

1. Identify several important mathematics concepts to be developed with beginning-mathematics students.

2. Create several mathematics activities to be used with beginning-mathematics students.

3. Explain strategies for developing the concept of number and related topics.

4. List some of the mathematical concepts that children exhibit upon entering kindergarten.

5. Describe some of the considerations for teaching geometry in kindergarten.

6. Discuss some of the preformal mathematical experiences that are necessary for developing concepts of number, measurement, and time.

Introduction

Good beginning programs in mathematics provide widely varied experiences for children to explore mathematics concepts. Games, songs, stories, and manipulative materials help to develop mathematical concepts and skills. Teachers of beginning mathematics also need to develop a child's social skills. Learning to cooperate with other children when building a block structure, developing a sense of completion when doing activities, and gaining a feeling of independence are equally important to the acquisition of specific mathematics concepts and skills. It is important that kindergarten teachers establish an enjoyable yet structured mathematics program for children.

Expectations

As children enter kindergarten, it is helpful to consider the kinds of mathematical knowledge that they have developed. Rea and Reys (1971) have reported on the mathematical knowledge of children prior to formal schooling. Over half the children in their study were able to identify numbers 1 through 8. Also, most children were able to identify pennies, nickels, and dimes before they started kindergarten instruction. On the other hand, only 29 percent of the children knew the day of the week, and only 20 percent of the children knew their birthday. Caution must be used in interpreting these findings because the early mathematical experiences of children vary widely. However, the central point is that children do come to school with some mathematical knowledge, and it is important to diagnose their level of understanding and then to begin teaching from that point.

Helping to guide the development of goals for kindergarten mathematics are research findings such as those of Kurtz (1978). Kurtz surveyed kindergarten teachers and developed a list of topics for development during the kindergarten school years. The following list represents a summary of topics that were viewed as important components of a kindergarten program.

Tentative List of Kindergarten Competencies

Rationally count to 20
Recognize numbers to 10
Identify sets of 0, 1, 2, 3, 4, and 5
Identify sets of 6, 7, 8, 9, and 10

Write numerals 0 to 5 in order
Write numerals 6 to 10 in order
Identify a circle, its inside and outside
Write numerals in order to 20
Identify sets for one more and one less
Join sets to form sums to 5
Join sets to form sums to 10
Separate two sets to form differences from 5
Add numerals to sums of 5
Tell time on the hour
Locate a day of the month on the calendar
Identify penny, nickel, and dime

A list of topics such as the preceding one is helpful for beginning teachers. However, additional experiences need to be developed in order to provide depth and breadth to a kindergarten program. Some children come to school with a rich assortment of mathematical understandings; other children have not had such experience. Therefore, a list of mathematical topics for kindergarten may be viewed as a map—some kindergarten classes and individual children may not move the entire distance along the map. However, having a map helps the teacher plan the journey and measure progress along the path. In this chapter we will consider many different topics in order to provide as comprehensive a map for young children as we can.

===== *MATH FACT 3.1* =====

Some primitive tribes count using "one," "two," and "many."

Preformal Mathematics

Much preformal mathematics work needs to be done at the kindergarten level. Children need to classify, order, and make patterns. Vocabulary is also important. In fact, the foundation of preformal mathematics needs to be carefully and slowly developed. Many publishing companies provide textbooks for kindergarten classes. These are helpful for beginning teachers but need to be supplemented with many experiences that involve manipulative objects. A thorough development of preformal mathematics lays a solid foundation for more abstract mathematical work.

Classification

Classification involves forming sets by determining relationships among elements. Noticing similarities and differences of objects is fundamental to the classification process. For example, given pictures of various foods, a child could form a set consisting of pictures of meats, another set consisting of pictures of vegetables, and a third set consisting of pictures of desserts.

Determining similarities and differences of objects and deciding whether to include an object in a given set are fundamental to the classification process (see Activity 3.1). Attribute blocks, which are shown in Fig. 3.1, are available through commercial mathematics distributors. They are useful for classification activities (see Activity 3.2). These blocks usually come in three or four shapes, such as triangular, square, and circular, and in different colors, sizes, and thicknesses. Children might sort all the triangular shapes into a set, or they might sort all the red shapes into a set. They might sort objects into a set and have other children guess why they sorted the objects in that way. Sorting all the thin triangles into a pile would involve using two attributes simultaneously.

Fig. 3.1 Attribute blocks. Photograph by author.

ACTIVITY 3.1   Classification Skill

Here is a teaching activity for developing classification skill.

Give a child a set containing a knife, fork, spoon, and toy plane. Ask the child to determine which item does not belong. Make up another activity in which three things have something in common but a fourth object is different in some way. Share your results with class members.

ACTIVITY 3.2   Classification by Shape

This is another teaching activity for developing classification skill.

Put different geometric shapes, such as a square, triangle, and circle, in a box. Have a student reach in and touch one, but do not let the child see it. Have the child describe the shape and try to guess what it is.

Household objects, such as bottle caps, toy cars, plastic soldiers, pencils, and crayons, can be used for classification activities. For example, broken crayons could be placed in one set, while intact crayons would form another set. Children can play games in which one child holds up a bottle cap and asks the class to find a similar cap. Likewise, the class could be asked to find a bottle cap that is different in some way from the one the child is holding.

Classification also involves a part-to-whole relationship, often called a *class inclusion relationship* (Inhelder & Piaget, 1958). For example, kindergarten children learn that knives, forks, and spoons "belong" in the category of kitchen utensils (Copeland, 1979). Other examples involve the children themselves (see Activity 3.3). The teacher might say, "Class, stand up." After the class is standing the teacher could say, "All the boys sit down." The boys are still part of the class, even though they are sitting down. Next, children wearing the color brown might be asked to sit down.

Many elementary school classmates have a day on which children can bring some of their pets to school. This is a great opportunity for classification activities. Children can develop the idea that all the dogs, cats, gerbils, and hamsters are part of the set described by the term "animals." Other classifications also are possible; for example, animals might be classified on the basis of color or size.

In summary, classification involves determining relationships among elements, finding features in common in a category, and distinguishing that category from other categories. Classification activities can be rather simple, such as determining that shirts and coats belong in the category called "clothes," or complex, such as finding thick, small, red circles among attribute blocks. In fact, Copeland (1974), a researcher of Piaget's theories, found that only 60 percent of 8- and 9-year-olds were successful with three attribute classification problems. For more detailed activities dealing with classification, the reader is referred to Burton (1985) and Copeland (1979).

In conclusion, a foundation of classification experiences is essential for later mathematical work. For example, questions on some standardized tests at the kindergarten level require that children know that kittens and puppies are included in the set of animals and that shirts and pants can be classified in the category of clothes. Children who do not understand these relationships are handicapped when they take formal, standardized achievement tests.

Furthermore, developing a concept of number is dependent on classification experiences at the preformal level. Seriation experiences help to provide a basis for ordering numbers and developing the meaning of ordinal numbers.

ACTIVITY 3.3   Classification by Attribute

Here is an idea that can help children develop attribute classification skill.

Have four children go out of the room. Put pencils in the left hand of each child. Then have the children come back into the classroom; see if the rest of the kindergarteners can observe the common attribute of the children. Make up some other guessing games for determining similarities and differences. Try some of these activities.

Seriation

Fig. 3.2

Seriation involves the ability to place objects in order according to some selected standard such as height, weight, or length. Experience in ordering concrete objects is important because it serves as a prerequisite for later work that involves ordering numbers. For example, children can arrange jar lids in order, from the smallest diameter to the largest diameter (see Fig. 3.2).

Books might be arranged in order on the basis of thickness; pencils might be arranged on the basis of length. Perhaps children could bring in old shoes and order those on the basis of length. Numerous examples of seriation activities for children are available in Baratta-Lorton's books *Workjobs* and *Workjobs II* (1972, 1979). These books provide excellent examples of hands-on experiences for kindergarten children.

Patterns

The determination of patterns is an essential feature of mathematical thinking. Even at the kindergarten level this activity can be fostered and nurtured. Gibb and Castaneda (1975) suggested that patterns for very young children may be made up of concrete objects, pictures, designs in weaving and stitchery, or symbols.

Fig. 3.3

Beads and string are useful for developing patterns. For example, a string could contain two black beads, then one white bead, two black beads, one white bead, and so on (see Fig. 3.3). Children might be asked what would come next.

Fig. 3.4

Attribute blocks might also be used. After being shown a square-circle-square-circle-square, children are asked what would come next (see Fig. 3.4).

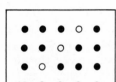

Fig. 3.5

A geoboard, made of pegboard and golf tees, is another material for developing patterns with young children (see Fig. 3.5). Make a pattern of golf tees, such as three red, one green, three red, one green; then ask the child what golf tee should be used next.

Physical movements are also useful patterning vehicles. Children could clap, whistle, and jump in order. Stop at some point in the sequence and ask which motion should come next. Also, children could clap once and then hop once, alternating in this way. Again, stop the action and ask what should come next.

Many examples of patterning are helpful for the development of mathematical thinking. Interested readers are referred to Burton (1985) for more examples.

Vocabulary

As children informally experience mathematics through classification, seriation, and patterns, vocabulary is developed. Terms that describe position, such as "under-over," "top-bottom," and "right-left," need to be developed. Terms that describe relationships, such as "bigger-smaller," "more-less," and "lighter-heavier," are also taught.

Many vocabulary terms can be taught informally or incidentally. For instance, children will go *inside* to their classroom. Creative teachers notice moments when they can develop preformal mathematical terms, such as when children are in line for lunch. A teacher might ask who is *between* Heather and Holly?

Summary

In conclusion, preformal mathematics is often developed at the kindergarten level. However, day care centers and parents can do the same kind of activities with even younger children. In contrast, some children with special learning problems, such as learning disabilities and mild mental retardation, might need experiences such as these even though their chronological age is several years beyond the kindergarten level.

Numbers and Counting

The development of a concept of numbers and the skill of rational counting are the cornerstone of the beginning-mathematics program. Often children come to school being able to rote-count—that is, they can say the number names in order, say, from one to ten, but are unable to count six objects rationally. When presented with six chips, they might say, "one, two, three, four, five, six, seven, eight, nine, ten." There is no association of the number names with objects in a way that determines the "how many-ness" of the set. Thus, the purpose of instruction is to help children develop rational counting skills.

According to Piaget, number concepts need to be established through repeated activities with objects. Children often are fooled by their perceptions, as indicated by the conservation of number example illustrated in Chapter 1. Fundamental to the development of number concepts is the relationship of one-to-one correspondence.

Fig. 3.6

A *one-to-one correspondence* between two sets is established when each element in the first set is matched with exactly one element in the second set. Likewise, each element in the second set is matched with exactly one element in the first set. A one-to-one correspondence is shown in Fig. 3.6.

The one-to-one correspondence between the set of plates and the set of forks helps establish the idea of "threeness"; that is, each set has three members. In fact, sets of three baseballs, three pretzels, three books, or three toy cars could each be matched in a one-to-one correspondence. The common feature or attribute of these sets is that they all contain three elements. Numerous experiences matching sets of objects in a one-to-one correspondence fashion need to be established. Also, when possible, children should use real objects. Placing forks next to a plate, hats on heads, or coats on hangers are some one-to-one correspondence possibilities (see Activity 3.4).

ACTIVITY 3.4   One-to-One Correspondence

This teaching activity can be used with kindergarten children to develop the idea of one-to-one correspondence.

Have five children come up to the front of the room. Put a hat on each child's head. Ask whether there are the same number of hats as there are heads. List some other activities that involve children with one-to-one correspondence experiences.

As children develop a concept of number through one-to-one correspondence activities, much experience counting individual groups or sets of objects is also provided. The notion of cardinal numbers or "how many" is gradually abstracted from the use of concrete objects. Initially, children should systematically touch the objects.

Care must be taken so that as the children touch each object, they say, "one, two, three, four, five, six." Finally, to provide closure, the children need to say that there are six objects in the set. Some kindergarten teachers report that even though some children can say the number names in order as they touch objects, they still may not recognize that the last number named indicates the number of objects in the group. This conclusion to the development of rational counting must be reinforced. Vary activities and sensory modalities to provide maximum practice effectiveness (see Activities 3.5 and 3.6).

ACTIVITY 3.5   Number Comprehension

Here is a teaching activity that you can easily construct.

Take shoeboxes and put a number on each, ranging from 0 to 9. Children are asked to read the numeral on each shoebox and "mail" the appropriate number of letters by inserting cards into the shoebox slots. For example, a "5" on the shoebox elicits a mailing of five cards.

ACTIVITY 3.6   Auditory Counting

This teaching activity emphasizes an auditory approach to counting.

Select one child from a small group of children. Tell the child to bounce a rubber ball as many times as he or she wants up to ten times. Tell the other children to listen carefully. The child who can state the number of bounces gets the ball. The process is then repeated.

Also, Piaget's theories suggest that after children learn to count rationally in a systematic way, they need to count objects that are placed in varied perceptual frameworks. Figure 3.7 illustrates this concept. For children with special learning problems it may be necessary to provide a systematic number design for a longer period of time before varying the arrangement (see Activity 3.7).

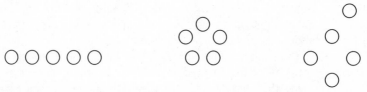

Fig. 3.7

ACTIVITY 3.7   Pocket Chart

This teaching activity can also be used as a bulletin board design.

Make a pocket chart from tagboard and cards that contain numerals, dots, and number words. Children can place the appropriate numeral card, card containing dots, and number word card in the correct slots on the pocket chart.

1	2	3	4	5	6	7	8	9	10
one	two	three	four	five	six	seven	eight	nine	ten
•	• •	• • •	• • • •	• . • . • .	• • • • • •	• • • • . • • •	• • • • • • • •	• • • • • • • • •	• • • • • • • • • • • •

In summary, rational counting initially involves numbers from 1 through 10. Since some children come to kindergarten class being able to count to 20 rationally, it is possible to teach rational counting beyond 10 without referring to place value. However, in this book we will consider a place value approach in the next chapter.

Finally, a special word on zero is in order. Zero is indeed a number—it is an element of the set of whole numbers {0, 1, 2, 3, 4, 5, 6 . . .}. A simple demonstration for illustrating the number zero is to take an empty box and ask the children how many candies they see. After some discussion (and disappointment), write the numeral "0" as a description of the number of candies in the box.

Order Relations

Order relations, in this case meaning the ordering of numbers, are developed along with the concept of numbers. In particular, we want children to be able to state that 7 is greater than 2 or that 5 is less than 10. Initially, this instruction needs to be verbal rather than symbolic. Using the inequality symbols (< for "less than" and > for "greater than") should be delayed until children have an intuitive grasp of order relations. Using Cuisenaire rods, which are colored rods used to develop a variety of mathematics concepts, staircases can be built to represent the order relationships of the numbers from 1 through 10. This approach is often called a *measurement approach* because Cuisenaire rods do not have indentations to show how many unit blocks make up a given rod. A child needs to place unit blocks next to a rod to determine the value of the rod. An example is shown in Fig. 3.8.

Thus, a visual image is seen for the ordering of numbers from 1 through 10. However, a problem may occur with this approach. Because there are no indentations on the rods, some children may see the red rod as one unit rather than two. An alternative method that allows for both a measurement approach and a counting approach was emphasized by Catherine Stern. A Stern counting board is shown in Fig. 3.9. The individual blocks fit together to give a view that looks like the measurement approach of the Cuisenaire rods, but discrete pieces can be seen so that children can count individual blocks. Children need to have experience with a variety of concrete approaches such as these (see Activities 3.8 and 3.9).

Order relations need to be emphasized concretely for numbers between 1 and 10. As children learn place value, place value models help to illustrate larger numbers and their order. This will be discussed in the chapter on place value.

Fig. 3.8 Cuisinaire rods. Photograph by author.

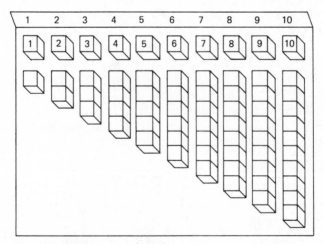

Fig. 3.9 Stern counting board.

ACTIVITY 3.8 ## Practicing Counting

You can use this activity when practicing counting. It should be used after a concrete, manipulative introduction to counting.

Make a walking number line by taking a 10-foot-long roll of paper and making squares about 1 square foot in size. Have a child walk to the square with a 3 on it; have another walk to the square with an 8 on it. Now have the children determine who is farther from zero.

0	1	2	3	4	5	6	7	8	9	10

Many other uses for the walking number line are available. See if you can invent some.

ACTIVITY 3.9 ## Practicing at the Semiconcrete Level

This teaching activity is perhaps at a semiconcrete level as compared with the Cuisenaire and Stern materials. However, it serves as a useful practice activity before children reach the abstract stage of order relations.

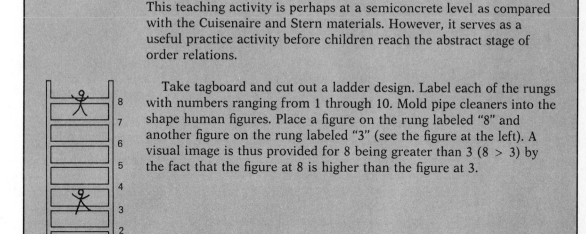

Take tagboard and cut out a ladder design. Label each of the rungs with numbers ranging from 1 through 10. Mold pipe cleaners into the shape human figures. Place a figure on the rung labeled "8" and another figure on the rung labeled "3" (see the figure at the left). A visual image is thus provided for 8 being greater than 3 (8 > 3) by the fact that the figure at 8 is higher than the figure at 3.

Numeral Formation

Children need to practice forming numerals correctly. Using primary paper and dotted numerals that children can color is one technique. Sandpaper

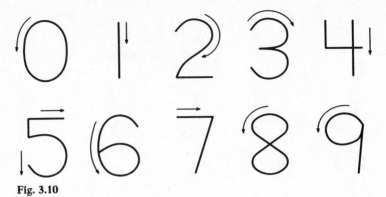

Fig. 3.10

with a number drawn on it is also helpful. Children can trace the numeral with their finger to practice the appropriate movement. Another technique for numeral formation is to use masking tape to construct large numerals on the floor. Children can walk along each numeral to trace the path of its construction (see Activity 3.10).

In general, numerals are drawn from the top down. Figure 3.10 shows some suggested motions.

Sometimes children will reverse numerals. Particular problems are often seen with Ɛ , ƨ , ϱ (3, 5, 9). There is no need for concern until about the middle of the second grade. If reversals continue at that point, a specialist in learning disabilities should be consulted.

ACTIVITY 3.10   Dominance Tests

Sometimes children with dominance problems have unusual difficulty writing numerals and doing cursive writing. Such a child may write numerals with the right hand yet reveal left-side hand and arm dominance. Here are some dominance tests for you to try with some elementary school children:

Hand dominance. Fold your hands in your lap. The thumb on top is probably your nondominant hand.
Arm dominance. Cross your arms on your chest. Your dominant arm is most likely the one closer to your body.

Ordinal Numbers

Ordinal numbers denote position. Rea and Reys (1971) noted that entering-kindergarten children exhibited a greater competence with cardinal-num-

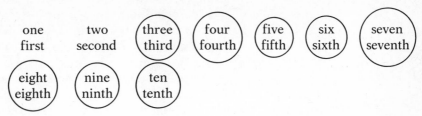

Fig. 3.11

ber concepts than with ordinal numbers. For example, more than 75 percent could count rationally to 10 but only 25 percent could identify the third ball in a row.

Ordinal numbers from first to tenth need to be developed in beginning-mathematics programs (see Activity 3.11). As children are lined up to leave the classroom, point out who is first, second, third, and fourth in line. Also, ordinal numbers can be illustrated by using toy cars arranged to show the order of a race's finish.

There is a parallelism between number words used in the cardinal sense and those used in the ordinal sense. As children grasp cardinal-number concepts, those concepts can help to gain ordinal-number understandings, especially from third to tenth.

Figure 3.11 shows the relationship between the terms used to refer to the cardinal and ordinal numbers. Notice that the looped portions show cardinal and ordinal names that sound alike.

ACTIVITY 3.11   Ordinal Numbers

This activity can be used to motivate a first-grade lesson on ordinal numbers.

Some children say that they have 11 fingers. Holding both hands up, such a child says, "ten, nine, eight, seven, six," while touching the fingers on his or her left hand. Looking at the right hand, the child says, "five." Then the child says, "Six plus five is eleven. So I have eleven fingers." How could this be? Diagnose the child's misconception of numbers.

Time

At the beginning-mathematics level, teaching time concepts is a difficult process. Copeland (1974) reported on Piagetian research that indicated that young children tend to focus on the measuring instrument rather than the duration of the time interval. For example, young children often think that it takes longer to cook a three-minute egg when measured by a timer than it does when the same three minutes is measured by a stopwatch. Children believe that since the stopwatch clicks quickly and seems to be moving faster, or further, than the timer, then it must measure a faster duration of time. Thus, teachers of young children must not rush children to read clocks and other time measurement instruments.

Initially, young children need to develop a sense of time duration. Children might guess how many blocks a classmate could stack in one minute, and then observe the results of this experiment. Television shows are popular with children. Thus, children might relate a half hour to the length of one of their favorite shows. Experiences with an hour might be developed by discussing an hour of TV shows and an hour of time during the school day. Children need experiences drawn from daily life to establish a sense of time duration (see Activity 3.12).

ACTIVITY 3.12   Relativity of Time

This activity helps us see the relativity of time. Also, we can, to some degree, determine how relaxed children are.

Put your head down on your desk and close your eyes. When you feel that a minute has passed, lift your head up. Your teacher will write on the board whether you are early or late with your estimate. No counting please. Try this activity with a 5- or 6-year-old child.

In a beginning-math program children need to become aware of the days of the week. A large calendar could be placed in the front of the room, and each day a child could mark off the day of the week. Thus, children will be acquainted with the day of the week as well as the month of the year. According to Gesell, Ilg, and Ames (1946), many children are unable to state the month, season, year, and day until around age 8. The same researchers indicated that topics such as morning, afternoon, and day of the week are well within the understanding level of most 5-year-olds.

After a solid foundation of time duration activities, children can begin to read a clock and relate it to their daily activities. Initially, a clock exhibiting only the hour marking should be displayed. A clock face can easily be constructed with a paper plate, colored paper for the clock hands, a brass fastener for holding the clock hands, and magic markers for indicating the numerals.

Fig. 3.12

The clock hands can be moved by children to parallel their daily activities. For example, school lunch starts at 12 o'clock. School starts at 9 o'clock. A favorite cartoon show begins at 4 o'clock. Again, care must be taken not to rush this activity with beginning-mathematics students. Informal reading of the clock at hour intervals should be emphasized. Not until the end of the third grade are children expected to read a clock to the hour and nearest minute.

================= *MATH HISTORY 3.1* =================

For thousands of years, an hour has been divided into 60 minutes and a minute into 60 seconds. This is considered to be a result of the ancient Babylonian system, which used a base of 60.

Also, perhaps a word on digital clocks is in order here. Most school materials for the reading of clocks still emphasize the clock face rather than the digital clock. The reason for this is that a sense of time before or after a given time, say, 4 o'clock, can be viewed. A digital clock reading "2:00" does not give any visual cues for time before or after the indicated time. Many children who have been given digital clocks for presents can read the clock; however, it is still necessary to give the child a sense of time duration and to relate the digital clock to daily activities. Some elementary school textbooks emphasize the traditional clock face but pair the digital clock with the traditional clock (see Fig. 3.12).

Money

By the onset of kindergarten, many children have had some experience with money. Perhaps they have been given pennies, nickels, or dimes from significant adults. Even so, the complexity of making change requires abstract thinking and needs to be delayed until children have developed rational counting, as well as some facility with addition and subtraction (Burton,

1985). At the first grade level, it is possible to use the classroom store activity in which children buy products and make change.

During the kindergarten year, children need to be able to identify a penny, nickel, and dime. Introduction of the quarter and dollar can also be undertaken. Whenever possible, use real money. Sometimes play money may have distorted relative sizes, for example a very large picture of a penny may confuse children when they see that the real coin is smaller than the play money pictures.

The concept of trading becomes an important idea as children mature through kindergarten and the start of first grade. Trading games, such as the one diagrammed in Fig. 3.13, can help children understand the relationships of coin values. In this game, children use a number cube with numerals from 1 through 6. After rolling a 5, for example, a child counts five pennies and puts them on the board in the penny column. However, the main rule of this game is to show, in any column, the least number of coins possible. Therefore, five pennies are traded for one nickel. Again, the number cube is rolled. Suppose a 3 is rolled. Now, three pennies are placed in the penny column; no trade is possible this time. Each time the number cube is rolled, trades are made if possible, and the smallest denominations of coins are shown. Play continues until a dime is placed on the board in the dime column. Variations of this activity are possible, such as trading until a quarter or dollar is obtained.

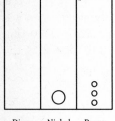

Dime   Nickel   Penny

Fig. 3.13

Games such as the previous one can be played with an entire class or used in a learning station with small groups of children. As children play matching and trading games to develop an understanding of coin value relationships, they become ready for the classic classroom store game. Here children can use money (perhaps play money at this time) to buy simulated products that have been cut out of newspaper or magazine ads.

=============== *MATH HISTORY 3.2* ===============

The issue of paper money was begun during the Roman Empire but lapsed and was not revived until the seventeenth century, when England and France began it again.

Measurement

Research by Hiebert (1984) suggests that young children have trouble with many measurement tasks that we, as adults, take for granted. In particular, young children need to experience and work with gross comparisons such as longer and shorter, more or less, heavier and lighter. They need to see that a unit can be repeatedly used to measure length, weight, capacity, or volume. Also, an extremely difficult idea for children, which is usually not learned until at least age 8, is the notion that if it takes many small units to measure something, then it will take fewer large units to measure the same thing. A later chapter devoted entirely to methods and activities for teaching measurement will discuss measurement in more detail. However, at this point some fundamental considerations for beginning-mathematics programs can be considered.

=========== *MATH HISTORY 3.3* ===========

A thousand paces were to the Romans *milia passum,* which we now call a "mile."

Length

Premature use of rulers should be avoided (see Activity 3.13). Initially, young children need to do a great deal of measuring using nonstandard or arbitrary units (see Activity 3.14). Some of the kinds of questions that can be posed are the following:

1. How many hand lengths is the table?

2. Can you find something longer than your book?

3. How many pencil lengths long is the room?

4. Can you find something taller than you?

Activities such as these help children to use a unit repeatedly, which is a prerequisite for using an inch or centimeter ruler at a later time. When beginning to use a ruler in class, be sure to use one with either inch or centimeter markings, not both. Young children are confused with all the markings that are on an "adult" ruler (some adults are, too). Also, when introducing the foot, why not cut out a design of a human foot (exactly 12 inches long) and let children measure their height? This gives them a nice visual recollection of how many feet tall they are.

Metric units are sometimes introduced in kindergarten classes. As with customary units like the foot and inch, specific names of units should be kept to a minimum—"centimeter" is sufficient for the level of development of many of the children. Also, for children with special learning problems, vocabulary and activities need to be modified so that children are not overloaded with names, symbols, or visual distractions—particularly a ruler with multiple markings on it.

ACTIVITY 3.13   Linear Measurement

This diagnostic activity helps you determine a child's readiness for linear measurement. If a child thinks that the two arrangements of sticks are unequal, then you need to avoid premature use of measuring rulers.

Take four sticks of equal length and arrange them as shown below:

Then rearrange them like this:

Ask the child if the path is the same length.

ACTIVITY 3.14   Arbitrary Measurement Units

This experience helps you appreciate the arbitrary nature of measurement units.

Invent a unit for measuring length. Use it to estimate the size of three objects in the room; then actually measure the objects. Record the results for both your estimates and your actual measurements. Discuss your unit and results in the class. How could you vary this activity for use with children of primary school age?

Weight (Mass)

As in the measurement of length, the emphasis for weight-measuring activities is on comparisons, such as comparing the weight of a pencil with that of a thumbtack. Units such as the pound or gram may be introduced, but the major purpose of the activities is to develop estimation and comparison experience. Here are a few activities for developing weight measurement experiences:

1. Fill boxes with popcorn, sand, or paper. Have the children use a balance with a pan on each side to compare the weights of each box and determine the heaviest or the lightest box.

2. Have the children collect four things that they feel are heavier than their math book. Again, compare the weights by using a balance with two pans (no fair weighing the teacher on the pan).

The term "weight" is used by many elementary teachers. *Weight* depends on a gravitational field and tends to fluctuate, whereas *mass* is the amount of matter in a body and is constant. For practical purposes, the distinction at the early elementary school level is unimportant. The term "weight" is probably preferred because it is usually consistent with what children are learning at home.

Capacity and Volume

Piaget has suggested that many young children have trouble conserving liquid capacity measures. That is, they think that a small glass of water has less water than an equal amount of water poured into a larger glass. Although the amount of water is the same, children are influenced by the size of the glass container.

Similarly, as with length and weight measurements, children need to do many experiments filling and emptying liquid and volume containers. Estimation, or "guessing," the result is, again, an important activity for young children Here are some sample questions and experiments for children to try:

1. How many glasses of water will fill the pitcher?

2. Find two jars that each hold more water than the milk carton.

3. How many scoops of sand will fill the cereal box?

4. How many teaspoons of sugar will fill a cup?

Any household objects such as margarine containers, ketchup bottles, soda bottles, or cans can be used for experiments such as this. If the children are unable to perform some of these experiments on their own, then the teacher can set up a demonstration area and can lead the class through the experiment by calling on individual children to perform a part of an activity, such as measuring a teaspoon of water (see Activity 3.15).

ACTIVITY 3.15   A Cooking Application of Measurement

Many kindergarten teachers have children mix food items together for snacks. Here is one such activity.

For this activity you do not need to cook. Mix together two parts nonfat dry milk, one part peanut butter, and one-half part honey. Roll this mixture into small balls and, if desired, roll in powdered sugar. This makes a nutritious candy for children during the kindergarten day.

Temperature

Having a thermometer in the room can help children gradually learn temperature reading. Nevertheless, at first, children should relate to weather conditions in a general way. Comments such as, "It is cold today," or "It is hot today," can be made by the teacher. Also, a teacher can say, "Put a coat on before you go *outside*. It is *cold outside*." Comments such as these help to teach informal terms of temperature.

Although Rea and Reys (1971) reported that over half the entering kindergarten students in their sample were able to identify the purpose of a thermometer, reading some of the degree markings and relating them to daily life requires at least another year of school. Therefore, the teacher might announce the temperature and say that it is cold or hot, but he or she should not expect children at the kindergarten level to be proficient in reading a thermometer.

Geometry

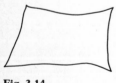

Fig. 3.14

Geometric experiences for young children are important elements of a beginning-mathematics program. To this end, a survey of geometric topics for the elementary school will be presented in a later chapter. At this point, however, some preliminary observations can be made. Children at the age of 5 usually can reproduce the design of a square shape. Prior to the age of 4, a square is often drawn with "ears" at one or more corners, as shown in Fig. 3.14.

Rea and Reys (1971) have indicated that the majority of children entering kindergarten could do the following geometric tasks:

1. Match objects to similarly shaped objects.

2. Match objects to similarly shaped drawings.

3. Match objects to similar shapes in a form board (a board where the designs are outlined).

4. Correctly identify inside and outside areas of geometric shapes.

5. Correctly identify squares and circles.

6. Correctly identify lines, sides, and corners.

7. Make accurate comparisons in terms of length and distance.

8. Correctly reproduce lines, parallel lines, and perpendicular lines.

Although these research findings indicate that many kindergarten children can perform the aforementioned tasks, it should be noted that these findings are tentative and do not suggest that these topics should be omitted in kindergarten. On the contrary, these topics should most assuredly be developed during the kindergarten year as essential prerequisites for mathematical work at later grade levels.

Another point of view on geometric experiences for young children is presented by those who advocate an informal study of topology. *Topology* studies geometric properties that do not change when subjected to motions. For example, when you take a balloon and mark an "X" on the outside of it, there is no amount of pushing or pulling that can force the X to the inside of the balloon. The notions of inside and outside are thus topological concepts. Other examples of topological relations are those of closed and open, between, and connectedness (all in one piece), as well as separation and class inclusion. Some writers who have studied Piagetian research (Robinson, 1975) suggest that children have an earlier understanding of topological relations than they have of Euclidean geometry, which is based on straightness and measurement. Of course, these topics must be treated in an informal manner that is consistent with the developmental stage of children. A simple, informal, yet powerful example of topological relations is described in Activity 3.16, which uses a balloon to illustrate several key concepts.

ACTIVITY 3.16 Topological Concepts

This activity helps illustrate the notion of "betweenness," which is a fundamental example of order relations along a path, and also presents some key topological concepts.

Inflate a balloon and draw a face on its surface. Several topological concepts can be developed. Children can find something *inside* the face—the eyes are an example of this. Something open is the nose.

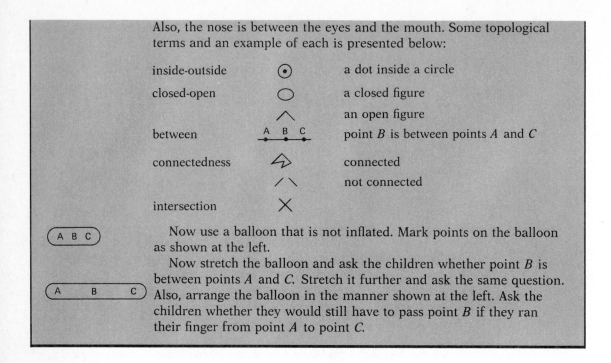

Also, the nose is between the eyes and the mouth. Some topological terms and an example of each is presented below:

inside-outside		a dot inside a circle
closed-open		a closed figure
		an open figure
between	A B C	point *B* is between points *A* and *C*
connectedness		connected
		not connected
intersection	X	

Now use a balloon that is not inflated. Mark points on the balloon as shown at the left.

Now stretch the balloon and ask the children whether point *B* is between points *A* and *C*. Stretch it further and ask the same question. Also, arrange the balloon in the manner shown at the left. Ask the children whether they would still have to pass point *B* if they ran their finger from point *A* to point *C*.

Numerous topological activities for young children are contained in Edith Robinson's essay (1975) in the NCTM yearbook entitled *Mathematics Learning in Early Childhood.*

As has been noted, children need to identify squares, circles, triangles, and rectangles during the kindergarten year. The study of these shapes is a part of Euclidean geometry because straightness and measurements are involved. Initially, recognition of these shapes is important. At a later point in the elementary school, the measurement of angles and sides will assume greater importance.

Sometimes teachers will use flips, slides, and turns to develop perceptual awareness. For example, take a triangle positioned as shown in Fig. 3.15. Now rotate or turn the triangle. Is it still a triangle? Of course, we as adults say yes, but some very young children do not. Therefore, sliding shapes, flipping them, or rotating them provides a varied perceptual approach to recognition of shapes that have been traditionally associated with Euclidean geometry. Other examples of what is often called transformational geometry will be developed in a later chapter.

In summary, geometry in the kindergarten can be developed from topological ideas to Euclidean concepts. The work of Rea and Reys (1971), Robinson (1975), and other writers has suggested some specific topics for inclusion in an early geometry unit.

Fig. 3.15

Microcomputers

Some innovative kindergarten and first-grade programs have developed activities for young children to use with a microcomputer. For gifted young children, the LOGO computer language has been used and individual teachers have reported some interesting findings (see Activity 3.17). To date, however, systematic research considering the learning capabilities of young children with the microcomputer has been lacking. Interested readers are referred to Clements (1985) for a description of the techniques that are currently available for using microcomputers with young children. In particular, Clements offers some suggestions for evaluating commercial software programs for use with young children.

ACTIVITY 3.17   Computer Usage

Elementary school children often have experiences with the BASIC computer language as well as the LOGO computer language. LOGO is often used with primary age children.

This LOGO program will draw a square on the screen. Although most initial LOGO programs teach directionality as well as memory for designs, some gifted 5- and 6-year-olds can actually construct programs such as the following:

To Square

```
FD 50 RT 90
FD 50 RT 90
FD 50 RT 90
FD 50 RT 90
END
```

Summary

Numerous concepts and skills need to be developed in a structured kindergarten mathematics program. This chapter has considered the major areas that should be included in a beginning-mathematics program. Children need a thorough understanding of preformal mathematics before embarking on a study of the concept of numbers. Concrete manipulative experiences are necessary to develop number relationships as well as topics such as time, money, measurement, and geometry. Awareness of relevant research relating to children's developmental stages has also been emphasized in this chapter.

The degree to which beginning topics are introduced, developed, or mastered will, of course, depend largely on both the teacher's skill and the child's prior experiences. However, as this chapter has pointed out, it is important for young children to enjoy exploring mathematics and investigating relationships in a concrete manner. A good teacher realizes the importance of a child's first attempts with mathematical thinking and encourages and accepts a child's work. A warm, supportive attitude can help children to feel good about their beginning-mathematics work, and this can help provide a solid first step in their walk through school mathematics.

Good teachers have known this for a long time. In fact, over 2500 years ago Laotse, a Chinese philosopher, said this:

> Therefore the Sage is good at helping men;
> For that reason there is no rejected person.
>   He is good at saving things;
>   For that reason there is nothing rejected.
> ——This is called stealing the Light.*

Discussion Questions

1. Choose five of the kindergarten competencies and develop an activity for each competency.

2. Based on the list of kindergarten competencies, develop a brief test that could be administered to kindergarten children to determine their degree of competency in these areas.

3. Read two articles that discuss skills needed by children before beginning a mathematics program. Compare and contrast the articles.

4. Read some of the literature related to Piaget's stages of intellectual development. Under which level or levels do the skills discussed in this chapter fall?

5. Discuss the role of a textbook in kindergarten and first-grade mathematics classes. How would you advise that the textbook be supplemented?

6. Construct at least two manipulative learning aids designed to develop rational counting, order relations, or numeral formation skills.

*Source: Laotse. (1948). The wisdom of Laotse (p. 156). Translated by Yu-T'ang, L. New York: Random House (Modern Library). Used with permission of publisher.

7. Read Evelyn Sowell's article from the March 1987 issue of *Arithmetic Teacher* entitled "Developmental Versus Practice Lessons in the Primary Grades." Using the idea in this article as a basis, construct a developmental lesson plan for one of the topics presented in this chapter.

8. Read Spiker and Kurtz's article in the February 1987 issue of *Arithmetic Teacher* entitled "Teaching Primary-Grade Mathematics Skills with Calculators." One interesting activity for promoting facility with ordinal numbers is the following:

> Add the first, third, and sixth numbers in these rows. Check your sums.

12	3	9	15	18	8	7	<u>29</u>
40	11	6	14	3	0	9	<u>46</u>

Develop some other hand calculator activities for beginning mathematics students to investigate.

References

Baratta-Lorton, M. (1972). *Workjobs.* Menlo Park, Calif.: Addison-Wesley.

Baratta-Lorton, M. (1979). *Workjobs II.* Menlo Park, Calif.: Addison-Wesley.

Biggs, E. E., & Maclean, J. R. (1969). *Freedom to learn.* Reading, Mass.: Addison-Wesley.

Burton, G. M. (1985). *Toward a good beginning: Teaching early childhood mathematics.* Menlo Park, Calif.: Addison-Wesley.

Clements, D. H. (1985). *Computers in early and primary education.* Englewood Cliffs, N.J.: Prentice-Hall.

Copeland, R. (1974). *How children learn mathematics.* New York: Macmillan.

Copeland, R. (1979). *Math activities for children.* Columbus, Ohio: Merrill.

Gesell, A., Ilg, F., & Ames, L. B. (1946). *The child from five to ten.* New York: Harper & Row.

Gibb, E. G., & Castaneda, A. M. (1975). Experiences for young children. In J. Payne (ed.), *Mathematics learning in early childhood.* The Thirty-Seventh Yearbook of the National Council of Teachers of Mathematics. Reston, Va.: NCTM.

Hiebert, J. (1984). Why do some children have trouble learning measurement concepts? *Arithmetic Teacher, 31,* pp. 19–24.

Inhelder, B., & Piaget, J. (1958). *The growth of logical thinking from childhood to adolescence.* London: Routledge, Kegan, Paul.

Kamii, C., & DeVries, R. (1976). *Piaget, children and numbers.* Washington, D.C.: National Association for Education of Young Children.

Kurtz, V. R. (1978). Kindergarten mathematics: A survey. *Arithmetic Teacher, 25,* pp. 51–53.

Rea, R. E., & Reys, R. E. (1971). Competencies of entering kindergartners in geometry, numbers, money and measurement. *School Science and Mathematics, 17,* pp. 389–402.

Robinson, E. (1975). Geometry. In J. Payne (Ed.), *Mathematics learning in early childhood,* the thirty-seventh yearbook of the national council of teachers of mathematics. Reston, Va.: NCTM.

Roper, A. (1977). *Metric recipes in the classroom.* Palo Alto, Calif.: Creative Publications.

CHAPTER 4

Teaching Numeration and Place-Value Concepts

Objectives

After reading this chapter you will be able to:

1. Identify characteristics of the Hindu-Arabic numeration system.

2. Create activities for students to use when studying place value.

3. Model place-value concepts using concrete models.

4. Compare and contrast several different systems of numeration.

5. Identify several estimation activities for students to do.

6. Analyze several materials useful for developing place-value concepts.

After students develop an understanding of cardinal numbers for numbers 1 through 10, counting greater-valued numbers and developing place-value concepts become increasingly important. This chapter focuses on the concepts and skills that maturing children need to understand and master as they learn to extend numeration and place-value concepts.

Refinements of Counting

In order to develop readiness for later work with operations, children need to develop a more sophisticated method of counting. For example, skip counting or counting by twos is useful as a readiness activity for multiplication. A walking number line can be placed on the floor and children can skip a numeral as they move along the number line; each time they land they can say the number name on which they have landed. To make a walking number line, simply draw blocks on a roll of paper and place numerals in the square areas.

Counting by threes and then by fives are also useful readiness activities. Particularly, counting by fives helps second graders to effectively read a clock. Further, counting backward from a number is helpful in laying a foundation for subtraction. Children can be given a number such as 8 and asked to count backward from that number. Also, starting at a number, for example 5, and counting forward from that number helps to provide readiness for addition of whole numbers.

The concept of odd and even numbers can be developed in an intuitive, concrete fashion. Rectangular grid paper can provide good models for odd and even numbers. Figure 4.1 illustrates the pattern that will develop. Children may offer the generalization that odd numbers always have a single square "hanging" from the diagram and even numbers have squares that fit in "evenly"!

The notion of zero as representing the number or quantity for an empty set is an important number concept. Teachers must be careful to use proper terminology to develop this number name—be sure to say "zero," not "oh." Children need to be reinforced many times that zero is indeed a number and a member of the set of whole numbers {0, 1, 2, 3, 4 . . .}.

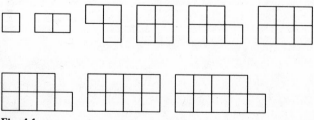

Fig. 4.1

Another concern when refining initial counting experiences is that the mathematics materials available today do not make as much of a distinction between number and numeral as they did in the past. However, it is important for elementary school teachers to be aware of the distinction and to use appropriate terminology in the classroom. *Number* represents an abstraction or idea regarding the "how manyness" of a set. We have a concept of "five," which is an abstraction. On the other hand, writing the *numeral* 5 is a symbol for the idea. We could have used other symbols, words, or notations to express the idea of "fiveness." For young children, this distinction requires a level of abstraction that, needless to say, most of them lack. When children are counting or performing operations such as addition or subtraction, there is nothing wrong with them saying that they are counting numbers or writing number names as answers.

Estimation activities, even for first-grade students, help to enrich the development of number and counting concepts. For example, teachers can scatter a set of 30 tacks on a table and ask children to look at them for several seconds. Then, the children can write down a guess of how many tacks they saw. Although estimation activities are of value, random guessing and specific counting should not be encouraged. By grouping the objects in some way such as sets of five or ten, children are discouraged from random guessing and specific counting and instead experience strategies for estimation.

Another activity for estimation involves placing between 5 and 20 chips on an overhead projector, turning on the light for a few seconds so that the students can see the arrangement, and then turning off the light. After recording their estimates, the children can compare their results and strategies. Teachers need to remember that exact answers are not important here; instead, approximations and visual groupings—the concept of "about"—are to be emphasized. Many good activities for estimating can be found in Van deWalle and Thompson (1985).

A Brief History of Numeration

Before studying specific methods for developing numeration and place value, a brief history of numeration is presented so that we can more greatly appreciate our own numeration system. Also, many of these historical topics can serve as a basis for historical reports by students, thus linking mathematics and social studies in an interdisciplinary manner.

Early humans first began to count orally. As time went on, numeral symbols were developed to help organize and keep records of larger amounts, and grouping made larger quantities more manageable.

One of the earliest forms of number recording survives from Babylonian civilization (2400 B.C.). Cunneiform or wedge-shaped characters were used to express numbers. The Babylonians used a base of 60, called a *sexigisimal system;* that is, place value was expressed on the basis of multiples of 60. Since the Babylonians did not have a symbol for zero, their numerals were difficult to interpret, and this was further confounded by the fact that they used a base-10 system for numbers less than 60, then shifted to a base-60 system for numbers greater than 60. Table 4.1 shows the Babylonian symbols for our numerals 1 through 10.

Here is an example of a Babylonian numeral:

$$(21 \times 60 \times 60) \quad + \quad (12 \times 60) \quad + \quad 13$$

◄ ◄ ▼   ◄ ▼▼   ◄ ▼▼▼

In the Babylonian base-10 and base-60 systems, the number 23, for example, could be written as ◄◄▼▼▼. However, ◄◄▼▼▼ could also be interpreted as $(2 \times 60) + 3$, or 123. Custom and context often dictated interpretations of Babylonian numerals, and only priests and kings were able to decipher the Babylonian notation.

The Egyptians also developed a numeration system but theirs was based on hieroglyphics, or picture writing. Several Egyptian symbols, their names, and our numeral equivalents are shown in Table 4.2.

The Egyptian system was cumbersome and time consuming to use. For instance, to express a number such as 3587, the Egyptians had to draw 23 pictures. Further, the Egyptian system did not have place value—∩II and II∩ both symbolized 12. Thus, the Egyptian system was more of a record-keeping than a numeration system and was not particularly efficient for computational exercises. Although the Egyptians made collections on the basis of groupings of tens, hundreds, thousands, and so on, the lack of place value was a fundamental deficiency of their numeration system.

Roman numeration, still in use today, was organized on the basis of multiples of 10. However, the Romans also lacked a place-value system such as our own. Table 4.3 lists some Roman numerals and our number equivalents, and then gives the derivations for some of the Roman symbols.

Table 4.1   Babylonian Symbols for Numerals 1 Through 10

Hindu-Arabic Numeral	Babylonian Symbol
1	▼
2	▼▼
3	▼▼▼
4	▼▼▼▼
5	▼▼▼▼▼
6	▼▼▼▼▼▼
7	▼▼▼▼▼▼▼
8	▼▼▼▼▼▼▼▼
9	▼▼▼▼▼▼▼▼▼
10	◄

Table 4.2   Egyptian Symbols for Numerals

Hindu-Arabic Equivalent	Egyptian Symbol	Name of Symbol
1	I	Stick or finger
2	II	
3	III	
4	IIII	
5	IIIII	
6	IIIIII	
7	IIIIIII	
8	IIIIIIII	
9	IIIIIIIII	
10	∩	Heel bone
11	∩ I	
20	∩∩	
23	∩∩III	
100	𝟗	Coiled rope or scroll
300	𝟗 𝟗 𝟗	
1,000	𝟈	Lotus flower or sheaf or wheat
10,000	𝒪	Pointing finger
100,000	𝒬	Pollywog or fish
1,000,000	𝒴	Person with arms raised in astonishment

Table 4.3   Roman Numeral Equivalency

Hindu-Arabic Equivalent	Roman Numeral	Derivation
1	I	Finger
2	II	
3	III	
4	IV	
5	V	Hand
6	VI	
7	VII	
8	VIII	
9	IX	
10	X	Crossed hands
11	XI	
12	XII	
20	XX	
22	XXII	
50	L	
100	C	Latin word *centum*
300	CCC	
500	D	
1000	M	Latin word *mille*

As seen in Table 4.3, the Romans used repetition of symbols as well as addition and subtraction procedures.

An intriguing and unique historical numeration system was that of the Central American Mayans. The Mayans, whose civilization may date back to 3000 B.C., exhibited a base-20 numeration system (perhaps because they went barefoot and saw 20 fingers and toes!) with place value and a symbol for zero. In contrast to the Babylonians, Egyptians, and Romans, the Mayans' recognition of a symbol for zero and the use of place value was quite remarkable. Unlike our notation, the Mayans wrote their place value notation in a top-to-bottom manner. An example is shown below.

$$
\left. \begin{array}{l} = \\ \otimes \end{array} \quad \begin{array}{l} 10 \times 20 \\ 0 \times 1 \end{array} \right\} \; 200
$$

Several Mayan symbols and our number equivalents are listed in Table 4.4. Note that the Mayan symbol for zero, $\otimes$, looks like a half-closed eye or a fist.

The Mayans probably used their numeration system for record keeping and calendar events rather than for computation purposes. (For a more detailed discussion of the Mayan system of numeration, see Bryket (1970).)

Table 4.4   Mayan Numeral Equivalency

Hindu-Arabic Equivalent	Mayan Symbol
1	•
2	••
3	•••
4	••••
5	—
6	$\overset{\bullet}{—}$
7	$\overset{\bullet\bullet}{—}$
8	$\overset{\bullet\bullet\bullet}{—}$
9	$\overset{\bullet\bullet\bullet\bullet}{—}$
10	=
20	$\overset{\bullet}{\otimes}$
21	$\overset{\bullet}{\vdots}$
100	$\overset{—}{\otimes}$
200	$\overset{=}{\otimes}$

Hindu-Arabic Numeration

Our system of numeration is called the *Hindu-Arabic system.* Early Hindu antecedents of our numerals were carved on temple blocks as early as 250 B.C. Credit for the invention of the symbol for zero and place value is usually given to the Hindus, but the exact date of origin is obscure. According to Benner (1969), sometime between the fifth and eighth centuries A.D. the Arabs modified and diffused the 10 Hindu symbols and the concept of place value to Western civilization. The creation of both a symbol for zero and a place-value system were important because they provided an efficient way of representing numbers *and* a highly effective method of computation.

Swenson (1973) notes that the first definite mention of the Hindu numerals and place-value system outside of India was made in 662 A.D. by Severus Seboket in western Syria. Also, Leonardo of Pisa recommended adoption of the Hindu-Arabic notation in a book called *Liber Abaci* written in 1202. Leonardo indicated that with place value and the symbols 0 through 9 any number could be written. Thus, we are indebted to the Hindu and Arabic cultures for our current numeration system. Imagine having to write or draw 26 characters to convey the numeral 4589! Instead, we use just four digits or numerals and convey the same idea through the system of place value. Commerce, industry, science—our whole modern culture—depends on an efficient and rapid use of numeration.

Contemporary Place-Value Numeration

At this point, we need to consider in more detail the concept of place value. What do we mean when we say our system is a place-value one? Simply, *place value* means that the positions of the digits in any numeral affects their value. For example, the numeral 24 is different from 42 because the digits are placed in different positions. Moreover, the 4 in the numeral 42 stands for 4 tens and in the numeral 24 it stands for 4 ones.

There are several terms that different writers use regarding place value and it is important to understand their meanings. The term *digits* usually refers to the symbols 0, 1, 2, 3, 4, 5, 6, 7, 8, and 9, which can be combined with place value to write numerals expressing many different numbers. For example, the numeral 2456 might be written to express the grouping shown here:

Thousands	*Hundreds*	*Tens*	*Ones*
2	4	5	6

Thus, each digit or numeral in a place-value system conveys far more information than it would in a system without place value. In our example, the numeral 2 in 2456 traditionally means 2 thousands, not 2 ones.

===================== *MATH HISTORY 4.1* =====================

An early form of Hindu numerals dates back to India at around 300 B.C. The equivalents of numbers 1 through 9 are shown below.

| 1 | 2 | 3 | 4 | 5 | 6 | 7 | 8 | 9 |

Most people would rather have $2000 than two $1 bills! Thus, the place-value notation system, by means of its positional emphasis, conveys a great deal of information. The discovery of zero, which allowed an efficient place-value structure to be constructed, was indeed ingenious. Numerals such as 207, for example, could now be written with zero as a place holder. Without zero, a vacant place would occur and 207 and 27 would be easily confused.

Consider also a numeral such as 3564, which is generally described as 3 thousands, 5 hundreds, 6 tens and 4 ones. However, we also use alternative methods of grouping, especially when doing computations. In this case the numeral 3564 could be described as containing 35 hundreds, 6 tens, and 4 ones. (Alternative methods of grouping are discussed later in the chapter.)

In summary, our system of numeration, which is of Hindu-Arabic origin, is a culmination of thousands of years of evolution. Its chief characteristics include the following:

1. Our collections for organizing our numeration system are made on the basis of powers of 10. The following table describes some of the place values:

$10 \times 10 \times 10 \times 10 \times 10$	$10 \times 10 \times 10 \times 10$	$10 \times 10 \times 10$	10×10	10	1
Hundred thousands	Ten thousands	Thousands	Hundreds	Tens	Ones

2. The existence of a symbol for zero allows numerals to be expressed in an unambiguous manner.

3. The system has place value, which means that the position of a digit in a numeral affects the value of that number.

4. The system is additive and multiplicative, which allows a numeral such as 257 to be expressed as $(2 \times 100) + (5 \times 10) + (7 \times 1)$.

=========== *MATH HISTORY 4.2* ===========

As the writing of numerals evolved, it became increasingly similar to our present form for writing numerals. For example, the West Arabic numerals shown here are from the eleventh century.

| 1 | 2 | 3 | 4 | 5 | 6 | 7 | 8 | 9 |

Strategies for Teaching Place-Value Concepts and Numeration

Although place-value concepts are extremely important in childhood education, a solid research base that describes their acquisition is lacking (Suydam & Dessart, 1980). In particular, Suydam and Dessart note a lack of research on the sequence of concepts needed to master place value for greater-valued numbers. During the late 1960s and early 1970s, it was generally accepted that the study of number systems such as a base-5 system would help children to develop an understanding of our own base-10 system. However, Glennon and Callahan (1968) reported that the advantages of supplementing instruction with other base numeration have not been demonstrated.

Current elementary school textbooks and journal articles can yield information about important strategies and concepts helpful to children in studying numeration and place value. Today the study of other number bases such as base 5 is seen as an enrichment activity for gifted mathematics students. Elementary mathematics textbooks need to be supplemented in order to provide a thorough explanation of base-10 numeration. There is a rich assortment of materials, activities, and strategies that can be useful to children and teachers alike as they develop base-10 numeration.

Initial Experiences

Trading and collection games can be helpful as readiness activities for place value. Each child (or a small group of children) can be given a bag and several popsicle sticks. Children are instructed to put five sticks in their bags and to observe how many sticks are left over. A record may be kept by the teacher and the list may look like this:

	Bag	Extra Sticks
John	1	2
Bill	1	0
Mary	1	3
Sue	1	4

The emphases in this activity are the notions of a group and that something is left over. At the kindergarten–first-grade levels, this activity is designed to provide readiness for base-10 place-value concepts.

Another activity that is a useful readiness technique is to give children some clay and popsicle sticks—one child receives six sticks, another seven sticks, another four sticks, and so on. Children are instructed to form animal shapes from the clay and to use four sticks for the legs. Recordings of the number of animals and of the leftover sticks are then made.

Chip-trading activities, available through Scott Resources, are also helpful for developing readiness for the concept of trading, vital to a thorough understanding of place value (see Activity 4.1). As children make trades of three yellow chips for one blue chip, they are building a foundation for more advanced work, such as trading 10 ones for 1 ten in base-10 numeration.

ACTIVITY 4.1   The Banker's Game*

The chip-trading activities available through Scott Resources are recommended. The Banker's Game is described here.

The Banker's Game can be played with two to four students. Each student is given one game board.

The chips should be thought of as money that can be traded like this:

1 blue = 3 yellow
1 green = 3 blue
1 red = 3 green

The person on the banker's left takes the first turn. A player gets chips from the banker by throwing a die, asking the banker for that number of yellow chips, and making any possible exchanges. For example, suppose the first player rolls 5. That player asks the banker for five yellow chips, and then trades three yellow chips for one blue chip. The player places the chips on his or her chip till.

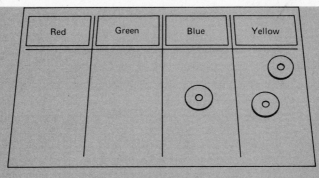

The second person now takes a turn. The player throws the die, receives yellow chips, and makes any exchanges possible.

Play continues in this manner for as many rounds as it takes for a player to get the red chip.

The winner is the person who first trades for the red chip, and he or she becomes the banker for the next game.

*Used by permission of Scott Resources, P.O. Box 2121, Fort Collins, Colorado 80522.

It should be noted that the emphasis in collecting and trading games is to informally develop readiness for base-10 numeration. Although groupings other than 10 are explored, the games do not attempt to teach other number base numeration. Collecting and trading are the key activities to be explored.

Teaching Base-10 Place-Value Concepts

The teaching of place value for two-digit numbers needs to be developed in a concrete manner. Also, to learn base-10 place value, children need to be given a variety of examples and models from which to work. For instance, by using commercially produced base-10 blocks, a teacher can show the numeral 24 on an overhead projector in the way shown at the left. Children are to record this way:

Tens	Ones
2	4

24

Conversely, the teacher can ask a child to come to the overhead projector and display the concrete model for 35, 3 tens and 5 ones. However, it is important to provide experience in both directions; that is, children should view a model from which they can record the proper numeral, and they should be given a numeral from which they can construct a model. Further, children working at their desks rather than at the projector should be given graph-paper models of tens and ones and asked to show various two-place numbers.

Fig. 4.2

Other materials can be used as well. For example, the numeral 16 may be demonstrated by using plastic straws and rubber bands, as shown in Fig. 4.2. Children need to have straws and rubber bands at their desks to perform bundling activities for representing two-place numbers. Some mathematics educators prefer using bundling activities before base-10 blocks, whereas others prefer base-10 blocks. Regardless of which is first introduced, it is important to note that children need to use several kinds of concrete material. Thus, a rich perceptual base is provided for understanding the concept.

As children are developing place-value concepts, it is best to start with the "teens" and move along through the twenties, thirties, forties, and so forth. However, it should be noted that the terms *eleven, twelve, thirteen, fourteen, fifteen, sixteen, seventeen, eighteen,* and *nineteen* are more difficult for some children than are the twenties or thirties. The latter are rhythmic—*twenty-one, twenty-two, twenty-three,* and so on—whereas the teens—the words *eleven, twelve,* and *thirteen*—have no common prefix sound and are thus more difficult to learn. The teens are the only decade of two-digit numbers that show this anomaly and as such, extra attention needs to be paid to their number names.

When teaching place-value concepts it is important that the teacher is positioned in such a way as to view the numerals from the same direction as the students. For example, we usually speak of 24 as having 2 tens recorded on the *left* by the numeral 2; however, the teacher must remember that when facing a class his or her left side is the students' right side. A student teacher was once observed teaching a class place-value concepts. Using manipulative material, she held up a model for 100, and said that the hundred was on the far left. Unfortunately, since the class was facing her, the model was on their far *right!* Needless to say, the lesson did not go over very well. An overhead projector is a useful vehicle for developing place-value concepts because it displays materials on both the teacher's and students' left side.

Some materials used to develop place-value concepts are classified as *proportional* or *nonproportional.* Proportional materials, such as number blocks or straws and rubber bands, allow children to see that 10 ones blocks make up 1 ten block or that 10 straws are bundled into one group of 10. In contrast, nonproportional materials include an abacus and money. An abacus, often used to model place value, does not show how 10 beads are traded for 1 bead. That is, a child cannot line up 10 beads from the ones place and see an equal number, size, weight, or thickness in the bead representing 10. Likewise, money is a nonproportional place value device. Although ten $1 bills can be traded for one $10 bill and ten $10 bills can be traded for one

$100 bill, students cannot glue ten $1 bills together and check that their area, length, size, or thickness is equal to a $10 bill. Thus, nonproportional devices are more abstract than proportional devices. For first and second graders, proportional devices need to be used first. Later, after gaining experience with proportional devices, students can be introduced to nonproportional devices. For intermediate-level students, nonproportional devices can be helpful in reviewing some place-value concepts and in introducing decimals. Many children who have been mainstreamed need to use proportional devices for a long period of time before they can use nonproportional materials.

Concrete models for numbers in the hundreds can also be developed using base-10 blocks. An example for 232 is shown in Fig. 4.3. As with two-place numerals, children need many examples and models to acquire an understanding of three-place numbers. Children need to fit together 10 of the tens blocks to see that an exchange can be made with a hundreds block. Examples that require children to construct or draw models for a numeral and to write the numeral for a given diagram or model need to be performed.

A perceptual model that displays the numeral 156 with straws and rubber bands is shown in Fig. 4.4. Notice that when ten bundles of 10 have been obtained, the group is bound by a large rubber band and placed in a box labeled hundreds.

The thousands also can be concretely developed by using base-10 blocks. For example, the numeral 2456 can be visualized as shown in Fig. 4.5.

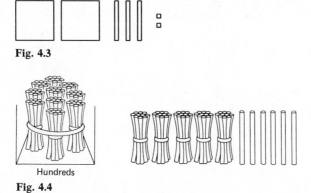

Fig. 4.3

Hundreds

Fig. 4.4

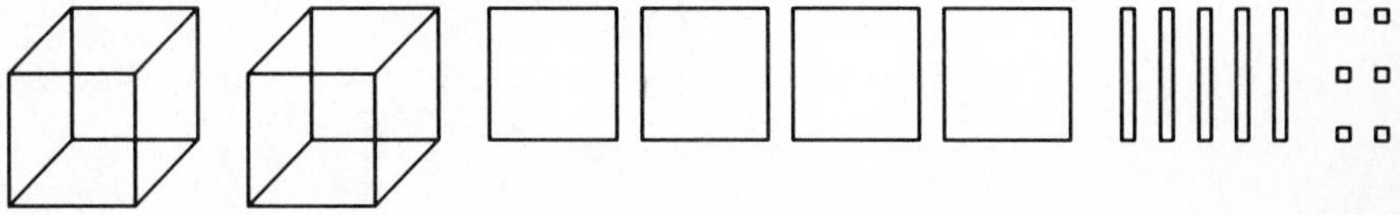

Fig. 4.5

Developing Place-Value Concepts with Nonproportional Materials

After children have gained an understanding of place value by using proportional materials, nonproportional examples can be developed. This section examines three nonproportional models: an abacus, a place-value pocket chart, and counting persons.

The *abacus,* used by the Romans over 2000 years ago, is a useful model for place-value topics. Figure 4.6 shows the numeral 2365 modeled on the type of abacus found in most schools.

A *place-value pocket chart* can be made by using tag board and envelopes. Envelopes are taped to the tag board at appropriate places. Colored construction paper is cut into small rectangles, with each color representing different values (e.g., red could represent ones, blue tens, and green hundreds). Figure 4.7 illustrates a place-value pocket chart for the numeral 56. Notice that 5 blue rectangles indicate 5 tens and 6 red rectangles show 6 ones. Similarly, 234 can be visualized by placing 2 green rectangles in the envelope slot under hundreds, 3 blue rectangles in the slot under tens, and 4 red rectangles in the slot under ones.

Counting persons may be cut out of wood to look like human figures. Clothespins may be attached to the hands to illustrate numerals, as shown in Fig. 4.8, which shows 423.

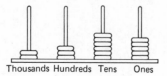

Thousands Hundreds Tens   Ones

Fig. 4.6

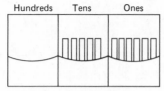

Fig. 4.7

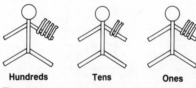

Hundreds   **Tens**   **Ones**

Fig. 4.8

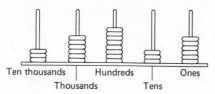

Fig. 4.9

Generally, most texts introduce first graders to numbers up to 100 and second graders to numbers up to 1000. Students in the third to fifth grades are introduced to numbers as large as one million. However, because concrete models of the proportional variety are useful only through the thousands, nonproportional devices are necessary to teach greater-valued numbers. For example, 36,836 can be shown on an abacus in the way shown in Fig. 4.9.

Extending Numeration

As children move to greater levels of abstraction with place-value concepts, expanded notation is used. At the primary level, a number such as 24 might be expressed as $20 + 4$. At the intermediate level, 2456 might be expressed in an expanded form such as $(2 \times 1000) + (4 \times 100) + (5 \times 10) + (6 \times 1)$. In the latter example, multiplication and addition are used to express numerals in expanded notation.

Often at the seventh-grade level numerals in expanded notation are expressed using exponential notation, which involves a base and an exponent. For example, $2^3 = 2 \times 2 \times 2 = 8$; that is, the exponent of 3 describes how many times the base of 2 is used as a factor. Therefore, 23,582 can be expressed as $(2 \times 10^4) + (3 \times 10^3) + (5 \times 10^2) + (8 \times 10^1) + (2 \times 10^0)$. (Note that any number having an exponent or power of zero is considered to be 1.) The evolution of expanded notation is not a substitute for concrete experiences; it only serves as a vehicle for using more abstract notation. When students understand concrete models through the thousands, greater-valued numbers can be investigated through expanded notation.

Reading numerals is a related activity that is abstract in nature. Children need to understand, for instance, that the symbol 24 can be read aloud as "twenty-four." Practice activities for reading numerals should be developed throughout the elementary school curriculum. Some elementary school textbooks, for example, ask students to write the numerals for the words *two thousand, six hundred, forty-three,* and so on. However, students should be able not only to translate names of numbers from words into numerical symbols but also to translate the symbols into words. That is, given the symbol 356, children should be able to write and say the words *three hundred fifty-six.*

A hand calculator can be used to develop some place-value skills. Wallace Judd (1976) has described a game called "Wipe Out" in which children are instructed to enter a number such as 85,467 into a calculator and then to "wipe out" the 5 and replace it with a 0 on the display. No other numbers are changed. The activity requires that the child recognize that the 5 occupies the thousands place. Thus, the equation $85,467 - 5,000 = 80,467$ yields the desired result. Judd's activity can be modified by asking students to write the number's name (in this case, *eighty-five thousand four hundred sixty-seven*) and then to perform the same activity with their calculators.

Practice in reading words for numbers also can be assisted by a calculator. One such activity asks students to enter into their calculators a number expressed in words, such as *seven thousand one hundred five,* and to turn the calculator upside-down in order to note a similarity between the numeral 7105 and the word *SOIL.* Examples such as this can be created to help relieve some of the drudgery involved in practicing the reading of number words and numerals.

Ordering greater-valued numbers is an activity that also needs to be developed. A hundreds board is useful in teaching the order of greater-valued numbers. It can be constructed by using paneling nails (nails with a small head) and key tags. The nails are hammered in in rows of ten and numbers are written on the key tags (or other suitable markers), which are then arranged as indicated in the chart below.

1	2	3	4	5	6	7	8	9	10
11	12	13	14	15	16	17	18	19	20
21	22	23	24	25	26	27	28	29	30
31	32	33	34	35	36	37	38	39	40
41	42	43	44	45	46	47	48	49	50
51	52	53	54	55	56	57	58	59	60
61	62	63	64	65	66	67	68	69	70
71	72	73	74	75	76	77	78	79	80
81	82	83	84	85	86	87	88	89	90
91	92	93	94	95	96	97	98	99	100

Children are asked to find the correct tags to complete a sequence such as 32, 33, 34, _____, _____; or they are instructed to find the missing numeral in a sequence such as 52, 53, _____, _____ 56. Other applications of a hundreds chart include asking students to find a pattern in the fifth row, in which the numerals have a 4 in the tens place; to locate numbers that have the same numerals in both the tens and ones places; and to search for secret numbers (e.g., to search for numbers that have an odd numeral in the tens place and an even numeral in the ones place).

Another useful practice activity for primary-aged children is a fishing game. Numerals such as 45, 142, 86, 12, among others, are written on fish-shaped pieces of tagboard. A paper clip is placed on each fish and a piece of wood with a string attached to a magnet is used as a fishing pole. Children close their eyes as they fish for two numerals (the magnet attracts the paper clip and a fish is "caught"). Each child must correctly read the numerals on the fish caught and state which fish has the greater number in order to keep the fish. Children can alternate in this activity and the child with the greatest number is proclaimed to have caught the "biggest" fish of the day.

Other useful games for teaching place value are described in Activities 4.2, 4.3, 4.4, and 4.5.

ACTIVITY 4.2   Place-Value Card Game

Materials: 50 blank cards (or cut 3″ × 5″ index cards in half).

Mark 25 cards with numerals and the other 25 cards with the corresponding place-value equivalents. For example, if the numeral card is 86, the place-value equivalent card would have 8 tens and 6 ones written on it.

Directions:

1. The game may be played with 2 to 4 students.

2. The dealer shuffles and distributes all of the cards face down to the players. Each player should have an equal number of cards.

3. The players do not look at the cards but pile them face down.

4. To begin, each player turns his or her top card over and the card with the "greatest" (or "least") place value wins all the cards shown.

5. The player with the most cards at the end of the game is the winner.

ACTIVITY 4.3   Number Accordions*

This activity, designed by Shirley Zielsche, is a novel approach to help children understand place value.

For two-place numbers, take a file folder, cut out a rectangular strip, and then label and fold it as shown below.

When the number accordions are folded, the child will see 35. Unfolding the accordians shows 3 tens + 5 and helps reinforce place value. For three-place numbers, the following folds are shown.

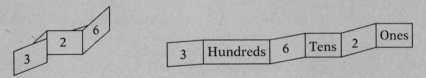

Reading larger numbers can be facilitated by combining the folded numerals with a chart such as this:

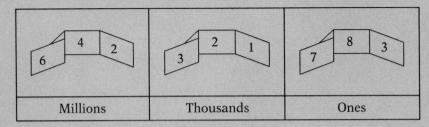

Millions	Thousands	Ones

The numeral shown in the diagram is read as 642 million, 321 thousand, 783.

*Adapted from Zielsche, S. (1970). Understanding place value. *Arithmetic Teacher*, *17*, pp. 683–684. Used with permission of the National Council of Teachers of Mathematics.

ACTIVITY 4.4   Lunch Bag Pocket Charts

A classroom teaching activity for practicing place-value concepts can be constructed by using a paper bag and note cards with numerals.

Take a paper lunch bag, place it on its side, and fold it over about 2 cm. Staple the fold so that the length of the bag is marked off in thirds. Next, place note cards in each of the pockets. Each child is given a "pocket" chart and cards, and is asked to show various numbers by calling off place-value names (e.g., 23 tens, 8 ones).

ACTIVITY 4.5   Number Sequencing

This computer program, written in Atari BASIC, can be used by second graders to practice number sequencing. With minor adaptations it can be used with several other microcomputers.

```
10    REM NUMBER SEQUENCING
20    FOR Z = 1 TO 50
30    LET X = INT (RND(1) * 1000 + 1)
40    PRINT ''WHAT NUMBER COMES RIGHT AFTER''
50    PRINT X
55    PRINT: PRINT
60    INPUT Y
70    IF Y = X + 1 THEN GO TO 200
80    GO TO 150
150   PRINT: PRINT ''TRY ANOTHER ANSWER''
160   PRINT: PRINT
170   GO TO 40
200   PRINT: PRINT ''GOOD WORK''
210   NEXT Z
```

Refinements of Place Value and Numeration

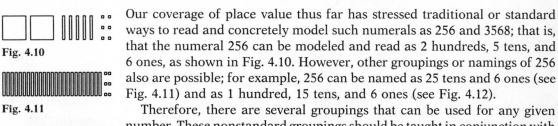

Fig. 4.10

Fig. 4.11

Fig. 4.12

Our coverage of place value thus far has stressed traditional or standard ways to read and concretely model such numerals as 256 and 3568; that is, that the numeral 256 can be modeled and read as 2 hundreds, 5 tens, and 6 ones, as shown in Fig. 4.10. However, other groupings or namings of 256 also are possible; for example, 256 can be named as 25 tens and 6 ones (see Fig. 4.11) and as 1 hundred, 15 tens, and 6 ones (see Fig. 4.12).

Therefore, there are several groupings that can be used for any given number. These nonstandard groupings should be taught in conjunction with place-value concepts, as they will be of value when other mathematics skills are learned. For example, this skill is extremely useful when learning addition and subtraction with regrouping. Consider this subtraction example:

$$\begin{array}{r} 256 \\ -94 \end{array}.$$

Often students are taught to regroup and record like this:

$$\begin{array}{r} \overset{1}{2}\overset{15}{5}\,6 \\ -\ 9\ 4 \end{array}$$

Notice that $\overset{1}{2}\overset{15}{5}$ 6 is actually an expression of 256 as 1 hundred, 15 tens, 6 ones. Sometimes students are taught to make these "marks" without an understanding of what they mean, which can cause learning problems if students confuse or omit a step. Thus, place-value concepts, necessary for computational achievement, need to be refined by illustrating numbers with several groupings.

Consider another example of this approach using the numeral 24. Second graders often are able to state that 24 has 2 tens and 4 ones. But to understand a subtraction exercise such as $24 - 7 = 17$ students must first be able to group numbers in several ways. Consider the place-value assumptions that children make as they attempt to solve the equation $24 - 7 = 17$.

$$
\begin{array}{cc}
24 & \cancel{2}^{1}4 \\
-\ 7 & -\ \ 7 \\
\hline
 & 1\ 7 \\
\end{array}
$$

Again, $\cancel{2}^{1}4$ is a representation of 24 as 1 ten and 14 ones. Thus, as a culminating activity for place value at the primary age level, children need to see that

and

both represent 24 (see also Activity 4.6).

For children with special learning problems it is important to specify carefully each step in the grouping process. Also, for some children an alternative subtraction algorithm might be used—one that does not stress these place-value concepts.

ACTIVITY 4.6   Graph Paper Models

This activity illustrates how teachers can demonstrate several ways to group concrete material.

Large-block graph paper can be used to illustrate various groupings of numbers. Can you show 372 with three different place-value groupings? Use scissors to cut up your models.

Another area of refinement for numeration occurs when one considers estimation and large numbers such as the millions and billions. Estimation activities involving quantities can be performed throughout the elementary school curriculum (see Activities 4.7, 4.8, and 4.9). At the intermediate level, jars filled with objects such as candy, cereal, or beans can be used. Children are asked to estimate the number of items in the jar and class discussion focuses on strategies for estimating, such as weighing the jar or looking at some smaller volume portion of the jar. As estimation activities are developed it is necessary to discourage both random guessing and extremely specific activities such as counting each item in the jar. Strategies such as estimating how many beans are in a cup and then estimating how many cups are in the jar should be developed.

ACTIVITY 4.7   Estimating and Grouping

In this activity estimation is related to the notion of grouping.

Fill a medium-sized jar with pinto beans. Have students estimate the number of beans in the jar. Discuss strategies and name the best estimator.

One strategy is to begin by estimating how many beans lie in a layer 1 cm high and then to estimate how many 1 cm-high groups there are.

ACTIVITY 4.8   Estimation Strategies

How many children can stand on the school playground? Develop a plan to solve this estimation activity.

ACTIVITY 4.9   Estimating Strategies for Large Numbers

Plans for estimating large numbers can be developed and verified by using a hand calculator. The following questions help students relate large numbers to everyday life.

How much is a million cents?
How many years is a million years?
How many times does your heart beat in a lifetime?

Other questions that might be answered by estimation techniques include the following.

1. How many hamburgers does the class eat in one year?
2. How many fans see major league baseball games each year?

3. How many plays does the average record get before its owner sets it aside?

4. How long would one million $1 bills stretch?

5. How high would one billion $1 bills be?

6. How much water would a leaky faucet waste in one year?

The estimation activities presented in Activities 4.7, 4.8, and 4.9 are designed to give children a visual sense of what large numbers are like. Fourth, fifth, and sixth graders too often study numbers in the millions and billions without much comprehension of what the numbers mean. Today we are bombarded by terms in the news media that describe large-valued numbers. Distances of space flights, corporate earnings reports, and attendance figures for concerts and sports are some of the experiences that we have with large-valued numbers. Children need to engage in many estimation activities and visual experiences with large numbers in order to develop coping skills for living in a society of great distances and quantities. Activities 4.10, 4.11, 4.12, and 4.13 are also useful in teaching estimation skills.

ACTIVITY 4.10   Estimate the Price

This activity is designed to develop estimation skills. It can be done with college students to simulate the experience of elementary students.

Objective: Estimation of prices
Materials: Empty grocery containers and 3″ × 5″ index cards
Procedure:

1. Separate the class into groups of approximately five students each.

2. Give each group an index card containing a list of five grocery items.

3. Display the five empty containers with their respective prices on a desk in front of the class.

4. Allow the students 60 seconds to "buy" $10 worth of items.

5. Two rules are stated: (a) paper and pencil calculations are not allowed; (b) the groups can purchase no more than three items of any one kind.

6. Each group must choose a recorder to write their selections on the note card.

7. At the end of 60 seconds, the note cards are collected and the group closest to $10 wins.

Strategies for estimating can be discussed at this point. Also, the activity may be repeated by changing the target amount to $15 or by using other items.

ACTIVITY 4.11 Great Numbers

This activity can help to reinforce students' ability to order large numbers. It is designed for use with a small group of students but can be varied for larger group participation.

Take a paper bag and put ten cards into it, each card having one numeral from 0 through 9 on it. Each child in the group should then construct this grid on a piece of paper:

Draw a card at random from the bag. Suppose the card is a 5. Each child can position the 5 in any place he or she wants. For example, one child might show this:

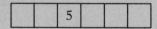

Replace the card, shake the bag, and draw another card. Suppose the card is a 6. A child might now show this:

The game continues in this way until six cards have been drawn. The child with the greatest number is the winner.

Play this game in class. Then see if you can adapt it for children studying three-place numbers.

ACTIVITY 4.12 ## Using a Thermometer to Show Greater-Valued Numbers

This activity is useful in teaching numbers greater than 10. A thermometer is a useful device for demonstrating greater-valued numbers to children.

Make a large thermometer by taking a piece of tagboard and a ribbon that has half its length colored red and half colored white. Fit the ribbon through two slits made in the tagboard and move it up to show different temperatures. By showing that 80° is hotter than 30° students see that 80 is greater than 30.

ACTIVITY 4.13 ## Diagnosing Place-Value Errors

Knowledge of place value affects students' ability to do computational work, as this diagnostic activity shows.

Look at the incorrect work that a child has done in this partially completed exercise.

$$
\begin{array}{r}
456 \\
-\ 89 \\
\end{array}
\qquad
\begin{array}{r}
\overset{3}{\cancel{4}}\,\overset{15}{5}\,\overset{1}{6} \\
-\ \ 8\ 9 \\
\end{array}
$$

Can you diagnose the place-value error? Clearly state the difficulty and suggest how it might be corrected.

Summary

This chapter presents various materials and techniques useful for extending numeration concepts and developing place-value concepts. Historical methods of numeration have been shown to trace the growth of numeration to the present day. Concrete models for illustrating place-value concepts and activities designed to provide an enjoyable learning environment are presented. Place-value concepts help children to acquire computational skill as well as to understand numbers for effective living in twentieth-century society. Again, a thorough understanding of place value helps to insure success with addition, subtraction, multiplication, and division of whole numbers.

Discussion Questions

1. Using diagrams to illustrate base-10 blocks, show each of the following numbers with three concrete models:
   a. 204   c. 35
   b. 186   d. 1253

2. Write the numeral 856 in three ways, using words, expanded notation, and exponents.

3. Explain why a thorough knowledge of place value is necessary for understanding whole number operations. Give examples of specific addition, subtraction, multiplication, and division exercises where place value understanding is important.

4. Explain several materials that can be used to exhance children's beginning knowledge of place-value concepts.

5. Read some journal articles that describe the teaching of other number bases such as base 5 or base 6. Develop an initial presentation on this topic for use with gifted sixth-grade students.

6. Display on a bulletin board some of the contributions of the historical numeration systems investigated in this chapter.

7. Construct a place-value pocket chart that can be used to illustrate various base-10 numerals.

8. When dealing with perceptually handicapped students, which type of place-value materials are most appropriate, proportional or nonproportional materials?

References

Ashlock, R. B. (1986). *Error patterns in computation: A semi-programmed approach.* Columbus, Ohio: Merrill.

Benner, C. V. (1969). Hindu-Arabic numeration systems. In *Historical topics for the mathematics classroom: The thirty-first yearbook of the National Council of Teachers of Mathematics* (pp. 46–49). Reston, Va.: NCTM.

Bergamini, D. (1963). *Mathematics.* New York: Time.

Burton, G. M. (1984). Teaching the most basic basic. *Arithmetic Teacher, 31,* pp. 20–25.

Byrket, D. R. (1970). Early Mayan mathematics. *Arithmetic Teacher, 17,* pp. 387–390.

Glennon, V., and Callahan, L. (1968). *A guide to current research in elementary school mathematics.* Washington, D.C.: Association for Supervision and Curriculum Development.

Heddens, J., & Speer, W. (1988). *Today's mathematics.* Chicago: Science Research Associates.

Judd, W. (1976). Instructional games with calculators. *Arithmetic Teacher, 23,* pp. 516–518.

Suydam, M., & Dessart, D. J. (1980). Skill learning. In R. Shumway (ed.), *Research in mathematics education* (pp. 207–243). Reston, Va.: NCTM.

Swenson, E. (1973). *Teaching mathematics to children.* New York: Macmillan.

Van deWalle, J., & Thompson, C. (1985). Estimate how much. *Arithmetic Teacher, 32,* pp. 4–8.

Zielsche, S. (1970). Understanding place value. *Arithmetic Teacher, 17,* pp. 683–684.

CHAPTER 5

Mathematics Anxiety

Objectives

After reading this chapter you will be able to:

1. Describe characteristics of mathematics anxiety.

2. Identify several ways to measure levels of mathematics anxiety.

3. Create several possible corrective strategies for elementary school students exhibiting mathematics anxiety.

4. Perform a muscular tension relaxation exercise.

5. Perform a breathing exercise designed to produce a more relaxed state of being.

Introduction

In recent years mathematics anxiety has become a concern of educators. Fear of mathematics, avoidance of mathematics-related occupations, and excessive tension when taking mathematics exams are some of the problems associated with mathematics anxiety. Also, concern with equitable mathematics education of females and minorities has been related to mathematics anxiety clarification. For example, groups of science and mathematics educators have been attempting to promote the involvement of females in mathematics.

Mathematics anxiety in contrast to a negative attitude toward mathematics, is often accompanied by such physical symptoms as sweaty palms, increased muscle tension, and increased heart rate. Whereas attitudes regarding mathematics often reflect relative likes and dislikes, mathematics anxiety is characterized as a more powerful emotion (Aiken, 1978). In order to be able to help students who suffer from this problem, elementary school teachers first must determine if they themselves exhibit symptoms of mathematics anxiety. In addition, strategies for alleviating students' mathematics anxiety need to be incorporated into the elementary school mathematics classroom.

Equity in Elementary School Mathematics

Several reports have related mathematics achievement to differential treatment of females and males in mathematics classes (Becker, 1981; Fennema & Peterson, 1985). For example, Fennema (1980) noted that teachers tend to pay more attention to the mathematical work of boys than to that of girls. Further, even though the achievement levels of boys and girls are comparable, it has been shown that boys receive more remedial help through mathematics clinics than do girls. Even subtle biases in the elementary school classroom can shift females' attitudes away from mathematics, as described by Fennema (1980, p. 171) in the following scenario:

> (John and Sue, seated side by side in a mathematics class, are working on a mathematics problem.)
> John: Sue, have you got this problem?
> Sue: If you find the square root of A, you'll get the answer?
> Teacher: Has anyone figured out how to get the answer?
> (John and Sue's hands both go up.)
> Teacher: John, how did you get it?
> John: If you find the square root of A, you'll get the answer.
> Teacher: That's right! Did everyone see how John got the answer?

Teachers need to be careful to communicate and reinforce mathematics work and to avoid sexual and racial stereotyping. Specifically, praise and encouragement of the value of mathematics activities need to be provided to female and minority students. Further, the mathematics anxiety of each student should be carefully evaluated, monitored, and corrected. Kaseberg, Krinberg, and Downie (1980) describe the *EQUALS* program, which is designed to create a community of educators who actively encourage female participation in mathematics. The references section at the end of this chapter contains numerous problems and activities for promoting participation of women in mathematics.

Measuring Mathematics Anxiety

Psychologists have been studying the concept of anxiety for many years and today there are more than 5000 published works on the subject (Speilberger, Anton, & Bedell, 1976). Often, investigators have emphasized their personal theoretical positions, which has resulted in an almost bewildering number of terms, concepts, and theories. However, the three major ways of measuring anxiety are the following:

1. *Indirectly.* Here the emphasis is on observing "anxiety signs" such as hair pulling, nail biting, and foot tapping.

2. *Semidirectly.* A paper-and-pencil instrument is administered to a person in order to diagnose his or her level of anxiety. High scores on the instrument are considered to reflect high levels of anxiety.

3. *Directly.* Physiological laboratory instruments such as the galvanic skin response, which measures palmar sweating, are administered. The measurement of palmar sweating and muscle tension is seen as evidence of sympathetic nervous system ascendancy and, thus, as an anxiety indicator. Conversely, low heart rates, reduced palmar sweating, and low muscle tension levels are viewed as evidence of parasympathetic nervous system ascendancy, and, therefore, a relaxed state of being.

Just as there are several ways to measure general anxiety, so it is possible to measure the more specific state of anxiety called *mathematics anxiety* in three ways. For elementary schoolteachers, observational experience (indirect measurement) and mathematics anxiety instruments (semidirect measurement) seem to provide the most potential use in the identification of children exhibiting mathematics anxiety symptoms.

However, it is also important for elementary school teachers to become aware of their own levels of mathematics anxiety. Some prospective elementary school teachers exhibit very low levels while others show higher degrees of the condition (Sovchik, Steiner, & Meconi, 1981). Many of the activities presented in this chapter are designed to make students of teaching aware of their own levels of anxiety, which is the first step toward reducing anxiety (see Activities 5.1 and 5.2).

ACTIVITY 5.1   Assessment of Feelings About Mathematics

Answer the following questions by stating "true" or "false." Answer them after responding to the first thought that enters your mind.

_____ 1. I am always extremely careful and neat when I do mathematics.

_____ 2. Very often I ask the instructor for the correct procedure or answer to a math problem.

_____ 3. I prefer to answer mathematics questions quickly.

_____ 4. I feel uncomfortable when talking about mathematics with my classmates.

_____ 5. I feel nervous when doing mathematics exercises at the board.

_____ 6. My parents expect me to do extremely well in mathematics.

_____ 7. I get angry when I don't get a mathematics problem correct the first try.

_____ 8. My stomach churns when I study mathematics or take a mathematics test.

_____ 9. The only thing that is important in mathematics is getting the correct answer.

_____ 10. When I do well in mathematics, it is mostly good luck.

_____ 11. I avoid mathematics homework.

_____ 12. I am a failure if I don't get a very high grade in mathematics.

_____ 13. Mathematics is by far the most important subject in the school curriculum.

_____ 14. My hands sweat a great deal when I take a mathematics test.

_____ 15. I would like to study statistics.

_____ 16. I have a brother or sister who is much better than I am in mathematics.

_____ 17. I have always been an inferior mathematics student.

If you had ten or more true answers, you may be a candidate for mathematics anxiety. Discuss your results with members of the class.

ACTIVITY 5.2　Teacher's Level of Mathematics Anxiety

This activity is designed to help you become aware of your level of mathematics anxiety.

1. Choose the description that best describes you when you study mathematics.
   a. totally relaxed
   b. fairly relaxed
   c. relaxed but alert
   d. fairly tense
   e. very tense

2. Choose the description that best describes you when you take a mathematics test.
   a. totally relaxed
   b. fairly relaxed
   c. relaxed but alert
   d. fairly tense
   e. very tense

3. Is there a difference in your rating for questions 1 and 2? List some reasons why.

4. List five reasons why you are tense when studying mathematics.

5. List five reasons why you are tense when taking a mathematics test.

Characteristics of Mathematics Anxiety

Mathematics anxiety is viewed as a situation-specific form of anxiety. Although studying mathematics or taking a mathematics exam can yield some of the same characteristics as general anxiety, the symptoms are apparent only in the mathematics classroom. For example, anxious people are often withdrawn and preoccupied with themselves. They may neglect to exchange even a cursory "hello" with their co-workers or neighbors. In the same way, students anxious about mathematics may be extremely quiet and withdrawn in mathematics classes. Of course, any such assessment requires observation of not one but several characteristics. The following characteristics of mathematics-anxious students have been developed by integrating general anxiety symptoms from psychological studies (Phillips, Martin, & Meyer, 1972).

Excessive Cautiousness.　Students who are extremely cautious often have extremely neat work, are afraid to take a moderate risk, and seem to be unable to problem-solve when something unique or creative is needed. Obviously, some neatness in mathematical work is necessary, but when this becomes the end rather than the means, it can yield a learning problem.

Dependence.   Children who seem to always cling to the teacher and are seemingly always asking whether they are right about a mathematics answer are exhibiting a dependency characteristic. Sometimes elementary school teachers encourage this by emphasizing correct answers rather than processes.

Reduced Responsiveness to the Environment.   Children who seem to be daydreaming in mathematics class may be anxious about their mathematics performance. They may use this as a defense against feelings of inadequate mathematics performance. As teachers, it is important to avoid having children work in isolation. They need some experience working with classmates on mathematics work.

Deterioration of Complex Problem-Solving Processes.   Students exhibiting mathematics anxiety may be able to recall basic facts well or perform rote learning tasks such as copying numerals, but they invariably have difficulty with problem solving in mathematics. Unable to suspend judgment or to reflect, these students seem to have difficulty looking at alternatives or developing a plan of attack in a word problem.

Schools need to examine the emphasis placed on speed in mathematics work. The most important problems in one's life are not solved quickly. Elementary school teachers may need to reexamine the emphasis on speed, which was valuable perhaps when calculators and computers were not as much a part of the mathematics curriculum.

Extreme Fear of Failure.   Mathematics anxiety causes some elementary pupils to experience a paralyzing fear of failure. Perhaps these students come from homes where extremely high goals are expressed for mathematics achievement. In some cases, children may equate love with success in school. This can yield a high level of tension, especially in a subject such as mathematics. Elementary school teachers need to be careful in how they utilize competition among students. For example, the teacher should not ask a child afraid of failure to work a problem quickly at the chalkboard.

Rejection by Family.   Some children receive little or no support system at home. Separation and divorce may emotionally affect children in an adverse manner. However, even when both parents are living in the home, rejection may also occur when parenting skills are lacking. Children may be pushed too hard to succeed and may be praised too little and criticized too often. Parents sometimes compare siblings in terms of their performance in mathematics. These subtle forms of rejection can be more devastating than more apparent ones.

Teachers need to be careful not to compare students unfavorably. For instance, the comment "Sally understands. Why don't you, Billy?" is a comparative question that will not facilitate Billy's learning. Also, teachers need to correct the child's performance, not the child. Sally is not a good or bad person because her mathematics performance is acceptable or weak. Separating the child's performance from the child's person is a helpful way of decreasing rejecting comments.

Hostility.   Students exhibiting mathematics anxiety may display anger. For example, if they do not solve an exercise or problem quickly, they may flare up in anger. Elementary school teachers need a calm attitude and a patient approach to mathematics exercises and problems.

Expectations May Exceed Skill.   Mathematics anxiety can be caused by a gap between expectations and realistic talents. Throughout our lives we become anxious about achieving certain goals, and in some cases our anxiety increases as it becomes apparent that we may not have the talent or skill needed to achieve those goals. In the elementary school classroom a child may hope to be the highest scoring mathematics student in the school but the child's skill in mathematics may fall short of that expectation. As a result, the child will experience mathematics anxiety. To help students set realistic goals, elementary school teachers need to realize that each child is unique in his or her mathematics ability.

Physiological Symptoms.   Elementary school students who exhibit such anxiety signs as hair pulling, eye tics, headaches, stomachaches, and increased breathing levels during mathematics classes or exams may be experiencing mathematics anxiety.

Compulsive Behavior.   Compulsive behaviors are nontask related and may direct the person's activity in a negative manner. For example, some mathematics students have been observed arranging their multicolored pencils in various ways during a mathematics exam. Likewise, students who make a ritual of studying for mathematics exams by spending most of their time finding the right kind of paper, sharpening pencils, setting up and cleaning their desks, and so on are also exhibiting compulsive behavior.

Elementary school teachers need not only to help students prepare to study but they must encourage students to indulge in mathematical task-related behavior as well. Solving problems, working with manipulative material, and making estimations need to be emphasized. Also, children need to be assured that their mathematical work is enjoyable, interesting, and worthwhile.

Avoidance Behaviors. Sells (1978) has reported that 57 percent of males entering a California college had taken four years of high school mathematics, whereas only 8 percent of females had had four years of high school mathematics. Sells concluded that because females had avoided four years of high school mathematics their opportunities in college had been dramatically limited. Further, Sells noted that in several cases females were subtly counseled to avoid mathematics work in school and, therefore, were selectively filtered out of high status college majors. Often, students' avoidance of mathematics homework, exams, and courses can reveal a form of mathematics anxiety. Students may feel threatened and attempt to avoid a situation of potential failure.

Elementary school teachers also should be aware of their own feelings of mathematics avoidance. For instance, certain mathematics topics may be skipped not because students do not understand them but because the teacher is fearful of teaching the topics incorrectly. Elementary school teachers need to evaluate their own feelings of avoidance in order to be sure that the topics avoided in the mathematics curriculum are, indeed, troublesome for children's learning.

Low Self-esteem. Low self-esteem is characterized by such comments as "I've never been able to score well on a mathematics test" or "I can't do math." Children with low self-esteem often indulge in a kind of substitute learning; that is, instead of attending to mathematical tasks they repeat and relearn phrases such as "I can't do it." This negative self-talk intrudes on the learning of mathematics.

As simple as it may sound, a useful strategy here is to ask the child to say out loud, "I can do math." This sets a readiness for further mathematical work and breaks the cycle of rote, negative memorizations of inferiority. Also, teachers need to avoid humiliating children with mathematics. For example, a child with low self-esteem should not be asked to say the multiplication tables in front of the class. Humiliation can make mathematics learning seem like punishment, and harmful learning effects may be observed later.

Finally, elementary school teachers need to be careful of making such statements as "If you are good today, you won't have any mathematics homework," as children may believe that being "good" means that they do not have to do mathematics work.

In summary, the characteristics of mathematics anxiety are not mutually exclusive; that is, they overlap in many cases. However, observation of several of these characteristics may indicate that certain corrective measures are needed.

Strategies for Coping with Mathematics Anxiety

The first step in the solution of a problem, and perhaps the most important part, is the recognition that a problem exists. Thus, elementary school teachers need to become aware of potential mathematics anxiety in their students as well as in themselves. Observation of several of the characteristics of mathematics anxiety can be a start. Elementary school teachers need to ask themselves how comfortable they are teaching mathematics. If they are uncomfortable with mathematics teaching, then there are several options available. One is to ask other teachers how they teach a particular topic. Attending summer workshops at local colleges or universities is another way to develop confidence in teaching mathematics. Publications such as those issued by the National Council of Teachers of Mathematics (NCTM) are often useful in developing new ideas.

Several other strategies cluster around the topic of competition. Some interpersonal competition is necessary, but excessive competition can be detrimental to mathematical work. As noted earlier, asking students to solve computational exercises at the blackboard quickly is a form of competition that may be detrimental to anxious mathematics students.

Timed tests are necessary at certain stages of mathematics study but their excessive use can be detrimental. Students who are asked to answer basic fact questions in six or less seconds sometimes feel that most mathematics questions are speed-oriented. In an age of hand calculators and computers, the emphases should be concept development, estimation, and problem-solving skills. Thus, rapid computation is not as important as it was in a less technological-oriented society.

The teacher's attitude toward competition can help to foster a more relaxed and interesting classroom. Researchers have found that extremely high levels of competition are sometimes associated with physical illness (Pelletier, 1977). Cooperation as well as moderate competition are necessary; thus, at times children need to solve problems together so that valuable social skills are developed.

Competition is prevalent in mathematics testing situations. A teacher was observed giving a class a ten-minute quiz. The teacher, a graduate school professor, was observed walking around the classroom, peering over each student's shoulder, and announcing the remaining amount of time. This negative example illustrates some test administration policies that need to be considered. First, clear and calm directions presented in a relaxed manner are necessary. Also, walking around may be useful but crouching over students' shoulders may cause more harm than good. Finally, students need help in allocating their testing time but this help should not be excessive.

Another strategy for treating mathematics anxiety is emphasizing process rather than product. Students need much experience working with concrete materials, doing experiments, and solving problems with more than one solution. Activities 5.3, 5.4, and 5.5 provide some examples of problems designed to emphasize more than one solution and are examples of creative, enjoyable classroom activities.

ACTIVITY 5.3   Alternative Solutions

How many ways can you express 100 using exactly 6 nines and any combination of the four fundamental operations? One example is provided for you.

$$100 = 99 + \frac{99}{99} \qquad 100 = (9 \times 9) + \square$$

$$100 = \square$$

ACTIVITY 5.4   Organizing a Party's Budget

List several ways that you can spend $45 for a class party. Use a newspaper or catalog to explain your purchases.

ACTIVITY 5.5   Creative Responses

How many ways can you use a rectangular box? List as many unique ways as you can. Do not worry about finding a "perfect" answer. Have some fun with this.

Other techniques helpful in treating mathematics anxiety are breathing, creative imaging, and progressive relaxation exercises (see Activities 5.6, 5.7, and 5.8). These techniques can be especially effective prior to a mathematics test. The activities should be practiced often, especially with mathematics anxiety students.

ACTIVITY 5.6   Natural Breathing

1. Begin by sitting or standing up straight in good posture.
2. Breathe *slowly* through your nose.
3. As you inhale, first fill the lower section of your lungs. Your diaphragm will push your abdomen outward to make room for

the air. Second, fill the middle part of your lungs as your lower ribs and chest move forward to accommodate the air. Third, fill the upper part of your lungs as you raise your chest slightly and draw in your abdomen slightly to support your lungs. These three steps can be performed in one smooth continuous inhalation, which, with practice, can be completed in a couple of seconds.

4. Hold your breath for a few seconds.

5. As you exhale *slowly,* pull your abdomen in slowly as the lungs empty. When you have completely exhaled, relax your abdomen and chest.

6. Pause and then repeat the exercise several times.

ACTIVITY 5.7 Progressive Relaxation

1. Curl both fists, tightening biceps and forearms. Now relax.

2. Wrinkle up your forehead. At the same time, press your head as far back as possible, roll it clockwise in a complete circle, and then reverse. Wrinkle up the muscles of your face like a prune; frowning, eyes tightly squinted, lips tight, tongue pushing up against the roof of the mouth, and shoulders hunched. Now relax.

3. Arch back as you take a deep breath into the chest. Hold. Relax. Take a deep breath, pressing out the stomach. Hold. Now relax.

4. Pull feet and toes back toward the face, tightening shins. Hold. Now relax. Curl toes, simultaneously tightening calves and thighs. Now relax.

ACTIVITY 5.8 Creative Imagery

Imagine yourself in mathematics class, ready for an exam. See yourself as prepared, ready with pencil and paper, calm and relaxed. See yourself as ready, having studied the major concepts and skills. Look at the test and visualize the easy questions that can be answered first. Now the longer questions are visualized and answered correctly. You are calm as the test is being taken. Say quietly to yourself that you are doing well on the test. See yourself completing the test and leaving the classroom.

Another category of treatment techniques for students with mathematics anxiety is the use of humor in alleviating stress and anxiety in the classroom. In a well-documented case, writer and editor Norman Cousins reviewed how he overcame a serious illness by emphasizing humor in the form of movies and old television situation comedies. After Cousins laughed, doctors noticed that his medical test results seemed to improve. In fact, after a medical treatment program with humor as one of the components, Cousins made a thorough recovery (Cousins, 1979). It seems that humor can be a valuable antidote to illness.

In mathematics classes, elementary school teachers need to have a sense of humor, not in a sarcastic, punitive way but in a creative one that emphasizes a common humanity. Often elementary teachers hear jokes from children, some of which are good examples of creative behavior. Activities 5.9, 5.10, and 5.11 are designed to emphasize subtle shifts of meaning, riddles, and enjoyable, motivating experiences in mathematics.

ACTIVITY 5.9   Solving Riddles

Why did the automobile carry a television set?

$$\overline{2}\ \ \overline{12} \qquad \overline{5}\ \ \overline{4}\ \ \overline{2} \qquad \overline{2}\ \ \overline{6}\ \ \overline{4}$$

$$\overline{10}\ \ \overline{6}\ \ \overline{12}\ \ \overline{1} \qquad \overline{12}\ \ \overline{8} \qquad \overline{2}\ \ \overline{6}\ \ \overline{4}$$

$$\overline{9}\ \ \overline{12}\ \ \overline{9}\ \ \overline{11}$$

Solve this riddle by substituting the letter value for the number value. (The activity is used *after* children have mastered basic division facts.)

A	$3\overline{)27}$	D	$4\overline{)44}$	H	$6\overline{)36}$
G	$4\overline{)20}$	T	$4\overline{)8}$	R	$20\overline{)40}$
E	$8\overline{)32}$	W	$87\overline{)87}$	O	$5\overline{)60}$
N	$2\overline{)16}$	S	$5\overline{)50}$		

ACTIVITY 5.10   Television Quiz*

Name the television show that the answer for each exercise suggests. Some of the programs are no longer on the air, so you may have to consult a TV historian!

1. Has four equal sides and four right angles. _____

2. $1 \times 2 \times 3 \times 5 \times 2 =$ ___ _____

3. $3000 \times$ ___ $= 9000$ _____

4. $84 \div 0 =$ ___ _____ .

5. How many angles does an octagon have? _____

Can you create an exercise that suggests a current television show?

*Adapted from Leonard, R. (1978). From the file: Computation. *Arithmetic Teacher, 25,* p. 33. Used with permission of the National Council of Teachers of Mathematics.

ACTIVITY 5.11   Humorous Assumptions

Answer the following questions.

1. If there are twelve 22¢ stamps in a dozen, how many 2¢ stamps are there in a dozen? _____

2. How far can a deer run into a forest? _____

3. A friend has two coins that total 55¢. One of them is not a nickel. What are the two coins? _____
_____

A final technique for treating mathematics anxiety is to utilize activities that emphasize movement on the part of the students (see Activity 5.12). Exercise is a well-known antidote for anxiety. The body's neuro-chemistry is believed to have a more harmonious balance as a result of exercise. Implications for elementary school mathematics classrooms might include a metric system track meet held outdoors or a nature hike with emphasis on collecting data about leaves and trees.

ACTIVITY 5.12   Estimating Movement*

How long would it take you to

	Guess	Test
Say "Happy New Year" 20 times?		
Snap your fingers 10 times?		
Tie your shoe 20 times?		

Go back and study your guesses. Are you close to the test results?

Use the data you have collected to determine if the following claims are true or false:

Dan said "Happy New Year" 30 times in 40 seconds?	yes	no
Bill snapped his fingers 30 times in 3 seconds?	yes	no
Denise tied her shoes 10 times in 30 seconds?	yes	no

Discuss what concepts and skills this activity is designed to teach.

*Adapted from Tabler, M., & Jacobson, M. (1980). Ideas. *Arithmetic Teacher, 28,* p. 28. Used with permission of the National Council of Teachers of Mathematics.

Summary

This chapter describes some of the characteristics of mathematics anxiety as well as some teaching strategies useful in reducing the harmful effects of this problem. Measurement instruments and specific relaxation techniques can be incorporated into the elementary school mathematics classroom to help children who exhibit excessive tension when studying mathematics or taking mathematics exams. Specific mathematical activities that yield a more relaxed and creative classroom environment are suggested.

Discussion Questions

1. List the major techniques that elementary school teachers can use to discover the mathematics anxiety levels of their students.

2. Briefly describe at least eight characteristics of elementary school students who seem to exhibit symptoms of mathematics anxiety.

3. Assume that an elementary school student has been described as exhibiting mathematics anxiety. Describe several teaching strategies that can aid the student.

4. Perform a progressive muscular relaxation exercise.

5. Perform a breathing relaxation exercise.

6. Describe two mathematical activities that you could use with elementary school pupils who seem to be anxious about mathematics.

7. Read a journal article describing the conditions and therapies for mathematics anxiety.

8. Make up a short (ten-item) mathematics anxiety inventory and administer it to an elementary school student. Analyze your results.

9. Make a bulletin board display of famous female mathematicians.

10. The March 1984 *Journal for Research in Mathematics Education* reviewed the National Assessment of Educational Progress results on minorities and mathematics. Read this report and describe some techniques for improving the attitudes of mathematics avoidance groups.

References

Aiken, L. R. (1978). Update on attitudes and other affective variables in learning mathematics. *School Psychology Digest, 7*(2), pp. 60–65.

Barnes, E. (1980). Demystifying math. *American Education, 16*(9), pp. 6–8.

Becker, J. R. (1981). Differential treatment of females and males in mathematics classes. *Journal for Research in Mathematics Education,* 12, pp. 40–53.

Brush, L. (1980). *Encouraging girls in mathematics.* Cambridge, Mass.: Abt Books.

Brush, L. (1981). Some thoughts for teachers on mathematics anxiety. *Arithmetic Teacher, 34*(4), pp. 37–39.

Cousins, N. (1979). *An anatomy of an illness as perceived by the patient: Reflections on healing and regeneration.* New York: Norton.

Davis, M., McKay, M., & Eshelman, E. (1982). *The relaxation and stress reduction workbook.* Oakland: New Harbinger.

Donady, B., & Tobias, S. (1977). Math anxiety. *Teacher, 95*(3), pp. 71–74.

Fennema, E. (1980). Teachers and sex bias in mathematics. *Mathematics Teacher, 33*(3), pp. 169–173.

Fennema, E. (1981). Women and mathematics: Does research matter? *Journal for Research in Mathematics Education, 12*(5), pp. 380–385.

Fennema, E., & Peterson, P. L. (1985). Autonomous learning behavior: A possible explanation of gender-related differences in mathematics. In L. D. Wilkinson & C. B. Marrett (eds.), *General influences in classroom interaction* (pp. 17–35). Orlando, Fla.: Academic Press.

Fox, L. H. (1981). Mathematically able girls: A special challenge. *Arithmetic Teacher, 28*(6), pp. 22–23.

Hill, J. (1980). The nonsexist classroom. *Instructor, 84*(7), pp. 78–80.

Hodges, H. L. B. (1983). Learning styles: Rx for mathaphobia. *Arithmetic Teacher, 30*(7), pp. 17–20.

Jacobson, E. (1974). *Progressive relaxation.* Chicago: University of Chicago Press.

Kaseberg, A., Kreinberg, N., & Downie, D. (1980). *Use EQUALS to promote the participation of women in mathematics.* Berkeley, Calif.: University of California Press.

Kogelman, S., & Warren, J. (1978). *Mind over math.* New York: Dial Press.

Lazarus, M. (1974). Mathophobia: Some personal speculations. *The National Elementary Principal, 52*(2), pp. 16–22.

Leonard, R. (1978). From the file: Computation. *Arithmetic Teacher, 25,* p. 33.

May, R. (1977). *The meaning of anxiety.* New York: Simon & Schuster.

Pelletier, K. R. (1977). *Mind as healer, mind as slayer.* New York: Delta.

Phillips, B. N., Martin, R. P., & Meyer, J., (1972). Interventions in relation to anxiety in school. In C. D. Speilberger (ed.), *Anxiety: Current trends in theory and research* (pp. 410–464). New York: Academic Press.

Richardson, F. C., & Suinn, R. M. (1972). Mathematics anxiety rating scale: Psychometric data. *Journal of Counseling Psychology, 19*(11), pp. 551–554.

Sells, L. (1978). Mathematics: A critical filter. *The Science Teacher, 45*(2), pp. 28–29.

Sovchik, R. J., Steiner, E., & Meconi, L. J. (1981). Mathematics anxiety of preservice elementary mathematics methods students. *School Science & Mathematics, 81,* pp. 643–647.

Speilberger, C. D., Anton, W. D., & Bedell, J. (1976). The nature and treatment of test anxiety. In M. Zuckerman & C. D. Speilberger (eds.), *Emotions and anxiety: New concepts and applications* (pp. 317–345). New York: Wiley.

Tabler, M. & Jacobson, M. (1980). Ideas. *Arithmetic Teacher, 28,* p. 28.

Tobias, S. (1978). *Overcoming math anxiety.* New York: Norton.

Tobias, S., & Weissbrod, C. (1980). Anxiety and mathematics: An update. *Harvard Educational Review, 50*(1), pp. 63–70.

CHAPTER 6

Teaching Mathematics to Exceptional Children in the Regular Classroom

Objectives

After reading this chapter you will be able to:

1. Identify strategies for teaching mathematics to exceptional children who have been mainstreamed into the regular classroom.

2. Explain some of the characteristics associated with children who have been mainstreamed into the regular classroom.

3. Explain current legislation that requires exceptional children to be mainstreamed into the regular classroom.

4. Identify characteristics of gifted elementary school mathematics students.

5. Explain some of the mathematical thinking strategies that gifted mathematics students utilize.

6. Create some sample learning activities for use with gifted elementary school students.

Teaching the Mildly Handicapped Student

Public Law 94–142 was passed by the United States Congress in November 1975 and reauthorized in 1986 (Education for All Handicapped Children, 1975; Education of the Handicapped Act Amendments, 1986). This landmark legislation guarantees a free appropriate public education to all handicapped children regardless of the severity of the handicapping condition. Prior to P.L. 94–142, schools could exclude handicapped children who did not easily fit into existing special education classes. P.L. 94–142 not only requires that all school-aged handicapped children receive an education, but that their education take place in the least restrictive environment available.

============ *MATH HISTORY 6.1* ============

In 1975, Congress commissioned a study on the status of education for handicapped children. The findings showed that of the 8 million handicapped children in the United States, half were not receiving the services necessary to provide them equal educational opportunity. One million handicapped children were totally excluded from the public schools and receiving services in segregated settings or they were receiving no education at all. P.L. 94–142 was passed as a result of this study.

Education in the least restrictive environment means that ". . . to the maximum extent appropriate handicapped children be educated with non-handicapped peers." For many mildly handicapped children, placement in the least restrictive environment means spending part of the day in the regular class with their nonhandicapped classmates. Placing special education students in regular classes is often called *mainstreaming,* which refers to their return from segregated classes to the educational mainstream. As an elementary school mathematics teacher, you will be expected to teach both regular class students and mainstreamed handicapped students with equal effectiveness.

P.L. 94–142 also requires that a nonbiased, multifactored assessment be performed before a child is placed in a special education class. This assessment looks at the child's abilities in different areas and the child's current level of achievement. The results of the assessment are used in writing an Individual Education Plan (IEP) for the child. Each child receiving special education services must have an IEP that includes the child's current level of performance, annual education goals and short-term objectives, the amount of time the child will spend in the regular classroom, and other important information about the child's program. IEPs must be reviewed and updated at least annually.

To make the mainstreaming experience a good one for both student and teacher, it is important to foster cooperation between the special education teacher and the regular classroom teacher. Whenever possible, the parents should also be included by sharing information and helping to set goals. As an elementary school mathematics teacher, you can gain much information about the children mainstreamed into your class by using the resources available to you: test reports, the IEP, the special education teacher, and the parents. The information you can gain will help eliminate a duplication of effort and assure that you are all working to reinforce the same objectives for the mainstreamed children.

The two groups of handicapped children most likely to be mainstreamed are also the two largest diagnostic categories. They are the specific learning disabled and the mildly retarded; collectively they are called the *mildly handicapped.*

Specific Learning Disabilities (SLDs)

A *specific learning disability (SLD)* is defined by P.L. 94–142 as

> . . . a disorder in one or more of the basic psychological processes involved in understanding or in using language, spoken or written, which may manifest itself in an imperfect ability to listen, think, speak, read, write, spell, or to do mathematical calculations. The term includes such conditions as perceptual handicaps, brain injury, minimal brain dysfunction, dyslexia, and developmental aphasia. The term does not include children who have learning problems which are primarily the result of visual, hearing, or motor handicaps, of mental retardation, of emotional disturbance, or of environmental, cultural, or economic disadvantage. [sec. 5(b) (4)]

In essence, SLD children have the intellectual ability to do at least average academic work but for some reason, often unknown, fail to learn under normal learning conditions. They often demonstrate uneven patterns of performance, doing well in some areas and poorly in others. In some cases, SLD children have a pattern of behavioral characteristics that may interfere with learning. Some of these characteristics include hyperactivity, distractibility, short attention span, and impulsivity. By carefully arranging environmental conditions to control these behaviors, you may enhance the likelihood of academic success.

It is important to note that not all SLD children demonstrate these characteristics. Many SLD children are totally free from such learning interferences, and the reason for their academic failure is unknown.

Mild Mental Retardation

The American Association on Mental Deficiency (AAMD) defines *mental retardation* as ". . . significantly subaverage general intellectual functioning existing concurrently with deficits in adaptive behavior and manifested during the developmental period" (Grossman, 1973). According to the AAMD, the category of mild mental retardation includes the IQ range 55–70. In different states this group may be called educable mentally retarded (EMR) or developmentally handicapped (DH). Each state defines the specific IQ range and terminology to be used (see Activity 6.1).

The single most notable characteristic of the mildly retarded is that they learn at a slower rate than normal children. While the SLD child may have an uneven pattern of performance, doing well in some areas and poorly in other areas, the mildly retarded child tends to lag behind evenly in all academic areas. Mildly retarded children may also demonstrate some of the same behavioral characteristics identified with some SLD children.

ACTIVITY 6.1   Standards for Special Education

Write to the Division of Special Education of your state's Department of Education and request a copy of the standards for special education. This will contain the definitions for learning disabilities, mental retardation, and other handicapping conditions that are used in your state. It will also provide information about services available to handicapped students.

Mildly handicapped students, whether learning disabled or retarded, may exhibit certain behavioral and/or learning characteristics that interfere with their ability to keep pace with the coursework in the regular classroom. You can help the mildly handicapped child by structuring your classroom and lessons to control for these interferences.

Distractibility

Children who are distractible have great difficulty keeping their attention on the task at hand. Instead, they focus their attention on extraneous motion, noise, and visual distractors in the room. To help children attend to their assigned work, you must eliminate unnecessary distractions.

In most elementary classrooms, teachers use bulletin boards, chalkboards, wall space, even windows to educate, motivate, and decorate. While this practice creates a stimulating learning environment for most children, it unfortunately creates a too-stimulating environment for the distractible child. This child requires a controlled environment in which he or she can concentrate.

The traditional method of reducing distractions is to place the child in a private study booth or carrel. This, however, is an undesirable strategy to use in the regular classroom. It draws unnecessary attention to the child in a negative manner. A less noticeable way to control attention is the use of preferential seating; by placing the child away from windows, colorful bulletin boards, and busy traffic patterns, the child has fewer distractions with which to contend. At first it may be desirable to place the child's desk so that it faces an empty wall with the student's back to the class. This should be done in a matter-of-fact manner so as not to ostracize the child from the rest of the class. Controlling distractions might require restructuring the classroom slightly so that there is a quiet area free of decoration. This is usually a temporary arrangement. As the child gets used to the classroom atmosphere, decorations can gradually be reintroduced one at a time, working toward returning to a normal level as the child learns to stay on task.

It is necessary to consider not only where the child's desk is placed but what is placed on it. When the child is supposed to be listening to a lesson or to directions, there should be nothing distracting on the desk. As the teacher you can control these distractors. If the child does not need a pencil then it should be put away, not left on the desk where the child will be fiddling with it instead of listening to the teacher. If the child does not need a worksheet, do not distribute it until it is time to start working on it. If it is passed out early, the child may be looking at the paper and not listening to directions. By planning ahead as to when to pass out materials, the teacher can help the child focus on the lesson or directions.

Elementary classrooms are full of colorful pictures and fanciful drawings to keep student interest high. This is also true of the pages in elementary math textbooks. Imagine how difficult it is for the child who has trouble concentrating to ignore those balloons floating up the side of the paper or the cute little train chugging across the bottom of the page. Why should the child concentrate on "boring" addition exercises when all this entertainment is available?

The obvious solution is to remove these drawings from the page. By removing unnecessary distractions from the worksheet, you make it easier for the child to focus his or her attention on the work to be done. Although this book advocates the use of concrete materials for introduction of new concepts, worksheets still can be used for practicing skills at the abstract level. Thus, we have provided several examples of how to handle practice assignments in this section. Many of the same considerations can be made when working with concrete materials. Consider the following example:

1. Use a window cut in a plain sheet of paper that allows only one exercise to be seen at a time, as shown at the left.

2. Frame out distracting decorations when photocopying worksheets.

3. Develop your own worksheets that are free of distractions.

Short Attention Span

Closely related to distractibility is the problem of short attention span. Some children can stay on task for only a short period of time; their attention span is inappropriately short. To keep such children on task, it may be necessary to include several short activities in each math instruction period and to switch activities frequently. Although all the activities used during the math class will be related to math instruction, they can employ different modalities to keep the child's attention on the work. The goal is always to lengthen the attention span by gradually increasing the amount of time the child is required to spend on each activity.

Again, the math materials that accompany your textbook may not be appropriate. The typical math worksheet contains about 25 to 30 exercises, and for the child who has a short attention span this may seem like an overwhelming task. There are several ways to circumvent this problem. Consider the following:

1. Cut the worksheet into several strips that include only a few exercises and give the strips to the child one at a time.

$$\begin{array}{cccc} 8 & 5 & 3 & 7 \\ +1 & +1 & +1 & +1 \end{array}$$

$$\begin{array}{cccc} 1 & 1 & 1 & 1 \\ +2 & +7 & +9 & +6 \end{array}$$

$$\begin{array}{cccc} 4 & 8 & 9 & 2 \\ +1 & +1 & +1 & +1 \end{array}$$

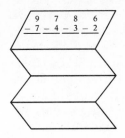

2. Fold the worksheet into accordion pleats so that only one row of exercises is visible at a time.

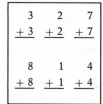

3. Develop your own materials that remove distractions and contain only a few clearly written exercises.

Another method of controlling attention is to consider the order in which you schedule your daily lessons. Children tend to be able to stay on task for longer periods of time when they are fresh. By organizing your teaching schedule so that the lessons that require the most sustained attention are taught early in the day, you can help the child with attention problems stay on task.

Hyperactivity

Hyperactivity is defined as constant and excessive motor activity. Recently, there seems to be a tendency to use this term loosely to describe all active children. The term *hyperactivity* should be reserved to describe children with extremely high activity levels. Many "normal" children and adults use movement to release pent-up energy. Look around your class and notice how many of your fellow students are tapping their foot in the air or moving some other body part. As long as these movements do not distract the learner or other students, they usually go unnoticed. Some hyperactive children are also able to control their behavior and the hyperactivity does not present a problem in the classroom. Hyperactivity is only a problem when it interferes with learning.

There are several methods currently employed by physicians, parents, and teachers to help manage the hyperactive child's behavior level. These methods can be classified as: (1) diet interventions, (2) medication, and (3) environmental interventions.

Diet Interventions.   The basic theory underlying the use of diet interventions is the belief that the hyperactivity is the result of an allergic reaction to something the child has eaten. Some diet programs focus on a single food element (e.g., sugar) while others have a broader focus.

The most well-known diet intervention is the K–P Diet developed by Dr. Benjamin Feingold (1975). This diet removes all artificial preservatives, flavorings, colors, and additives from the child's diet. It also eliminates natural and artificial salicylates that are found in some fruits and vegetables. This is a very strict diet that requires parents to spend much time purchasing and preparing natural foods. Although some parents claim to see drastic improvement in their child's behavior, the diet itself may cause an improvement in the behavior of some children while the increased family interaction due to the diet effort may cause improvement in other children. Research has not shown the diet to be effective.

Medication. In 1938, it was discovered that stimulant medications have a paradoxical effect on the behavior of hyperactive children. Instead of raising their activity level, as would be expected, the drugs have a calming effect. In the 1950s, pharmaceutical companies began vigorous marketing efforts praising the benefits of stimulant medications in controlling hyperactive behavior. As a result, stimulant medication became the treatment of choice.

One reason that these medications are so popular is that they are effective in controlling behavior and in most cases cause no side effects. Short-term side effects such as loss of appetite and insomnia occur in a small percentage of children. Long-term side effects are not known and for this reason most children are medicated only for school; that is, they do not take medication on weekends or over vacation.

Although medication is often effective in controlling behavior and improving attention span, there are some serious concerns about its use. Some feel that we may be teaching children that they are not responsible for controlling their own behavior and that they must rely on outside help such as drugs. Concerns with dosage and administering the medication on schedule can also be problematic. It is generally felt that medication should be used only in cases where attempts at improving behavior through use of environmental controls have been unsuccessful.

Environmental Interventions. There are many ways to structure the environment to control hyperactivity. One formal method of arranging the environment to increase desired behaviors is behavior modification. Basically this method rewards the child for appropriate behavior and, whenever possible, ignores inappropriate behavior. It requires a consistent effort on the part of the teacher but, when used correctly, is very effective. By working with parents the same method can be used both at home and at school and can teach the child to control his or her own behavior. You will need to work closely with your school psychologist to develop an individualized plan that will work with the hyperactive child in your class.

There are other, less formal ways to use environmental interventions in the classroom. As we all know, children learn from our example. If the teacher sets a calm, even pace, the children will likely follow this example. If the teacher sets a hectic, frenetic pace, the children's behavior will likely reflect this pattern. Hyperactive children are even more prone to react to a teacher's behavioral cues. By setting a calm, consistent example, you help the hyperactive child control his or her own activity level.

Allowing the child to get up from the desk and move around can help the hyperactive child work off some of the excess energy. Even normal children become fidgety when required to sit for extended periods of time. This is especially true for hyperactive children. By planning activities that allow students to be active learners you can let them use up extra energy while teaching math concepts at the same time. Activities such as working problems on the chalkboard or using a walking number line allow the child to move about while working on their lesson (see Activity 6.2). Musical number games such as *The Number March* by Hap Palmer, available from Educational Activities, Inc., also employ rhythm and movement to teach concepts.

ACTIVITY 6.2   Using Physical Exercise

Create a learning activity that introduces or reinforces a mathematics concept by having the students move around the classroom or use large motor muscles. The activity may involve one student, a small group of students, or the whole class. For example, numeration or introductory geometry can be taught by having a large group of students represent large numbers or geometric shapes.

Impulsivity

Impulsivity is defined as acting on impulse without consideration of the consequences of the action. Simply put, impulsive children act without thinking. This characteristic can be seen in both their classroom behavior and their academic work. Behaviorally, they may talk out in class, be out of their seats, and generally appear to ignore rules even when they are aware of the consequences of their actions. Academically, they may blurt out the first answer that pops into their heads, fail to read directions, or begin working before directions are given and may finish their work quickly but with answers that appear to have been randomly chosen.

Impulsive children may have particular difficulty with worksheets that require the child to switch from one operation to another; for example, a sheet that randomly mixes addition and subtraction exercises on one page. In a case such as this you must consider your objective for giving this assignment. If your objective is for the child to identify the proper operational sign and then compute the correct response, then this worksheet is appropriate. However, if your objective is simply for the child to have practice in calculating, then this particular worksheet is not appropriate. A better approach would be to use separate pages for each type of problem. Sometimes it is necessary to clarify our objectives so that we do not unnecessarily and unfairly penalize the mildly handicapped child.

To help control impulsivity you must employ strategies that require the child to slow down and think before responding. Possible strategies include:

1. Cut the directions from the top of the worksheet and give them to the child first. After the child has read directions, he or she may begin.

2. Read the directions to the child and ask the child to repeat them before beginning.

3. Pass out worksheets and have a minute of quiet time for reading directions before getting out pencils.

The suggestions for controlling distractibility given on pages 130–132 are also helpful in controlling impulsivity.

Auditory Perception

Auditory perception refers to the child's ability to interpret what is heard. Children with auditory perception problems are not hard of hearing. Although they have normal hearing acuity, they still have problems identifying, understanding, sequencing, or remembering what is heard. In the elementary classroom, some mathematics practice involves paper and pencil tasks and is visual in nature. There are, however, two aspects of mathematics instruction that tend to be highly auditory in nature: explanations and directions.

To assist the child with auditory perception problems it is best to make sure that explanations and directions are not given using only oral communication. Adding visual and/or tactile kinesthetic cues helps the child to compensate for the weakness in the auditory area.

Specific activities that require the child to listen carefully and use hearing can actually help strengthen auditory weakness. Some activities to strengthen auditory perception while practicing math concepts include the following:

1. Drop beans into an empty can to create auditory addition exercises.

2. Clap out simple patterns and see if the child can discover the auditory pattern. If necessary, a visual chart can be used as a guide.

3. Tape record simple problems and allow the child to hear them only once.

Visual Perception

Visual perception is the ability to attach meaning to what is seen. Children who experience problems in the area of visual perception may have difficulty identifying, understanding, sequencing, or remembering what is seen (see Activity 6.3). Because these problems do not involve visual acuity, glasses are usually not beneficial.

As an elementary mathematics teacher, you may see students who have unusual difficulty with number formation and reversals, copying exercises from the board, or keeping rows and columns of numbers straight. Many of the errors they make may be the result of these problems rather than an inability to correctly compute the answer. If you copied the wrong numbers or put them in the wrong column, then you obviously will not come up with the answer the teacher wants.

For some children, exercise programs to improve these visual skills are helpful. For other children, this may remain a long-term problem and some intervention on the part of the teacher is required. Do not penalize the children by requiring them to copy exercises from the board if this is an overwhelming task. They may spend the entire class time trying to copy the exercises and still not copy them correctly. Instead, give the children a written copy and allow them to skip the copying and get straight to work. The following strategies may also be helpful:

1. For students who have difficulty keeping columns straight, have them use a sheet of notebook paper turned sideways. Use one space for each column.

2. For children who have difficulty with both rows and columns, use graph paper to keep both rows and columns straight.

3. Use the child's auditory strength. Songs and rhymes that reinforce math facts can help the child who has a visual weakness. An example is the Independent Drill Mastery Tapes available through DLM Teaching Resources.

ACTIVITY 6.3 Follow the Maze

To experience what it is like to have difficulty with visual perception, try the following exercise.

You will need a pencil, a blank sheet of paper, a small mirror, and a partner. You are going to follow the maze below using a special procedure:

1. Sit across the table from your partner.

2. Place the maze on the table in front of your partner but close enough that you can reach it.

3. Have your partner hold the blank sheet of paper under your chin so that you cannot cheat by looking directly at the maze.

4. Hold the mirror about a foot above the maze. Now take your pencil and complete the maze by looking only in the mirror.

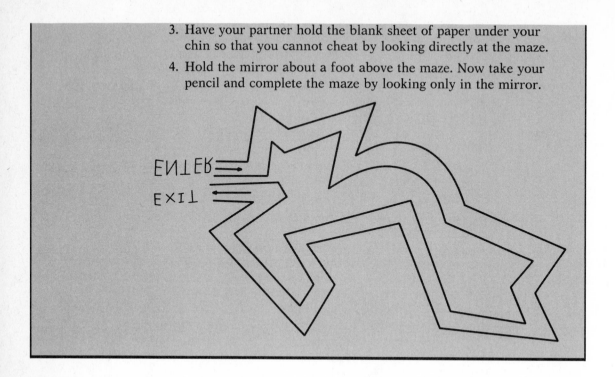

Fine Motor Problems

Some children have unusual difficulty with the fine motor control needed to form letters and numbers. This may be especially evident when they are required to write in a small space. Some of these children may be experiencing a developmental lag in this area and exercise, practice, and maturity may help lessen their fine motor problems. Other children may have a more severe problem called *apraxia*. Apraxia is defined as ". . . difficulty in fine motor output or in performing purposeful motor movements" (Lerner, 1985).

The child who has fine motor problems may know the correct answer but may not be able to write it neatly in the small space provided on most worksheets. The effort and time required to complete a worksheet may unduly tire the child. In this situation it is probably best to arrange another way of responding. Some ways to minimize the fine motor requirements include the following:

1. Use number stamps and an ink pad to answer on worksheets where small numbers are required.

2. Take sheets of circle stickers (available in school supply stores) and

write numbers on the stickers. The child can choose the correct number; peel off the sticker and stick the answer on the worksheet.

3. Develop worksheets that are set up in a matching format with exercises down one side and answers down the other side. The student draws a line from the problem to the correct answer.

Strategies that help develop fine muscle coordination in the elementary mathematics classroom include doing problems on the chalkboard, using large pencils or pencil grips, or using a clothespin number line (see Activity 6.4). In this activity you tie evenly spaced knots (3 to 4 inches apart) in a clothesline and hang the line in the classroom. Between each knot, tightly wrap a small piece of masking tape and use a permanent marker to identify the number for each space. Old-fashioned spring-type clothespins are moved up and down the number line to solve simple addition and subtraction exercises. This activity strengthens the small finger muscles while teaching mathematics.

If it is necessary to totally eliminate the motor output aspect of the lesson, other strategies are needed. The teacher can use a tape recorder to present the problems and the children can record their responses. Of course, if the teacher has the time, the entire lesson can be presented orally and the children can respond directly to the teacher. This method may be especially desirable for tests.

ACTIVITY 6.4   Creative Worksheets

> Develop a learning activity that allows the student to respond in a manner that does not require writing the answer in a small space. Be creative; there are many possibilities. These activities are useful not only for children with fine motor problems but for all students. They can be used at learning stations to give practice and reinforce concepts, and the students often view them more as a game than as work.

Reading Problems

Some mildly handicapped children experience most of their learning difficulties in reading. But eventually reading problems begin to affect other academic areas, including mathematics. This is especially true when the child must read directions or story problems. Errors in reading may cause the child to answer incorrectly when he or she actually knows how to solve the problem correctly.

Sometimes it may be necessary to try to lessen the effect of a reading problem on the child's mathematics performance. The following suggestions may be helpful:

1. Develop a mathematics chart or dictionary that lists key words often used in directions and story problems and gives a corresponding symbol or visual cue.

2. Underline potential key words in story problems. A color code can be used, such as red for subtraction, green for addition, and so on; just be consistent in color-coding. Remember that key words may *suggest* an operation, but, the context of the language determines the actual selection of the operation. Thus, be careful when using key or clue words when solving story problems.

3. Assign a peer tutor to sit near the child and assist in reading direction and story problems.

Resistance to Change

Some handicapped children exhibit a behavioral characteristic called *rigidity,* or *resistance to change.* Once they are comfortable in a certain environment or with a certain response pattern, they find it difficult to adapt to new situations. Consistency on the part of the teacher can play an important role here because the child knows what to expect. An organized classroom is also helpful because the child knows where things are and can rely on this remaining the same from day to day.

The following suggestions may help structure the environment for this child:

1. Develop a routine manner in which you present lessons. Once the child is used to the routine, he or she feels comfortable.

2. Do not change bulletin boards, redecorate the classroom, or move the children's desks around when the child is not present. If the child can see the change being made or can participate in making the change, then it is easier for the child to adjust.

3. Do not mix several different types of operation exercises on one page.

Conceptual Difficulties

Some mildly handicapped children will have more than the usual amount of difficulty with certain mathematical concepts. Although these will vary from child to child, teachers have been able to identify some concepts that seem to be especially problematic. Several of these are described here. (Suggestions on how to teach these concepts are described in Chapter 3.)

One-to-One Correspondence.   The use of many concrete and motor activities is useful to reinforce the concept of one-to-one correspondence prior to beginning more difficult mathematics instruction. Games that require one-to-one matching of objects include dropping one bean into a can for each number counted and clipping one clothespin on a line.

Greater Than (>) and Less Than (<)   While the concept of greater than (>) and less than (<) may be somewhat easy for many children, some special education children have extreme difficulty with it. For many special education children, the use of > and < symbols should be eliminated. (Several strategies for teaching greater than and less than are treated in Chapter 3.) Certainly, practice with number games can help reinforce the concept. The card game *War* and other similar games can be used for this purpose. *War* can be played by following the general rules for this game with one additional feature. When two cards are placed face up, the first student who names the greater value gets to keep the cards.

The Concept of Zero.   The concept of zero is a difficult idea for children with conceptual difficulties. An empty box may serve as an example of a quantity described by the number zero.

Long Division.   Perhaps it is because there are so many steps required in the long-division process that these students have so much difficulty with remembering all the steps in the correct sequence. If the child experiences extreme and continuing difficulty with long division, it may be more efficient to allow the use of a hand calculator for these exercises.

Missing Addends.   Some elementary school mathematics programs introduce exercises with missing addends $(3 + \square = 5)$ as early as the first grade. Although the handicapped child may have memorized the number facts to correctly answer the original problem $(3 + 2 = 5)$, he or she may be lost when asked to fill in missing addends. Several conceptual problems may be interfering with the child's ability to solve these exercises, including the inability to reverse a process or to generalize and apply previously learned knowledge. If the child has extreme difficulty with this concept, it may be best not to frustrate the child by forcing him or her to complete these exercises. Try coming back to these exercises later when the child may have developed the necessary conceptual framework.

General Comments

The reasons for mainstreaming will vary from child to child. In some cases, the child is ready to return to the regular class for academic instruction. In other cases, it is felt that the child will benefit from social interaction with peers. It is important to remember that because a child is ready to be mainstreamed *does not mean* that the child should be expected to do all of the same work in exactly the same way as the regular students. Adaptations of the curriculum, assignments, and teaching strategies will be necessary. If the child did not need special help, he or she would not be in the special education program. The following general suggestions may be helpful in adapting to the needs of a handicapped child:

1. Try to identify the cause of the child's learning problem. In this way you can adapt your lessons appropriately. For example, identify the reason behind addition errors (copied problem incorrectly, applied wrong process, uneven columns, conceptual difficulty, and so on). You can then work on remediation.

2. Establish a clear routine that you follow. Be consistent in your approach.

3. Clearly define the objective of your lesson and then make sure that you are not confusing the child by introducing additional requirements. For example, do not mix addition and subtraction problems on one page or add another objective to the task.

4. Use concrete materials to introduce and reinforce concepts.

5. Allow the student enough time to complete assignments and tests. This may mean that the child gets fewer problems or more time than other students.

6. Give the student lots of practice with concepts and facts. Do not assume that the child has mastered a concept just because he or she has demonstrated the ability on one occasion. These children need to "overlearn," so review often.

When you accept a handicapped child into your classroom, you are accepting responsibility for that child's education. This child will have distinct learning problems that will challenge you as a teacher. You will need to be creative in order to effectively adapt your teaching to the child's abilities. But, it is your responsibility to adapt your teaching strategies to the child's needs, not to force the child to adapt to you.

Teaching the Gifted Mathematics Student

Increasing concern for the education of gifted elementary school students has been observed in recent years. Gifted students represent a national resource, providing us with future leaders, scientists, and heads of government. Sometimes, gifted students are a wasted treasure. For example, Davis and Rimm (1985) have cited research that indicates that some high school dropouts are gifted students. Gifted students, often bored by routine classroom instruction, can represent an underachieving segment of the school population. It is important for teachers to recognize the gifted students in their classes and to provide them with the best possible educational alternatives. Similarly, talented females and minorities need to be identified and provided with an enriched educational experience. Thus, the purpose of this section is to help elementary school mathematics teachers understand how to recognize gifted mathematics students, and, correspondingly, to develop strategies and activities to assist these students in realizing their fullest potential.

Characteristics of Gifted Mathematics Students

As elementary school teachers observe gifted mathematics students there are several traits that emerge that characterize these students. The following list of characteristics was derived, in part, from the writing of Krutetski (1976), Hershberger and Wheatley (1980), Greenes (1981), and Johnson (1983):

1. Spontaneous formulation of problem sensing
2. Data organization ability
3. Flexibility in handling data
4. Mental agility, or fluency of ideas
5. Originality of interpretation
6. Ability to transfer ideas
7. Ability to generalize abstractions by observing structural patterns
8. Excellent short- and long-term memory
9. Independence
10. Task perseverance, or motivation
11. Self-confidence
12. Ability to think visually

Although the preceding list is not exhaustive, it contains enough information to allow us to characterize the gifted mathematics student fairly well.

Consider the following examples of how gifted children think. The examples illustrate how the preceding list of characteristics can be applied to specific cases of gifted children's thinking. A sixth grader was posed with the following problem:

> Two workers made the same amount of money for work they had done. One worker was paid $12 per day while the other worker was

paid $20 a day. If one worker worked six more days than the other, how many days did each one work to obtain an equal amount of money?

The sixth grader began to organize the data by generating the following sets of multiples:

Worker paid $12 a day	$12, 24, 36, 48, 60, 72, 84, 96, 108, 120, 132, 144, 156, 168, ⟨180,⟩ 192, . . .
Worker paid $20 a day	$20, 40, 60, 80, 100, 120, 140, 160, ⟨180,⟩ 200, . . .

The multiples listed represent cumulative wages for each working day. That is, after one day the first worker made $12, after two days $24, after three days $36, and so on. Likewise, the second worker earned $20 after the first day, $40 after the second day, $60 after the third day, and so on. From this list of wages the sixth-grade child noticed that the multiples had a common value of 60, but the child quickly disregarded this equality of wages by saying, "The first worker worked only five days and the second only three. I need a difference of six days." Continuing, the child saw that at the $180 mark the wages were again the same, but that the first worker worked 15 days and the second worked 9 days to earn that $180. Thus, the second condition of the problem was met, namely, that the workers have a six-day difference of work time. The sixth-grade child then announced that the problem was solved: one worker worked 15 days; the other, 9 days.

The work of the child in our example shows several of the characteristics of gifted elementary mathematics students. First, the child has the ability to organize data. Second, the child exhibited flexibility in handling the data. It is important to note how the sixth grader thought that $60 might represent a potential solution. However, the child was flexible enough to consider another condition of the problem; that is, the fact that there must be a six-day difference in working time. Third, the child also was able to transfer the idea of common multiples to a rather original use. Finally, the child worked confidently, without distraction, until the solution was apparent.

Consider another example of a gifted elementary school student's work, presented by Greenes (1981). The following description of a spontaneous formulation of a problem focuses on the thought processes of a fifth-grade student named Marcie.

Marcie's fifth-grade class was reading about the Statue of Liberty. It was mentioned that the Statue's mouth is 36 inches wide. Marcie wondered what was the length of the arm of the Statue holding the flaming torch. It was suggested by the teacher that Marcie look this information up in a reference book in the library. Marcie, however, felt that she could compute the length. Measuring the width of her own mouth, Marcie found that her mouth was about two inches wide, or $1/18$ the width of the Statue's mouth. Marcie then measured the length of her own arm and multiplied by 18. This approximated the length of the Statue's arm.*

Greenes's example shows how gifted children spontaneously develop problems. They are curious, energized by questions that they feel compelled to answer. Marcie used several strategies to solve her problem. In general, gifted mathematics students use several thinking strategies, often simultaneously, to help resolve the questions they have defined. Marcie applied the concept of ratio to a new situation; that is, she was original in her transferring of the ratio concept to a new situation. Also, notice the personality characteristic of independence that Marcie exhibited. Even though the teacher suggested that the answer could be found in a reference book, Marcie persisted and solved the problem in her own way.

Bright, gifted elementary school students are able to observe patterns and structural relationships that help them to make generalizations. Consider the following problem:

$$\frac{271 + 272 + 273 + 274 + 275}{5} =$$

A gifted fourth grader might recall a useful, fundamental generalization about division—that is, that division involves taking a set of objects and forming equal-sized subsets. In less mathematical language, we break something up to form equal parts. Thus, the following generalization is appropriate for these exercises:

$$\frac{273 + 273}{2} = 273$$

$$\frac{273 + 273 + 273}{3} = 273$$

$$\frac{273 + 273 + 273 + 273}{4} = 273$$

Considering the original example,

$$\frac{271 + 272 + 273 + 274 + 275}{5} =$$

---

*Greenes, C. (1981). Identifying the gifted student in mathematics. *Arithmetic Teacher*, *28*, p. 15. Used with permission of the National Council of Teachers of Mathematics.

we know that

$$\frac{273 + 273 + 273 + 273 + 273}{5} = 273.$$

A gifted child might almost instantaneously restructure the elements of this problem by noting the following:

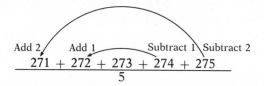

A compensation that achieves a structural balance is developed by noting that $271 + 2 = 275 - 2$, and that $272 + 1 = 274 - 1$. Now, the restructuring of this exercise yields:

$$\frac{273 + 273 + 273 + 273 + 273}{5} = 273.$$

A gifted child's ability to see a deep and fundamental generalization about division of whole numbers, coupled with an original way to restructure or organize the data, yields a solution of 273. How many of us would try to add the numbers and then divide by five?

Gifted elementary school mathematics children are exciting to teach. Even at the kindergarten level, their talents are readily apparent. For example, classifying and comparing sizes of objects may be performed by the gifted student with eight or nine objects, whereas the so-called "average" student may be able to arrange in size only three or four objects (see Activities 6.5 and 6.6). Novel solutions—multiple approaches often referred to as *divergent thinking*—are observed early in the elementary school years. The quality and depth of mathematical thinking exhibited by gifted mathematics students is a rich treasure for student and teacher alike. Activities 6.7, 6.8, and 6.9 offer more ways to enrich the gifted student's learning.

ACTIVITY 6.5   Measuring Creativity

This activity is similar to those designed to measure creativity in elementary school mathematics students.

You are given a large barrel of water, a 9-liter can, and an 8-liter can. There are no markings to indicate a lesser amount on either can, such as 7 liters or 6 liters. How can you exactly measure 10 liters of water?

ACTIVITY 6.6   Spatial Relationships

This exercise can help children to develop spatial relations ability. It can also help you to become more visually aware.

Consider these four diagrams:

Which one of the preceding shapes can you observe in the designs below? (You may see a different figure in each design.) Shade the figure that you see in each design.

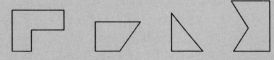

Spatial relationship ability is related to mathematical ability, particularly when studying geometry.

ACTIVITY 6.7   Similarities

This activity focuses on obvious similarities of geometric figures; for example, one answer is that they all have an interior and an exterior.

List some ways in which the following geometric figures are alike: square, rectangle, equilateral triangle, and rectangular prism.

ACTIVITY 6.8   More Spatial Relationships

This is creative spatial relationship activity for gifted elementary school mathematics students.

The nine dots in the diagram to the left represent animals. How can you draw two squares so as to completely enclose each animal in an individual stall?

ACTIVITY 6.9   Developing Creativity

> In four minutes, list as many unusual uses for the numeral 2715 as you can.
>
> Invent some other creative, open-ended questions for use with gifted elementary schoolchildren.

Selection of Gifted Students

Selection criteria for gifted students differ among school districts. Thus, it is difficult to cite specific criteria to use when selecting gifted students. For example, Stanley (1979) has reported on the mathematical precocity experiment conducted at Johns Hopkins University in which over 20,000 students, primarily seventh and eighth graders, were tested using the Scholastic Aptitude Test (SAT). Only the top 1 percent of students were selected to be accelerated through the traditional high school mathematics curriculum. Some gifted mathematics students were able to take college-level mathematics while still in high school. However, Renzulli, Reis, and Smith (1981) have described what they call a "revolving door" model by which 25 percent of the school population is placed in a talent pool and enter a resource room to work on individual projects. After completion of the projects, students revolve back to the regular classroom. Renzulli et al. advocated that the gifted children talent pool be identified on the basis of three measures: *superior IQ, creativity,* and *task perseverance* or *motivation.*

IQ.   Generally, gifted elementary mathematics students are two to five years ahead of their classmates on the mathematics subtest of a standardized achievement test such as the Iowa Test of Basic Skills. However, it is not sufficient to use only one measure when deciding on students' inclusion in a gifted mathematics program. The three identification categories of Renzulli, Reiss, and Smith (1981) are helpful here. An intelligence test, preferably an individual IQ test, should be administered. Further, group intelligence tests tend to be less reliable for young children than individually administered tests. Group intelligence tests also require speed as a factor since all are timed. An individual IQ test such as the WISC-R eliminates some of the drawbacks associated with group tests. Although cutoff scores for inclusion into a gifted program vary among school districts, an IQ of at least 120 should be required.

Creativity.   Creativity is another area that should be measured as a requirement for admission into a gifted mathematics program. Often gifted elementary mathematics students are curious—they want to know why things work. They are problem sensors as well as problem solvers. For example, a gifted elementary math student might wonder how much $1 million weighs or if an odd number added to another odd number yields an even sum. Questions such as these often arise spontaneously from creative children. Generally, when creative people set out to solve a problem, they are flexible, original, emit a large number of responses (fluency), and can elaborate on their solution process. However, the flip side of these positive attributes is that creative children may not be passive receivers of information in a classroom. In fact, they can be quite active, somewhat undisciplined at times, and raise numerous questions. Creativity measures such as the Torrance Test of Creative Thinking (Torrance, 1966) can be useful for measuring creativity of elementary schoolchildren.

Task Perseverance and Motivation.   Task perseverance or motivation can be measured by teacher checklists, self-rating schemes, or parent ratings. However, these measures can be the most unreliable of the Renzulli, Reiss, and Smith (1981) triad for identification. Obviously, it is possible that some parents may have a biased perception of their child's mathematical ability. Likewise, some elementary school teachers may find a creative child to be bored by routine work such as computational practice. Thus, they may incorrectly rate the child low on motivation when in reality the child is able to function with mathematics at a higher level than his or her classmates. To bring some structure to motivational rating, interested readers are encouraged to consult the Scale for Rating Behavioral Characteristics of Superior Students in Renzulli and Hartman (1981) and Renzulli (1983). In effect, the scale is comprised of items like "This child is easily bored with routine tasks." These items are designed to provide a structured teacher evaluation of a child's motivational level. To encourage accurate teacher evaluations of students, it is suggested that the ratings be done in November of the academic year. In this way, teachers will know their students well enough to make knowledgeable ratings.

Teachers' Expectations.   A final concern about teacher ratings rests on the notion of teacher expectations. In particular, minorities and females need to be rated fairly. Ernest (1976) has reported that 41 percent of the teachers interviewed in a study believed boys were more proficient in math than girls, and none of the teachers interviewed thought girls were better in math. Thus, teacher ratings need to be freed from racial and sexual biases.

Teacher Attitudes

By this time, you may be impressed by the intelligence and creativity of gifted elementary mathematics students. In fact, you may have some trepidation about encountering these children in your classroom. Let us consider some suggestions for providing a creative, exciting classroom environment for gifted mathematics students.

First, although an elementary school teacher should have a good understanding of elementary school content, methods, and materials, it is not necessary that the teacher be gifted in mathematics. More important is an open, curious, questioning attitude. Teachers need to sense individual differences among children and have a knowledge of materials and supplementary problems that can enhance a gifted child's potential. Teachers should encourage divergent ideas and self-initiated projects, maintain a high level of enthusiasm for the teaching of mathematics, and, because gifted mathematics students can be independent, support these students against peer conformity pressures. Do not be afraid to occasionally wander off the teaching schedule and try something different when a student has posed an interesting question. Realize that elementary school mathematics involves far more than teaching computation. Understanding the content of mathematics, problem solving, active learning through experiments and questioning experiences are only some of the important learning experiences beyond that of computational skills. Elementary school teachers need to see the overall picture regarding mathematical thinking in order to broaden and deepen the gifted mathematics student's school experience.

Many resources are available to help the teacher of gifted elementary school students. Some of these are listed in the references at the end of this chapter, as well as in the appendices at the end of this book. However, some additional sources are listed here to help you compile activities, experiments, and problems to use with gifted students. Some of the companies or organizations listed have valuable materials in their publication catalogs. You are urged to write them to obtain a catalog.

National Council of Teachers of Elementary School Mathematics
1906 Association Drive
Reston, VA 22091

Arithmetic Teacher (February 1981 issue)
Issue devoted to the challenge of teaching the mathematically able student.

Fisher, Lyle. *Super Problems.* Palo Alto, CA: Dale Seymour Publications, 1982.

Seymour, Dale. *Favorite Problems.* Palo Alto, CA: Dale Seymour Publications, 1982.

Arithmetic Teacher (February 1987 issue)
Issue devoted to using the hand-held calculator with elementary school students.

Teaching Statistics and Probability. 1981 Yearbook of the National Council of Teachers of Mathematics. Reston, VA: NCTM, 1981.

Computers in Mathematics Education. 1984 Yearbook of the National Council of Teachers of Mathematics. Reston, VA: NCTM, 1984.

Burns, Marilyn. *The Book of Think.* Boston: Little, Brown, 1976.

Burns, Marilyn. *The I Hate Mathematics Book.* Boston: Little, Brown, 1975.

Cook, Marcy. *Think About It.* Palo Alto, CA: Creative Publications, 1982.

Creative Publications
P.O. Box 10328
Palo Alto, CA 94303

Gifted Child Quarterly, a journal specializing in gifted education.

In summary, teachers of gifted elementary school students need to express an open, flexible, and supportive attitude. Further, they should be familiar with the many supplementary articles, materials, organizations, and companies that produce mathematics materials. Some sample activities for children at various grade levels in a gifted program are given later in the chapter.

Program Options for Teaching the Gifted Mathematics Student

Since schools vary in their delivery systems for teaching gifted mathematics students, our emphasis has been to familiarize you with the various identification procedures, characteristics of gifted mathematics students, and materials and methods for teaching gifted elementary school mathematics students. In short, the assumption has been that you are likely at some point to teach gifted elementary school mathematics students, either in the regular classroom or in a special program. Therefore, it will be necessary for you to consider some program options for teaching gifted elementary school mathematics students.

Acceleration.　Any strategy for gifted elementary school mathematics students that results in advanced placement or credit can be defined as an *acceleration* strategy. For example, skipping a grade in school and taking first-year algebra in the eighth grade for high school credit are acceleration strategies. Also, early admission into kindergarten is an acceleration strategy.

Enrichment.　Strategies that supplement or go beyond the standard grade-level work but that do not result in advanced placement or credit are considered *enrichment* strategies. A microcomputer BASIC language programming course for gifted fourth-grade students constitutes an enrichment experience, as does a special unit of probability and statistics taught to gifted fifth-graders. Other enrichment strategies include independent projects, learning centers, field trips, and Saturday and summer programs.

Magnet Schools.   A *magnet school* usually offers a specialized curriculum to both gifted and "regular" students seeking special training in a trade or skill. Many large urban school districts provide this alternative by having special schools for math, science, business, and trade skills. Students from all corners of the school district may attend the magnet schools.

Special Schools for the Gifted.   Special schools for the gifted are a variation of the magnet school idea. Here, however, the schools serve only gifted students of the school district. These types of schools are most common in large urban school districts.

Private Schools.   Private elementary, junior high, and high schools often have gifted programs of their own. These may be special classes, a learning resource center, special Saturday programs, summer programs, or field-trip experiences.

Special Classes.   In a given elementary school, gifted elementary mathematics students may be scheduled into a special class to study mathematics with other gifted mathematics students. The special-class approach highlights a controversial issue that affects many of the program modifications for gifted mathematics students. On one hand, special classes help the gifted mathematics student to interact with other similarly gifted students. Thus, there can be a payoff of intellectual stimulation. On the other hand, other students may resent these gifted students and label them as "brains," thus affecting the overall socialization process of the gifted mathematics student.

"Pull-out" Programs.   Gifted mathematics students are "pulled out" of the regular classroom for two or three hours per week to study special topics such as microcomputers, probability and statistics, mathematical problem solving, and number theory. Often these children meet in a special room called a *mathematics resource room*, which contains numerous types of mathematics materials.

Regular Classrooms.   The regular classroom approach places its major emphasis on the classroom teacher's ability to form meaningful, instructionally valid grouping schemes. Sometimes groups are formed, in the case of homogeneous grouping, by school policy based on test data. There may be a high math ability group, a middle group, and a low group of fourth graders, for example, formed by the school testing program. However, the so-called high math group may, at most, contain three or four gifted mathematics students. Thus, it is incumbent on the teacher to recognize the truly gifted mathematics students and to provide appropriate enrichment experiences.

In the case of heterogeneous grouping, where students in the class can have a grade range of five to six years, the situation becomes even more complex. A teacher posed with this dilemma can consult the criteria for selection of gifted students that is operative in the school district. Then, after assessing the data available for each child, a determination is made regarding the existence of a group of gifted elementary mathematics students. Particular attention should be paid to the identification procedures outlined earlier in the chapter.

There are a myriad number of program options for gifted elementary school mathematics program. Most of these options have been developed by central office personnel or a given school district or consortium. For most elementary school teachers, the essential organizational ideas can be distilled to the point of recognizing gifted mathematics students, regardless of the school's or district's organizational scheme, providing mathematical experiences of quality.

Strategies for Teaching the Gifted Mathematics Student

As we consider the teaching of gifted mathematics students, our concern is with our goals for these children. Hershberger and Wheatley (1980) have summarized the goals of a gifted mathematics program in the elementary school as follows:

> Development of problem-solving skills
> Development of thinking-learning skills
> Stimulation of intellectual curiosity
> Exploration of advanced topics
> Participation in determining problems to be investigated
> Development of spatial ability
> Development of visuo-intuitive thinking
> Development of logical-analytical ability
> Development of a healthy self-concept
> Development of computational ability

Our broad goal for gifted elementary mathematics students is to help them develop their fullest mathematical potential. This may be done, for example, by teaching a unit of microcomputer programming to enhance the development of logical-analytical ability. However, the basic mathematics curriculum of the regular classroom, if explored in sufficient depth, can contribute to many of the goals for gifted children. For example, several of the geometric activities presented in this chapter can assist the development of spatial ability and may serve as supplements to regular classroom work (e.g., see Activities 6.6 and 6.8). In addition, the activities can further the development of the goals for gifted mathematics students.

Activities for Teaching the Gifted Primary-grade Students (K–3)

Gifted primary-grade children need to explore mathematics in order to develop their individual creativity and knowledge of mathematical thought. The goals of a gifted mathematics program can serve as guidelines for the development of quality enrichment material. Often a mathematical experience illustrates several of the means toward the attainment of a goal. For example, a problem-solving experience may also develop spatial and logical-analytical abilities. With this overlapping of goals in mind, consider the following sample activities for gifted primary-grade students.

Sample Problems and Activities

1. If you offer to sweep the basement floor for 5¢ the first day, and each day for a week you charge twice as much as the day before, how much will you make after two weeks?

2. Mike the Monkey is at the bottom of a 14-foot well. Every day he climbs up 2 feet but slides back 1 foot at night. In how many days will he reach the top?

3. For this problem-solving activity you need a balance and eight clay balls, one of them containing a weighted object to make it heavier than the other seven balls. Use the balance to find the ball that is heavier than the other.

4. I'm thinking of two numbers whose sum is 36 and differ 8. What are the numbers?

5. Draw a picture of your favorite animal. Then create a story problem involving the numbers 8 and 5 and your favorite animal.

6. How many of the 100 multiplication facts have even sums?

7. Using a hand calculator, find three numbers whose sum is 57. Find several possible answers.

8. How many squares do you see in the diagram below?

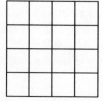

9. How many triangles do you see in the diagram below?

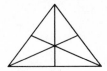

10. Loop the numbers for these sequences on the hundreds chart shown below. Then, in the blank spaces, write the next four numbers in sequence.

1	3	5	7	9	____	____	____	____
5	10	15	20	25	____	____	____	____
8	16	24	32	40	____	____	____	____

Can you find other patterns on the hundreds chart?

Hundreds Chart

①	2	③	4	⑤	6	⑦	8	⑨	10
⑪	12	⑬	14	⑮	16	17	18	19	20
21	22	23	24	25	26	27	28	29	30
31	32	33	34	35	36	37	38	39	40
41	42	43	44	45	46	47	48	49	50
51	52	53	54	55	56	57	58	59	60
61	62	63	64	65	66	67	68	69	70
71	72	73	74	75	76	77	78	79	80
81	82	83	84	85	86	87	88	89	90
91	92	93	94	95	96	97	98	99	100

11. Use a hand calculator to estimate how many pizzas you will eat in a lifetime.

12. Is it likely that two people in your class have the same birthday? How can you find this out? What would happen if you tried this with another class?

13. Program a microcomputer to add any two numbers for you.

These activities are only some of the many experiences that primary-aged gifted children can have to help them develop problem-solving skills.

Numerous resources are available for helping these children grow in a supportive mathematical climate, but a mathematically curious teacher is the cornerstone of any gifted mathematics program. Be sure to compile supplementary activities, experiments, and materials (see Activities 6.10 and

6.11). Be open to questions. Be curious and questioning about mathematics. Seek to be emotionally supportive of children who exhibit great learning potential in mathematics. These attitudes will help these children on their road to more advanced mathematics.

ACTIVITY 6.10 Number Tricks

Number tricks such as this are interesting means of motivating the study of mathematics. For gifted elementary students the emphasis might be on exploring why these tricks work.

Pick any number. Now double it. Add 15. Add the original number; divide by 3. Subtract the original number. You should always end up with 5. Can you explain why this trick works?

ACTIVITY 6.11 Hand Calculators

Hand calculator activities such as this can be useful in promoting problem solving with gifted elementary school students.

A rectangle has a length 4 meters more than its width. If W stands for the width of the rectangle, write and solve an equation that states the area is 154 square meters.

Activities for Teaching the Gifted Intermediate-grade Student (4–6)

Often intermediate-grade students with mathematics ability show levels of abstraction and deductive ability that many first-year high school students lack. *Levels of abstraction* refers to the fact that many of these children are capable of quickly passing through the concrete and semiconcrete stages of development to the abstract stage. *Deductive ability* implies that these children are capable of putting together a sequence of logical thoughts, such as that required for programming in the BASIC computer language. The activities presented here emphasize problem solving, visual-spatial ability, logical-analytical reasoning, and problem formation. The activities for intermediate-grade students are of course more complex and represent more sophisticated mathematical thought than those for primary-grade students.

Sample Problems and Activities

1. How many times would you use a 9 to number the pages of a 999-page book?

2. If the mouth of the Statue of Liberty is 36 inches wide, how long is the arm that holds the torch?

3. Collect data over a 2-week period to determine which local television station has the best record for accurately predicting the weather.

4. Use a hand calculator to determine the amount of water wasted by a dripping faucet in one year.

5. The Hindu Pyramid Puzzle, shown below, has seven discs of increasing size.

Photograph by author.

You should move the entire set of discs to one of the adjacent rungs by following these rules: (a) move one at a time and (b) always place a smaller disc on top of a larger disc.

6. What is the maximum number of pie pieces obtained by 1, 2, 3, 4, and 5 cuts? Can you generalize a rule that allows you to predict how many pieces are made by n cuts?

7. Write a microcomputer program for finding the factors of a given number. Use either the BASIC or the LOGO language.

8. Solve the following problem:

This is a mixed up basketball team. Can you help sort out the players and positions? Use the following information to help you understand the players' names and positions and to find the captain of the team.

Points	9	18	27	12	16
Position Played	——	——	——	——	——
Player's Name	——	——	——	——	——

a. The left guard is the low scorer.
b. The forwards score less than the center and right guard.
c. The captain plays right guard.
d. John plays center.
e. Eric and Terry each score less than the center.
f. The left forward scores more than Bill but less than John.
g. The captain is the highest scorer.
h. Bob scores the same amount of points as Bill and John combined.

9. Investigate the idea of a 5-minute clock. Use 0, 1, 2, 3, and 4 as the numerals. Explore how to add and multiply in this system. Also, construct an operation table for $+$ and $\times$ in this system and determine the basic properties that are evident. That is, are the systems commutative? Do they have an identity element?

10. How many triangles are there in the diagram below?

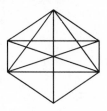

11. Work through *The Factory,* an excellent spatial relationship program available through Sunburst Communications.

These problems and activities are only some of the many experiences that gifted intermediate-grade children can have. Interested readers are referred to the sources listed at the end of the chapter for other strategies and activities. Activity 6.12 offers a problem that gifted children would enjoy.

ACTIVITY 6.12 Mathematical Patterns

Extending sequences by observing a mathematical pattern can be a useful activity for gifted elementary school mathematics students.

Try these sequences. Extend the pattern to fill in the missing numbers.

4	6	8	9	10	12	___	
2	3	5	7	11	13	___	___
3	7	15	31	63	___	___	

Microcomputer Experiences for Gifted Mathematics Students

The use of microcomputers to develop powerful mathematical ideas is a helpful component for the education of the gifted in mathematics. We have at our disposal two approaches for using microcomputers with gifted mathematics students. First, commercial software programs are improving to the point that some good, thoughtful commercial programs are available that develop visual-spatial thinking skills, logical reasoning, and problem-solving skills. One of the better programs is *The Factory,* available from Sunburst Communications. This program requires, among other skills, students to use visual-spatial skills as they rotate, punch, and paint a hypothetical object created in a simulated factory. Another good program for gifted mathematics students is *Teasers by Tobbs,* also available from Sunburst. Here, various logical alternatives are tried as guessing and checking is utilized to find missing elements of addition and multiplication tables. Finally, *The King's Rule,* produced by Sunburst, requires students to find patterns to extend increasingly difficult number sequences. These and other microcomputer programs that emphasize problem solving and simulate application situations are valuable for gifted students in the upper elementary school grades.

Another avenue for increasing mathematical thinking is to have students write simple computer programs. These programs can help students to develop the concept of a variable, a powerful mathematical idea. Also, students observe patterns and can develop their visual-spatial potential. Also, the ability to generalize, an ability linked to a growing knowledge of the concept of a mathematical variable, should be developed.

At the primary-grade level, some elementary schoolteachers are having children write simple programs in the LOGO language. At first, most of this work involves moving a "turtle" in various directions such as forward, left, and right. Designs are copied and patterns are observed as children try to duplicate designs. Clithero's (1987) description of how Instant LOGO was used with primary-aged children provides several examples of how patterning and visual memory experiences can be provided for selected primary-aged children. Interested readers are referred to Clithero's 1987 article as a good source for beginning LOGO activities.

After exploring the construction of some predetermined designs, gifted children can create their own programs. The sample program that follows shows how some gifted children can create a triangle image by logically linking together several LOGO commands. Angular measurement is involved in this program as well as the notation of a variable. In our example we have selected n to represent a movement of any length, thus the generalizing power of creating a triangle of various dimensions is available.

```
To Triangle: n
Forward: n
Right 120
Forward: n
Right 120
Forward: n
Right 120
```

Once again, we are viewing the notation of a variable as a growing process primarily, at this point, for gifted primary-grade children. Gifted children can put together programs and create rather involved designs such as putting a triangle on top of a square to form the image of a house.

The LOGO language has great potential for gifted primary mathematics students. Patterning, visual-spatial training, logical thinking, generalizing, and creativity are some of the valuable goals that can be achieved by using the LOGO language with exceptional children. There are a variety of LOGO languages for young children, two of the most popular being the EZ-Logo and Instant LOGO languages. A helpful article designed to help teachers choose the most appropriate LOGO language for their students is provided by Harvey (1987). (See also Activity 6.13.)

ACTIVITY 6.13   Locating Suitable Software Programs

Write several commercial software suppliers letters requesting software catalogs. Compile a list of programs suitable for use with gifted elementary school students. Addresses for commercial suppliers are listed in Appendix C of this book.

At the intermediate-grade level, programming in the BASIC language is more often observed. For gifted mathematics students, simple programming can teach a great amount of mathematical thinking skills. For example, fifth and sixth graders study the concept of percent and often are asked to solve application problems such as the one that follows.

A coat marked at $189.95 is on sale for 25 percent off the marked price. What is the sale price?

Gifted children can be taught to write the following program to solve this problem.

```
10  P = 189.95
20  D = P * .25
30  S = P - D
40  Print P, D, S
```
Run
```
    189.95    47.487    142.463
```

Although at this point you may not be skilled in interpreting computer programs, the letters P, D, and S allow us to develop the concept of a variable in this program. Also, a child writing this program needs to link a chain of statements together and thus is developing logical analytical skill. To further the development of the concept of a variable, we can change the program by using the Input statement available in the BASIC language, as shown here:

```
10  Input P
20  Input PER
30  D = P * PER/100
40  S = P - D
50  Print P, D, S
```

Do not be too concerned if the specific statements in BASIC are somewhat ambiguous to you at this time. The important point is that with this latter program we can find the selling price for almost any item that has been marked down at any relevant percentage. This is indeed a powerful example of the concept of mathematical generalization!

Thus, as gifted children explore programming they can develop logical-analytical skills, generalizations, and, if desired, skill with constructing various spatial-geometric forms. This brief introduction to the use of programming for gifted students is meant to show you how mathematical thought can be developed by using microcomputer languages. Many gifted elementary students can pursue, on their own, the creation of new problems and geometric forms. Thus, the creativity of finding and solving original problems is enhanced for these children.

Summary

This chapter describes several strategies for teaching mathematics to exceptional children in the elementary school. Children with learning problems such as those who are educably mentally retarded as well as those who are gifted in mathematics are considered. It is hoped that the methods, materials, and resources suggested in this chapter will help you to create interesting and educationally sound learning experiences for these students.

Discussion Questions

1. Read the research report by Bley in the April 1987 *Arithmetic Teacher* and describe the suggestions made for teaching word problems to children with learning disabilities.

2. Compile a file folder resource unit of problem-solving activities, spatial relationship activities, and microcomputer programs. Use this resource unit with some gifted elementary school students.

3. Consult the microcomputer laboratory at your university to find out what software is available for use with gifted elementary school mathematics students. If possible, work through *The Factory, King's Rule,* and *Teasers by Tobbs.*

4. Discuss with class members some strategies for individualizing an elementary school classroom containing exceptional children who have been mainstreamed.

5. What types of children are most likely to be mainstreamed? What specific teaching strategies can you use when teaching them?

6. Develop a lesson plan for introducing the system of integers to fourth-grade children who are considered gifted mathematics students.

7. List some specific strategies that you can use to help gifted children avoid peer-group pressure to underachieve.

8. Discuss how you can encourage gifted females and other minorities to excel in mathematics.

References

Bley, N. (1987). Research report: Problem solving and learning disabilities. *Arithmetic Teacher, 34,* p. 35.

Clithero, D. (1987). Learning with logo "instantly." *Arithmetic Teacher, 34,* pp. 12–15.

Davis, G., & Rimm, S. (1985). *Education of the gifted and talented.* Englewood Cliffs, N.J.: Prentice-Hall.

Edge, D. (1986). Uninterrupted sustained arithmetic. *Arithmetic Teacher, 34,* pp. 12, 15.

Education for All Handcapped Children Act of 1975 (P.L. 94–142). (1975, November 28).

Ernest, J. (1976). Mathematics and sex. *American Mathematical Monthly, 83,* pp. 595–614.

Federal Register. (1977). *42,* p. 163.

Feingold, B. G. (1975). *Why your child is hyperactive.* New York: Random House.

Fennel, F. (1984). Mainstreaming and the mathematics classroom. *Arithmetic Teacher, 32*(3), pp. 22–27.

Fox, L. (1981). Mathematically able girls: A special challenge. *Arithmetic Teacher, 28,* pp. 22–23.

Greenes, C. (1981). Identifying the gifted student in mathematics. *Arithmetic Teacher, 28,* pp. 14–17.

Grossman, H. (ed.). (1973). *Manual on terminology and classification of mental retardation.* Washington, D.C.: American Association of Mental Deficiency.

Harvey, B. (1987). Finding the best logo for your students. *Classroom Computer Learning, 7,* pp. 48–51.

Hayes, M. L. (1975). *Oh dear, somebody said "learning disabilities"!* Novato, Calif.: Academic Therapy Publications.

Hershberger, J., & Wheatley, G. (1980). A proposed model for a gifted elementary school mathematics program. *Gifted Child Quarterly, 24* (Winter), pp. 37–40.

Hofmeister, A. M. (1978a). *Independent drill for mastery: Fundamentals of addition and subtraction.* Allen, Tex.: DLM Teaching Resources.

Hofmeister, A. M. (1978b). *Independent drill for mastery: Fundamentals of multiplication and division.* Allen, Tex.: DLM Teaching Resources.

Johnson, M. L. (1983). Identifying and teaching mathematically gifted elementary school children. *Arithmetic Teacher, 30,* pp. 25–26, 55–56.

Keating, D., & Schaeffer, R. (1975). Ability and sex differences in the acquisition of formal operations. *Developmental Psychology, 11*(4), pp. 531–532.

Krutetski, V. A. (1976). *The psychology of mathematical abilities in school children.* Chicago: University of Chicago Press.

Lerner, J. W. (1985). *Learning disabilities: Theories, diagnosis, and teaching strategies.* Boston: Houghton Mifflin.

Mercer, C. D. (1987). *Students with learning disabilities* (3rd ed.). Columbus, Ohio: Merrill.

Mercer, C. D., & Mercer, A. R. (1981). *Teaching students with learning problems.* Columbus, Ohio: Merrill.

Palmer, H. (1969). *Learning basic skills through music,* Vol. I. Freeport, N.Y.: Educational Activities.

Payne, J. (1981). The mathematics curriculum for talented students. *Arithmetic Teacher, 28,* pp. 18, 21.

Rathmell, E., & Leutzinger, L. (1981). Classroom activities for able students: In kindergarten, first, and second grades. *Arithmetic Teacher, 28,* pp. 48, 54.

Reisman, F. K. (1982). *A guide to the diagnostic teaching of arithmetic* (3rd ed.). Columbus, Ohio: Merrill.

Renzulli, J. S. (1983). Rating the behavioral characteristics of superior students. *Gifted Child Quarterly* (September/October), pp. 30–35.

Renzulli, J. S., & Hartman, R. K. (1981). Scale for rating the behavior characteristics of superior students. In W. B. Barbe & J. S. Renzulli (eds.), *Psychology and education of the gifted* (3rd ed.) (pp. 243–248). New York: Irvington.

Renzulli, J. S., Reis, S. M., & Smith, H. L. (1981). *The revolving door identification model.* Mansfield, Conn.: Creative Learning Press.

Schulman, L. (undated). Classroom activities for able students: In third and fourth grades. *Arithmetic Teacher, 28,* pp. 49, 56–57.

Stanley, J. C. (1979). The study and facilitation of talent for mathematics. In A. H. Passow (ed.), *The gifted and the talented* (pp. 169–185). Chicago: National Society for the Study of Education.

Torrance, E. P. (1966). *Torrance tests of creative thinking.* Bensenville, Ill.: Scholastic Testing Service.

Trafton, P. (1981). Overview: Providing for mathematically able students. *Arithmetic Teacher, 28,* pp. 12–13.

CHAPTER 7

Hand Calculators and Computers in Elementary School Mathematics

Objectives

After reading this chapter you will be able to:

1. Explain the role of hand calculators in the elementary school mathematics curriculum.

2. Describe criteria for selecting a hand calculator to use with elementary school pupils.

3. Identify hand calculator activities to use with elementary school students to teach problem solving.

4. Identify hand calculator activities to use with elementary school students to practice computation.

5. Compare and contrast hand calculator activities in order to select an activity that develops a specific curriculum objective.

6. Identify hand calculator activities to use with elementary school students that introduce mathematics concepts.

7. Explain procedures and criteria for evaluating microcomputer software.

8. List several ways that computers have affected the world in which we live.

Hand Calculators in Elementary School Mathematics Classrooms

Hand calculators have emerged as a strong force in the elementary school mathematics curriculum. Estimates indicate that over 75 percent of 9-year-olds either own their own calculators or have one available to use (Suydam, 1980). Millions of Americans use hand calculators when shopping or banking, and calculators have appeared even on wrist watches that can be purchased for less than $30 at retail stores. With the tremendous number of calculators available to the American public, it is necessary for schools to provide educational experience with hand calculators for children.

Historically, the French mathematician Blaise Pascal invented a calculating machine in 1642 that was the forerunner of today's electronic marvel. With the price of an efficient hand calculator dropping to below $10, school systems have begun integrating hand-calculator activities into the mathematics curriculum. Major textbook publishers have included hand-calculator activities in recent elementary school mathematics textbooks. The National Council of Teachers of Mathematics (NCTM) has suggested that calculators be available for appropriate use in all mathematics classrooms and has recommended that imaginative uses of the calculator be developed for exploring, discovering, and developing mathematics concepts (NCTM, 1980). Practicing computation and checking answers are seen as only part of the many instructional uses for the calculator.

Pros and Cons of Hand Calculator Usage

One of the major objections offered by opponents of the use of hand calculators is the concern that children will become so dependent on them that their mathematics achievement scores will decline. Perhaps this is one of the reasons that fewer than 20 percent of elementary school teachers have used hand calculators during mathematics instruction (Suydam, 1982). As we will see, hand calculator usage does not adversely affect achievement of basic skills in mathematics.

There have been numerous research studies investigating the effects of hand calculator usage on the achievement of basic skills in elementary school mathematics. Over 175 studies have investigated hand calculator usage in schools, and at least 75 of these studies explored the question of whether calculators harm achievement and found that they do not (Suydam, 1983). In all but a few studies, achievement scores were as high or higher when calculators were used for instruction as when they were not used. In these studies, calculators were not used on tests. Further, Hembree (1986) integrated 79 research studies on hand calculators and concluded that in grades K–12 (except in grade 4), students who use calculators in concert with traditional instruction maintain their skills with paper and pencil. In fact, using calculators can improve the average student's basic skills. Thus, research firmly supports the use of calculators at the elementary school level.

Continuing, potential objections against using hand calculators in elementary schools often stem from these perceptions: lack of availability, maintenance and security problems, and projected deterioration of students' computational skills. As noted earlier, calculator availability has increased greatly in the last few years. In fact, some calculators made today can be displayed on an overhead projector screen, and an example of one is shown in Fig. 7.1. Thus, an alternative for a financially depressed school district might be to display and use one of these calculators on a screen. This would alleviate any security or potential damage problems and at least provide some calculator experience to elementary students. Certainly, at the very least one calculator could be shown and its functions demonstrated to students. Further, if students cannot bring calculators from home, then perhaps a math lab with locked doors and file cabinets could be organized to provide security.

Finally, as mentioned earlier, research studies have indicated that elementary students' computational ability is not damaged by temperate use of hand calculators. Mathematics educators encourage reasonable paper and pencil computational practice. In fact, at the primary level, much use of manipulative materials for concepts and operations is encouraged. Thus, there is no intention of making the hand calculator a substitute for legitimate computational practice.

The effectiveness of hand calculators as a means of teaching problem solving, estimation, number patterns, and consumer mathematics, among others, far outweighs the fears of calculator opponents. However, it should be noted that hand calculators are an instructional tool, not an instructional panacea. Using a calculator every day throughout elementary mathematics classes is hardly the way to teach most mathematical topics. A judicious blend of hand-calculator activities during certain segments of the math class, or a separate unit on hand calculators, is a more balanced way of teaching.

Fig. 7.1

Criteria for Selecting a Hand Calculator

It is important to note that with the wide variety of hand calculators available for purchase, certain fundamental criteria are useful in determining which calculators are best for elementary school students. There is no need to have a sophisticated, confusing array of keys on a hand calculator for elementary school students. The following criteria may be helpful when selecting a calculator.

1. *Cost.* Good hand calculators can be purchased for less than $10.

2. *Algebraic logic.* Algebraic logic means that the solution for 2 + 3 = 5 is punched into the calculator in the same manner as it is taught in elementary school. For example, first the 2 symbol key is punched, then the + key, then the 3 key, and finally the = key. Hand calculators that use reverse polish notation (RPN) are not recommended. These are more sophisticated hand calculators, often useful in senior high school mathematics or college courses but confusing to elementary school students.

3. *Clear key.* This key allows the display to be cleared.

4. *Clear entry key.* When given a long list of numbers to add, a mistake might be made when entering a number. A clear entry key allows a student to correct the entry without having to go back and reenter all the preceding numbers.

5. *No dual-purpose keys.* Addition, subtraction, multiplication, and division keys should be separate. Also, the hand calculator keys should be simple. There is no need for sine, cosine, and exponential types of keys on a hand calculator for elementary school students.

6. *Large keys.* There is little need to have a petite calculator for children. Their small muscle development requires a larger key system.

7. *Warranty.* A suggestion here is to buy from major discount retailers or to use a catalog from a reputable school supply company.

8. *Eight-digit display.* At least eight digits should fill the display screen of the calculator.

9. *Easy-to-read display.* Numerals need to be large, clearly formed, and bright enough so students can see them clearly.

10. *Division by zero.* Since this is impossible, a hand calculator should flash or exhibit an error symbol such as a large E. Some hand calculators show 0.0.0.0.0, which may be a confusing result.

In summary, selection of a hand calculator for elementary school students requires consideration of criteria that can yield an instructional tool of great value.

Instructional Strategies for Using Hand Calculators

Many strategies for using a hand calculator with elementary school students are be developed in this section. It is suggested that you bring a hand calculator to class and try these activities in order to have firsthand experience before you try them with children.

Develop Understanding of Computational Algorithms and Mathematics Concepts

Although it is best to initially develop understanding of computational algorithms through the use of concrete and semiconcrete models, hand calculators can be used to support and consolidate developmental understanding. Activities 7.1, 7.2, and 7.3 show how the calculator can be used in this way.

ACTIVITY 7.1   Patterns in Decimal Multiplication

Use your calculator to solve the following exercises.

$10 \times 0.3 =$ _____

$10 \times 0.4 =$ _____

$10 \times 0.6 =$ _____

$10 \times 0.7 =$ _____

Can you formulate a generalization about multiplying a decimal numeral by 10? Make up a similar guidesheet for developing a generalization about multiplying decimal numerals by 100.

ACTIVITY 7.2   Using a Calculator to Introduce Subtraction and Division

Enter 24 into your calculator. Now subtract 8. Continue subtracting 8 until you reach zero. How many subtractions did you make?

This activity uses a repeated-subtraction technique to show a meaningful introduction to division. Use repeated subtraction to show $45 \div 9 = 5$ on your calculator.

ACTIVITY 7.3   Repeated-Addition Technique

> Punch 4 into your calculator. Now add 4. Add 4 again. Your result should be 12.
>
> Here $4 + 4 + 4 = 3 \times 4 = 12$. You have used a repeated-addition technique for demonstrating multiplication. Try to show $6 \times 8 = 48$ by using the repeated-addition technique.

=== *MATH JOKE* ===

If two is company and three is a crowd, how much is four and five?

Formulate Generalizations from Number Patterns

Formulating generalizations is an important mathematical thinking skill. Activities 7.4, 7.5, and 7.6 demonstrate how a hand calculator can be used to help elementary students make mathematical generalizations.

ACTIVITY 7.4   Patterns in Multiplication

> Do the following multiplication exercises on your calculator. Fill in the answers.
>
> $15 \times 15 =$ _____
>
> $25 \times 25 =$ _____
>
> $35 \times 35 =$ _____
>
> $45 \times 45 =$ _____
>
> $55 \times 55 =$ _____
>
> Do you see a pattern to the products? Use this pattern to solve the following examples but do not use your calculator until you have completed the exercises. Then use your calculator to check your results.
>
> $65 \times 65 =$ _____
>
> $75 \times 75 =$ _____
>
> $85 \times 85 =$ _____

ACTIVITY 7.5   A Number Trick

This activity requires students to use observation and patterning skills. Teachers can use it to motivate students in that they will appear to be "lightning calculators."

Have a student write any six-place number.	321,583
You write:	678,416
The student will write any six-place number.	235,131
You write:	764,868
The student will write any six-place number.	<u>532,819</u>

Let the student use a calculator to find the sum of the numbers. You will not need one because instantly you will say that the sum is 2,532,817.

Examine the following procedure to see why this trick works.

$$
\begin{array}{l}
\left.\begin{array}{l} 321{,}583 \\ 678{,}416 \end{array}\right\} \leftarrow \text{sum is } 999{,}999, \text{ or } 1{,}000{,}000 - 1 \\[4pt]
\left.\begin{array}{l} 235{,}131 \\ 764{,}868 \end{array}\right\} \leftarrow \text{sum is } 999{,}999, \text{ or } 1{,}000{,}000 - 1 \\[4pt]
+\,532{,}819
\end{array}
$$

The sum of the top four numbers is 2,000,000 − 2. Note that all you need to do is place 532,819 in the appropriate places and then subtract 2.

$$
\begin{array}{l}
2{,}000{,}000 - 2 \\
\underline{+\,532{,}819} \\
2{,}532{,}819 - 2 = 2{,}532{,}817.
\end{array}
$$

The key to this number trick is to make sure your partial sums are 999,999, or 1,000,000 − 1. Try to construct similar number tricks and use a calculator to check your work. Try them out with children and see if they discover your procedure.

ACTIVITY 7.6   More Patterns in Multiplication

Use your calculator to perform the following multiplications. See if you can find a pattern.

$$1 \times 1 = 1$$

$$11 \times 11 = \underline{\hspace{1.5cm}}$$

$$111 \times 111 = \underline{\hspace{1.5cm}}$$

$$1111 \times 1111 = \underline{\hspace{1.5cm}}$$

Without using your calculator, solve the following exercise:

$$11{,}111 \times 11{,}111 = \underline{\hspace{1.5cm}}$$

Develop Problem-Solving Skills

Activities 7.7 through 7.10 emphasize how a hand calculator can be used to develop problem-solving skills.

ACTIVITY 7.7   Number Operation

This activity emphasizes number operation flexibility and creativity.

Using only the 4 numeral key, display the numbers from 1 to 10. You must use the 4 key exactly four times. You can use the $+$, $-$, $\times$, and $=$ keys.

$1 = (4 \div 4) + 4 - 4$ $6 = \underline{\hspace{3cm}}$

$2 = \underline{\hspace{3cm}}$ $7 = \underline{\hspace{3cm}}$

$3 = \underline{\hspace{3cm}}$ $8 = \underline{\hspace{3cm}}$

$4 = \underline{\hspace{3cm}}$ $9 = \underline{\hspace{3cm}}$

$5 = \underline{\hspace{3cm}}$ $10 = \underline{\hspace{3cm}}$

ACTIVITY 7.8   Numbers That Resemble Words

Textbook story problems can be supplemented by creative use of the hand calculator. Solve these story problems with your calculator and then turn the calculator upside down. If you have solved the problem correctly you should see a word!

1. A large cat named Chico ate a lot of cat food. Chico ate 25 fish each day for 323 days. How many fish did Chico eat? _____

2. The pitching staff for the Bears gave up 1558 doubles, 587 triples, 785 singles, and 577 home runs. How many hits have been given up? _____

3. The school orchestra has purchased a trumpet for $399, a piano for $2565, and a violin for $116. How much has the orchestra spent on musical instruments? _____

ACTIVITY 7.9   Collect and Interpret Data

Collecting and interpreting data can be a valuable problem-solving experience.

Find the number of hours you watch television each day of the week by completing the following table and then adding the figures on your calculator.

	Number of Hours of TV Viewing	Number of Hours Awake	Percent of Time Awake Watching TV
Sunday	_____	_____	_____
Monday	_____	_____	_____
Tuesday	_____	_____	_____
Wednesday	_____	_____	_____
Thursday	_____	_____	_____
Friday	_____	_____	_____
Saturday	_____	_____	_____

What patterns do you observe? For example, on what day do you watch the most television? How does this compare with the rest of your class?

Repeat this activity, but this time fill in the table for the entire class. What patterns emerge? For example, on what day does the class watch television the least? Raise as many questions as you can about this information.

ACTIVITY 7.10   Strategies for Winning

This activity is designed for two players. Be sure to follow the directions carefully!

Flip a coin to determine who starts. The first player enters a number from 1 to 10 into the calculator. The second player punches the add key and a number from 1 to 10. Play alternates in this way until a sum of 100 is reached. The first person to reach 100 wins.

After you have played this game several times, find a winning sequence of numbers to punch into the calculator so that you can guarantee your victory, assuming that you start first. Determining a winning strategy requires you to analyze the game structure. A useful problem-solving strategy in this case is to find a pattern by working backward from the last number that guarantees your victory.

=== **MATH HISTORY 7.1** ===

In 1751, Jedediah Buxton, an English colonist in America, calculated mentally the number of cubic inches in a block of stone 23,145,789 yards long, 5,642,732 yards wide, and 54,965 yards thick.

In 1724, Thomas Fuller, brought to Virginia as a slave, could mentally multiply two 9-digit numbers and state the number of seconds in a given period of time.

Fuller and Buxton never learned to read or write.

Reinforce Computational Practice

Activity 7.11 is designed to reinforce computational practice in addition, subtraction, and decimal operations.

ACTIVITY 7.11   Computational Practice

A hand calculator can help students practice computational exercises.

Use pencil and paper to solve the following exercises. After you have solved an exercise, punch in the answer and turn your calculator over. If you have done the exercise correctly you should see a word.

Children enjoy the self-checking feature of calculator "words" and are thus reinforced as they practice computation.

Addition

1. 154	2. 191	3. 3,175
+453	+147	+4,563

4. 63,471	5. 1,562
+13,874	+1,483

Subtraction

1. 2,959	2. 9,489	3. 11,925
−2,041	−1,411	−10,932

4. 6,959	5. 8,947
−1,451	−1,229

Operations on Decimals

1. 0.435	2. 2.283	3. 0.588
+0.326	+2.631	+0.216

4. 1.18	5. 0.89	6. 0.973
−0.25	−0.29	−0.569

Develop Estimation Skills

Estimation skills are important in our technologically oriented society. Activities 7.12, 7.13, and 7.14 show how a hand calculator can be used to reinforce estimates of computational exercises, restaurant gratuities, and surface areas.

ACTIVITY 7.12   Estimating Products and Quotients

Estimate the following products and quotients. Use your calculator to solve the exercises. Discuss how close your answers were to the actual product or quotient.

1. $29 \times 81 =$ _____

2. $4876 \div 62 =$ _____

3. $198 \times 211 =$ _____

4. $9898 \div 93 =$ _____

ACTIVITY 7.13   Estimating Percentages

Estimate the 15 percent gratuity that is paid at a restaurant. Then use your calculator to find the exact amount.

1. Bill: $11.87   4. Bill: $87.42
   Tip: _____   Tip: _____

2. Bill: $38.97   5. Bill: $23.81
   Tip: _____   Tip: _____

3. Bill: $42.35   6. Bill: $114.21
   Tip: _____   Tip: _____

Discuss effective strategies for solving these estimation activities.

ACTIVITY 7.14   Estimating Area Size

Develop a plan for estimating how many students can comfortably stand on your classroom floor. Use your calculator to help you solve this problem.

Solve Practical and Consumer-related Problems

Many practical problems such as finding the mean of a set of test scores or balancing a checkbook can be aided by using a hand calculator (see Activities 7.15 and 7.16).

ACTIVITY 7.15   Averaging Test Scores

An elementary school student obtained the following scores on six quizzes: 85, 93, 74, 89, 96, 72. What is the student's average (mean) score? Use your calculator to solve this problem.

ACTIVITY 7.16   Balancing a Checkbook

Find the balance for each checking account activity described in the accompanying table.

Check	Date	Checks Issued or Description of Deposit	Amount of Check (−)	√ T	Amount of Deposit (+)	Balance $231.86
86	3/20	O.K. Auto	$ 84.21			_____
	3/25	Paycheck deposit			$ 400.00	_____
87	3/26	Acme Records	14.96			_____
88	3/30	Jack's Food Warehouse	85.43			_____
89	4/2	All Bright Utilities	35.96			_____
90	4/4	Rental World	236.00			_____

Motivate Mathematical Curiosity

Calculators can be used to motivate mathematical curiosity. Activities 7.17 and 7.18 show how children can be challenged in an enjoyable manner.

ACTIVITY 7.17   Motivating Mathematical Curiosity

This is a motivational activity.

Enter your age into a calculator and then double it. Add 5. Multiply by 50. Add the amount of change in your pocket up to but not including $1. Now subtract the number of days in a year. Add 115. Divide by 100. Can you see your age and pocket change?

Discuss how you could use this activity in a mathematics class.

ACTIVITY 7.18   Magic Squares

Magic squares offer an enjoyable and instructive motivational activity for the elementary school classroom.

Use your calculator to add the numbers in each row and column, and then add along the diagonals.

156	832	468	1,144	780
1,040	416	1,092	728	104
364	1,300	676	52	988
1,248	624	260	936	312
572	208	884	520	1,196

Fill in the empty squares below so that a magic square results. (Rows, columns, and diagonals all yield the same result.)

400	☐	☐	550	375
500	200	525	350	375
175	625	325	☐	475
600	☐	☐	450	150
275	☐	425	250	☐

Discuss several other ways in which magic squares could be used.

ACTIVITY 7.19   Palindromes

Palindromes are words or numerals that read the same forward or backward, like *wow, radar, tot, 121, 252,* and *18,181.* Although palindromes are discussed in Chapter 9, hand calculators can be used to reduce the computational work associated with them. Thus, children can look for patterns when constructing palindromes.

The process of generating a palindrome is as follows:

1. Write any numeral.
2. Reverse the digits and add.
3. If the result is not a palindrome, reverse the digits again and add to the previous result.
4. Sometimes this process must be done several times before a palindrome is obtained.

Example:		
	1. Start with an arbitrary number:	651
	2. Reverse the digits:	156
	3. Add:	807
	4. Reverse the digits:	708
	5. Add:	1515
	6. Reverse the digits:	5151
	7. Add:	6666 (a palindrome)

Using your calculator, start constructing a palindrome from 46. Then make up a few of your own examples. Can you find any patterns that enable you to construct palindromes effectively?

Microcomputers in Elementary School Mathematics Classrooms

Microcomputers have influenced the content of mathematics in the elementary school mathematics curriculum. A fast computer can do more calculations in one minute than a person using a pencil and paper could do in a lifetime. Today, introduction of topics such as problem solving, estimation, and a reduction of paper and pencil calculations seems to be major content modifications of the elementary school mathematics curriculum. Similarly, children need to learn how to operate computers and use commercial software, and in some cases, particularly with able mathematics students, learn to write simple programs in the BASIC and LOGO languages. The widespread availability of microcomputers in elementary schools has prompted the National Council of Teachers of Mathematics to suggest that elementary school students have access to microcomputer experiences that integrate microcomputer activities with core mathematical content.

A Brief History and Examples of Social Uses of Computers

Counting aids such as the abacus have been used for centuries by various cultures. In 1642, Blaise Pascal developed the first gear-operated calculating machine, considered by many to be a true precursor of the electronic computer. In the early nineteenth century, an English mathematician and inventor, Charles Babbage, designed what he called an *analytical engine*. The machine was designed to store data and then print out the results automatically on a typewriter. Unfortunately for Babbage, the necessary precision to allow construction of such a machine was not available until the 1930s. Nevertheless, Babbage made a valuable contribution to computer development.

In the 1890s, Dr. Herman Hollerith developed a system for automatic data processing that used punch cards, electromagnetic counters, and a sorting box. Using this system to analyze the results of the 1890 census, Hollerith was able to do the analysis in 3 years, 4 years shorter than the previous census analysis. Hollerith started the Tabulating Machine Company, which in 1924 became known as the International Business Machine Company, known today as IBM.

In the 1930s, Dr. Howard Aiken, a professor at Harvard, developed the Mark I, which was completed in 1944. Mark I used electronic relays to perform 200 calculations per minute. However, it was very bulky and weighed 5 tons. The ENIAC computer, completed in 1946, utilized more electronic parts than the Mark I. However, although ENIAC was a technological advance capable of doing many rapid calculations, it weighed 30 tons, required the floor space of a small house, and consumed so much electrical power that the lights of West Philadelphia dimmed slightly when it was turned on! Needless to say, early computers were big, bulky, and utilized a great deal of electrical power.

Over the years, technological refinements occurred that increased the power but decreased the size and bulk of computers. So-called first-generation computers—the big, bulky computers of the 1940s—used vacuum tubes as long as your hand. The transistor, much smaller than a vacuum tube, reduced computers from the size of a house to the dimensions of a modest-sized room. Transistors also decreased the time necessary to access data and execute instructions. Transistors were utilized in the 1950s. Third-generation computers, making their appearance in the 1960s, utilized integrated circuits using silicon as a semiconductor. The electronic circuitry of an integrated circuit was about the size of a small stamp. By 1965, a third-generation computer could perform between 50 and 100 million operations per second.

Fourth-generation computers, the current class of computers, are smaller and faster than their predecessors. In 1971, the Intel Corporation developed the 4004 microprocessor. These chips, smaller than postage stamps, have speed of processing and memory built into them. They are sometimes called "computers on a chip." With the development of the microchip, the construction of microcomputers soon followed. Today's small desk-top computers approach the power of yesterday's large, expensive mainframe computers.

Today, computers affect all of our lives. Banks and savings and loans use computers to keep account records. Hospitals and medical personnel keep track of patient records, and, in some cases, diagnoses are made by computers programmed to detect pathological symptoms. Even professional baseball and football teams utilize computers to gather statistics on player performance and to make predictions of game situations. Schools are beginning to use microcomputers for a broad range of activities. Elementary school mathematics classes are a fertile field for students to learn about microcomputers. Later in this chapter we explore some specific microcomputer activities for children (see Activity 7.20).

Microcomputer Terminology

At the most basic level, a *computer* is a machine with a memory, which accepts information, works on the information to solve a problem, and puts out the answer. *Microcomputers* are distinguished from *mainframe* computers by their smaller size, weight, memory, and slower speed. Mainframe computers, on the other hand, are used to process payrolls for large corporations, schedule airline reservations for commercial airlines, and track aircraft in the Western Hemisphere for the Defense Department. However, as technology improves, we may find that small, lightweight microcomputers are soon capable of performing operations that were thought to be the sole responsibility of mainframe computers.

A microcomputer works in the following way:

Input	*Processing*	*Output*
Usually input is via a keyboard terminal that communicates a program or set of instructions to the microcomputer. Also, a disc-drive system can input programs stored on a floppy disc into the random access memory of the microcomputer.	The central processing unit contains three important elements: 1. Memory 2. Control 3. Arithmetic	Usually output for a microcomputer is printed on a printer or displayed on a television monitor.

We need to consider in more detail the central processing unit of a microcomputer. When you purchase a microcomputer for home or school, the computer's memory is usually described as 48K, 64K, or 128K. This number refers to the number of bytes that can be stored on a memory chip. Also, the

specific name for this primary memory is random access memory (RAM), the programmable memory of a microcomputer that is available when the microcomputer is turned on. Suppose we have a microcomputer with 64K random access memory. One kilobyte (1K) is 1024 bytes. One byte is equivalent to one character. That is, a character is a specific number, letter, or symbol such as the letter A. Thus, a 64K microcomputer has $64 \times 1,024$ or 65,536 characters available in its programmable memory. This means the microcomputer can remember a program containing approximately 33 pages of double-spaced text.

The control and arithmetic components of the central processing unit of a computer work together. The control unit figures out the meaning of the instructions in a program. The arithmetic unit performs the necessary logical and numerical calculations. In brief, the central processing unit has become a computer within a computer. Miniaturization has increased the power and speed of microcomputers while at the same time decreasing their size and weight.

ACTIVITY 7.20   Scrambled Computer Terms

The following are scrambled computer terms. Can you unscramble them to form computer-related words?

1.   DAARRWEH   _____
2.   REOMMY   _____
3.   EOUPTMRC   _____
4.   NITROOM   _____
5.   KDITTESE   _____

Strategies for Using Microcomputers with Elementary School Children

Initially, teachers can teach children how to operate and use commercial software. It is important to remember that commercial software programs need to be integrated into the mathematics curriculum as a means of enhancing and achieving our overall mathematics objectives. Commercial programs usually fit into three categories: (1) drill and practice, (2) tutorial, and (3) simulation and problem solving. We now consider some sample programs in each of these categories of computer-assisted instruction.

Drill and Practice Programs

Drill and practice programs are the most common commercial software programs available. They can serve as a useful supplement when practicing basic computational procedures.

Challenge Math, available from Sunburst Communications, motivates children to practice whole-number and decimal operations in the context of a mysterious mansion complete with sound and color accents. *Fact Track,* prepared by Science Research Associates, provides for practice of basic operations at varying levels of difficulty and time. Children can make choices to accommodate their personal achievement level. *Primary Math/ Prereading,* developed by the Minnesota Educational Computing Consortium, helps children to practice counting by punching in the correct number for a set of objects. If a child is correct, a smiling face appears. If the child is incorrect, the screen is modified to eliminate the incorrect numeral that was selected. Thus, the correct answer is reduced to a narrower range of options. (The computer software suppliers mentioned here and elsewhere in this chapter may be contacted at the locations given in Appendix C.)

In general, drill and practice programs can be helpful adjuncts to the review process. However, their repetitive nature may be boring after a period of time. Similarly, care must be taken to avoid the "glamor" of the review games so that worthwhile mathematical objectives are not shortchanged. We do not want children to spend all of their time reviewing materials they already understand just because a game format is attractive, exciting, and colorful.

Tutorial Programs

Tutorial programs are designed to introduce a mathematical concept or skill. In elementary school mathematics classes, the preferred mode of introducing a concept is at the concrete or semiconcrete level. Thus, there are some limitations to the use of tutorial microcomputer programs. Nevertheless, some tutorial microcomputer programs may serve as a helpful supplement to semiconcrete instruction. *Get to the Point,* available through Sunburst Communications, uses a game format to expose children to the concept of ordering decimals. *Explorer Metros,* also available from Sunburst Communications, helps to introduce estimation of metric system units. Students explore an alien planet while they estimate metric capacity, mass, length, and temperature units.

In general, there is a need for more and better-quality tutorial programs.

Problem-Solving Simulation

Perhaps the most valuable microcomputer programs are the problem-solving simulation programs. The potential for good quality, in-depth programs is, indeed, great. Some quality programs are mentioned in Chapter 6 for use with gifted mathematics students; however, additional sample programs are mentioned here.

Gertrude's Secrets, available from the Learning Company, challenges primary school children to solve classification problems by theorizing and experimenting. *More Teasers by Tobbs* presents an extension of the successful software program *Teasers by Tobbs.* Available from Sunburst Communications, *More Teasers* utilizes fractions and decimals as numerical examples in a grid arranged to have children discover missing numbers. *More Teasers* is useful with intermediate and middle school children. The extremely popular *Oregon Trail,* available from the Minnesota Educational Computing Consortium, is a simulation game that crosses several discipline areas. Although primarily a social studies simulation, *Oregon Trail* has enough applied mathematics that it is included in this review. Students reenact a trip along the Oregon Trail in 1847. Decisions regarding money expenditures, estimates of distances traveled, as well as probabilistic thinking are contained in this program. Its popularity and high motivational level make this an excellent program for getting elementary students interested in using a microcomputer.

In addition, research cited by Clements (1985) has indicated that computers can make the learning experience more exciting, satisfying, and rewarding for learner and teacher. Also, computers can be used to improve performance in specific subject areas such as mathematics. A skilled teacher can judiciously use computers to enhance and provide in-depth mathematical experiences for elementary school students.

Evaluation of Software

Today there are numerous commercial software suppliers (see Appendix C), producing some good-quality software as well as some inferior material. It is important for elementary school teachers to be able to evaluate software for potential use by children. Although there are some software review reports available, such as those available from Scholastic Magazines (P.O. Box 644, Lyndhurst, NJ 07071–9985), it is better for elementary teachers to evaluate software according to their students' unique needs.

The software evaluation form on pages 186–187 is a "commonsense" approach to software evaluation. A teacher can evaluate a piece of software in about 30 to 45 minutes. One of the first instructional considerations is the type of program being examined. Is the program a drill and practice program or a problem-solving program? Moreover, as you describe the type of program, consider your overall resources for teaching mathematics. Perhaps your school has a wide assortment of drill and practice games and a lack of quality problem-solving materials. Thus, it would probably enhance your overall educational materials collection to have a quality problem-solving program. Keep in mind as you go through a software evaluation what your major goals are for materials, specifically computer software. Most school districts have limited resources and, therefore, priorities must be made to purchase the most necessary software.

As we scan the software evaluation form, we note several instructor considerations. Some of these are self-evident, such as the quality of directions in the program. Readability is an obvious concern. Sometimes a program designed for primary-aged children contains sentences far beyond the children's reading level. So, a teacher is forced to explain the program to the child. This contradicts the purpose of allowing a child to work independently with a computer.

Programs should have instructional significance. They should be relevant. Students need to be able to easily terminate a program or switch among program options. Also, the program should be mathematically sound; words, terms, and concepts should be clearly portrayed.

Visual and auditory characteristics should be interesting and motivating without being "busy." Sometimes there is simply too much clutter on the screen. Appropriate use of color and sound are fine, but they should not detract from the stated mathematical objective. Sound, for example, should be reinforcing, not a cacophony of strident negative messages.

In summary, your overall priorities will help you to decide on the purchase of a particular software package. Hopefully, a careful analysis and evaluation of a software program can help to reduce the accumulation of poor-quality software (see Activities 7.21 and 7.22). A final suggestion is to attempt, whenever possible, to obtain a backup disc of the software you select. Often companies provide these when a purchase is made. Computer discs are fragile, and having a copy disc would surely save time and energy in the event a disc is lost or damaged.

Software Evaluation Checklist

Program Name: _____

Subject: _____

Commercial Source and Address: _____

_____

Target Student Group

I.   Grade level   _____

    Ability level   _____

    Individual, small group, large group   _____

Software Evaluation Checklist (*Continued*)

II.   Program type
      Drill or practice   _____
      Problem solving   _____
      Tutorial   _____
      Simulation   _____
      Other   _____

III. Instructor considerations of the software
      program

                            1   2   3   4   5
                            Poor   Excellent

      Quality of directions   _____
      Readability   _____
      Independence from instructor directions
      and intervention   _____
      Absence of system errors   _____
      Appropriate flexibility for students to
      terminate program   _____
      Appropriate flexibility for students to
      easily choose among program options   _____
      Instructional importance of the program   _____
      Appropriateness of the program for the
      student   _____
      Length of time needed to complete
      program   _____

IV.   Visual and auditory characteristics

                            1   2   3   4   5
                            Poor   Excellent

      Quality of still graphics   _____
      Quality of animation   _____
      Quality of color   _____
      Quality of sound   _____
      Use of game format   _____
      Motivational level   _____
      Degree to which cooperation of students
      is emphasized   _____

V.   What are the major strengths of this
      program?

      What are the major weaknesses of this
      program?

      What is your overall rating of the
      software? Do you recommend it for
      purchase?

ACTIVITY 7.21   Evaluating Microcomputer Software

> Locate a microcomputer program and systematically evaluate it using the software criteria identified in this chapter. Share your results with the class.

ACTIVITY 7.22   Collecting Microcomputer Materials

> Visit a computer store and obtain brochures and catalogs for microcomputers used with elementary school students. Familiarize yourself with the hardware and software options available. For best results, consult Apple, Tandy, Commodore, and IBM affiliates since most elementary schools buy from these sources.

Sample BASIC Programs

The BASIC computer language (*B*eginners *A*ll-purpose *S*ymbolic *I*nstructional *C*ode) is the most widely used microcomputer language. Some children, particularly gifted and talented intermediate and middle school students, may benefit by investigating and writing programs. The following sample programs are designed to illustrate some mathematical topics that can be approached by constructing programs in the BASIC language. Also, fundamental commands in the BASIC language are described within the context of the programs.

Program I

```
Objective:  Introduce Print Statement
Program:    15  FOR X = 1 to 5
            20  PRINT ''YOUR NAME''
            25  NEXT X
            30  END
```

How can you vary this program?

Program II

Objective: Counting to 100
Program: 20 FOR X = 1 to 100
           30 PRINT X
           40 NEXT X
           50 END

How can you vary this program?

Program III

Objective: Multiplication Exploration
Program: 10 INPUT A
           20 INPUT B
           30 PRINT A*B
           40 END

How can you vary this program?

Program IV

Objective: Addition Practice
Program: 5 FOR X = 1 TO 5
           10 INPUT A
           20 INPUT B
           30 PRINT A;''+'';B;''='';A+B
           40 NEXT X
           50 END

How can you vary this program?

These sample programs are meant to suggest just some of the many fine programs that elementary school children can explore and construct. Research so far has not put limits on young children's ability to write computer programs. In fact, for gifted and talented intermediate students, many school districts are providing experience for children to write programs. Shumway (1984) even has reported on first graders' ability to write simple programs in the BASIC language!

In summary, we have touched on the following BASIC language terms: PRINT, FOR-NEXT, INPUT, END, as well as some formatting use of semicolons. [Readers interested in further study of the BASIC language should consult Malone and Johnson (1981).] Writing programs should be fun for students. A creative expression and modification based on sample programs seems to be a good way to approach it.

LOGO Experiences

Some innovative elementary school mathematics programs are providing children with experiences with the LOGO computer language. A common feature of all LOGO language variations is that initially children move a "turtle" on the monitor screen to create geometric shapes. Students must sequence commands and generalize procedures as they move the turtle around the screen. Children can actively create their own learning environment as they create programs. For example, the following program moves the "turtle" to create a square shape:

```
DRAW
    FORWARD  50
    RIGHT  90
    FORWARD  50
    RIGHT  90
    FORWARD  50
    RIGHT  90
    FORWARD  50
    RIGHT  90
```

An example of a generalized procedure is the fact that this condensed program does the same thing. It creates the same square shape.

```
DRAW
    REPEAT 4[FD50 RT90]
```

Programs can be combined to form complex geometric figures. Fractions, number lines, and other topics can be investigated through LOGO as well.

An even more primary exploration of LOGO concepts is provided by EZ-LOGO, available from the Minnesota Educational Computing Consortium. EZ-LOGO is designed for children of ages 4 through 8. EZ-LOGO utilizes a "turtle" to draw various shapes. Children learn to estimate distances and degrees, to recognize patterns and symmetry, as well as to gain familiarity with the computer keyboard. Initial activities involve the presentation of mazes from which the child must sequence commands to extricate the "turtle." Directionality is developed by sequencing commands such as forward, right, left, and backward. Later, children are asked to duplicate designs that have been viewed and then removed from the visual screen. Culminating activities involve the construction and saving of designs that can be recalled later. EZ-LOGO prepares children for the LOGO language and enables them to explore fundamental concepts in self-directed, creative ways.

LOGO, in contrast to EZ-LOGO, is a computer programming language that allows children to construct their own programs. As noted earlier, children can influence and construct their own learning environment. Developed by Seymour Papert and his colleagues at MIT, LOGO has influenced the thinking of many educators about the possibilities of primary children creating their own programs.

Although it is not the purpose of this text to attempt a thorough explanation of the LOGO language, a sample program is shown below. [Readers interested in more information about the LOGO language are referred to Moore (1984), which provides many useful programming activities for children, and Clement (1985), which provides a good overview of the philosophical and learning theory orientation of LOGO.] Here is another sample LOGO program:

```
TO CURVE
REPEAT 9[FD8 RT10]
```

This program draws a curve. It uses three *primitives,* as they are called in the LOGO language. They are the commands forward (FD), right (RT), and REPEAT.

Summary

The National Council of Teachers of Mathematics (NCTM) has suggested that elementary schools utilize the hand calculator. This means more than a narrow view of using the calculator to develop computational skill and to check paper and pencil results.

This chapter includes activities designed to develop the meaning of operations; to teach estimation skills, problem solving, and consumer skills; to motivate curiosity; to practice computation; and to investigate mathematical patterns and generalizations. The activities are presented to show how the hand calculator can be integrated into the elementary school mathematics curriculum.

This chapter also describes some of the arguments against using a hand calculator in the elementary school. Particularly, the achievement declines that have been feared by some have not materialized. In fact, students using hand calculators have experienced a much broader study of mathematics than a narrow, computationally based curriculum could provide. Criteria for obtaining a calculator for elementary school children is provided.

This chapter also presents an overview of the impact that computers have had on our society as well as of their importance in the elementary school mathematics curriculum. Sample commercial software and suggested evaluation criteria are demonstrated. BASIC and LOGO, two relevant computer programming languages for children, are discussed and some sample programs are given.

Discussion Questions

1. List three reasons for using a hand calculator in elementary school.

2. Describe at least one specific activity for teaching problem solving with a hand calculator.

3. List at least five criteria for selecting a hand calculator in elementary school.

4. Describe a calculator activity for use with elementary school students that reinforces computational practice.

5. Describe a calculator activity for use with elementary school students that teaches them to investigate patterns and generalizations.

6. Read a current journal article that describes how hand calculators are used in the elementary school mathematics curriculum. Discuss your findings with your fellow students.

7. Discuss several ways that the hand calculator can be used with children who have been mainstreamed into the regular elementary school mathematics classroom. List some specific teaching activities.

8. Select a current elementary school mathematics textbook and observe how hand calculators are treated in the text.

9. Develop a file of quality software for teaching mathematics. Annotate this list by describing the source of the software, price, and content.

10. Construct a bulletin board display showing the influences of microcomputers on our society. Show pictures of computers, key terms, and related occupational options.

References

Albrecht, B. (1972). *My computer likes me.* Beaverton, Oreg.: Dilithium Press.

Bartalo, D. B. (1983). Calculators and problem-solving instruction: They were made for each other. *Arithmetic Teacher, 30*(5), pp. 18–21.

Billings, K., & Moursund, D. (1979). *Are you computer literate?* Beaverton, Oreg.: Dilithium Press.

Clements, D. H. (1985). *Computers in early and primary education.* Englewood Cliffs, N.J.: Prentice-Hall.

Duea, J., & Ockenga, E. (1982). Classroom problem solving with calculators. *Arithmetic Teacher, 24*(6), pp. 50–51.

Gibb, E. G. (1975). Calculators in the classroom. *Today's Education, 64*(2), pp. 42–44.

Grossnickle, F. E., (1983). *Discovering meanings in elementary school mathematics.* New York: Holt, Rinehart & Winston.

Hembree, R. (1986). Research gives calculators a green light. *Arithmetic Teacher, 34*(1), pp. 18–21.

Hoffman, R. I. (1975). Don't knock the small calculator—Use it! *Instructor, 75*(1), pp. 149–150.

Immerzeel, G., & Ockenga, E. (1977). *Calculator activities for the classroom.* Palo Alto, Calif.: Creative Publications.

Judd, W. (1974). *Games, tricks, and puzzles for a hand calculator.* Menlo Park, Calif.: Dymax.

Kinzer, C. K., Sherwood, R. D., & Bransford, J. D. (1986). *Computer strategies for education.* Columbus, Ohio: Merrill.

Lappan, G., Phillips, E., & Winter, M. J. (1982). Powers and patterns: Problem solving with calculators. *Arithmetic Teacher, 30*(2), pp. 42–44.

Malone, L., & Johnson, J. (1981). *BASIC discoveries.* Palo Alto, Calif.: Creative Publications.

Meyer, P. I. (1980). When you use a calculator you have to think! *Arithmetic Teacher, 27*(5), pp. 18–21.

Moore, M. L. (1984). *LOGO discoveries.* Palo Alto, Calif.: Creative Publications.

Morsund, D. (1981). *Calculators in the classroom: With applications for elementary and middle school teachers.* New York: Wiley.

National Council of Teachers of Mathematics. (1980). *An agenda for action: Recommendations for school mathematics of the 1980s.* Reston, Va.: NCTM.

Reys, R. E. (1980). Calculators in the elementary classroom: How can we go wrong? *Arithmetic Teacher, 27*(3), pp. 38–40.

Seymour, D. (1981). *Developing skills in estimation.* Palo Alto, Calif.: Dale Seymour Publications.

Shumway, R. (1984). Young children, programming, and mathematical thinking. In V. Hansen & M. Zweng (eds.), *Computers in mathematics education* (pp. 127–134). Reston, Va.: NCTM.

Suydam, M. N. (1976). *Classroom ideas from research on computational skills.* Reston, Va.: NCTM.

Suydam, M. N. (1980). *Education: Third annual state-of-the-art review.* Columbus, Ohio: Calculator Information Center, The Ohio State University, p. 3.

Suydam, M. N. (1982). *The use of calculators in precollege education: Fifth annual state-of-the-art review.* Columbus, Ohio: Calculator Information Center, The Ohio State University.

Suydam, M. N. (1983). Achieving with calculators. *Arithmetic Teacher, 31*(3), p. 20.

Usiskin, Z. (1983). Arithmetic in a calculator age. *Arithmetic Teacher, 30*(9), p. 2.

Wheatley, G. (1980). Calculators in the classroom: A proposal for curricular changes. *Arithmetic Teacher, 28*(4), pp. 37–39.

Wiebe, J. H. (1981). Using a calculator to develop mathematical understanding. *Arithmetic Teacher, 29*(3), pp. 36–38.

CHAPTER 8

Addition and Subtraction of Whole Numbers

Objectives

After reading this chapter you will be able to:

1. Use concrete models for developing addition and subtraction concepts with elementary school students.

2. Identify mathematics concepts that serve as the foundation for elementary school mathematics.

3. Develop models that illustrate addition and subtraction as inverse operations.

4. Explain a variety of materials used to develop addition and subtraction with elementary school students.

5. Organize and teach basic addition and subtraction facts.

6. Create games and activities designed to reinforce the development of beginning addition and subtraction.

Introduction

After elementary school students develop greater understanding of and skill with counting, the operations of addition and subtraction are introduced. The concept of addition can be introduced as a more rapid and efficient means of counting forward. On the other hand, the concept of subtraction, can be introduced as a means of more efficiently counting backward.

Primarily, researchers have studied the relationship between counting and addition. Houlihan and Ginsburg (1981) found that when given an addition sentence such as $3 + 4 = \square$, most first graders started from 1, counted to 3, and then continued counting until they reached 7. As the first graders grew in mathematical maturity, they were able to begin counting from the first addend; in our example, from 3. Second graders, when given an example such as $3 + 6 = \square$, were able to count forward from 6, the larger addend, to find the desired result of 9. Thus, children seem to develop increasingly efficient means of relating counting to addition.

Throughout history societies have developed algorithms, or procedures, for addition and subtraction operations to meet more sophisticated counting and tallying needs. Thus, the operations of addition and subtraction are fundamental for effective living in advanced technological societies.

===================== *MATH HISTORY 8.1* =====================

The term *magic square* refers to a square array of numbers that have an interesting property—the numbers along any row, column, or diagonal add to the same sum. About 2200 B.C. the Lo Shu magic square was known to the Chinese. In 1514, German painter and engraver Albrecht Dürer made an engraving called "Melancholia," which was the magic square shown below.

16	3	2	13
5	10	11	8
9	6	7	12
4	15	14	1

Research on skill learning (Suydam & Dessart, 1980) has indicated that a complete understanding of operations such as addition and subtraction takes several years of elementary schooling. First, a thorough understanding involving concrete and semiconcrete models is necessary. Then application and practice of skills are necessary. This chapter considers several methods and materials for developing understanding and efficient use of addition and subtraction operations of whole numbers.

Preliminary Considerations

Although this text treats the concept of sets through an informal approach, a few explanations about sets will help prospective elementary schoolteachers by providing some background in the foundations of elementary school mathematics.

First, a *set* is a mathematically undefined term that usually refers to a collection or group. In everyday life we speak of a set of people, cars, or numbers. Usually brackets are used to designate sets: {a, b, c} is a set consisting of the letters *a, b, c,* as elements or members. In many contemporary elementary school mathematics series, the notation and terminology of sets is downplayed. In fact, at the primary school level, children should manipulate objects as they form groups or collections. Symbolism of set concepts is advised only in rare instances. However, a theoretical knowledge of sets is necessary for elementary schoolteachers so that they know the underlying rationale behind many of the topics that are taught in elementary school mathematics.

Another concept from set theory that is used to develop mathematical concepts is that of the *subset*. For example, let $A = \{1, 2\}$, then set $B = \{1\}$ is considered to be a subset of A. This can be symbolized by saying $A \subseteq B$. A set can have several subsets including the original set itself. For our example, the following list considers the subsets of set A.

$A = \{1, 2\}$ . . . the set itself

$B = \{1\}$

$C = \{2\}$

$D = \emptyset$ . . . called the null set or empty set

The term *proper subset* refers to a subset that is *not* the original set itself. Thus, sets *B, C,* and *D* are considered proper subsets of set A. The symbol showing that *B* is a proper subset of *A* is this: $B \subset A$. Although precise terminology and symbols are not taught to primary-aged schoolchildren, elementary teachers should know that part-to-whole relationships developed in classification activities, as well as in later work with division of whole numbers and concepts of fractions, are all supported by the foundation of set-subset relations.

Union and intersection of sets are two operations that have practical significance to the development of elementary school mathematics concepts. The *union* of two sets results in a third set in which all of the elements of *either* set are members. For example, let $A = \{a, b, c,\}$, and $B = \{e, f, g,\}$, then $A \cup B = \{a, b, c, e, f, g\}$. The symbol $\cup$ is read as "union." The *intersection* of two sets results in a third set that is formed by selecting the elements *common* to both sets. For example, consider $A = \{1, 2, 3, 4\}$, $B = \{5, 6, 4, 2\}$, then $A \cap B = \{4, 2\}$, where $A \cap B$ contains elements that are members of set A *and* set B. The symbol $\cap$ is read "intersection." Two sets, such as $A = \{4, 6\}$ and $B = \{1, 2\}$, with no elements in common are said to be *disjoint*.

As teachers model addition of whole numbers with concrete objects, often two sets are formed and then a third set is formed by joining the two sets. In effect, a union of two sets has taken place. Figure 8.1 shows a flannel board with cutouts of lollipops being used as concrete material. Note that modeling addition of whole numbers as the union of two sets requires that the two sets be disjoint, with no elements in common. Verbal descriptions for concrete models are helpful. For example, in the example given in Fig. 8.1, the teacher would say something like "Johnny had three lollipops and Sue gave him two lollipops. How many lollipops does Johnny have now?"

In describing situations that illustrate addition of whole numbers, elementary school teachers need to choose their words carefully so as not to confuse students. For instance, note the confusion that this verbal description could create: "Bill has three friends. Steve has two friends. How many friends do they have altogether?" Although the teacher might expect five as an answer, the child would be correct by answering three, four, or five friends. Further, if the two sets in the example are not disjoint, then multiple interpretations may be available. For instance, Bill might have these friends {Howie, Dave, Dan}, and Steve might have two friends who are common to Bill's friends—Steve's friends might be {Dave, Dan}. For this situation Steve and Bill have three friends altogether! Thus, whenever verbal descriptions of whole-number addition are presented, care must be taken to insure that the two sets are disjoint.

In conclusion, prospective elementary teachers need to be acquainted with some of the terms related to sets so that they can use these ideas functionally. That is, there is little need for children to use abstract terminology and notation, but as teachers use concepts of sets to help children develop mathematical concepts, they must be aware of the correct terminology and applications. In particular, the addition example $3 + 4 = 7$ contains an addend (3), another addend (4), and the sum (7). An informal approach to teaching addition would not require that children immediately memorize the terms *addend* and *sum*. However, at some point it is wise for teachers to use this terminology when describing addition examples.

2 + 3

2 + 3 = 5

Fig. 8.1

Introducing Addition of Whole Numbers

Elementary school students' initial experiences with addition need to be concrete. For example, the teacher might use magnetic tape attached to discs on a chalkboard as a model for addition. Some of the key procedures are outlined here.

The teacher points to a set of objects (see the diagram to the left) and asks the class how many they see on the left side of the diagram. The question is repeated for the set on the right side.

The teacher joins the two sets and asks the students how many objects now appear.

As children begin to study addition of whole numbers, many concrete experiences are required. A teacher can give each child a set of ten counters and have them form sets of three and four counters. Children can join the sets and individually count the result. After a while, children will refine their ability to determine the number of elements in the newly formed set. For our example, some children will be able to recognize three counters and count from there saying, "four, five." Others will be able to recognize the entire set of five immediately.

Folsom (1975) has suggested that partial counting experiences can be valuable semiconcrete activities for developing understanding of whole-number addition. For example, cards with dots can be displayed, such as

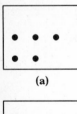

(a)

(b)

(c)

Fig. 8.2

those shown in Fig. 8.2a-c. Children are asked to state how many dots they can immediately recognize without touching or counting individual dots. This helps children to recognize the number of elements in the union of the two modeled sets.

After students have had several concrete and semiconcrete experiences, the addition sign (+) and equals sign (=) may be introduced. As shown in Fig. 8.3a-b, the teacher can begin by suggesting that the addition sign denotes a joining or combining operation and that the equals sign means that the resultant set has the same number of discs as the two original sets.

Finally, some inexpensive concrete materials for introducing addition of whole numbers include tongue depressors, popsicle sticks, and other household materials, which students should have available at their desks.

━━━━━━━━━━━━━ *MATH HISTORY 8.3* ━━━━━━━━━━━━━

The addition symbol is thought to be an abbreviation for the Latin word *et,* meaning "and." A manuscript dated 1417 uses this symbol.

Materials and Strategies for Beginning Addition

There are a number of materials that can be used to develop beginning addition concepts. Some of these materials are available through commercial suppliers whereas others can be easily constructed.

Unifix Cubes.   Unifix cubes are small cubes that interlock to form combinations that illustrate addition examples (see Fig. 8.4). The cubes are available from several of the educational suppliers listed in Appendix B.

oooo	oo	oooooo
4 +	2	6

(a)

oooo	oo	oooooo
4 +	2 =	6

(b)

Fig. 8.3

3   +   2   =   5

Fig. 8.4

Cuisenaire Rods. Cuisenaire rods, useful for developing addition concepts, are shown in Fig. 8.5 in a color-number combination. Cuisenaire rods also allow several number combinations to be explored. For example, a list of names for 5 and the corresponding rod equivalents are shown in Fig. 8.6.

Hanger and Clothespins. A model for addition can be easily made from hangers and clothespins (see Fig. 8.7). Children place clothespins on the hanger and slide them together to form sums.

Brown		8
Dark green	Red	6 + 2

Fig. 8.5

Yellow					5
Green		Red			3 + 2
Red		Red		White	2 + 2 + 1
Red		Green			2 + 3
Red		White	White	White	2 + 1 + 1 + 1
White	White	White	White	White	1 + 1 + 1 + 1 + 1

Fig. 8.6

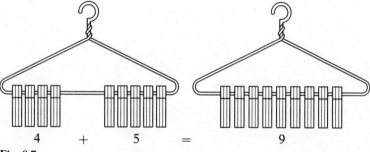

Fig. 8.7

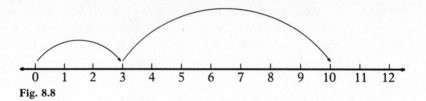

Fig. 8.8

Number Line.   The number line is more of a semiconcrete material than a concrete manipulative. After initial exposure to concrete material, a number line can be useful when illustrating addition examples. The addition example $3 + 7 = 10$ is shown on the number line in Fig. 8.8.

Number Balance.   A number balance, most often commercially produced, can be helpful in illustrating addition examples. Number balances are used after students have developed concrete and semiconcrete understandings of addition. As indicated in Fig. 8.9, $4 + 2 = 6$ is modeled by placing weights on the hooks below the numerals 4 and 2. Then, after placing a weight on the hook below numeral 6, the balance will look as it does in Fig. 8.10.

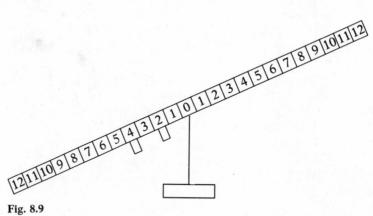

Fig. 8.9

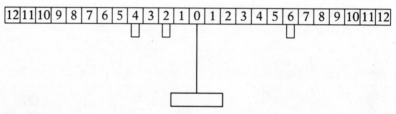

Fig. 8.10

After much development work at the concrete and semiconcrete levels, students are ready to begin practicing the recall of addition facts at the abstract level (see Activities 8.1 and 8.2).

ACTIVITY 8.1   Envelope Computer Game

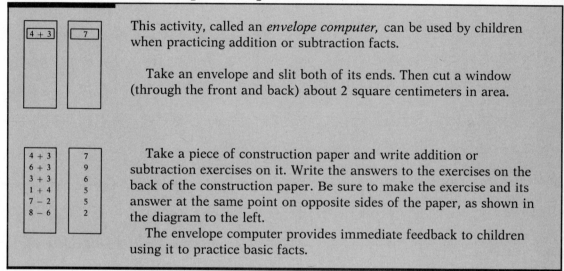

This activity, called an *envelope computer,* can be used by children when practicing addition or subtraction facts.

Take an envelope and slit both of its ends. Then cut a window (through the front and back) about 2 square centimeters in area.

Take a piece of construction paper and write addition or subtraction exercises on it. Write the answers to the exercises on the back of the construction paper. Be sure to make the exercise and its answer at the same point on opposite sides of the paper, as shown in the diagram to the left.

The envelope computer provides immediate feedback to children using it to practice basic facts.

ACTIVITY 8.2   Magic Squares

This activity is motivational as well as useful when practicing basic facts at an abstract level.

To construct a 3 × 2 magic square, make a design like that in the diagram below.

Put numbers in sequence along the paths of the arrow, as shown here.

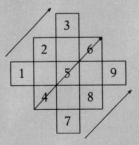

A partially completed square looks like this:

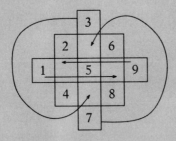

The numbers remaining outside the square are placed in the empty cells in the way shown by the arrows in the diagram below.

The completed magic square looks like this:

2	7	6
9	5	1
4	3	8

Introducing Subtraction of Whole Numbers

After students have developed an understanding of addition, many elementary school programs develop the operation of subtraction. Subtraction is the inverse operation of addition. In addition, we are given two addends and we obtain a sum. Conversely, subtraction is performed when we are given a sum, an addend, and our objective is to find a missing addend. The following diagram shows the inverse relationship of addition and subtraction.

$$2 \quad + \quad 3 \quad = \quad 5 \qquad 5 \quad - \quad 2 \quad = \quad 3$$

addend   addend   sum   sum   addend   addend

Some second- and third-grade teachers use the following terminology:

$$\begin{array}{r} 7 \\ -\ 2 \\ \hline 5 \end{array}$$ minuend
subtrahend
difference

Although the use of these terms is correct, it does not help to develop the relationship of addition and subtraction. Further, children experiencing a great amount of vocabulary development are burdened with more identification terms.

There are four fundamental subtraction situations that can be concretely modeled for children. The first situation is the *take-away model.* In daily life we often see this used in situations such as, "Five boys were playing basketball, three went home. How many are left?"

As indicated in the diagrams to the left, a teacher can place five chips on the overhead and pull two chips to the right side to illustrate 5 − 2. The remaining three chips serve as a model for the answer of 3.

As with addition, children need to have bags of chips so that they can solve subtraction examples at their desks. Children with bags of ten chips, for instance, can place seven chips on their desks, remove three, and determine how many are left, thus illustrating 7 − 3 = 4.

A second subtraction situation that children need to observe is *comparison.* This appears in daily life when, for instance, a teacher says, "I have 42 students in my class this year. Last year I had 26 students. What is the difference in my two classes?" A concrete model for comparison can be made from flannel board and shapes, as shown in Fig. 8.11. The teacher can say that there are five comic cutouts in one row and three in the other. The class can be asked a question such as, "What is the difference in the two rows of comic characters?" Matching the two rows leaves two comic characters

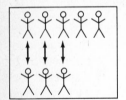

Fig. 8.11

in the first row without partners. Thus, comparing two sets results in an incomplete match. The objects that cannot be matched represent the differences in the two sets.

A third subtraction situation is that of determining how much more needs to be added to make a sum. For example, the missing addend approach to subtraction symbolizes this form; that is, $7 - 2 = \square$ can be represented in an equivalent sentence as $2 + \square = 7$. We often see this type of subtraction performed in grocery stores. Suppose you buy some merchandise that costs 68¢. If you pay with a $1 bill, the cashier might give change by first giving you two pennies, saying "70 cents"; then a nickel, saying "75 cents"; and finally a quarter, saying "one dollar." In symbolic terms, the cashier has solved $68 + \square = 100$, a subtraction sentence written in what some mathematics educators call a *related addition form*.

This "how many more" form of subtraction can be easily modeled by placing bottle caps next to an empty box on a table. The teacher tells the students that there are three bottle caps but that seven are needed for a complete collection. The students are asked how many more bottle caps are needed. As the class watches, the teacher slowly drops the four bottle caps into the box.

A fourth subtraction situation to which students should be exposed is the *set-subset* situation. Here language is important, in that students need a good grasp of class inclusion concepts (part to whole) in order to understand this form. Consider this example:

Bill has seven toy cars, four of them black and the rest white. How many are white?

A model for this subtraction situation might be to use blocks, as shown in the diagram to the left. The teacher can say that there are seven blocks, four of which are black and the rest white. The teacher then asks, "How many blocks are white?"

In summary, it is important that children have experience with a variety of subtraction models and situations. Many teachers start with the take-away approach. However, after a while it is necessary for students to be acquainted with the other subtraction types as well, because the language and context of many problem-solving situations in life are not of the "take-away" variety. Although many of the subtraction situations described here may seem simple, they contain subtle shifts of meaning, language and context that can be difficult for children. Thus, as elementary school mathematics teachers, we need to make these experiences meaningful for students. Suydam (1985) has cited research that indicates children need to experience a variety of subtraction situations, and that reliance on only the take-away approach is detrimental to maximum achievement. Further, with some mainstreamed children from special education classes, we need to pace the various subtraction situations appropriately. Finally, children need practice associating subtraction sentences with manipulative activities. First, given a subtraction sentence such as $8 - 5 = \square$, children need to demonstrate a solution with concrete materials. Next, after watching a demonstration of a concrete action on objects, students need to write the appropriate subtraction sentence.

MATH HISTORY 8.5

In a mathematics methods book entitled *How to Teach Arithmetic,* published in 1914, Joseph Brown describes the Austrian method of subtraction. If, for example, 6 is to be subtracted from 13, one thinks of what number must be added to 6 to make 13. Brown also notes that this method, called the *making change* method, dates to the sixteenth century.

Materials and Strategies for Beginning Subtraction

The materials used for introducing beginning addition can be adapted when teaching beginning subtraction concepts.

Number Line.   A number line, used after a concrete representation of subtraction has been developed, can be used in two ways. The first way is depicted in Fig. 8.12. This approach for $9 - 5 = 4$, requires a movement to the right on the number line to 9 followed by a movement to the left of five units. The result is 4.

An alternative approach for using the number line is to use the related addition technique. For example, $7 - 2 = \square$ can be written in an equivalent

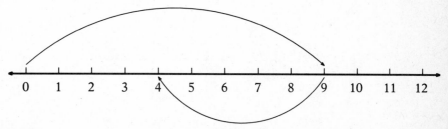

Fig. 8.12

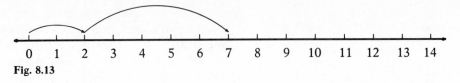

Fig. 8.13

form as 2 + □ = 7. As shown in the number line in Fig. 8.13, the first addend, 2, is modeled. Then the question "How many more units do I need to go to get to seven?" is asked. The movement takes up five units and the missing addend of 5 is identified. Thus, the solution for 7 − 2 = □ and 2 + □ = 7 is seen to be 5.

Cuisenaire Rods.   Cuisenaire rods are useful for developing solutions to the "how many more" subtraction situation. For example, a subtraction example such as 3 + □ = 5 can be shown by the following procedures.

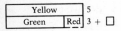

The yellow rod symbolizing 5 is placed on a table. Below it is placed the green rod, which shows 3. The task is to find a rod that, when placed down, will extend the distance to the end of the yellow rod. The red rod, which shows 2, is the correct rod.

Number Balance.   A number balance can be helpful when modeling subtraction, particularly for a sentence such as 5 + □ = 7, which is diagramed in Fig. 8.14a-b.

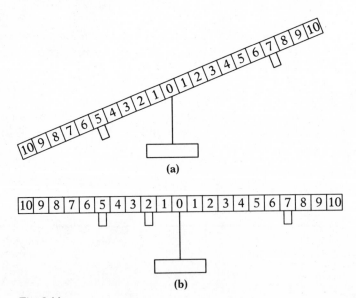

Fig. 8.14

Dot Cards.   Dot cards can be made of file-folder material, tagboard, or even plain paper. Simply put some dots on the paper and fold at the creased line, as shown in Fig. 8.15a. When the card is folded at the line we see that $6 - 2 = 4$, as shown in Fig. 8.15b.

Hangers and Clothespins   Take a hanger and place some clothespins on it. Slide off a subset of clothespins to illustrate a subtraction example. Figure 8.16a-b show $8 - 5 = 3$.

After a careful conceptual development of subtraction at the concrete and semiconcrete levels, children can begin to practice at the abstract level (see Activities 8.3, 8.4, 8.5, and 8.6).

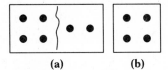

(a)   **(b)**

Fig. 8.15

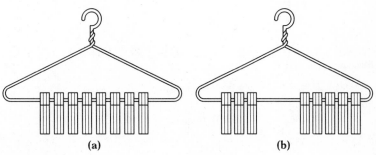

(a)   **(b)**

Fig. 8.16

ACTIVITY 8.3   Deliver the Mail

This game can help children practice basic addition and subtraction facts.

8	9	5
6	7	12
4	2	14
3	10	13

Take a box with subdividers and label each subsection as shown in the diagram to the left. Make up a set of cards with addition or subtraction facts on them. Children are instructed to "mail" the correct card to its appropriate address (answer). Thus, the card with $4 + 5 = \square$ would be delivered to the space labeled with the numeral 9.

ACTIVITY 8.4   Introducing the Calculator

This hand calculator activity can help children estimate and find sums to basic addition and subtraction facts. It can also serve as one of the initial introductory activities for using a hand calculator (see Chapter 7).

Predict the sum for each of the following. Then use your calculator to calculate the sums.

a. $4 + 5 = \square$ e. $8 + 6 = \square$
b. $3 + 8 = \square$ f. $7 + 4 = \square$
c. $7 - 2 = \square$ g. $12 - 3 = \square$
d. $9 - 3 = \square$

ACTIVITY 8.5   Addition and Subtraction Envelopes

This activity can help children as they begin to practice basic addition and subtraction facts. To make this device you need a 9″ × 12″ mailing envelope and 9″ × 12″ insert cards. The procedure for the activity is:

1. Cut the front of the 9″ × 12″ mailing envelope in half so that a pocket forms.

2. Then cut five holes in the bottom front half.

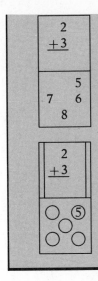

3. Make 9″ × 12″ cards with an exercise at the top and the answer choices at the bottom. The correct answer choice should coincide with *one* of the five holes on the bottom half of the envelope.

4. A child should look at the exercise on the card insert (2 + 3) and then determine the correct answer from four number choices, in this case (7, 5, 6, 8). The child will insert the card into the card holder and the correct answer will show through one of the holes.

ACTIVITY 8.6 Sunshine Subtraction

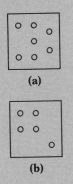

(a)

(b)

This is an outdoor educational activity that can be used to support introductory lessons on beginning subtraction. Make cards with several holes punched out of them, as shown to the left.

Take the children outside on a sunny day and use one of the cards to demonstrate how shadows can be formed by the sun streaming through the holes in the cards. For example, holding card (a) perpendicular to the sun's rays will yield seven shadow dots. Now tilt the card so that two of the shadow dots are cut off, as shown in card (b). Notice that five shadow dots are now visible.

This example can illustrate 7 − 2 = 5. Have the children use the cards to demonstrate several other basic subtraction examples.

Addition and Subtraction as Inverse Operations

The development of the inverse-operation relationship between addition and subtraction can be illustrated in a concrete manner. Often children are taught to "check" their work. For example, 6 − 2 = 4 can be checked by adding 2 + 4 and obtaining 6. The reason why the check for subtraction "works" is because of the inverse-operation relationship between addition and subtraction.

Consider our example in more detail. A solution for the inverse-operation relationship is diagramed here:

| | | | | | Original set of six toothpicks
| | | | | | Solution for 6 − 2 = 4 leaves four toothpicks
| | | | | | Sliding the toothpicks back is a model for 4 + 2 = 6

The original set of six objects has two objects removed, thus modeling 6 − 2 = 4. The return of these objects to their original position is a model of the check for subtraction, in this case 4 + 2 = 6. Thus, addition in one sense brings objects together whereas subtraction takes them apart. They work in concert because checking subtraction by addition restores the original model to its exact numerical value.

Vertical Format for Addition and Subtraction

Fig. 8.17

It is necessary that children see addition and subtraction exercises in both the vertical and horizontal frameworks. Current elementary school textbooks publishers are showing exercises written in both ways. At the first-grade level, children are solving $7 + 2 = \square$ or $\begin{array}{r} 7 \\ +2 \\ \hline \end{array}$.

Sometimes children have difficulty realizing that both the horizontal and vertical frameworks require the same response. The teacher can make this clear by using concrete material. For example, paper clips can be attached to a piece of tagboard and held vertically, as shown in Fig. 8.17. By sliding the paper clips together, $\begin{array}{r} 7 \\ +2 \\ \hline \end{array}$ is illustrated.

Basic Properties for Operations

In recent years, the emphasis on basic properties for operations has decreased. However, elementary school teachers need to be acquainted with these properties so that they have the necessary background in mathematics. Although not all of these properties need to be stressed in the classroom, it is recommended that teachers know their meaning.

The basic properties of addition of the set of whole numbers are listed in Table 8.1.

Subtraction does not exhibit the same basic properties as addition. For

Table 8.1 Basic Properties of Addition

Basic Property for Addition	*Example*
Closure	
$a + b = c$	For any whole numbers *(a* and *b)*,
$7 + 5 = 12$	their sum is also a whole number *(c)*.
Identity of 0	
$a + 0 = 0 + a = a$	When zero is added to any number, the
$6 + 0 = 0 + 6 = 6$	result is the original number.
Associative Property	
$a + (b + c) = (a + b) + c$	We add two numbers at a time. Thus,
$2 + (3 + 4) = (2 + 3) + 4$	when adding three numbers we have a
$2 + 7 = 5 + 4$	choice. Note that the parentheses help
$9 = 9$	to clarify our steps.
Commutative Property	
$a + b = b + a$	The sum remains the same even if the
$3 + 6 = 6 + 3$	addends are interchanged.
$9 = 9$	

example, subtraction is not closed; that is, if we subtract any two whole numbers the difference is *not* necessarily a whole number. The equation $3 - 7 = {}^-4$ shows a negative integer as a result. Also, subtraction is not commutative. For example, $3 - 7 \neq 7 - 3$.

In general, basic properties are usually developed for addition and multiplication. Also, informal use of these basic properties is suggested. In particular, the *commutative property* of addition is very useful for helping students memorize basic addition facts. In the primary grades, it is not necessary that students say the word *commutative,* but they should be able to signify that the order of the addends does not affect the sum. Later in the chapter we examine how the commutative property helps students to memorize basic addition facts.

The *associative property* helps students when doing column addition such as $\begin{array}{r} 3 \\ 4 \\ +6 \end{array}$. Again, it is debatable whether first and second graders should use the word *associative.* However, they can use the property informally by adding from top to bottom or bottom to top in an example such as $\begin{array}{r} 5 \\ 3 \\ +2 \end{array}$.

In conclusion, the prospective elementary school teacher should have a working knowledge of the terms used to describe the basic properties. Most children do not need to learn the names of these properties until the fifth or sixth grade, but elementary teachers should, at all times, use correct vocabulary at earlier points in the elementary mathematics curriculum.

Organizing and Memorizing the Basic Facts of Addition and Subtraction

Even though we are living in a technological age of hand calculators and microcomputers that reduce somewhat the drudgery of computational work, elementary school students still need to memorize certain basic addition and subtraction facts.

Just what are these basic facts that children need to memorize? Table 8.2 shows the 100 basic addition facts.

Table 8.2   Basic Addition Facts

+	0	1	2	③	4	5	6	7	8	9
0	0	1	2	3	4	5	6	7	8	9
1	1	2	3	4	5	6	7	8	9	10
2	2	3	4	5	6	7	8	9	10	11
3	3	4	5	6	7	8	9	10	11	12
4	4	5	6	7	8	9	10	11	12	13
⑤	5	6	7	⑧	9	10	11	12	13	14
6	6	7	8	9	10	11	12	13	14	15
7	7	8	9	10	11	12	13	14	15	16
8	8	9	10	11	12	13	14	15	16	17
9	9	10	11	12	13	14	15	16	17	18

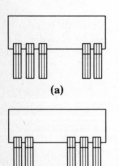

(a)

(b)

Fig. 8.18

The arrows indicate how to read the table. To find the sum of 5 + 3, we locate 5 on the vertical column to the extreme left of the table, read upward to locate the + sign, and proceed to the right to locate 3. The intersection of the row containing 5 and the column containing 3 yields the sum of 8. Notice that the sums are symmetric about the diagonal line. For example, 2 + 3 = 5 and 3 + 2 = 5. These appear as mirror images of each other, indicating the commutative property of addition. Thus, when memorizing the basic addition facts, the actual number of different facts to be memorized is reduced from 100 to 55. An early development of the commutative property will serve students well, for if they know the answer to 4 + 5 = 9 then they will automatically know that 5 + 4 = 9.

An easy way to develop the commutative property for addition is to take clothespins and put them on a piece of tagboard, and then slide them together to show the sum. Figure 8.18a uses 3 + 2 = 5. Now rotate the card so it looks like Fig. 18b. Bring the pins together again, and now 2 + 3 = 5.

After working several examples of this type, students can generalize the idea that the order of the addends does not affect the sum.

Students' thinking strategies can help to guide the organization of basic facts (see Activity 8.7). Rathmell (1978) has described three strategies that children use when memorizing basic facts as follows:

1. "Counting on" means that 2 + 3 would be solved by counting from 2. The child says 3, then 4, and finally 5.

2. Recognizing an unknown fact to be one more or one less than a known fact. An example of this is 3 + 4. Since children seem to quickly memorize doubles such as 3 + 3 = 6, the near double of 3 + 4 would be memorized as one more, or 7.

3. Compensating is a strategy that is useful for facts that have a sum greater than ten. For example, 8 + 6 is thought of as having the same sum as 10 + 4. The addend, 8, is *increased* by 2 so that it is thought of as 10. The addend 6 is *decreased* by two and thought of as 4. Thus, the sum is 14.

ACTIVITY 8.7   How Children Think

Mental arithmetic emphasizes thinking strategies and thus contributes to the growth of mathematical ideas.

Answer each exercise mentally. Focus on a strategy to help you.

1. 5 + 7 + 3 + 5 + 6 + 3 + 4 = ___
2. 8 + 9 + 3 + 2 + 1 + 7 + 6 = ___
3. 7 + 4 + 3 + 6 + 9 = ___

Make up several of these and try them with third-grade children. Observe the manner in which the children try to solve the exercises.

There are several ways to organize the basic addition facts for memorization. For example, emphasizing the commutative property of addition as well as thinking strategies can help students memorize these facts effectively. This plan requires that students gain mastery with one set of facts before moving on to another group. Notice that although 55 facts are listed in Table 8.3, the use of the commutative property, where it is applicable, brings the total number of facts to 100.

Table 8.3 Organizing Basic Addition Facts

Identity	One More Than	Two More Than	
1 + 0	2 + 1	3 + 2	
2 + 0	3 + 1	4 + 2	
3 + 0	4 + 1	5 + 2	
4 + 0	5 + 1	6 + 2	
5 + 0	6 + 1	7 + 2	
6 + 0	7 + 1	8 + 2	
7 + 0	8 + 1	9 + 2	
8 + 0	9 + 1		
9 + 0			

Doubles	Near Doubles	Unclassified	
0 + 0	3 + 4	3 + 5	
1 + 1	4 + 5	3 + 6	4 + 6
2 + 2	5 + 6	3 + 7	4 + 7
3 + 3	6 + 7	3 + 8	4 + 8
4 + 4	7 + 8	3 + 9	4 + 9
5 + 5	8 + 9	5 + 7	6 + 9
6 + 6		5 + 8	7 + 9
7 + 7		5 + 9	8 + 6
8 + 8			
9 + 9			

The unclassified facts, perhaps the most difficult for children to memorize, need special attention. Some children with special needs may take longer to memorize these facts. From an elementary teacher's perspective, these facts would be good to include as a quick diagnostic test for determining a child's mastery of basic addition facts. It is likely that a child who can correctly answer these facts would be proficient with the other groups. Likewise, corrective teaching might be started with these facts, especially if a fifth or sixth grader exhibits difficulty with them.

Another strategy especially useful with certain types of special education students has been presented by Kramer and Krug (1973). An example such as   2 would be solved in the following way.

$\quad$ +3

Large dots are placed on the numerals, which children count.

After a while, the dots are made smaller.

Finally, the dots are removed.

A modified list of these dot numerals is presented in Fig. 8.19.

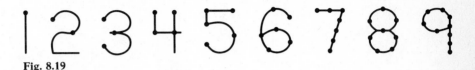

Fig. 8.19

The 100 basic subtraction facts do not exhibit a commutative property, so children must memorize them. The same table that was used for the addition facts can also be used for identifying the 100 basic subtraction facts (see Table 8.4). This time we must read inside the table—to the left to find one of the addends and above to find the missing addend. We have isolated the subtraction fact $10 - 7 = 3$.

Table 8.4   Basic Subtraction Facts

+	0	1	2	3	4	5	6	7	8	9
0	0	1	2	3	4	5	6	7	8	9
1	1	2	3	4	5	6	7	8	9	10
2	2	3	4	5	6	7	8	9	10	11
3	3	4	5	6	7	8	9	10	11	12
4	4	5	6	7	8	9	10	11	12	13
5	5	6	7	8	9	10	11	12	13	14
6	6	7	8	9	10	11	12	13	14	15
7	7	8	9	(10)	11	12	13	14	15	16
8	8	9	10	11	12	13	14	15	16	17
9	9	10	11	12	13	14	15	16	17	18

As with addition, the basic subtraction facts need to be organized. This is done by arranging the facts by differences, as shown in Table 8.5. Initially, a teacher can focus on one of the groups shown in Table 8.5. However, to insure memorization, the facts eventually should be practiced at random.

Table 8.5 Organizing Basic Subtraction Facts

Difference of Zero	*Difference of One*	*Difference of Two*
0 − 0 = 0	1 − 0 = 1	2 − 0 = 2
1 − 1 = 0	2 − 1 = 1	3 − 1 = 2
2 − 2 = 0	3 − 2 = 1	4 − 2 = 2
3 − 3 = 0	4 − 3 = 1	5 − 3 = 2
4 − 4 = 0	5 − 4 = 1	6 − 4 = 2
5 − 5 = 0	6 − 5 = 1	7 − 5 = 2
6 − 6 = 0	7 − 6 = 1	8 − 6 = 2
7 − 7 = 0	8 − 7 = 1	9 − 7 = 2
8 − 8 = 0	9 − 8 = 1	10 − 8 = 2
9 − 9 = 0	10 − 9 = 1	11 − 9 = 2

Difference of Three	*Difference of Four*	*Difference of Five*
3 − 0 = 3	4 − 0 = 4	5 − 0 = 5
4 − 1 = 3	5 − 1 = 4	6 − 1 = 5
5 − 2 = 3	6 − 2 = 4	7 − 2 = 5
6 − 3 = 3	7 − 3 = 4	8 − 3 = 5
7 − 4 = 3	8 − 4 = 4	9 − 4 = 5
8 − 5 = 3	9 − 5 = 4	10 − 5 = 5
9 − 6 = 3	10 − 6 = 4	11 − 6 = 5
10 − 7 = 3	11 − 7 = 4	12 − 7 = 5
11 − 8 = 3	12 − 8 = 4	13 − 8 = 5
12 − 9 = 3	13 − 9 = 4	14 − 9 = 5

Difference of Six	*Difference of Seven*	*Difference of Eight*	*Difference of Nine*
6 − 0 = 6	7 − 0 = 7	8 − 0 = 8	9 − 0 = 9
7 − 1 = 6	8 − 1 = 7	9 − 1 = 8	10 − 1 = 9
8 − 2 = 6	9 − 2 = 7	10 − 2 = 8	11 − 2 = 9
9 − 3 = 6	10 − 3 = 7	11 − 3 = 8	12 − 3 = 9
10 − 4 = 6	11 − 4 = 7	12 − 4 = 8	13 − 4 = 9
11 − 5 = 6	12 − 5 = 7	13 − 5 = 8	14 − 5 = 9
12 − 6 = 6	13 − 6 = 7	14 − 6 = 8	15 − 6 = 9
13 − 7 = 6	14 − 7 = 7	15 − 7 = 8	16 − 7 = 0
14 − 8 = 6	15 − 8 = 7	16 − 8 = 8	17 − 8 = 9
15 − 9 = 6	16 − 9 = 7	17 − 9 = 8	18 − 9 = 9

Another popular method used to help children memorize basic addition and subtraction facts is to use the number family approach, shown in the following example.

$$1 + 6 = 7 \qquad 7 - 6 = 1$$

$$6 + 1 = 7 \qquad 7 - 1 = 6$$

The number family approach pairs addition and subtraction examples and attempts to reinforce their inverse-operation relationship. Number families can be formed because of the following mathematical principle:

$$a + b = c \quad \text{implies} \quad c - b = a$$

$$b + a = c \quad \text{implies} \quad c - a = b$$

These statements are examples of inverse operations. However, with some mainstreamed children this approach can be confusing. Some children need to practice addition examples in isolation, only later to be followed by subtraction examples. For children who grasp addition and subtraction rather quickly, the number family approach is especially useful.

Estimation Strategies

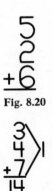

Fig. 8.20

Fig. 8.21

Addition exercises such as the one shown in Fig. 8.20 are developed in many textbook series at the second-grade level. These exercises, applications of the associative property of addition, are opportunities for developing mathematical thinking skills. Although, as noted earlier, students can start at the top and work down or reverse the order, there are other strategies that can better increase their flexibility with numbers. For example, consider Fig. 8.21. Children can be taught a skill of "catching tens." Recognizing that 3 + 7 = 10, a child can then add four to obtain the sum of 14.

Estimation strategies, extremely important in today's technological world, build on the development of thinking strategies in mathematics. In Chapter 9 we develop some specific techniques to guide the development of estimation ability. However, even when developing beginning addition and subtraction, strategies such as "counting on," adding 1 to a known fact, compensation, and "catching tens" can be taught so that children begin to gain number flexibility and estimation skills.

A game that helps students develop skill with estimation involves placing numerals on a card, as in Fig. 8.22. Children loop as many sums of 10 as they can within about one minute. After experiences such as this, children in the fourth grade and above can utilize this skill to add several addends, such as the exercise in Fig. 8.23.

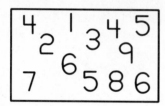

Fig. 8.22

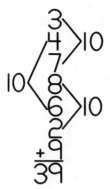

Fig. 8.23

General Comments

Some general guidelines for helping children memorize addition and subtraction facts are listed here.

1. Develop a small set of facts and achieve mastery with these before moving on.

2. Use many verbal descriptions of situations where addition and subtraction apply. Examples should be drawn from the children's world; for example, "Mary had four comic stickers, Sally gave Mary three. How many does Mary have?"

3. Be patient. Do not put children under constant time pressures. Especially with shy children or mainstreamed children, it is necessary to be supportive and encouraging.

4. Be careful with dittoes or textbook pages. Sometimes 40 exercises are too many when 20 would be sufficient.

5. Examine some software programs for use with a microcomputer. The novelty of this approach may aid retention. (See Activity 8.8.)

6. Play games and activities for quick recall of facts. (Activities 8.9, 8.10, 8.11, 8.12, 8.13, and 8.14 give some examples.)

7. Diagnose which facts are troublesome for children. Do not just show flash cards; rather, identify the facts that children need to practice.

8. Use intermittent practice. Perhaps you can give a child a paper bracelet with a cutout of the fact that you want to practice that day. Ask the child what the sum or difference is when he or she is in the lunch line, going home, and so on. Do not restrict learning of mathematics to the mathematics time period.

9. Emphasize thinking skills such as "counting on," compensation, doubles, near doubles, "catching tens," and so forth.

10. Relax—there are many areas of mathematics with which children can be successful even if they do not have instantaneous recall. A person with a Ph.D. in mathematics once reported that he did not have instantaneous recall of the multiplication facts. However, he knew the multiples of 5 and used a strategy that he had invented to obtain the other facts!

11. Remember that a meaningful, sensory, and concrete approach to addition and subtraction is helpful to children when memorizing basic addition facts. Research by Brownell and Moser (1949) and more recent findings of Suydam (1984b) support the idea that achievement in mathematics is increased by using manipulative material to provide meaningful and structured instruction.

ACTIVITY 8.8   Computer-Assisted Memorization

This microcomputer program was written for an Atari computer. The program is designed for children to use when practicing basic addition facts.

Basic Language Addition Practice Program

```
100    REM ADDITION PRACTICE
200    LET A = INT (10*RND(1))
210    LET B = INT (10*RND(1))
220    PRINT:PRINT
230    PRINT A; ''+''; B; ''=''
300    INPUT C
400    IF C = A+B THEN 600
450    PRINT ''I GET ANOTHER ANSWER''
470    GO TO 230
600    PRINT ''GREAT WORK''
610    GO TO 200
```

ACTIVITY 8.9   Matching Domino Cards

A variation of dominoes can be constructed to help children practice addition and subtraction facts.

In our variation, five domino cards are passed out to four players. One card is placed face up on the center of a table. A player tries to match two equal number values. A sample play is shown here.

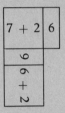

Continuing, the next player tries to play off of any of the values that are observed. If the player cannot make a play, he or she draws one card and loses a turn. Play goes to the next player who sees that a match can be made. The game ends when one player's cards have been discarded. A sample game is shown here.

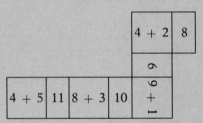

Domino cards are easy to make. Some 40 cards should be made containing basic addition or subtraction facts. The cards should be made so that each one has several possibilities. For example, 5 = 4 + 1 = 3 + 2 = 5 + 0 has several possible addend combinations. This idea can be adapted for any situation that requires a matching, such as matching pictures of fractions with their symbols. A sample set of addition facts to be used on the cards is shown below and on the following page.

10/2 + 3	5 + 3/9	8/1 + 8
10/4 + 1	10/2 + 2	2 + 7/6
5/4 + 6	2 + 6/5	7/2 + 4
7 + 3/9	4 + 4/10	1 + 5/9
8/3 + 2	8 + 1/7	7 + 2/6
6/3 + 5	2 + 1/7	6/4 + 5

5/3 + 7	0/1 + 4	4 + 2/10
10/4 + 3	5 + 4/8	7/1 + 9
9 + 1/4	8/1 + 8	7/1 + 9
5 + 2/4	5/4 + 6	2 + 7/6
9/3 + 1	3/5 + 5	8 + 2/8
6/6 + 4	10/1 + 2	1 + 6/9
6 + 1/3	3 + 6/8	7 + 1/7
1 + 3/10	4/6 + 3	1 + 7/2
8/1 + 1	3 + 4/8	6 + 2/5
10/3 + 3	9/2 + 5	2 + 8/7

ACTIVITY 8.10   Concentration

"Concentration" is a good game for developing skill in recalling basic addition and subtraction facts.

Prepare a set of cards with equations and the sum or difference on separate cards. Then place the cards face down and let a team or child pick a pair of cards. If they have obtained a match, then they keep the cards. If a match is not located, the cards are placed *face down* and play alternates to the next child or team. (Children need to remember basic facts as well as where the matching facts are located.) Play continues until all the cards are off the board.

A sample set of cards for you to make is shown in the diagram below. However, you may wish to make a set of cards that focuses on particular facts with which your students have trouble.

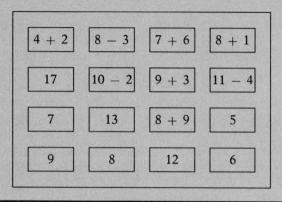

ACTIVITY 8.11   Math Match

Here is another game for practicing the basic addition and subtraction facts.

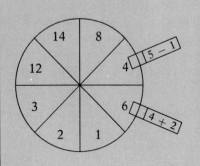

Take a circular piece of cardboard and divide it into eight sections. Write a number in each section, and then write equations on clothespins. Children are to match the clothespins with appropriate sums or differences. Two number sentences are shown in the diagram: $5 - 1 = 4$ and $4 + 2 = 6$.

ACTIVITY 8.12   Less Is More

This game involves strategy as well as knowledge of basic addition facts.

Give students a ditto sheet that looks like this:

Extra

| 1 | 2 | 3 | 4 | 5 | 6 | 7 | 8 | 9 | ☐ |

| 1 | 2 | 3 | 4 | 5 | 6 | 7 | 8 | 9 | ☐ |

| 1 | 2 | 3 | 4 | 5 | 6 | 7 | 8 | 9 | ☐ |

| 1 | 2 | 3 | 4 | 5 | 6 | 7 | 8 | 9 | ☐ |

Total _____

Take two dice with the numerals 1 through 6 on them. Roll them and call out the sum; for example, 2 and 6 would be called out as 8. On their sheets, children cross out addends that add up to 8. For example, students could cross out 2 and 6, 3 and 5, or 1, 2, and 5, among other choices. Any combination of addends that yields 8 is allowed. We have shown the option of crossing out 2 and 6. A total of 5 rolls is made for each row. Any excess numbers that have not been crossed out are added and placed in the extra box. Repeat the entire process for the second row, rolling the dice 5 times. After completing the fourth row, have the students sum their excess amounts. The student with the smallest number wins.

"Less Is More" can be adapted for use with young children by using only the first row.

ACTIVITY 8.13 Matho

This game is a variation of the popular game of bingo. The directions for playing this game are as follows:

1	13	11	6
10	4	8	16
7	15	12	3
14	5	9	2

1. Have children fill in grids by placing numbers from 1 through 16 in the cells (see the diagram at the left).

2. Using flash cards, the teacher calls out basic addition and subtraction facts. After calling the fact, the card is laid down.

3. If the player has a correct answer on the grid, a disc is placed over it.

4. The first player who has four discs in a row, column, or diagonal says "matho."

5. The teacher compares the answers to the cards that have been laid down.

ACTIVITY 8.14 Number Cards

This can be a useful enrichment activity for first- and second-grade children who are memorizing basic addition facts.

Make up a number card and have children loop adjacent numbers that yield a specified sum. An example of one such card, on which a few sample numbers have been looped, is shown to the left. Students should loop as many numbers as they can that have a sum of 8.

Numeral cards can be made of tagboard and laminated. Children can use grease pencils for marking.

Summary

This chapter examines the materials and methods for introducing addition and subtraction to elementary school students. A brief overview of set theory and number properties is considered to give prospective teachers a mathematical background for the topics taught. Thinking skills are emphasized for basic fact development and sample organizations for basic addition and subtraction facts are provided. Finally, some guidelines for helping children memorize facts are offered.

Discussion Questions

1. Discuss the value of simultaneously introducing addition and subtraction facts to children. Consider, specifically, the simultaneous presentation of addition and subtraction facts to special education children who have been mainstreamed into the regular classroom.

2. Explain why the check for subtraction that is traditionally taught in elementary schools works. That is, children are taught, for example, that $5 - 2 = 3$ is correct if $2 + 3 = 5$.

3. List several prerequisite skills that children should master in order to be ready for an initial presentation of beginning addition and subtraction examples.

4. List several concrete materials for children to experiment with in order to explore beginning addition and subtraction exercises.

5. Construct three games designed to help children practice recall of basic addition and subtraction facts.

6. Read the February 1987 *Arithmetic Teacher* for ideas on how to use a hand calculator to help children practice addition and subtraction facts. Here is one innovative example:
   Place the appropriate sign between the two numbers.
   a. 7   3 = 10   c. 8   7 = 15
   b. 8   2 = 6   d. 5   2 = 3

7. Describe how thinking skills such as "counting on," estimating the reasonableness of results, and doubles and related doubles can help children master basic fact memorization.

8. Read some microcomputer software catalogs (see Appendix C) and develop a list of programs that can help children master basic addition and subtraction facts.

References

Ashlock, R. B., Johnson, M. L., Wilson, J. W., & Jones, W. L. (1983). *Guiding each child's learning of mathematics.* Columbus, Ohio: Merrill.

Brown, J. C., & Coffman, L. D. (1914). *How to teach arithmetic.* Chicago: Row, Peterson.

Brownell, W., & Moser, H. E. (1949). Meaningful vs. mechanical learning: A study in grade III subtraction. *Duke University Research Studies in Education, 8.* Durham, N.C.: Duke University Press.

Folsom, M. (1975). Operations on whole numbers. In J. Payne (ed.), *Mathematics learning in early childhood* (pp. 161–190). Reston, Va.: NCTM.

Houlihan, D. M., & Ginsburg, H. P. (1981). The addition of first and second grade children. *Journal for Research in Mathematics Education, 12* (March), pp. 95–106.

Kennedy, L. M. (1984). *Guiding children's learning of mathematics.* Belmont, Calif.: Wadsworth.

Kramer, T., & Krug, D. A. (1973). A rationale and procedure for teaching addition. *Education and Training of the Mentally Retarded, 8,* pp. 139–145.

Rathmell, E. C. (1978). Using thinking strategies to teach the basic facts. In M. Suydam (ed.), *Developing computational skills* (pp. 13–38). Reston, Va.: NCTM.

Reys, B. (1985) Mental computation. *Arithmetic Teacher, 33,* pp. 43–46

Reys, R. (1985) Estimation. *Arithmetic Teacher, 33,* pp. 37–41.

Suydam, M. (1984a). Learning the basic facts. *Arithmetic Teacher, 32,* p. 15.

Suydam, M. (1984b). Manipulative materials. *Arithmetic Teacher, 33,* p. 27.

Suydam, M. N. (1985). Addition and subtraction: Processes and problems. *Arithmetic Teacher, 33,* p. 20.

Suydam, M. N., & Dessart, D. J. (1980). Skill learning. In R. Shumway (ed.), *Research in mathematics education* (pp. 207–243). Reston, Va.: NCTM.

CHAPTER 9

Addition and Subtraction Algorithms

Objectives

After reading this chapter you will be able to:

1. Analyze an addition and subtraction sequence to determine when to begin initial teaching of algorithms.

2. Demonstrate an algorithm for addition using concrete models.

3. Demonstrate the decomposition method of subtraction using concrete models.

4. Identify several materials for developing addition and subtraction algorithms.

5. Apply estimation strategies to computational applications of daily-life situations.

Introduction

This chapter extends the operations of addition and subtraction to include greater-valued numbers. Algorithms for addition and subtraction are modeled and sample sequences that display a hierarchy of examples are provided. The term *algorithm,* believed to be derived from the name of a ninth-century Persian mathematician, Al-Khowarizmi, is defined as a set of procedures for obtaining a result. An algorithm is used to answer an exercise such as 247.

$$\begin{array}{r} 247 \\ +356 \\ \hline \end{array}$$

As we extend the operations of addition and subtraction we need to approach examples from concrete and semiconcrete perspectives. Several methods including estimation skills are used to examine the examples presented here. Although addition and subtraction are inverse operations and thus related, we consider addition first and then look at extending subtraction. For many students, especially for some mainstreamed students, it is advisable to teach addition separate from and before subtraction. Of course, students need to understand both operations in order to deal with real-world problems effectively, but initially there is a need to develop and practice skills without overloading students' memories.

Developing Addition Algorithms

Extending addition beyond the basic facts requires a sequential approach. The following sequence for addition contains sample items that are hierarchical in nature. That is, elementary school students need to learn the early examples first before they can master the more involved exercises. Each example builds on the concepts and skills learned in previous ones. Note that nonregrouping examples such as 24 are considered to be easier for

$$\begin{array}{r} 24 \\ + 2 \\ \hline \end{array}$$

children than regrouping examples such as 35. Further, to make interpre-

$$\begin{array}{r} 35 \\ + 7 \\ \hline \end{array}$$

tation of the sequence samples easier, specific examples are given rather than general rules such as adding two 3-place numbers by regrouping from the tens to the ones place.

Sample Sequence for Addition

Non-Regrouping Examples

1. 50 (extension of the   2. 34   3. 123   4. 234
    +20 basic facts)   +3   + 5   +31

Regrouping Examples

1. 24	2. 35	3. 453	4. 563
+7	+16	+92	+182

5. 472	6. 896
+248	+758

The preceding sample sequence for addition is only one example of many that can be created. Most important is that the sequence be arranged to flow from easier examples to more involved ones. For example, a child would have to master item 1 in regrouping before being able to calculate item 6 in regrouping.

Developing Non-Regrouping Addition Examples

Assuming that students have mastered the basic addition facts and have an understanding of place value, the initial extension of the basic facts involves modeling exercises such as $30 + 40 = 70$. This equation can be modeled easily as indicated in the following diagram. We need to show 3 ten blocks and 4 ten blocks. Collecting these gives us 7 tens, or 70.

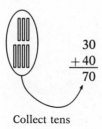

$$\begin{array}{r} 30 \\ +40 \\ \hline 70 \end{array}$$

Collect tens

Consider also the following procedure for modeling the exercise   234
with base-10 blocks.   +31

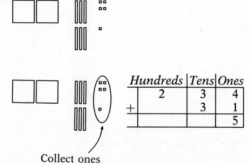

Hundreds	Tens	Ones
2	3	4
+	3	1
		5

Collect ones

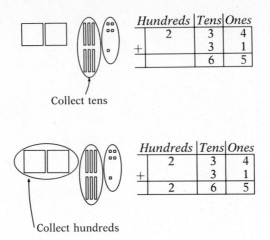

Collect tens

Hundreds	Tens	Ones
2	3	4
+	3	1
	6	5

Collect hundreds

Hundreds	Tens	Ones
2	3	4
+	3	1
2	6	5

In this example, note that the concrete manipulation of numbers is linked to the recording of the symbols. Eventually the concrete material will not be needed and the exercise will be solved in an abstract manner. Also, some elementary textbook series link the semiconcrete model (the diagram) with a verbal approach using the number words *hundreds, tens,* and *ones.* Thus, our design for the solution of 234 + 31 = ☐ reflects this approach.

When modeling addition of greater-valued numbers, a variety of materials need to be used. Number blocks are used in many teaching situations, and several popular elementary school textbooks use pictures of number blocks as illustrations of the semiconcrete level. Some mathematics educators favor the use of straws and rubber bands, with ten straws bundled to show 10, as a prominent place-value device. The abacus is sometimes used to model addition of greater-valued numbers as well. Graph paper displayed on the chalkboard can illustrate hundreds, tens, and ones when color-coded. In fact, Bley and Thornton (1982) have suggested that color is a good guideline for teaching learning disabled mathematics students. To model 25 + 23, a color-coded diagram might be developed as follows.

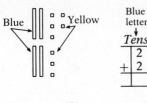

Tens	Ones
2	5
+ 2	3

Use graph paper with a blue ten piece. Yellow squares can be used for ones. Attach a piece of magnetic tape to the back of the models and place them on the chalkboard.

Tens	Ones
2	5
+ 2	3
	8

Collect ones and record.

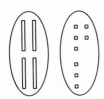

Tens	Ones
2	5
+ 2	3
4	8

Now collect tens and record.

In conclusion, concrete and semiconcrete models are needed for developing non-regrouping examples in addition. After experience at these levels, children need to practice solving addition of greater-valued numbers in an abstract manner (see Activities 9.1 and 9.2).

A note of caution is in order at this point. Note that children can work by starting from either the left or right side and still obtain a correct answer.

$$243$$
$$+121$$
$$364$$

starting point
from right side

$$243$$
$$+121$$
$$364$$

starting point
from left side

However, teachers should emphasize that working from the right side of the example to the left side is the correct movement. Although working from left to right does not affect the solution in non-regrouping examples, a left-to-right approach can yield much confusion when regrouping examples are considered (see Activity 9.3).

ACTIVITY 9.1 Find the Number Pattern

This activity integrates adding and subtracting greater-valued numbers with searching for patterns. It can be used as an enrichment activity.

Find the Pattern		
21	35	29
54	68	62
81	95	89
42	56	50
83	97	—
22	—	—

Create some number patterns similar to the one shown to the left for use with children who have mastered multidigit addition and subtraction.

ACTIVITY 9.2   Bottle Cap Math Practice

A useful device for helping children practice computational algorithms can be easily constructed.

Take a plastic half-gallon bottle and make a semicircular cut about 3 centimeters from the neck of the bottle (see the diagram to the left).

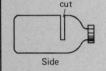

Take several 5″ × 8″ note cards and write addition and subtraction exercises in the way shown at the left.

Write the sum or difference at the bottom center section of the card. After you have inserted cards into the cut of the bottle only the exercise can be seen, as in our example of 25 + 8. The students must then solve the equation. They can check their results by unscrewing the bottle cap and looking into the bottle. The answer (33 in this case) will appear as shown to the left.

ACTIVITY 9.3   Teacher's Assessments

Teachers often need to make daily diagnostic assessments and corrections. Can you determine a child's procedure for these addition exercises?

$$
\begin{array}{cccc}
35 & 46 & 52 & 43 \\
+\ 8 & +\ 9 & +\ 8 & +\ 2 \\
\hline
33 & 45 & 50 & 45
\end{array}
$$

How would you correct this computational error? List some possibilities.

Developing Regrouping Addition Examples

Let us first consider regrouping in addition by way of a concrete, manipulative example. The procedures that follow are used to solve 24 + 7. Place-value pocket charts with tagboard pieces for tens and ones are the materials used. Two students are selected—one serves as a recorder while the other manipulates the concrete material. The remaining members of the class are asked to manipulate similar concrete materials at their desks.

Tens   Ones

Tens	Ones
2	4
+	7

Give the pieces to the child who will manipulate the tagboard; draw a chart with the heads "tens" and "ones" for the child who will record the actions.

Tens	Ones
2	4
+	7
	1

The first child collects ones and then trades 10 ones for 1 ten. The second child records the result.

Tens	Ones
2	4
+	7
3	1

As the first child collects the tens, the second child records the sum of 31.

Place-value knowledge becomes extremely important as addition of greater-valued numbers is developed. In our example, the first child needs to recognize that 11 ones can be regrouped as 1 ten and 1 one. A brief review of place value may help you to organize the development of a lesson on regrouping in addition (see Chapter 4). Further, your lessons should include many examples of how addition is applied to the child's own experience. Situations such as the following are most valuable: "Bonnie delivered 24 newspapers. She then delivered seven more papers. How many papers did Bonnie deliver?"

Let us consider another concrete model, this one involving 243 + 89. Here is a possible situation.

Hundreds	Tens	Ones
2	4	3
+	8	9

Mary sold $243 worth of tickets for the afternoon play and $89 worth of tickets for the evening performance. How many dollars did Mary earn for the school?

Hundreds	Tens	Ones
2	4	3
+	8	9
		2

Collect ones.

Regroup 12 ones as 1 ten, 2 ones.

Hundreds	Tens	Ones
2	4	3
+	8	9
	3	2

Collect tens. Thirteen tens may be regrouped for 1 hundred, 3 tens.

Hundreds	Tens	Ones
2	4	3
+	8	9
3	3	2

Collect hundreds. You have 3 hundreds. The completed exercise indicates a sum of 332.

After students observe the teacher presenting examples, they need to actively manipulate concrete materials at their desks to consolidate their learning of addition. This is the most important part of the instructional process for greater-valued addition examples. After many experiences manipulating concrete materials and interpreting semiconcrete models, many children are ready for a transition to the abstract stage. Following are some helpful practice activities for transition to the abstract stage. (See also Activities 9.4, 9.5, 9.6, and 9.7.)

$$
\begin{array}{r}
24 \\
+7 \\
\hline
11 \\
20 \\
\hline
31
\end{array}
\qquad
\begin{array}{r}
186 \\
+\ 98 \\
\hline
14 \\
170 \\
100 \\
\hline
284
\end{array}
$$

Partial sums eliminate the need to remember a regrouped value. However, a meaningful approach for this method requires that children recognize that $24 = 20 + 4$.

================ *MATH HISTORY 9.2* ================

The word *one* is derived from the Latin *unus* (meaning "one"), which is found in *uniform* (meaning "one form, alike") and many other words beginning with *uni-*, as in *unicorn*, *unit, unique*, and *universe*.

The word *two* is derived from the Latin *duo* (meaning "two"), which is found in *duet* (music for two) and many other words beginning with *du-*, as in *duplex, dual*, and *duplicate*.

Lined paper can be helpful in the transition to the algorithm stage, especially for children who make place-value errors. For example, if a child solves $35 + 8$ as shown to the left, lined paper can be used to show how the hundreds, tens, and ones correctly line up. This technique can help bridge the gaps between concrete experience, textbook diagrams (semiconcrete), and the abstract level.

$$
\begin{array}{r}
35 \\
+\ 8 \\
\hline
313
\end{array}
$$

Tens	Ones
3	5
+	8
4	3

The child is required to write only one numeral in a place-value position.

ACTIVITY 9.4   Teacher–Child Interaction

This activity is designed to help you role-play a teaching interaction.

Imagine that you are asked to teach a child how to concretely model $235 + 81 = \square$. Draw diagrams to simulate base-10 blocks and list the key questions of your procedure.

ACTIVITY 9.5   Search for Palindromes

Studying palindromes is a useful enrichment activity and also serves as a unique form of computational practice.

A *palindrome* is a number that reads the same forward and backward, such as 141 and 252. The number 89 is not a palindrome. To find a palindrome, do the following:

1. Start with an arbitrary number: 75
2. Reverse the digits: 57
3. Add: 132
4. Reverse the digits: 231
5. Add: 363 (A palindrome!)
6. Repeat steps 1–5 as many times as necessary to obtain a palindrome.
7. Find all the palindromes from 1 through 100.

ACTIVITY 9.6   Identify Patterns in the Calendar

This calendar activity can help motivate practice of two-digit addition.

Take a calendar and mark off a square as shown in the diagram below. What happens when you add numbers along the diagonal? Mark off some other squares and see if you obtain the same pattern. Can you find any other patterns in the calendar?

March

					1	2
3	4	5	6	7	8	9
10	11	12	13	14	15	16
17	18	19	20	21	22	23
24	25	26	27	28	29	30
31						

ACTIVITY 9.7   Greater Sum Game

Like Activity 9.6, this activity promotes meaningful practice of two-digit addition.

Ask children to write each of the numbers below on a separate card.

85	96	43	16	32	96	43	76
42	31	92	19	46	81	53	81
51	78	81	81	75	32	61	42

Shuffle the cards and place them face down. A child draws two cards and adds the numbers. Then, the next child draws two cards and adds, and so on. The child with the greater sum gets a point. Play continues until four points have been scored.

Estimation Strategies for Addition

$$\begin{array}{r} 38 \\ + \ 7 \\ \hline 315 \end{array}$$

As children experience a variety of methods for addition of greater-valued numbers, estimation activities need to be included. Sometimes students will produce absurd answers to a rather easy exercise, such as the one shown at the left.

In Chapter 8, the need for children to use thinking strategies when studying basic addition facts is demonstrated. A strategy such as counting on from 38 would at least indicate to a child a "ballpark" estimate of the expected answer. Children need to develop number sense, a flexibility of approach, in order to avoid the errors that occur as a result of rote, mechanical procedures.

Research has indicated that replacing computational drill with instruction in estimation does not have an adverse effect on computation skills (Schoen et al., 1981). Consider also that we rarely need paper and pencil for computational work when shopping. Although we may, at times, use hand calculators, we more often estimate prices when shopping. For example, suppose you want to purchase only one item priced at 2/$1.99. Rather than dividing $1.99 in half, you are more likely to estimate the inclusive price at $2 to arrive at your calculation of $1 for one item.

According to Suydam (1984), good estimators have the following characteristics:

1. Good recall of the basic facts

2. Ability to change data to a mentally manageable form

3. Tolerance for error

4. Ability to adjust an initial estimate

5. Ability to translate a problem to a more mentally manageable form

In our example, a more mentally manageable form for the data is to treat $1.99 as if it were $2 because it is much easier to work with an even, whole number. Persons who feel that they must always be exact have a diminished level of tolerance for error. Good estimators first seek to get close to the answer; later they use a hand calculator or microcomputer for a more exact answer. (See Activity 9.8.)

ACTIVITY 9.8 Compensation Strategies

Here are some mental arithmetic exercises that utilize a compensation strategy.

To add 83 + 39, think of 83 + 40 = 123; then subtract 1, yielding 122.

Mathematically, here is what is being done:

$$83 + (40 - 1) = (83 + 40) - 1 = 123 - 1 = 122.$$

In effect, one number is rounded so that it is a multiple of 10. The addition is then compensated by adding or subtracting the difference between the rounded value and the original number.

Try these:

1. 45 + 29 = ___

2. 93 + 39 = ___

3. 35 + 62 = ___

4. 98 + 53 = ___

R. E. Reys (1985) has provided many good examples of estimation activities that illustrate some of the characteristics of good estimators. Suppose our job is to estimate the total of this list of bills:

$84.91
35.18
42.16
53.85
+98.99

Reys suggests using *front loading* (i.e., 84 + 35 + 42 + 53 + 99 = about 310) and then *adjusting* (the cents are about $3). Our estimate of the total is $313. The same set of bills could be estimated using a rounding strategy, as shown here:

$84.91 ⟶ about $85 ⎫
   35.18 ⟶ about   35 ⎬ over $100 ⟶ adjust to $110
   42.16 ⟶ about   42 ⎫
   53.85 ⟶ about   54 ⎬ about $100
+98.99 ⟶ about   99 ⟶ about $100

Our estimate of the total is $310.*

Since many routine computations have been taken over by computers and calculators, children and adults need to have good estimation skills to cope with the contemporary marketplace. For example, suppose you want to purchase a new automobile with a sticker price of $9,000. The salesperson uses a calculator to add the amounts for sales tax and options and arrives at a total price of $13,532. As a consumer you need to be able to judge the reasonableness of this result by estimating the sales tax and the cost of the options, even if it is not the exact amount. Therefore, your ability to judge the reasonableness of a result is quality of estimation ability.

Developing Subtraction Algorithms

Extending subtraction beyond the basic facts requires a sequential approach. A hierarchy of examples, each example building on the concepts and skills of the previous ones, can be developed. To that end, a sample sequence is given here.

Sample Sequence for Subtraction

Non-Regrouping Examples

1. 60 (extension of the   2. 35   3. 148   4. 256
   −20 basic facts)   − 2   − 3   −21

5. 847
   −532

*Adapted from Reys, R. (1985). Estimation. *Arithmetic Teacher*, *33*, pp. 37–41. Used with permission of the National Council of Teachers of Mathematics.

Regrouping Examples

1. 24   2.   84   3. 146   4. 239
    −7   − 38   −39   −48

5. 352   6. 1001
    −85   − 98

As in the addition sequence, the flow of items is from least difficult to more difficult. That is, non-regrouping examples are generally developed prior to regrouping examples in elementary school mathematics programs. Likewise, mastery of an item such as 146 − 39, involving one regrouping, is necessary before children can learn how to calculate an item with two regroupings such as 352 − 85. Again, several sample items are selected and concrete models are used to illustrate how to teach them.

=========== *MATH HISTORY 9.3* ===========

The word *subtraction* comes from the Latin words *sub* (meaning "below") and *trahere* or *tract* (meaning "to draw from"). Thus, drawing one number down from another is the literal translation of the Latin derivatives.

The Methods of Decomposition and Equal Addition

Before examining the concrete models, some comment about the methods used for subtraction with regrouping is needed. Essentially, there are two popular ways in which subtraction with regrouping is taught—the methods of decomposition and equal addition. The more popular approach is the *decomposition method,* which looks like this:

$$
\begin{array}{c c c c}
\begin{array}{r}35\\-7\\\hline\end{array} &
\begin{array}{r}^{2}\cancel{3}\,^{1}5\\-\ 7\\\hline\end{array} &
\begin{array}{r}^{2}\cancel{3}\,^{1}5\\-\ 7\\\hline 8\end{array} &
\begin{array}{r}^{2}\cancel{3}\,^{1}5\\-\ 7\\\hline 2\ 8\end{array}
\end{array}
$$

According to Sherrill (1979) and Suydam and Dessart (1980), the decomposition method, when taught in a meaningful way, yields higher achievement than the equal-addition method. The *equal-addition method* for subtraction of greater-valued numbers is less frequently used. This technique, which emphasizes speed, is performed in the following manner:

$$
\begin{array}{c c c}
\begin{array}{r}35\\-7\\\hline\end{array} &
\begin{array}{r}3\,^{1}5\\-1\ 7\\\hline\end{array} &
\begin{array}{r}3\,^{1}5\\-1\ 7\\\hline 2\ 8\end{array}
\end{array}
$$

A compensation feature is applied here. In effect, a 10 is added to the ones place of the top number, the minuend, yielding 15. To compensate for this, a 10 is added to the bottom number, the subtrahend, changing 7 to 17.

Although these subtraction procedures are the most popular, interested readers may want to consider learning more about Barton Hutchings's low-stress algorithms (1976). These algorithms may be helpful with children who have had difficulty learning operations taught in a contemporary manner.

Developing Non-Regrouping Subtraction Examples

The decomposition method is used for the subtraction examples in this book. Suppose that we want to concretely model $60 - 20 = \square$. A child can be chosen as the recorder while you demonstrate the concrete model on the overhead projector.

> Develop a situation such as, "Sixty dollars was made from the class auction. Twenty dollars was spent on refreshments. How much money is left?"

> Show 6 tens, or 60, then remove 2 tens or 20, to show the money that was spent. Ask students how much money remains. Then have the recorder record the 4 tens, or 40.

Notice that in modeling a subtraction example with the decomposition method the bottom number, the subtrahend, is *not* concretely modeled. An oral description is provided instead because a concrete model causes confusion. For example, if we were to show the concrete model, which includes the subtrahend, the following difficulties would occur.

If we remove 2 tens, then we have shown that $60 - 20 = 60$!

$$\begin{array}{r} 60 \\ -20 \\ \hline 60 \end{array}$$

Suppose we remove 2 tens from both the top and bottom models. Here we have obtained 40 but we have removed 40 rather than 20. Remember the exercise is $60 - 20 = \square$!

$$\begin{array}{r} 60 \\ -40 \\ \hline 40 \end{array}$$

Therefore, when using decomposition as a subtraction method, the bottom number (the subtrahend) should not be shown concretely.

Another non-regrouping example can now be considered. Although base-10 blocks, straws and rubber bands, and graph paper—all proportional models—are generally preferred, the abacus is sometimes used for modeling addition and subtraction. In the interest of portraying a variety of materials, we will use the abacus for modeling $245 - 31 = \square$.

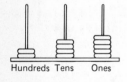

Hundreds Tens Ones

Show 245 on the abacus. Remove one bead from the ones place, then three beads from the tens place.

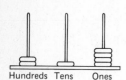

Hundreds Tens Ones

Ask a child to record the results of each step, concluding with the difference of 214.

Developing Regrouping Subtraction Examples

Regrouping in subtraction builds on place-value concepts. For example, when solving $24 - 7 = \square$, a child needs to know that 24 can be shown as 2 tens, 4 ones, or as 1 ten, 14 ones. Let us develop a model for $24 - 7 = \square$. This time we will use an alternative material, beansticks, which are made from tongue depressors or popsicle sticks on which beans are glued.

$\begin{array}{r} 24 \\ -7 \\ \hline \end{array}$ We show 24 as 2 beansticks, each having 10 beans, and 4 individual beans. A key question is, "Can we take seven beans away from this model?" The answer from the class is that we cannot do so.

$\begin{array}{r} 24 \\ -7 \\ \hline \end{array}$ We now ask, "What can we do? Can we exchange one of our beansticks for ten beans?" Let us do that.

$\begin{array}{r} 24 \\ -7 \\ \hline 7 \end{array}$ Have a child remove 7 beans. How many beans are left? A child can record a 7 as a representation of the remaining 7 beans.

24　　How many tens are left? Record the one remaining 10.
−7
___
17

In our example it is important to point out clearly that a regrouping must take place. Sometimes after studying regrouping in subtraction students assume that *all* subtraction exercises are to be regrouped. Then, solutions such as the one below are diagnosed by observant teachers.

$$24 \longrightarrow \overset{1\,1}{2}4 \longrightarrow \overset{1\,1}{2}4$$
$$\underline{-2} \qquad \underline{-2} \qquad \underline{-2}$$
$$ 112$$

Indicate to children that a regrouping takes place only when it is impossible to remove the desired amount from the top number or minuend. A regrouping then allows us to make the appropriate removal of material. Once again, it is important that children perform actions on concrete material so they can thoroughly understand the concept (see Activity 9.9). Be sure to allow children to use blocks, straws and rubber bands, and other concrete material at their desks for modeling subtraction examples.

Consider yet another example, this time using the more conventional base-10 blocks. The example to be solved is $146 - 39 = \square$.

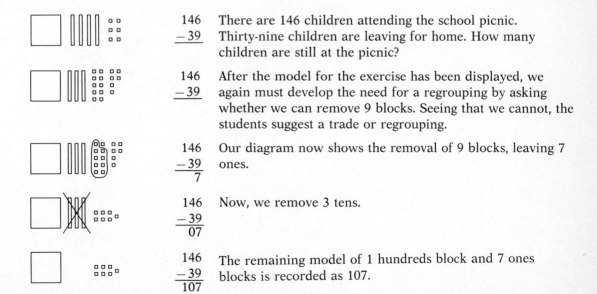

146　　There are 146 children attending the school picnic.
−39　　Thirty-nine children are leaving for home. How many
　　　　children are still at the picnic?

146　　After the model for the exercise has been displayed, we
−39　　again must develop the need for a regrouping by asking
　　　　whether we can remove 9 blocks. Seeing that we cannot, the
　　　　students suggest a trade or regrouping.

146　　Our diagram now shows the removal of 9 blocks, leaving 7
−39　　ones.
___
　7

146　　Now, we remove 3 tens.
−39
___
　07

146　　The remaining model of 1 hundreds block and 7 ones
−39　　blocks is recorded as 107.
___
107

ACTIVITY 9.9   Diffy Board*

A unique form of practicing subtraction exercises and integrating strategic decision making is the following.

Write any four numbers in the four circles at the corners of the largest square (see the diagram below). Find differences for any two adjacent corners. Continue from outer to inner squares. The object is to choose the original four numbers so as to reach the innermost square before all four differences on any square become zero. Try this several times and see if you can discover any patterns.

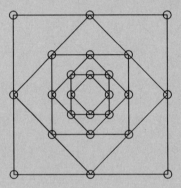

*Adapted from Wills, H. (1971). Diffy. *Arithmetic Teacher*, *18*, p. 65. Used with permission of the National Council of Teachers of Mathematics.

A final point needs to be made about certain examples that are often troublesome to students in the middle grades, such as $1001 - 99 = \square$. Often three regroupings are developed with a process that looks like this:

$$\overset{0\ \ \overset{9}{1}\overset{9}{0}\overset{9}{0}1}{\cancel{1001}}$$
$$-\ \ \ 99$$
$$\overline{\ \ 902}$$

Children are instructed to do the following:

Since 9 cannot be subtracted from 1, go to the next place, the tens, to make a regrouping. Since there are no tens, go to hundreds. Since there are no hundreds, go to thousands. Regroup one of the thousands as 10 hundreds. Then regroup one of the hundreds as 10 tens. Finally, regroup one of the tens as 10 ones. Now you can begin to subtract.

The preceding instructions are quite confusing! However, if students have a good understanding of place value, the exercise can be solved easily. We will concretely develop this approach.

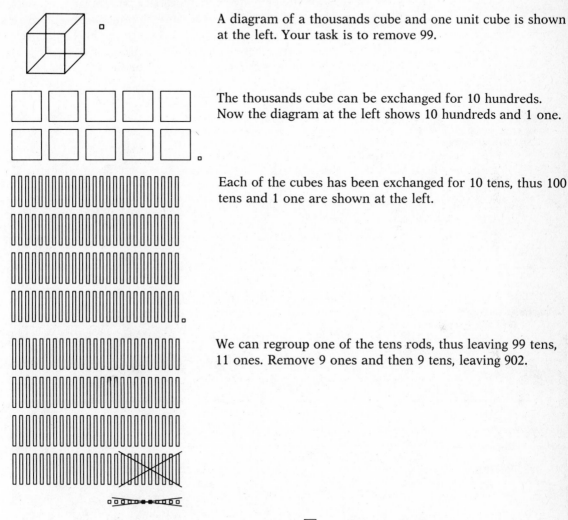

A diagram of a thousands cube and one unit cube is shown at the left. Your task is to remove 99.

The thousands cube can be exchanged for 10 hundreds. Now the diagram at the left shows 10 hundreds and 1 one.

Each of the cubes has been exchanged for 10 tens, thus 100 tens and 1 one are shown at the left.

We can regroup one of the tens rods, thus leaving 99 tens, 11 ones. Remove 9 ones and then 9 tens, leaving 902.

Symbolically, $1001 - 99 = \square$ is solved in this fashion:

$$
\begin{array}{r}
1001 \\
-\ 99 \\
\hline
902
\end{array}
$$

The underlined value represents the thinking of 100 as 100 tens. Thus, if children have experience with many ways of grouping numbers, an example that once had been difficult may now be solved in a less cumbersome manner. Admittedly, this approach requires a good understanding of place value. Even so, a goal of place-value knowledge is, indeed, a major goal of the school curriculum.

To refine the development of subtraction, practice with the algorithm is needed. However, sometimes some intermediate techniques are used before children practice an algorithm at the abstract level. After a thorough development of concrete and semiconcrete models, these procedures can be employed to help solidify the abstract stage of the algorithm. (See Activities 9.10, 9.11, and 9.12.)

ACTIVITY 9.10   Diagnosing Subtraction Errors

Teachers often make diagnostic decisions when evaluating children's mathematical work. Can you determine a child's procedure for these subtraction exercises?

$$\begin{array}{r} {}^{2\,1\,1}\!\!\not{3}32 \\ -\ 16 \\ \hline 2126 \end{array} \qquad \begin{array}{r} {}^{4\,1\,1}\!\!\not{5}41 \\ -\ 27 \\ \hline 4124 \end{array} \qquad \begin{array}{r} {}^{5\,1\,1}\!\!\not{6}83 \\ -\ 54 \\ \hline 5139 \end{array}$$

ACTIVITY 9.11   Concrete Modeling of Subtraction

Imagine that you are to develop a meaningful procedure for using concrete material to teach a multidigit subtraction example with regrouping. Draw diagrams illustrating how base-10 blocks can be used to solve $243 - 85 = \square$.

ACTIVITY 9.12   Hangman

This activity reinforces systematic guessing, a useful problem-solving strategy.

Make up an equation such as $27 - 18 = 9$. Put this on the chalkboard or overhead: __ __ __ __ __ = __. Children are to guess the operation and the equation. For each incorrect answer, a body part is drawn. The object is to guess the equation before the body is completed.

$$\begin{array}{r} 35 \\ -\ 2 \\ \hline 213 \end{array}$$

Lined Paper.   The use of lined paper, or graph paper, helps to preserve place-value relationships. For example, some children will solve an example like $35 - 2 = \square$ in the way shown at the left.

Tens	Ones
3	5
−	2
3	3

Lined paper helps to focus on the relationship of tens and ones. Children can only record *one* numeral in the appropriate place, as shown at the left.

Verbal or Number Word Approach.   To solve $54 - 9 = \Box$, a textbook might utilize a verbal or number word approach. In this approach, spaces are left blank so that students can regroup a set of tens as a set of ones, as shown below. Also, seeing the word *tens* is thought to be a reinforcement of necessary place-value knowledge.

	5 tens	4 ones			4 tens	__ ones
−		9 ones		− __ tens		9 ones
					4 tens	__ ones

Estimation Strategies for Subtraction

Concurrent with the development of subtraction algorithms is the need to estimate differences. For example, the mathematics results of the Third National Assessment of Educational Progress (Lindquist et al., 1983) revealed that only about 20 percent of the 9-year-olds tested could figure $58 - 9 = 49$ mentally, whereas 70 percent could subtract a similar example using pencil and paper (the results of the remaining 10 percent were not given in the report). Several general strategies for estimation are developed in the addition section earlier in the chapter. Some of these are appropriate for estimation of subtraction results. In particular, the strategies of *compensating, rounding,* and *judging the reasonableness* of *results* can be used for subtraction.

Suppose, for example, that you enter a store with $20 and want to purchase some record albums. Would you be able to buy three albums? Obviously, you need to find out how much each one costs. Suppose that each record album costs $8.99. Using the *rounding strategy,* you would estimate each record album at $9 and three at $27. Therefore, you would conclude that it is not possible, or unreasonable, for you to purchase three record albums with your $20.

To teach students how to *judge the reasonableness of differences,* a listing of a series of statements such as the following is helpful. Students are asked to respond to each item by marking "true" or "false." Afterward, a class discussion is undertaken to examine the reasoning behind the students' choices.

1. Texas has a greater population than New York.

2. A million seconds is greater than a week.

3. Most 11-year-olds watch television 8 hours a day.

4. The average fifth grader eats 329 hamburgers a year.

5. College professors make more money than professional baseball players.

Rounding is an important strategy for estimating subtraction results, particularly with checking accounts. For example, if the checkbook reads $865.29 and a check for $79.67 is written, the estimate could be done by treating the checkbook amount as about $880 and the check as $80. Thus, there is about $800 in the account.

Compensation is a helpful strategy when estimating subtraction. For example, $22 - 8 = \square$ could be solved in the following way:

$$
\begin{array}{llll}
22 & \text{add 2} \longrightarrow \text{yields 24} \longrightarrow & 24 \\
\underline{-8} & \text{add 2} \longrightarrow \text{yields 10} \longrightarrow & \underline{-10} \\
& & & 14
\end{array}
$$

In summary, estimation activities need to be developed throughout the mathematics curriculum. They are helpful in developing real-world applications, and the development of number sense and flexibility helps to teach appropriate computational skills. (For more information on estimation activities, interested readers should consult Seymour, 1981. See also Activities 9.13, 9.14, 9.15, and 9.16.)

ACTIVITY 9.13   Equation Loop

This activity creatively practices recognition of addition and subtraction number sentences. The teacher can place numerals on tagboard and laminate the board. Children can use grease pencils as they draw loops around equations.

Equation Loop

24 = 18	82	45	37	53
0	+ 6	37	19	27	26
6	43	14	13	26	39
18	9	27	8	18	14
12	6	7	21	19	25
18	14	16	30	37	3

Using the operations of addition or subtraction, students should loop as many equations as they can. They may move horizontally, vertically, or diagonally, and in an "L" shape, as shown in the table.

ACTIVITY 9.14   How Much Is the Check?

This activity promotes the skill of estimating a restaurant check.

Menu

1. Two eggs, any style.
   Bacon or sausage.
   Toast and jelly.
   $2.10

2. Buttermilk
   pancakes with
   butter and syrup.
   $1.40

3. French toast with
   butter and syrup.
   $1.75

4. Fluffy omelettes
   served with toast
   and jelly.

Cheese	$ 2.55
Ham & cheese	$ 2.99
Western	$ 2.85
Fresh mushroom	$ 2.75

Side Orders

Hot or cold cereal	$ .55
Hash browns	$ .65
One egg	$ .55
Two eggs	$ .95
Toast and jelly	$ .45
Bacon	$ 1.30
Sausage	$ 1.30
Ham	$ 1.30

Beverages

Coffee	$ .40
Sanka	$ .40
Hot tea	$ .40
Hot chocolate	$ .50
Cold milk	$ .45

Juices

Orange juice	$ .50
Tomato juice	$ .50
Grapefruit juice	$ .50

Answer the following question by estimating.

Suppose you are having breakfast at a restaurant with three friends. They ordered combinations 1, 2, and 3. You ordered a cheese omelette. Each of you had a cup of coffee and one person had a glass of orange juice. What is the total bill?

Make up an estimation question from this data. Use it with an elementary school student.

ACTIVITY 9.15   Calculator Estimation

This activity practices estimation skills in conjunction with a hand calculator.

Estimate the following addition and subtraction exercises. Then use a hand calculator to check your results. How good an estimator are you?

	Estimate	*Hand Calculator Result*
1.	2496 + 3858	
2.	8951 − 2899	
3.	85698 + 99999	
4.	56831 − 42519	

Discuss your strategies with other members of your class.

ACTIVITY 9.16 Find More Patterns

This activity is designed for enrichment. Using addition or subtraction, you need to find a pattern for each row of numbers in the table below.

Find the Pattern

43	21	64
57	35	92
62	40	102
81	59	140
51	22	___

Summary

This chapter describes the methods and materials used for developing algorithms of addition and subtraction. Emphasis is placed on concrete and semiconcrete models to develop understanding of the steps involved. Situations drawn from daily life that illustrate addition and subtraction are presented. Finally, specific estimation strategies provide a setting for applications and are helpful in insuring computation mastery. Practice of algorithms at the abstract level is recommended but, whenever possible, applications are needed so that practice does not degenerate into a 50-item form of meaningless drill.

Discussion Questions

1. Draw base-10 blocks to illustrate a concrete approach to 125 + 37 = ☐.

2. Draw base-10 blocks to illustrate a concrete approach to 235 − 48 = ☐.

3. What prerequisite skills are necessary for effective mastery of an addition exercise such as 298 + 57 = ☐.

4. Make up a lesson plan for teaching the addition of a two-place number with a one-place number involving regrouping from the ones to the tens place.

5. Research the literature to find alternative algorithms for addition and subtraction. Specifically, read Barton Hutchings's nonthematic essay on low-stress algorithms in the *1976 Annual Yearbook of the National Council of Teachers of Mathematics.* For a free publication list you can write to NCTM, 1906 Association Drive, Reston, VA 22091.

6. Develop a list of problems that require estimation procedures for their solutions. Consult recent articles in the *Arithmetic Teacher* to help you compile your list.

7. Write a word problem involving addition of whole numbers and another involving subtraction of whole numbers.

8. What special, unique strategies would you use for teaching addition and subtraction to exceptional children who have been mainstreamed into the regular classroom?

References

Ashlock, R. (1986). *Error patterns in computation.* Columbus, Ohio: Merrill.

Bley, N., & Thornton, C. A. (1982). Help for learning disabled students in the mainstream. In L. Silver (ed.), *Mathematics for the middle grades* (pp. 20–34). Reston, Va.: NCTM.

Hutchings, B. (1976). Low-stress algorithms. In D. Nelson (ed.), *Measurement in school mathematics* (pp. 218–239). Reston, Va.: NCTM.

Lindquist, M. M., Carpenter, T. P., Silver, E. A., & Matthews, W. (1983). The third national mathematics assessment: Results and implications for elementary and middle schools. *Arithmetic Teacher, 31,* pp. 14–19.

Reys, B. (1985). Mental computation. *Arithmetic Teacher, 33,* pp. 43–46.

Reys, R. E. (1985). Estimation. *Arithmetic Teacher, 33,* pp. 37–41.

Schoen, H. L., Friesen, C. D., Jarret, J., & Urbatsch, T. D. (1981). Instruction in estimating solutions of whole number computations. *Journal for Research in Mathematics Education, 12,* pp. 165–178.

Seymour, D. (1981). *Developing skills in estimation—Books A & B.* Palo Alto, Calif.: Dale Seymour Publications. (Available from Dale Seymour Publications, P.O. Box 10888, Palo Alto, CA 94303.)

Sherrill, J. M. (1979). Subtraction: Decomposition vs. equal addends. *Arithmetic Teacher, 27,* pp. 16–17.

Smith, D. E., & Ginsburg, J. (1972). *Numbers and numerals: A story book for young and old.* Reston, Va.: NCTM.

Suydam, M. (1984). Research reports: Estimation and computation. *Arithmetic Teacher, 32,* p. 35.

Suydam, M., & Dessart, D. (1980). Skill learning. In R. Shumway (ed.), *Research in mathematics education* (pp. 207–243). Reston, Va.: NCTM.

Wills, H. (1971). Diffy. *Arithmetic Teacher, 18,* p. 65.

CHAPTER 10

Teaching Problem-Solving Strategies

Objectives

After reading this chapter you will be able to:

1. Recognize the difference between teaching problem solving and teaching computational exercises.

2. Identify characteristics of good problem solvers.

3. Apply a broad range of problem-solving strategies to solve a variety of problems.

4. Develop teaching strategies designed to help children solve word problems.

5. Create a classroom environment that encourages children to effectively solve problems.

6. Create problems to supplement elementary school textbook problem-solving experiences.

Introduction

Problem solving is the most important element in the elementary school mathematics curriculum. The National Council of Teachers of Mathematics (NCTM), in its *Agenda for Action* (1980), recommends that problem solving serve as the focus of school mathematics. The NCTM also suggests that performance in problem solving yields a higher level of individual and national mathematical competence.

Although concern with mathematical problem-solving ability has been raised throughout the twentieth century, the unique societal and industrial changes of our time demand an even greater emphasis on an enlarged viewpoint of problem-solving skills and applications. Naisbitt (1982) pointed out that the fastest growing area for employment is computer science. It is predicted that by 1995, a division c   r will occur between what experts call jobs for "thinkers" and those considered low-level service occupations. Jobs in law, accounting, and computer science, among others, will be highly paid, whereas jobs in traditional industries such as steel, rubber, and automobiles will decline. In fact, between 1980 and 1985, according to a newspaper account (Jacobson, 1985), 1.5 million manufacturing jobs were lost. The same report predicted that since rapid change will occur, workers will need to be retrained every 5 to 10 years. Thus, the labor market will increasingly require workers who can think critically and learn and apply new information. Schools must share this responsibility by providing students with the ability to solve problems. To that end, elementary school mathematics offers a rich opportunity for the development of problem-solving experiences.

The term *problem solving* is an all-encompassing term that needs clarification. Activities such as solving word or nonroutine problems or puzzles, applying mathematics to problems of the "real world," and creating and testing mathematical conjectures can all be considered problem-solving activities (Branca, 1980). However, solving a number sentence such as $25 + 8 = \square$ is better described as an *exercise,* not a problem. Problem solving, sometimes meaning different things to different people, is an activity that attempts to resolve a situation in which an answer is not immediately apparent. Computational exercises usually do not require more than the recall of a memorized result or set of procedures and thus are not examples of problem-solving activities. The National Council of Supervisors of Mathematics has described problem solving as "a process of applying previously acquired knowledge to new and unfamiliar situations" (NCSM, 1977, p. 20).

=== *MATH HISTORY 10.1* ===

Over 2200 years ago, the brilliant Greek scholar Eratosthenes devised a way of estimating the circumference of the earth.

Developing a Classroom Environment for Problem Solving

Teaching children problem-solving strategies begins when the elementary teacher models an inquisitive, questioning, and supportive manner. The 1983 and 1988 results of the National Assessment of Educational Progress point out that elementary school children seem to perform well with routine computation and single-step story problems (Lindquist et al., 1983; Kouba et al., 1983). On the other hand, the results of the third and fourth National Assessment seem to indicate a need to increase the curricular attention of nonroutine problem solving and higher-order mathematical thinking skills. Children need to develop strategic ways of thinking about problems rather than passively memorizing and repeating the teacher's procedures.

Elementary school teachers need to allocate time so that students have ample opportunities to solve puzzles and nonroutine problems. Children need to raise questions, gather data, and develop a broad repertoire of problem-solving strategies. Although the story problems found in most elementary textbooks are a useful means of applying mathematics concepts and skills, they should not constitute students' only problem-solving experiences. William Brownell, writing in 1942, claimed that some elementary school textbook problems are a "disguised drill." For example, after a chapter on multiplication has been completed, often all the story problems are applications of multiplication. Thus, children apply computational skills in a narrow sense. Students need to have experience solving a variety of problems, using a variety of methods. Several sample problems and strategies are described in this chapter.

Further, teaching problem solving requires teachers to reconsider their methods of questioning. In particular, Rowe (1978) has gathered research data that indicates the average time between a teacher's question and a student's response is about 1 second. On the average, 10 or 12 questions were raised in 1 minute. Clearly, teaching problem solving requires a slower pace. Children need to understand a problem and to formulate a method of solution without being burdened by time pressure. Actually, good problem solvers tend to be less impulsive. They suspend judgment and do not rush their work. Very few of life's major problems are solved in 6 seconds or less. All one has to do is look at the evening news and see a discussion of the country's economic trends to see that a clear-cut, easy, and quick solution usually is not rendered within 6 seconds! Therefore, a patient and open approach is needed for teaching problem solving.

In summary, in order to develop a problem-solving environment in an elementary school classroom, a teacher needs to help children raise questions, develop strategies for solving problems, and most significant, allocate time for solving a wide variety of problems. Students can learn to solve problems only if they are confronted with problems to solve. Children, even at the primary level, must experience the process and solve many problems.

Helpful ways to encourage and stimulate problem-solving interest include, among others, creating a problem of the day from newspaper topics or by involving students in a problem-solving newsletter.

================= *MATH HISTORY 10.2* =================

Elbert Francis Cox (1896–1969) was the first black American to obtain a Ph.D. in mathematics. He obtained his Ph.D. from Cornell University and was head of the mathematics department at Howard University for 32 years.

Characteristics of Good Problem Solvers

Research has shown that good problem solvers share some common traits (Suydam, 1980). By determining the traits that good problem solvers possess, we can help students maximize their problem-solving potential by constructing learning experiences that teach these abilities. Some of the most common characteristics of good problem solvers include the following:

1. Ability to understand mathematical concepts and terms.
2. Ability to note likenesses, differences, and analogies.
3. Ability to identify critical elements and to select correct procedures and data.
4. Ability to note irrelevant detail.
5. Ability to visualize and interpret quantitative or spatial facts and relationships.
6. Ability to estimate and analyze.
7. Ability to generalize on the basis of a few examples.
8. Ability to switch methods readily.
9. Higher scores for self-esteem and confidence.
10. Lower scores for test anxiety and less impulsive.

As we work through the problems in this chapter and develop strategies for solving them, several of these traits are illustrated.

A Model for Solving Problems

A model for solving problems can be developed by considering the work of mathematician George Polya (1945), who has developed strategies that are extremely useful when solving problems. Routine problems such as those found in elementary mathematics textbooks as well as nonroutine, or process, problems can be solved by considering Polya's four-stage method:

George Polya's 4 Stage method for solving problems

I. Understand the problem

    A. What is given?
    B. What is wanted?
    C. Can you draw a diagram?
    D. Can you select appropriate notation?

II. Devise a plan

    A. Do you know of a similar problem?
    B. Can you restate the problem in your own words?
    C. Can you make a table?
    D. Can you make a simpler problem?
    E. Can you write a number sentence?
    F. Can you work backward?
    G. Can you make a model?

III. Carry out the plan

    A. Can you guess and check?
    B. Do you see a pattern?
    C. Can you use any of the other strategies from part II?

IV. Look back

    A. Can you generalize?
    B. Can you check the solution?
    C. Can you find another solution?
    D. Can you find another way to solve it?

To illustrate this procedure, we can look at a simulated classroom situation that applies Polya's method of problem solving to the solution of a problem typically found in many elementary school textbooks. Consider the following problem and teacher-student interaction.

There are 26 rows in the Palace Theater. Each row has 58 seats. How many seats are there in all?

I. Understanding the problem

The teacher's role is very important at this stage. Some of the questions that can be asked are these:

a. How many seats are there in each row of the theater?

b. How many rows are there?

c. What is the given information?

d. What do we want to find?

e. Can anyone restate the problem in their own words?

II. Devising a plan

The teacher, along with the children, might come up with these plans:

a. Make up a simpler problem. Try a problem which has eight seats in each row and six rows. How many seats are there in the theater?

b. Can you add 58 + 58 + 58 . . . until you have added 58 a total of 26 times?

c. Can you make a table to help you find the answer?

Rows	1	10	20	21	22	23	24	25	26
Seats	58	580	1160	1218	1276	1334	1392	1450	1508

d. Could you draw a diagram of the theater seating by having 26 rows with 58 seats in each row?

e. Could we use graph paper to show a model of 26 rows of 58 seats?

f. Can the problem be solved by writing a multiplication sentence and then solving it. For example, what is the solution of $26 \times 58 = \square$?

III. Carrying out the plan

At this point, children will complete the plan that they have selected. It can be informative to have class members use different plans and then see if the obtained results agree.

IV. Looking back

Children can explain their work. Also, a check of different methods can be performed to determine if the same result has been observed or new problems can be created such as this one: "If ticket prices for the Palace Theater are $5 for adults and $2.50 for children, how much money is collected for tickets when children occupy every seat in the theater?"

Attention should be paid to alternative solution strategies, creation of new problems, checking results, and generalizations such as the appropriate use of the multiplication algorithms.

Although the preceding problem is similar to a standard textbook problem, it serves as a good organizing example of a problem-solving method appropriate for a wide range of problems, including process or nonroutine problems. Additional examples of Polya's method are described by Leblanc (1977). Once again, a skillful teacher needs to be patient and allow children time to devise plans and solutions. In addition, a teacher needs to have a flexible attitude when using this method. Sometimes, a teacher has a solution strategy in mind. Children may not explain their ideas clearly or they may come up with an ingenious idea unforeseen by the teacher. This type of experience can be threatening to some teachers. Therefore, when in doubt, have students explain their work to the class. Usually, another class member will be able to explain it to the group.

Problem-Solving Strategies and Sample Problems

In this section we develop problems and some of the strategies that can elaborate and clarify Polya's four-stage model of problem solving. Although a problem often yields several solution strategies, we attempt here to emphasize one solution strategy for each problem. Also, a strategy is described in terms of its placement in Polya's four-stage problem-solving model. That is, if a strategy seems helpful in understanding or planning a solution, then it is noted. Likewise, a strategy of primary use in carrying out a plan or looking back is noted. Since solving a problem requires insight and ingenuity, a hard and fast classification of strategies is difficult to create. However, several of the strategies considered here can be classified in terms of Polya's stages as follows:

1. Make a table or graph
2. Look for a pattern
3. Make a diagram
4. Work a simpler problem
5. Guess and check
6. Work backward
7. Make a model

8. Find another solution

9. Offer various perspectives

10. Determine wanted and given information

11. Write a number sentence

12. Estimate

Make a Table or Graph.   The strategy of making a table can be helpful in systematizing information. It is often used in conjunction with the strategy of making a simpler problem. In Polya's problem-solving model, making a table fits under the category of devising a plan. Following are problems whose solutions emphasize the making of a table.

> Last year, 64 teams entered the NCAA Basketball Tournament. The format of the tournament was a single elimination plan. How many games were played to determine the national champion?

Using a simpler problem strategy and systematizing our results in a table yields the following information.

Teams	2	3	4	5	. . . .	64
Games	1	2	3	4	. . . .	63

For a simpler problem of two teams, we can quickly see that one game needs to be played. If three teams are entered, then a solution can be diagramed like this:

Team 1
Team 2 }   2 games are played
Team 3

Continue to draw diagrams and solve the situation for four teams, then five teams. A table systematizes the result and a pattern emerges. The number of games is one less than the number of teams. Thus, with 64 teams, 63 games need to be played.

Here is another problem that can be solved in a systematic fashion by using a table.

> How many ways can you make 25¢ in change?

Tabulating results in a table helps to provide a systematic way to approach this problem. We first note that only one quarter can be used. Next, we list all the possibilities that occur for one nickel, two nickels, three nickels, four nickels, and five nickels. Having accounted for all the possibilities for nickels, we then consider the outcomes available for dimes. Finally, we conclude with the only possibility, which occurs for zero quarters, zero nickels, and zero dimes, namely, 25 pennies (see the table below). Our table helps to guide our thinking as we account for all possibilities and recorded results.

Quarters	Nickels	Dimes	Pennies
1	0	0	0
	1	2	0
	1	1	10
	1	0	20
	2	1	5
	2	0	15
	3	1	0
	3	0	10
	4	0	5
	5	0	0
	0	1	15
	0	2	5
	0	0	25

Graphing is an aid to problem solving because it also helps to systematize results. Actually, collecting data and displaying it in graphical form is used in many advanced research studies. We can simulate this activity even at the primary-grade level (K–3). Consider Activities 10.1 and 10.2 for use with primary-aged children.

ACTIVITY 10.1   Make a Graph

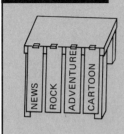

Question: What are your favorite television programs?
Data Collection: On the edge of the teacher's desk, tape the
                  names of several popular television shows
                  (see the diagram at the left).

Give each child a cube and ask students to walk up and place their cubes on the desk above the label of their favorite television show. As

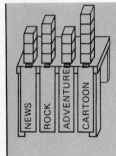

each child places a cube on top of the other cubes, a concrete graph appears similar to the one shown at the left.

Some follow-up questions that can be asked include "Which television show is the most popular?" "If we guessed what show the children at Harper School liked the most, what would be our best guess?"

Other questions that can be asked and then graphed are:

1. What are your favorite animals?

2. What are your favorite meals?

3. What are your favorite sports teams?

4. What are your favorite rock bands or singers?

ACTIVITY 10.2 Make a Table*

This problem can be solved by using the strategy of making a table.

In our garage we have bicycles, tricycles, and cars. I saw that there were 12 wheels in the garage. What vehicles were there?

*Used with the permission of L. J. Meconi and R. Steinen.

Look for a Pattern.   Looking for patterns is a basic mathematical thinking technique. Often a table helps to arrange information so that a trend can be more readily seen. As we carry out the plan of our solution strategy, looking for patterns is helpful. Study the following problem.

What is the twenty-fifth triangular number?

Triangular numbers are constructed in this way:

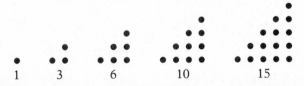

Each triangular number can be expressed in this way:

T_1 (first triangular number): $1 = 1$

T_2 (second triangular number): $3 = 1 + 2$

T_3 (third triangular number): $6 = 1 + 2 + 3$

T_4 (fourth triangular number): $10 = 1 + 2 + 3 + 4$

T_5 (fifth triangular number): $15 = 1 + 2 + 3 + 4 + 5$

A pattern emerges that suggests the sixth triangular number would be found by adding up the first six counting numbers. Thus, $T_6 = 1 + 2 + 3 + 4 + 5 + 6 = 21$. This generalization can be checked by drawing a diagram like the one to the left and counting the dots. Therefore, the twenty-fifth triangular number, found by observing a pattern, is $T_{25} = 1 + 2 + 3 + 4 + 5 + 6 + \ldots + 25$. A formula developed by Karl Freidrich Gauss, a famous eighteenth-century mathematician, allows for easy computation of this sum. To add the first n counting numbers, multiply n (the last number) by $n + 1$ (the next highest number) and divide by 2. Thus, $(25 \times 26) \div 2 = 325$, and so the twenty-fifth triangular number is 325.

Problems suitable for primary-aged children can emphasize mathematical patterns. Colored beads can be strung along a wire to show a pattern such as the one diagramed in Fig. 10.1. As children try to determine the next bead in a sequence of beads, they are laying a valuable foundation for the development of problem-solving ability. Later, a similar but more abstract pattern might be observed by intermediate-aged children. For example, find the next number in the sequence shown in Fig. 10.2. Observing the differences between successive numbers is a helpful strategy to use when confronted with a set of numbers that exhibit a potential pattern. Applying that technique to this problem yields the recognition that the differences seem to double. In other words, the difference between 47 and the next number in the sequence should be 48. Thus, the next number is 95. (See Activity 10.3 for another mathematical pattern that children can solve.)

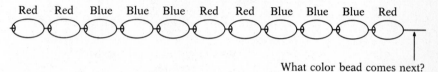

Fig. 10.1

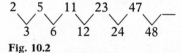

Fig. 10.2

ACTIVITY 10.3   Patterns with a Hand Calculator

This activity utilizes a hand calculator to help find patterns.

Use a hand calculator to help you do this problem. If you receive $1 one day, $2 the second day, $4 the third day, $8 the fourth day, and $16 the fifth day, how much money will you have after 14 days?

Make a Diagram.   Making a diagram is an essential strategy for understanding a problem as well as designing and carrying out your plan. A wide range of problems, including standard textbook problems, can be resolved by the use of diagrams or pictures. Following are some examples of problems whose solutions are derived, in part, by the use of diagrams as aids.

Adrienne set her watch at 7:30 A.M. At 1:30 P.M. she noticed her watch had lost 4 minutes. Predict how many minutes her watch will lose by 7:30 A.M. the following day.

Simulate the movement of the clock by using the diagrams shown at the left as a reference. For each 6 hours of movement, 4 minutes are lost. Thus, 4 + 4 + 4 + 4 or 16 minutes are lost in 24 hours, and in 6 hours the watch lost 4 minutes.*

Here is another example of drawing a diagram as an aid to problem solution.

If it takes 1 minute to make each cut, how long will it take to cut a 10-foot pole into ten equal pieces?

An immediate answer might be 10 minutes, but drawing a diagram like the one on the following page to simulate the cutting of the pole shows the error of this answer. The ninth cut yields ten pieces; thus it takes 9 minutes.

*Used by permission of the Ohio Department of Education.

Using pictures or diagrams is a good strategy for helping children solve textbook word problems. Pairing a picture with a word problem can help students gain important information about the problem. At the primary level, the rebus method, which uses pictures as part of a sentence, is used. Here is an example of a brief, three-line word problem suitable for primary-grade children (K–3).

Bob bought four 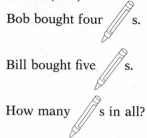 s.

Bill bought five ____ s.

How many ____ s in all?

Intermediate-grade students (4–6) can be exposed to a paragraph style for story problems. Again, a picture or diagram is used to help students understand the conditions of the problem.

Betty bought a new baseball glove and a ball. How much did they cost?

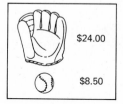

$24.00

$8.50

As children grow more mature, formal textbook problems, which are completely verbal, are solved. Then, children can draw their own diagrams and pictures to help aid their solution. (See Activity 10.4.)

ACTIVITY 10.4   Make a Diagram

Drawing a diagram can help solve this activity.

A cat is at the bottom of a 30-foot basement. Each day the cat climbs up 3 feet and each night it slides back down 2 feet. How many days will the cat take to climb out of the basement?

Work a Simpler Problem.   Sometimes a difficult problem can be reduced to a simpler, more manageable problem. The simpler problem can be studied to discover relationships that suggest solutions for the more complex case. Working a simpler problem can be part of our plan for solution because it helps us to understand the original problem. Study the following problem and its solution.

Place the numbers 1 through 19 into the 19 circles in the diagram below so that any three numbers in a row will give the same sum.

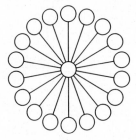

This problem, a rather difficult type of enrichment activity in elementary textbooks, seems to be complicated. Trial and error could be used, but the number of combinations that would have to be tried seems to be too great. Let us try a simpler problem.

Place the numbers 1 through 5 into the five circles in the diagram below so that any three numbers in a row give the same sum.

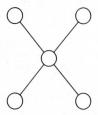

This problem can be made even simpler by noting that the number placed in the middle will appear in both sums. Thus, we can reduce the problem to finding pairs of numbers having the same sum, as shown here:

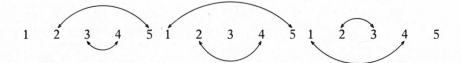

We have found three solutions for our simpler problem:

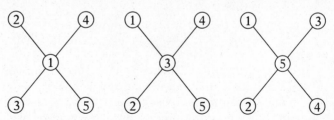

As we examine our solutions for the simpler case, we discover that a procedure involving averaging occurs. Moreover, it seems that after a number has been removed to occupy the center circle, then a pairing of smallest to largest, next smallest to next largest occurs. Further, if we selected any number other than the first, middle, or last for the center circle, we would destroy the averaging effect. Thus, the only three possibilities for the center circle are the first number, the middle number, or the last number. Now, let us use this information to solve the original problem (see Fig. 10.3). The solution is shown in Fig. 10.4.*

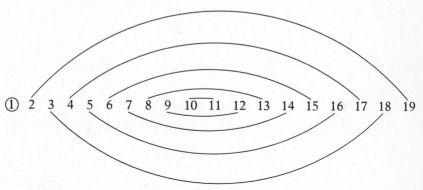

Fig. 10.3

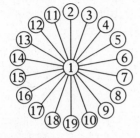

Fig. 10.4

*Used by permission of the Ohio Department of Education.

Another problem that emphasizes a strategy of working a simpler problem is this:

How many line segments connect 15 points?

Drawing line segments to 15 points is confusing as well as cumbersome. Making a simpler problem by using a table to systematize results and drawing a diagram are strategies useful to the solution of this triangle. We start by working some simpler problems and recording results in a table.

Two points yield one line segment.

Three points yield three line segments.

Four points yield six line segments.

Five points yield ten line segments.

Aha! It looks like these could be triangular numbers again.

Six points yield 15 line segments.

Extending the pattern by noting that successive differences between numbers are increasing by one yields 105 line segments for 15 points.

Points	1	2	3	4	5	6	7	8	9	10	11	12	13	14	15
Line Segments	0	1	3	6	10	15	21	28	36	45	55	66	78	91	105

              2   3   4   5   6   7   8   9   10   11   12   13   14

Another way to solve this problem is to make a generalization. For example, with five points a line segment can be drawn from one point to four other points. Since we can start at any one of the five points, we have four options at each point, or $5 \times 4 = 20$ line segments. However, this is twice the number needed because a count is being made in two directions:

$$A \longrightarrow B$$
$$A \longleftarrow B$$

Thus, $(5 \times 4) \div 2 = 10$ is the required number of line segments determined by five points. In general, if we have n points and can draw line segments from any one of these points to $n - 1$ points, the product $n \times (n - 1) \div 2$ is a generalization that can yield the number of line segments for any given number of points. The generalization can be restated more clearly as: To find the number of line segments that can be drawn from a given number of points, multiply the number representing the number of points by a number one less, then divide by 2.

Textbook word problems can also be used to illustrate the strategy of working a simpler problem. Solving a simpler problem can develop an understanding of the problem situation and, consequently, a selection of an operation can be advanced, as shown in the following problem.

> Mary mows lawns on Saturdays. She works for $2\frac{1}{3}$ hours before lunch and $1\frac{1}{5}$ hours after lunch. How much longer does she work in the morning?

We can make up a simpler problem such as:

2 hours before lunch 2
1 hour after lunch $\underline{-1}$
                          1 hour (approximately)

The operation to be used is subtraction, as shown here:

$$2\frac{1}{3} = 2\frac{5}{15}$$
$$\underline{-1\frac{1}{5}} = \underline{1\frac{3}{15}}$$
$$1\frac{2}{15} \quad \text{hours longer in the morning}$$

=========================== *MATH HISTORY 10.3* ===========================

Karl Friedrich Gauss, an eighteenth-century mathematician, related the story of how his elementary school teacher gave his class a problem of adding the first 100 counting numbers. Gauss, only 10 years old at the time, answered the question immediately by observing that $1 + 100 = 101$, $2 + 99 = 101$, $3 + 98 = 101$, and so on. Since there are 50 such pairs of numbers, Gauss obtained 5050 as a result.

Guess and Check. Blind, random guessing is not advocated, but systematic and approximate guessing and checking are often useful strategies for the planning and executing stages of problem solving. Consider the following problems, the first of which can be used with third graders.

Heather has 8 more stickers than Holly. When they count all their stickers, they have 24. How many stickers does Holly have?

Although this problem could be solved by other means, we employ a guessing and checking strategy to illustrate the strategy's systematic approach. Our thinking might be as follows:

We cannot have more than 24, so we need a pair of numbers whose difference is 8 and whose sum is 24. We try some combinations:

Difference of 4 $\longrightarrow$ 14 + 10 = 24
Difference of 6 $\longrightarrow$ 15 + 9 = 24
Difference of 8 $\longrightarrow$ 16 + 8 = 24

So, Heather has 16 stickers and Holly 8.

The following problem can be enjoyable for intermediate-grade children.

Form dollar words (letter values yielding a sum of 100) by using the following design:

A B C D E F G H I J K L M N O P Q R S T U V W X Y Z
1 2 3 4 5 6 7 8 9 10 11 12 13 14 15 16 17 18 19 20 21 22 23 24 25 26

The word *TURKEY* is a dollar word because the letter values are 20 + 21 + 18 + 11 + 5 + 25 = 100. Numerous other words can be found but patience as well as a strategy of guessing and checking are required. One of the author's sixth-grade classes once found 30 words by using a dictionary to help guide their hunches. (See Activity 10.5.)

ACTIVITY 10.5 Guess and Check

This activity emphasizes a systematic guessing and checking procedure.

Bill and Steve live in towns that are separated by 120 km of straight road. They decide to meet at 12 noon. Bill rides his bike at 15 km an hour and Steve rides at 25 km an hour. They want to leave their homes at the same time. What is the latest time that they can leave their homes in the morning to be sure to meet at noon?

Work Backward. Sometimes a problem contains a series of actions that are better understood and clarified by working backward from the end to a desired point in the action sequence. The strategy of working backward is a valuable and sometimes neglected strategy for solving problems. Following are two sample problems whose solutions are dependent on a working-backward strategy. (See also Activity 10.6.) The working-backward approach is best classified in the planning and carrying out stage of Polya's (1945) model for problem solving.

> A water lily doubles itself in size each day. From the time the original plant is placed in a pond until the surface is completely covered takes 30 days. How long will it take for the pond to be half covered?

If we attempt to solve this problem by reading the information in sequence from the beginning, difficulties arise immediately. Actually, the problem is an easy one if we remember the clue about when to use the working-backward strategy. Here a sequence of actions is performed, namely, doubling the water lily's size each day. We note the pond is full on the thirtieth day. Thinking backward, we know that the pond is half full on the twenty-ninth day.

Here is another problem that is easily solved by applying the working-backward strategy.

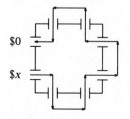

$0

$x

> A man enters a funhouse at the gate labeled x (see the diagram to the left). He pays \$1 to enter, loses half the money in his possession while inside, and pays \$1 to exit.
> The man continues along the path and enters another door of the funhouse. Once again he pays \$1 to enter, loses half of the money in his possession while inside, and pays \$1 to leave.
> Continuing, the man enters the funhouse two more times, each time paying \$1 to enter and exit and losing half of his money while inside the funhouse. At this point, the man has no money left. How much money did he have when he started?

Starting at the beginning of the sequence of actions in this problem produces a complicated mathematical problem. However, we can easily work the problem by working backward, remembering that the opposite of losing \$1 is gaining \$1, and noting that the opposite of halving is doubling. The diagram at the left shows the solution values.

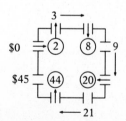

$0

$45

Working backward suggests that the man must have spent his last \$1 exiting the funhouse. If he lost half of his money and was left with \$1 then he must have had \$2 before he lost half. Continuing our backward movement, the man must have had \$3 before he entered the final entrance to the funhouse. Similarly, we add $1 and double amounts at appropriate places in our backward trek. This leaves us with $45 as the amount with which the man started.

ACTIVITY 10.6   Work Backward

Try a working-backward procedure to solve this problem.

Thirty matches are placed on a table. You can pick up 1 to 6 of the matches. The second player also picks up 1 to 6 matches. The player who picks up the last match wins.

If you are starting the game, how can you insure a victory?

Make a Model.   Making a model is a strategy that involves using objects or simulating the problem's actions in some way, sometimes by drawing a diagram as an aid. Thus, a helpful aid for understanding and devising a solution plan is found. Following are three problem examples that can be solved by making a model.

Sixteen toothpicks form five squares of the same size and shape. Move exactly three toothpicks to form four squares having the same size and shape.

A model of this problem is constructed by using actual toothpicks to represent the situation. This allows us to pick up and move toothpicks and thus reduces mental and visual confusion that can occur if we try to simulate the movement of toothpicks mentally.

The corner square is removed by moving two toothpicks.

Place them on top of one of the other squares. Now remove a toothpick to remove another square.

Put it with the other two toothpicks to form another square. We now have four squares.

Geometric problems such as this are often amenable to a solution that builds a model with concrete objects such as sticks and chips.

Here is another problem that illustrates the use of a concrete model as a means of finding a solution.*

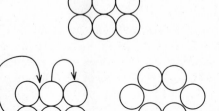

With two rows of three coins, move only two of the coins to make a circle.

Coins or chips can be used for experimenting with solutions. The result is shown to the left.

Making a model or acting out a problem are good strategies when solving standard textbook problems such as the following.

> There are 14 students in the class. Every two students will share a pair of scissors. How many scissors are needed?

To model this problem, the teacher can bring a box of scissors to class and select 14 students to participate. A pair of scissors can be passed out to two students, then another pair of scissors to two more students, and so on. The class can then count out that seven pairs of scissors have been distributed. Modeling or acting out word problems is an excellent strategy for teachers to use to help children discover the correct operation to use in a word problem.

Find Another Solution.   Problems that illustrate several solution possibilities are useful examples of how mathematical thinking can yield several answers. Some people feel that mathematics always has one exact answer. Although mathematical thinking can yield precise answers to problems, many problems yield approximate answers and multiple solutions.

Following are examples of problems that have several answers (see also Activity 10.7). Often the strategy of finding another solution is viewed as part of the "looking-back" stage in Polya's problem-solving model.

> Susan has $1 in her pocket made up of seven coins. What are the coins?*

*Used by permission of the Ohio Department of Education.

A table can help to systematize the results.

50¢	25¢	10¢	5¢	Total
1	1		5	100¢
1		4	2	100¢
	3	1	3	100¢

A benefit of using a table is to help us systematically account for all possibilities of the results. Although we are not attempting to prove that there are only three options for the answer, we can be reasonably sure that we have accounted for all possibilities because the design of our table helps us to look carefully at the options.

Here is a problem that can be used with primary-grade children.

How many ways can you put eight cubes on two plates?

Here, a concrete model would be used. Children could actually place cubes on plates and tabulate the results. However, it should be noted that all children at the first or second grade level will not be systematic in their approach. Remember, the goal of the preceding problem is to get children to come up with more than one answer. Some children may have several answers whereas others may have only two or three. To the degree that you can, encourage a systematic approach, but treat anything more than one answer with praise.

ACTIVITY 10.7   Find Another Solution

> Write an expression equal to 10 that uses exactly 5 nines and any operation symbols.

Offer Various Perspectives.   Problems that entail a change of perspective or view are often good examples of creative thinking. Open-ended problems—those with more than one answer—can be a valuable vehicle for developing novel, imaginative solutions (see Activity 10.8). Changing your point of view requires a complete and imaginative understanding of the problem. Consider this problem:

Using exactly four line segments, connect all the dots in the diagram to the left without picking up your pencil and without retracing an entire line segment.

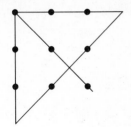

A change of view requires that you draw the segments *outside* of the square array of dots (see the diagram to the left). If your vision field stays within the square region of dots, then the solution is impossible.

At the primary-grade level, four blocks can be used and the following question asked:

How many buildings can you build with four blocks?

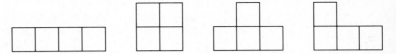

Several solutions are shown, but remember that we are encouraging creativity—a complete, systematic explanation is not to be expected of a first- or second-grade child.

ACTIVITY 10.8   Think of Imaginative Solutions

How many ways can you use a thermometer to measure the height of a building?

Determine Wanted and Given Information.   In essence, problem solving requires determining the existing information or conditions and then selecting a process to find the unknown or wanted goal. All problems require an understanding of wanted and given information (see Activity 10.9). Standard elementary textbook problems often require children to determine the given information and the wanted or unknown goals.

Often, elementary school textbooks pose a word problem and then list questions about wanted and given information, as the following problem illustrates.

The Drake School voted for a student council president. Heather received 234 votes and Bill received 163. How many more votes did Heather get than Bill?

What do you know?   Heather—234 votes
                                     Bill—163 votes

What do you want to know?   How many more votes were
cast for Heather than for Bill?

ACTIVITY 10.9 Identify Given and Wanted Information

> A bottle of soda pop costs 35¢. The soda pop costs 25¢ more than
> the bottle. How much of a refund is the bottle worth?

Write a Number Sentence.   Some problems can be effectively solved by
writing a number sentence. Often, the number sentence is considered part
of Polya's devise-a-plan stage. Textbook problems in elementary school
mathematics often require students to write and then solve a number sentence such as $85 + 7 = \square$. Selecting the operation or operations to use in
the number sentence is perhaps the most difficult aspect of solving textbook
word problems (Zweng, 1979).

Thus, students need to write number sentences to describe a problem,
with particular emphasis being placed on selecting the correct operation.
Before formal problem solving is taught, children need to hear many oral
examples of how addition applies to their daily lives. Also, meaningful instruction in operations through concrete models provides an understanding
of how operations work. Modeling or acting out word problems also helps
children lay a foundation for solving problems on their own. Finally, elementary textbooks help students write number sentences by designing problems and situations similar to the one that follows.

Loop one of the number sentences for this word problem:
There are eight striped clowns and six solid-colored clowns. How
many clowns are there?

$8 + 6 = \square$ $8 - 6 = \square$ $8 \times 6 = \square$

Estimate.   Estimation, a thinking skill, can also help to solving problems. Determining the reasonableness of an answer is a helpful strategy. A
standard textbook problem can include several choices of estimated answers (see Activity 10.10). Students are asked to loop the correct estimate
without actually computing the exact answer, as in the following example.

Bill sold tickets for a school play. On Monday he sold $984.78
worth of tickets. On Tuesday, he sold $692.14 worth of tickets. On
Wednesday, he sold $487.16 worth of tickets. How much money did
he collect for the school?

Loop the most reasonable answer:

    1. $2200   2. $220   3. $1500

ACTIVITY
10.10

Estimate the Discounted Price

Estimate the solution to this word problem.

A department store has an end-of-year sale during which all items are reduced by 35 percent. Karin wants to buy a blazer that lists for $119.99. How much will Karin pay for the blazer after the 35-percent reduction?

Supplementary Strategies for Standard Textbook Problems

Elementary school mathematics textbooks and commercial tests emphasize word problems that require children to read and solve problems. Although research has suggested that children able to read word problems often fail to solve them because of a lack of understanding regarding the selection and use of operations (Knifong & Holtan, 1977), a prudent teaching approach is still to emphasize reading for comprehension as one of the means for effectively solving word problems. Likewise, effective computational skills and a thorough knowledge of the meaning of operations are necessary for solving word problems. To supplement the strategies for teaching children how to solve word problems presented earlier in the chapter, several teaching strategies that further promote word problem-solving ability are given here.

===== *MATH HISTORY 10.4* =====

Here is how one child described her solution for a word problem in 1925:

If there are lots of numbers, I add. If there are only two numbers with lots of parts, I subtract. But if there are just two numbers and one is smaller than the other, it is hard. I divide if they come out even, but if they don't, I multiply.

Use Problems with Too Much Information. Use problems for which students must read critically in order to cross out extra information. Here is one example.

Cross out the extra information:

Mary took swimming lessons twice a week for 7 weeks. She also took piano lessons once a week for 12 weeks. How many swimming lessons did Mary take?

Use Problems with Too Little Information.   From a list of word problems students must determine whether there is sufficient information to solve the problem. Here are some examples of this technique.

Do you have enough information to solve this problem?

A basketball game started at 8:00 P.M. How long did the game last?

We do not have enough information. We need the time the game ended.

A ticket for a basketball game costs $4.50. Bill needs six tickets. How much will he spend?

Yes, there is enough information.

Use Problems Without Questions.   Problems without questions help children to read critically. They can make up a question for the information presented, as in the following example.

Bill and Mary go to the store. Bill has 48¢ and Mary has 36¢. They want to buy some candy that costs 86¢.

Several questions are possible for this information. Do they have enough money? How much more will they need? How much change will they get?

Have Children Invent Problems.   Children can create their own problems. At the primary-grade level, this may be done by using a combination of pictures and words. An example of this is shown in Fig. 10.5. At the intermediate-grade level, children can use information from the newspaper, the *Guinness Book of World Records,* and other sources to create problems for friends to solve.

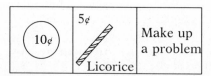

Fig. 10.5

Teach Reading and Mathematics.   Many of our examples illustrate this issue, but some additional guidelines are needed. For one, children must understand special mathematical vocabulary words such as *perimeter, area, power,* and *times,* to name a few. Also, children need to reread a problem. Often, the eye movements when reading word problems are more active; we do not only read from left to right. We scan, find information in a vertical and horizontal manner. Thus, children need to read problems at a slower rate than ordinary prose.

Clue phrases and words, such as *in all, left, from, all together,* are sometimes taught as if they designate operations. That is, sometimes students learn that when they see the words *take* or *take away* in a problem they should subtract. Consider the following problem.

> John had eight marbles. John took four marbles away from Steve. How many marbles does John have?

The preceding problem is solved by adding, not subtracting! Therefore, be careful when using key words for selecting operations. Barnett, Sowder, and Vos (1980) suggest that students underline *potential* key words in the first reading of a problem. In a second reading, the social context of the problem is examined to determine an operation choice. [Readers interested in more information about the relationship between reading and mathematics should consult Barnett, Sowder, and Vos (1980).]

Supplement the Textbook.   Supplement the textbook by creating your own problems. Use the names of children in your class, or famous personalities to enhance children's problem-solving interest. Also tape-record some problems so children with reading difficulties can attain some degree of success. Have a problem of the day or week on the bulletin board. Allow children to obtain extra credit for attempting and solving these problems. Finally, at times it is good to allow children to work in small groups as they solve problems, as this helps to teach them valuable social skills and cooperative behavior. It also promotes a sharing of problem-solving skills.

Emphasize Multiple-Step Problems at the Intermediate Level.   Research from the National Assessment of Educational Progress (Kouba et al., 1988) has shown that children are reasonably competent with routine, one-step problems. However, problems requiring more than one step cause children difficulty. Multiple-step word problems such as the one shown here need to be emphasized at the intermediate-grade level.

Mary needs to work on the computer for 25 hours. She worked $3\frac{1}{2}$ hours on Monday, 3 hours on Tuesday, $4\frac{1}{4}$ hours on Wednesday, and $3\frac{1}{4}$ hours on Thursday. How many more hours does Mary need to work in order to meet her goal of 25 hours?

Notice that this problem requires the student to use addition to find the number of hours that Mary has worked. Then, a comparison is made, using subtraction, to determine how much time Mary needs to work in order to achieve her goal of 25 hours.

Word problems that involve more than one step need to be emphasized at the intermediate-grade level, particularly in grades 5 and 6. Teachers need to examine a few problems carefully rather than rush through a set of ten problems. Quality, not quantity, is the guideline here. As Polya (1945) noted, "Solving problems is a practical skill like, let us say, swimming. We acquire any practical skill by imitation and practice" (p. 4). Elementary school teachers need to model effective problem-solving skills and attitudes as well as provide moderate, in-depth practice of multistep word problems. (See Activities 10.11 and 10.12.)

ACTIVITY
10.11　　Tic-Tac-Toe

Put these numbers on the tic-tac-toe board at the left.

38　17　18　15　3　45　51　93　105

Variations

Solve each problem listed below. Put an X on the answer on the tic-tac-toe board. The player who obtains a row, column, or diagonal line marked with Xs is the winner.

I bought 6 records for $8.50. How much money did I spend?
I had 74 baseball trading cards. I gave 15 to Sue. Sue gave me 34 baseball trading cards. How many cards do I now have?
I bought items in the store for $.50 and $12.50. How much change will I receive from a $20 bill?
There are three football teams with 35 players on each. How many players are there?
Mary's father is 45 years old. How old will he be in 6 years?
Holly swam 15 laps before lunch. After lunch she swam 18 more laps. She must swim 71 laps in order to qualify for the swim meet. How many more laps does she need to swim?

Cheeseburgers are needed for lunch at the picnic. There are seven children, eight parents, and three teachers. If each person eats one cheeseburger for lunch, how many are needed?

A quarterback has thrown 24 times and gained 360 yards. How many yards does the quarterback average on each throw?

There are 12 children at a slumber party. If everyone there eats an ice cream cone that costs 65¢, how much money will be needed to pay for these treats?

ACTIVITY 10.12

Invent a Word Problem

Make up a word problem that involves a two-step operation for its solution.

Use a Hand Calculator. A hand calculator can be a helpful aid when solving a variety of problems. Chapter 7 devotes considerable attention to a wide range of curriculum objectives that can be developed by using a hand calculator. For the special case of teaching word problems, a hand calculator helps to focus a child's attention on the critical information presented in the problem situation as well as the important task of selecting an appropriate operation. Computational ability is minimized, and, thus, children are helped to developed an understanding of the appropriate selection of operations. Even though the hand calculator will perform the calculation, a child must know what keys to push, and a necessary skill for solving word problems is practiced.

Summary

Teaching techniques for developing children's ability to solve problems are developed in this chapter. Numerous strategies for solving problems are pointed out so that prospective teachers can gain firsthand experience with a wide variety of problems. Some of these problems will be useful to you, others may not. However, it is the central point of this chapter that children can, indeed, be taught strategies for solving problems.

A teacher's attitude is the key to a successful problem-solving program. If a teacher is impatient with children or is afraid to take a risk, then children will sense this. It is sometimes risky to pose a new problem and then find out that you have solved it incorrectly. However, some mathematicians have worked for years trying to solve problems that have resisted solution! The important point is to take time to solve several problems well. Assembly-line thinking will not help children to be good problem solvers. Quality in terms of an in-depth analysis of a problem is to be sought. This chapter provides some problem material and guidelines for successful problem-solving experiences.

Discussion Questions

1. Construct two word problems suitable for primary-grade children. Also, construct two multistep problems for intermediate-grade children. Bring these problems to class and examine the quality of the sample problems produced by your classmates.

2. Make up a story problem. Then design a series of questions to help students through the four stages of problem solving that are outlined in this chapter. Your questions should consider these stages: understanding the problem, devising a plan, carrying out the plan, and looking back.

3. Collect some problem-solving materials for developing each of the strategies developed in this chapter. Two useful resource books are *The Book of Think* (1976) and *The "I Hate Mathematics" Book* (1975) by Marilyn Burns. Also, consult the *Arithmetic Teacher* for sample problems available in the "Problem Solving Tips for Teachers."

4. Read "Problem Solving Tips for Teachers" by Phares O'Daffer in the May 1985 issue of *Arithmetic Teacher*. Try the problems presented in the article with your class.

5. Solve this problem:

   S, H, and *E* are different digits. Replace the letters with numbers to make the statement true. $(HE)^2 = SHE$

6. Solve this problem:

   Move three toothpicks to make three squares.

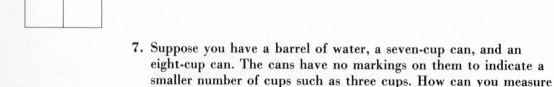

7. Suppose you have a barrel of water, a seven-cup can, and an eight-cup can. The cans have no markings on them to indicate a smaller number of cups such as three cups. How can you measure nine cups of water using only the seven-cup can and the eight-cup can?

8. Collect riddles and puzzles to use as a problem of the week. Consult *Think About It* by Marcy Cook (1982).

9. Write to the National Assessment of Educational Progress, Suite 700, 1860 Lincoln Street, Denver, CO 80295, for current research on problem solving.

References

Barnett, J., Sowder, L., & Vox, K. (1980). Textbook problems: supplementing and understanding them. In S. Krulik and R. Reys, (eds.), *Problem solving in mathematics* (pp. 92–103). Reston, Va.: NCTM.

Branca, N. (1980). Problem solving as a goal, process, and basic skill. In S. Krulik and R. Reys (eds.), *Problem solving in school mathematics* (pp. 3–8). Reston, Va.: NCTM.

Brownell, W. A. (1942). *Problem solving. The psychology of learning. Forty-first Yearbook, Part II. National Society for the Study of Education.* Chicago: University of Chicago Press.

Burns, M. (1975). *The "I hate mathematics" book.* Boston: Little, Brown.

Burns, M. (1976). *The book of think.* Boston: Little, Brown.

Cook, M. (1982). *Think about it.* Palo Alto, Calif.: Creative Publications.

Jacobson, A. (1985). Future jobs will go to those at the top, bottom of market. *Akron Beacon Journal* (July), p. 23.

Knifong, J. D., & Holtan, B. (1977). A search for reading difficulties among erred word problems. *Journal for Research in Mathematics Education, 8,* p. 229.

Kouba, V., Brown, C., Carpenter, T., Lindquist, M., Silver, E., & Swafford, J. (1988). Results of the fourth NAEP assessment of mathematics: Number, operations, and word problems. *Arithmetic Teacher, 35,* pp. 14–19.

Leblanc, J. (1977). You can teach problem solving. *Arithmetic Teacher, 25,* pp. 16–20.

Lindquist, M., Carpenter, T., Silver, E., & Matthews, W. (1983). The third national mathematics assessment: Results and implications for elementary and middle schools. *Arithmetic Teacher, 31,* pp. 14–25.

Meconi, L. J., & Steinen, R. (1974). *Teaching elementary school mathematics.* Dubuque, Iowa: Kendall/Hunt.

Meiring, S. (1980a). *Problem solving: A basic mathematics goal—A resource for problem solving.* Columbus, Ohio: Ohio Department of Education.

Meiring, S. (1980b). *Problem solving: A basic mathematics goal—Becoming a better problem solver.* Columbus, Ohio: Ohio Department of Education.

Naisbitt, J. (1982). *Megatrends.* New York: Warner Books.

National Council of Supervisors of Mathematics. (1977). Basic skills. *Arithmetic Teacher, 25,* pp. 19–22.

National Council of Teachers of Mathematics. (1980). *Agenda for action.* Reston, Va.: NCTM.

O'Daffer, P. (1985). Problem-solving tips for teachers. *Arithmetic Teacher, 32,* pp. 18–19.

Polya, G. (1945). *How to solve it.* Princeton, N.J.: Princeton University Press.

Rowe, M. B. (1978). Wait, wait, wait . . . *School Science and Mathematics, 78,* pp. 207–216.

Stevenson, P. R. (1925). Difficulties in problem solving. *Journal of Educational Research, 11,* pp. 95–103.

Suydam, M. (1980). Untangling clues from research on problem solving. In S. Krulik (ed.), *Problem solving in school mathematics* (pp. 34–50). Reston, Va.: NCTM.

Zweng, M. J. (1979). The problem of solving story problems. *Arithmetic Teacher, 27,* p. 2.

CHAPTER 11

Multiplication and Division of Whole Numbers

Objectives

After reading this chapter you will be able to:

1. Demonstrate a concrete procedure for introducing multiplication and division to elementary school children.

2. Explain several models and illustrations for developing beginning multiplication and division examples.

3. Demonstrate that multiplication and division are inverse operations.

4. Create several practice games and activities for developing skill with multiplication and division facts.

5. Relate multiplication and division sentences to justify the claim that division by zero is impossible.

Introduction

As children investigate mathematics in grades 3–5, major emphasis is placed on developing an understanding of and application skill with the operations of whole-number multiplication and division. Children need to experience these operations from the concrete base of actively manipulating objects in order to lay a foundation for abstraction. Research from the National Assessment of Educational Progress [see Lindquist et al., (1983)] has indicated that children's level of achievement with basic multiplication facts is reasonably successful overall. For example, in a timed situation, 75 percent of fourth graders correctly recalled the result for 3×8.

In this chapter we develop materials and methods for teaching multiplication and division operations to children. In a sense, multiplication can be conceived as a more rapid form of addition in that $3 \times 4 = 4 + 4 + 4$. Also, division can be thought of as an extension of subtraction in that $6 \div 2 = 3$ can be solved by repeated subtraction, as shown below.

$$
\begin{array}{l}
6 \\
\underline{-2} \rightarrow 1 \\
4 \\
\underline{-2} \rightarrow 2 \\
2 \\
\underline{-2} \rightarrow 3 \text{ groups of 2 have been subtracted.} \\
0
\end{array}
$$

Of course, multiplication and division of whole numbers stand on their own as legitimate operations. However, children must first understand addition and subtraction to develop skill with multiplication and division. Also, applications of multiplication and division operations should include examples related to the child's own world as well as to situations that the child will encounter later in life.

Research has revealed a rich variety of thinking strategies exhibited by children as they investigate beginning multiplication examples. Using a clinical interview technique, Katterns and Carr (1986) posed interesting, probing questions to 7- and 8-year-old children. Here is a sample of their results.

> When asked what the terms times or multiply meant, one child responded by saying, "You count them out. Say, if it says two times three, you count the three twice." Another child, responding to the same question, said that "times" tells you how many things there are and gives you an answer a bit quicker. The same child said that another word for "times" was lots. (p. 18–21)

On the basis of their research, Katterns and Carr recommend that children receive a great deal of concrete experience so that they can gain a thorough conceptual understanding of multiplication.

The first use of the symbol × for multiplication is attributed
to William Oughtred in 1631. Gottfried Leibniz, in 1698,
suggested using a raised dot as a symbol for multiplication.

In eighteenth-century France, J. E. Gallimard used this symbol
for division: ⫍⫎. The sign we use today (÷) is believed to
have derived from a simple fractional line embellished by an
upper and lower dot.

Introducing Multiplication of Whole Numbers

Set Model

An example such as 2 × 3 = 6 can be modeled, concretely, as two groups
of 3. The exercise below describes this approach.

Take two bowls or paper cups and place three marbles in each.
Thus, two groups of 3 are shown.

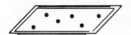

Now collect all of the marbles and place them on a tray. There are
six marbles on the tray.

The *set model* for multiplication requires that the first factor describes the
number of groups or sets and the second factor the size or number of
elements in each set. Some writers use the term *equivalent* (meaning the
same number of elements in each set) to describe multiplication. That is,
multiplication can be modeled by showing a specified number of equivalent
sets. With young children it is best to limit the use of terms; for example,
we would use the description *two groups of 4* to illustrate the multiplication
example 2 × 4 = ☐.

Children should have counters at their desks so that they can show a
concrete representation for examples such as 3 × 4 = ☐. Also, magnetic
tape attached to the back of discs makes a good chalkboard model for the
teacher. A teacher can show 3 × 4 = ☐ on the board by showing three
groups of 4. Similarly, children can use counters to illustrate the same
example at their desks. Next, the teacher and students can slide the discs
together to illustrate that 3 × 4 = 12.

Initially, a teacher needs to present a multiplication sentence such as 3 $\times$ 5 = □ and develop the symbol $\times$ as a new way of thinking about number operation. The collection of objects and the recognition of having five objects three times can help give meaning to the term *times*. Early multiplication experiences should be illustrated by way of number stories. For example, "Mary received three packages of candy. Each package had five candies. How many candies did Mary have?"

Array Model

Essentially, the *array model* is more specific than the set model. For the array model, an example such as 3 $\times$ 6 = □ is shown as three rows of six objects. Stickers or stars can be used to demonstrate an array model by asking students to paste three rows of six stars and to count the result. Some students will recognize that they can count 6 + 6 + 6 = 18 rather than count each star. Initially, though, this should not be stressed. The key idea here is to get children to associate a concrete representation with a symbolic number sentence. Again, a story relating to the array model is helpful. For example, "Barry has three bookshelves. On each bookshelf there are six books. How many books are on the shelves?" [Additional examples of how to use arrays for beginning multiplication can be found in Stuart and Bestgen (1982).]

Repeated Addition

Multiplication can be modeled as repeated addition. For example, 4 $\times$ 5 = 5 + 5 + 5 + 5—we have added 5 four *times*. Thus, this is why the multiplication tables are sometimes called the *"times" tables*. Although some children recognize that repeated addition can be used when working with concrete models, others need to have this pointed out to them. Often an abstract, paper-and-pencil activity is used in elementary mathematics textbooks that asks students to represent an example such as 4 $\times$ 8 as 8 + 8 + 8 + 8.

Number Line

A number line builds on the repeated-addition concept of multiplication. For example, 3 $\times$ 7 = □ would be shown on the number line as three groups of 7 (see Fig. 11.1).

Number Balance

A number balance can also be used when developing multiplication (see Chapter 8). To solve 2 $\times$ 4 = □, two weights are placed on the numeral 4 hook. The balance then looks as it does in Fig. 11.2. A weight is then placed

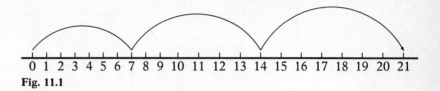

Fig. 11.1

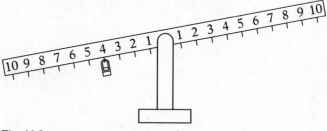

Fig. 11.2

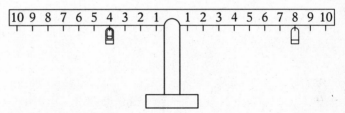

Fig. 11.3

on the hook near the numeral 8, on the right side of the balance. The balance is now level and $2 \times 4 = 8$ is shown (see Fig. 11.3).

Situation Cards

As children investigate beginning multiplication examples, situation cards, which show how multiplication applies to daily life, can be presented. For example, children can be asked to complete a card like the one on the next page, which illustrates the multiples of two at a semiconcrete level. At this point, reference should be made to the objects—do not write $2 \times 4 = \square$ or other multiplication sentences too quickly. The emphasis here is on providing readiness for later abstract work. (See Activities 11.1 and 11.2.)

Number of Persons	Number of Hands
1	2
2	4
3	_____
4	_____
5	_____
6	_____
7	_____
8	_____
9	_____

Situation cards can be laminated and drawings can be made of representative physical objects. Here is another example of a card.

Number of Trikes	Number of Wheels
1	2
2	6
3	9
4	_____
5	_____
6	_____
7	_____
8	_____
9	_____

Consider also these examples for constructing multiplication situation cards:

Multiples of 4—carts and wheels
Multiples of 5—school week and days
Multiples of 6—carton of soda pop and bottles
Multiples of 7—weeks and days of the week
Multiples of 8—spiders and legs
Multiples of 9—baseball team and players

ACTIVITY 11.1   Using Concrete Materials

This activity is designed to promote practice of introductory multiplication.

Use chips, straws, or any other suitable concrete material. Find a classmate and "role play" a teaching lesson on the introduction of multiplication. Use the set model and choose some examples, such as $2 \times 3 = \square$ and $3 \times 4 = \square$. Prepare your questions and be sure to let your classmate manipulate the concrete material.

ACTIVITY 11.2   Finger Multiplication

This is a motivational, enrichment activity.

To multiply any two numbers with a factor of 6, 7, 8, 9, or 10, do the following:

Suppose we want to multiply 7×8.

1. Subtract 5 from both numbers:
   ($7 - 5 = 2$ and $8 - 5 = 3$)

2. Raise as many fingers on each hand as the difference. Add the number of raised fingers to obtain the number of tens.
   2 + 3   5 tens

3. Multiply the number of closed fingers on each hand. $2 \times 3 = 6$ (thumbs are considered fingers).

4. Add $50 + 6 = 56$

Use finger multiplication to multiply 8×9.

Vocabulary and Symbolism

Although multiplication sentences are usually introduced horizontally ($2 \times 5 = 10$), the vertical format should be introduced shortly thereafter:

$$
\begin{array}{r}
5 \\
\times 2 \\
\hline
10
\end{array}
$$

Convention dictates that changing a multiplication expression from a horizontal to a vertical framework requires the number on the *left* (horizontal) to appear on the *bottom* (vertical). In most elementary textbooks, this is already done for you. But if you want to use concrete models for an expression such as   12 , you are advised to write it as 3×12 in order to preserve
                            ×3
a place-value relationship. (This is developed further in Chapter 12, where we study and develop concrete models for the multiplication algorithm.)

Along with symbolism, vocabulary needs to be introduced during beginning multiplication work. Some elementary textbooks still use the following terminology:

24	Multiplicand
×3	Multiplier
72	Product

However, when a student reaches the algebra level of school mathematics, much attention is paid to factoring and none to multiplicanding! Thus, in the interest of providing simple yet consistent language that prepares students for later mathematical experiences, we use the following terms widely applied in elementary mathematics textbooks:

2	Factor
× 3	Factor
6	Product

Thus, our introduction to multiplication defines it as an operation that associates two factors with a product. For children, a formal definition should be used only after sufficient concrete and semiconcrete learning experiences have been undertaken. (See Activity 11.3.)

ACTIVITY 11.3 Trace a Path of Multiples

Trace a path of multiples of 7. Begin at the square in the top left corner and enter adjacent squares.

Start

7	26	17	24	32
14	21	49	56	35
28	45	64	27	42
99	7	54	63	70
15	42	28	56	14
16	18	18	65	21
35	28	56	81	28

Finish

Properties of Multiplication

Commutative Property of Multiplication

Fig. 11.4

The *commutative property* of multiplication means that the order of factors does not affect the product. For example, 2 × 3 = 3 × 2 = 6. Although the order of the factors is changed, the product remains the same. This can be demonstrated to children by using a card with dots, as shown in Fig. 11.4. Three rows of four dots each show that 3 × 4 = 12. If the card is rotated, as shown in Fig. 11.5, four rows of three dots each show that 4 × 3 = 12.

Associative Property of Multiplication

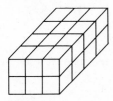

Fig. 11.5

The *associative property* of multiplication allows us to group three factors in two different ways. For example, to illustrate that 2 × (3 × 4) − (2 × 3) × 4 = 24, we can use a rectangular prism like the one in Fig. 11.6 to show the associative property. The rectangular prism has the following dimensions:

Height = 2 units
Width = 3 units
Length = 4 units

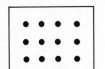

Fig. 11.6

We can find the volume by multiplying the height, length, and width of the prism. The expression 2 × (3 × 4) multiplies the width value and length value (3 × 4) and the height value of 2. We could also multiply height and width numerical values (2 × 3) followed by a multiplication of the length value (4). Other combinations are also possible. The point is that we can find the volume of the rectangular prism in two ways: 2 × (3 × 4) = (2 × 3) × 4, both of which yield a volume of 24.

Identity Element

The *identity element* for multiplication is 1. Any number multiplied by 1 results in the original number as a product. For example, 5 × 1 = 1 × 5 = 5.

Introducing Division of Whole Numbers

Division, the inverse operation of multiplication, can also be introduced with concrete, manipulative materials. Usually considered to be the most difficult of the four operations on whole numbers (Laing & Meyer, 1982), division requires careful modeling attention.

Measurement and Partitive Division

Two fundamental division situations are usually developed with children, the first being *measurement division*. The following scenario is an example of the type of situation that teachers can use to help children gain a concrete understanding of measurement division.

> The teacher displays six cubes and then asks how many children can each get two cubes. Distributing two cubes to one child, then two cubes to another child, and, finally, the last two cubes to a third child, the class discovers that all the cubes have been distributed. Each of the three children has two cubes; thus, $6 \div 2 = 3$.

Measurement division involves determining the number of groups that will occur when a specified subset of a set is distributed. Consider this measurement division situation:

> Eight players are going to form teams of two players. How many teams can be formed?

A teacher can act out this situation by actually forming teams of two from eight students.

As solutions to division situations are concretely solved, division sentences such as $8 \div 2 = 4$ can be written. However, care must be taken so that children can manipulate objects for the solution of beginning division sentences (see Activity 11.4). For example, each child can be given a bag of counters and asked to solve $8 \div 2 = \square$ by forming sets of two from eight counters. The recognition that four sets can be formed helps to solidify a firm understanding that can be applied later to abstract, symbolical questions.

The other fundamental division situation, *partitive division,* is described in the following simulation.

> The teacher selects two children from the class. After showing the class eight marbles, the teacher distributes them equally to the two children in a manner similar to dealing cards—one marble for one child, the next marble for the other child, and so on. Finally, each child has four marbles. Thus, $8 \div 2 = 4$.

A partitive division situation involves distributing a set of objects into a predetermined number of subsets. The number of elements or objects in each set is the answer to the division exercise. Here is another example of a partitive division situation:

> Twelve books are to be placed in three equally sized stacks. How many books are in each stack?

Although children need not be familiar with the terms *measurement* and *partitive division,* they should have ample experience with both types. Application problems often require ability in finding the number of equal-sized groups in a set or the number of elements in a predetermined subset of a set. An informal approach is advised for children; however, teachers need to be aware of the distinctions between the division examples presented here.

ACTIVITY 11.4 Role Playing

This activity is designed to promote practice in introductory division.

Use suitable concrete material and choose a classmate to role play an elementary school student. Pick an example such as 6 ÷ 2 = ☐ and guide the "student" through a measurement approach and then a partitive development. Prepare some questions and be sure the "student" has experienced manipulating the concrete material.

Relating Division to Multiplication

Since division is the inverse of multiplication, we can use our knowledge of multiplication to help solve division exercises. For example, a multiplication sentence such as 5 × 3 = 15 involves two factors multiplied to obtain a product. In the division sentence 15 ÷ 3 = 5, a product (15) and a factor (3) are given and the operation of division produces the missing factor (5). Thus, children need experience, at an abstract level, in determining missing factors. Number sentences such as those listed here are often used to help children relate division to multiplication:

$$21 ÷ 3 = \Box \qquad 3 × \Box = 21$$
$$21 ÷ 7 = \Box \qquad 7 × \Box = 21$$

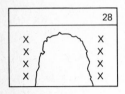

Fig. 11.7

Another useful device designed to relate multiplication and division has been described by Smith (1974): the use of "tiger bite" cards. Cards are made that have been "bitten by a tiger" (see Fig. 11.7). The total number of marks and rows on the card are known; in the figure there are 28 marks and 4 rows. Because the "tiger" has taken a bite out of the card, the class is asked to find the number of marks in each row. Relating multiplication to division results in this number sentence: $4 \times \square = 28$. Recognizing that $4 \times 7 = 28$ yields the missing elements.

Children need a great deal of experience relating multiplication to division. In fact, clinical research suggests that skill in relating division facts to multiplication can improve performance on tests of basic division (Kalin, 1983). For example, many children think of $27 \div 3 = 9$ in terms of 3 nines equaling 27. Thus, teachers are advised to relate division and multiplication as children attain the abstract level of concept development. (See Activity 11.5.)

ACTIVITY 11.5   Cuisenaire Rods

Use Cuisenaire rods for demonstrating division examples to small groups of children.

The orange rod has a value of 10. The red rod has a value of 2. We can show $10 \div 2 = \square$ by finding out how many groups of 2 will make up 10.

Place the orange rod on top of 5 red rods to show that 5 groups of 2 make up 10, and thus $10 \div 2 = 5$.

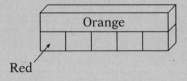

Red

Use Cuisenaire rods to solve the following division exercises.

$6 \div 2 = \square$

$8 \div 4 = \square$

$10 \div 5 = \square$

Repeated Subtraction

Division also can be developed through the method of *repeated subtraction*. An exercise such as $12 \div 4 = \square$ can be solved as shown here:

$$
\begin{array}{r}
12 \\
-\ 4 \\
\hline
8 \\
-\ 4 \\
\hline
4 \\
-\ 4 \\
\hline
0
\end{array}
$$

One group of 4

Two groups of 4

Three groups of 4

$12 \div 4 = 3$

The repeated subtraction model builds on the measurement division concept as successive groups of 4 are subtracted from the initial value of 12.

One possible reason for children's difficulty with division concepts and skills is that too little time is devoted to developing meaning through a variety of methods and materials and too much time is spent memorizing meaningless information.

Number Line

Another vehicle for understanding division concepts, more of a semiconcrete than concrete device, is the number line. The number line model, although not used widely in current elementary mathematics textbooks, can be helpful as an alternative modeling technique.

Consider this division sentence: $8 \div 2 = \square$. A number line model would backtrack from 8 in groups of 2 until reaching zero (see Fig. 11.8). Thus, $8 \div 2 = 4$.

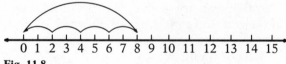

Fig. 11.8

Terminology and Symbolism

Initially, third-grade children write and read division sentences in the horizontal format (e.g., $18 \div 6 = 3$) from left to right. However, as early as the third grade children learn to read division exercises vertically, as shown here:

$$6)\overline{24}\ \ \ \ \ \ ^{4}$$

To read this exercise, we must look inside the division symbol and locate 24. Continuing, we read "24 divided by 6 is 4." To find the 6, we read left and then up to find the quotient. Needless to say, attention needs to be paid to this reading difference. For some special education students, it may be wiser to introduce only one division expression so to avoid reading problems. Some textbook series use diagrams to help students adjust to this reading difficulty.

$$45 \div 9 = ? \longrightarrow 9\overline{)45}$$

Think $? \times 9 = 45$

Since $5 \times 9 = 45$

Then $45 \div 9 = 5 \longrightarrow 9\overline{)45}^{\,5}$

Again, division sentences can be written in several ways. For example, $28 \div 7 = \square$ can be written in the following ways:

$7\overline{)28}$

$\square \times 7 = 28$ Related multiplication sentence

$7 \times \square = 28$ Related multiplication sentence

$\dfrac{28}{7}$ As a fraction

The number sentences $\square \times 7 = 28$ and $7 \times \square = 28$ are called *related multiplication* sentences. Notice that in both number sentences a factor is missing. Therefore, an alternative to the traditional dividend, divisor, and quotient terminology is apparent. We can use the same terms as we did for multiplication, but here we are given a product and a missing factor. Multiplication sentences provide us with a pair of factors and we need to state the product to solve the sentence. Conversely, division sentences require us to find a missing factor for their solution.

Related multiplication sentences can help teachers remember the difference between measurement and partitive division. Remember that for modeling multiplication sentences the first factor represents the number of groups and the second factor the elements in each group or set. Although the context of a mathematical problem dictates whether a division sentence can be interpreted as a measurement or partitive situation, the following guideline is helpful.

Measurement division	Looking for the number of groups of sets of 7 in 21.	$\square \times 7 = 21$
Partitive division	7 equal-sized groups are to be formed from 21 objects. We must find the number of elements in each group.	$7 \times \square = 21$

Open sentences for division need to be developed with children, particularly at the fourth- and fifth-grade levels. Of course, the examples should follow a concrete, informal approach to division. However, teachers need to know the distinction between these modeling situations. Researchers Grouws and Good (1976) have pointed out the need for these types of number sentences:

> Another important, but often overlooked, role for a mathematical sentence is that of a mathematical model for many perceptually different physical situations. In both the computational and modeling role the ability to solve open sentences is very important. (p. 155)

In summary, introductory division should be concretely modeled with symbols and terminology used minimally. After sufficient concrete and semiconcrete experiences (usually provided by textbook pictures), children can proceed to abstract symbols and alternative ways of writing number sentences. For some special education children, only one symbolic form may be most appropriate.

Basic Multiplication Facts

The basic facts for multiplication can be observed in Table 11.1. Notice that the basic multiplication facts exhibit a commutative property that helps children to memorize and recall the facts. For example, if a child knows that $4 \times 5 = 20$, then the commutative property for multiplication helps the child to realize that $5 \times 4 = 20$. The number of basic multiplication facts to be memorized is reduced from 100 to 55. The commutative property is illustrated in the table by a line segment. The indicated line segment separates the table into two symmetric halves. For example, the result, 12, of $4 \times 3 = \square$ and $3 \times 4 = \square$ appears as a mirror image at equal distances from the line.

Table 11.1 Basic Multiplication Facts

×	0	1	2	3	4	5	6	7	8	9
0	0	0	0	0	0	0	0	0	0	0
1	0	1	2	3	4	5	6	7	8	9
2	0	2	4	6	8	10	12	14	16	18
3	0	3	6	9	(12)	15	18	21	24	27
4	0	4	8	(12)	16	20	24	28	32	36
5	0	5	10	15	20	25	30	35	40	45
6	0	6	12	18	24	30	36	42	48	54
7	0	7	14	21	28	35	42	49	56	63
8	0	8	16	24	32	40	48	56	64	72
9	0	9	18	27	36	45	54	63	72	81

Organizing the multiplication facts for development with children follows the procedure of sequentially teaching the multiples of 1, 2, 3, 4, and so on through the 9s. A sample list of facts for the multiples of 9 is presented here:

$$0 \times 9 = 0 \qquad 5 \times 9 = 45$$
$$1 \times 9 = 9 \qquad 6 \times 9 = 54$$
$$2 \times 9 = 18 \qquad 7 \times 9 = 63$$
$$3 \times 9 = 27 \qquad 8 \times 9 = 72$$
$$4 \times 9 = 36 \qquad 9 \times 9 = 81$$

Several patterns occur in the multiples of 9. Observe that the sum of the digits for each product greater than zero is always 9. Can you find another pattern to this table? Whenever possible use patterns and thinking skills to help children memorize basic facts. For example, notice that the products for the multiples of 5 always end in 0 or 5. Also, the commutative property should be emphasized to help children relate facts to previously learned ones. Finally, thinking skills such as repeated addition should be used to obtain products for troublesome facts.

Numerous activities for teaching children basic multiplication facts are available (see Activities 11.6 through 11.10). Many of the games and activities useful for addition and subtraction practice can be easily adapted for multiplication practice. Ashlock and Washbow (1978) have suggested that practice games should involve a time constraint, provide immediate feedback, and have a minimal penalty for error.

ACTIVITY 11.6 Array Game

This activity, a reinforcement vehicle at the semiconcrete level, can be used to introduce multiplication facts.

Make a table as shown below on transparency acetate. Also make arrays of the basic multiplication facts that you want to practice. Some sample arrays are shown alongside the table.

Place the transparency on an overhead projector. Give an array to each child in the class. Call out a random fact, for example, 5 × 3.

The child who has the array card will place the card in the appropriate place in the table.

As the activity continues, ask children to record the multiplication facts on a sheet of paper.

ACTIVITY 11.7   Math Bingo

This is a useful practice activity for reviewing basic multiplication facts.

Math Bingo is played with two students. Make the following game boards.

×	4	5	6	7	8	9
4						
5						
6						
7						
8						
9						

×	4	5	6	7	8	9
4						
5						
6						
7						
8						
9						

Also construct two cubes with the numerals 4, 5, 6, 7, 8, and 9 on them. A child rolls two cubes and writes the product of the two numbers on the game board. Observing the two numbers that are face up on the cube, a child makes a choice. Suppose, for example, the numbers 5 and 6 appear on the cubes. The child may interpret them as $5 \times 6 = 30$ or $6 \times 5 = 30$. Thus, the product of 30 can be written in two places on the game board. The object of Math Bingo is to achieve the winning result of six products in a row either horizontally, diagonally, or vertically. An element of strategy is thus presented.

ACTIVITY 11.8   Review of Basic Facts Game*

This game, useful with children at the middle-school levels, can be used with children who have mastered the basic facts but need a quick review. The game also involves strategic thinking and is effective with capable elementary and middle-school students.

Construct 45 cards as shown below.

1
1

2	2
1	2

3	3	3
1	2	3

4	4	4	4
1	2	3	4

5	5	5	5	5
1	2	3	4	5

6	6	6	6	6	6
1	2	3	4	5	6

7	7	7	7	7	7	7
1	2	3	4	5	6	7

8	8	8	8	8	8	8	8
1	2	3	4	5	6	7	8

9	9	9	9	9	9	9	9	9
1	2	3	4	5	6	7	8	9

Four students can play the game. A dealer is chosen and the cards shuffled. Five cards are given to each player and one additional card is placed face up on the table. The remaining deck of cards is placed face down on the table.

Suppose this card is the card that is face up: $\boxed{\begin{smallmatrix}7\\2\end{smallmatrix}}$ The player on the dealer's left begins play by examining the card. Four potential operations are possible: addition, subtraction, multiplication, and division. The objective is to match an answer from a card in your hand with an answer on the face-up card. For our example, $7 - 2 = 5$; $7 \times 2 = 14$; $7 + 2 = 9$; no even division result is possible here. Observing the cards in your hand, you might come across this card: $\boxed{\begin{smallmatrix}5\\1\end{smallmatrix}}$. Since $5 \times 1 = 5$ on your card and $7 - 2 = 5$ on the face-up card, you can discard the card labeled $\boxed{\begin{smallmatrix}5\\1\end{smallmatrix}}$. Place this card on top of the $\boxed{\begin{smallmatrix}7\\2\end{smallmatrix}}$ card. Play moves to the next player who now has to find a

combination equal in value to a combination on the $\boxed{\begin{smallmatrix}5\\1\end{smallmatrix}}$ card. If a play cannot be made, then a card is drawn from the leftover stack. The first person to discard all of his or her cards wins.

*Adapted from Arnsdorff, E. (1972). A game for reviewing basic facts of arithmetic. *Arithmetic Teacher, 19,* pp. 589–590. Used with permission of the National Council of Teachers of Mathematics.

ACTIVITY 11.9   Punch and Check Cards

Punch and check cards provide an enjoyable way of practicing basic multiplication facts.

Cards designed to practice certain basic facts are constructed from tagboard. A child places a pencil through the hole near the answer of his or her choice. If the child is correct, a check mark is observed on the rear of the card. A sample card is shown below.

$9 \times 8 =$ ___ 1 27 56 72	$9 \times 7 =$ ___ 16 2 63 56	$9 \times 4 =$ ___ 5 13 28 36	$9 \times 2 =$ ___ 7 11 18 24
$9 \times 10 =$ ___ 19 22 90 8			$9 \times 11 =$ ___ 2 70 49 99
$9 \times 12 =$ ___ 3 21 108 0	Punch and Check		$9 \times 9 =$ ___ 18 0 81 76
$9 \times 1 =$ ___ 9 8 10 0	$9 \times 3 =$ ___ 27 6 12 18	$9 \times 5 =$ ___ 14 45 4 56	$9 \times 6 =$ ___ 54 15 3 72

Punch cards can be made to focus on a particular set of basic multiplication facts. Research suggests that practice focusing on a small number of facts is more successful (Davis, 1978). Thus, we need to diagnose and focus our instructional attention on selected facts.

ACTIVITY
11.10   Tic-Tac-Toe

Ask children to select nine of these numbers and place them on a tic-tac-toe diagram made from tagboard.

8	15	24	36
45	21	14	32
42	6	18	54

Take a set of multiplication flash cards. Call out exercises, such as 7×2. If a student has the product, he or she makes a mark. Play continues until a student has three marks vertically, horizontally, or diagonally. The game can be repeated several times to practice small sets of specific facts.

Basic Division Facts

The operations of addition, subtraction, and multiplication each have 100 basic facts, but division has 90 basic facts. Why? Because division by zero is impossible and thus 10 facts are eliminated from division.

One technique for explaining why division by zero is impossible is to focus on the related multiplication form. For example, $6 \div 2 = \square$ can be written as $\square \times 2 = 6$. We can see that a solution of 3 satisfies both open sentences. However, when we write $6 \div 0 = \square$ as a related multiplication sentence, we have $0 \times \square = 6$. Let us look closely at this related form. We know that any number multiplied by 0 is 0. So, no matter what number we might use to try to solve $0 \times \square = 6$, we can never do so. Therefore, $6 \div 0$ is considered to be impossible.

Another example that explains the impossibility of division by zero can be developed from a measurement division situation.

Imagine a box with eight cubes in it.

If the teacher reaches into the box and takes out two cubes with each grasp, how many reaches into the box need to be performed to empty the box? Four reaches of two marbles will empty the box, thus, $8 \div 2 = 4$.

Consider $8 \div 0 = \square$. This time the teacher will reach in and take zero cubes out with each reach into the box. How many reaches are needed to empty the box? We find that it is impossible to empty the box; thus $8 \div 0$ is impossible.

The 90 division facts that children need to memorize are shown in Table 11.2.

Table 11.2   Basic Division Facts

×	0	1	2	3	4	5	6	7	8	9
0	0	0	0	0	0	0	0	0	0	0
1	0	1	2	3	4	5	6	7	8	9
2	0	2	4	6	8	10	12	14	16	18
3	0	3	6	9	12	15	18	21	24	27
4	0	4	8	12	16	20	24	28	32	36
5	0	5	10	(15)	20	25	30	35	40	45
6	0	6	12	18	24	30	36	42	48	54
7	0	7	14	21	28	35	42	49	56	63
8	0	8	16	24	32	40	48	56	64	72
9	0	9	18	27	36	45	54	63	72	81

As shown in the example in Table 11.2, we must look into the table for the product, to the left for the given factor, and to the top for the missing factor. We have isolated $15 \div 5 = 3$. Notice that the first row of the table portrays the difficulty that occurs when we try to divide by zero, in that we obtain the following list of incorrect answers when we try to extract division exercises from the top row.

$0 \div 0 = 0$ $0 \div 0 = 5$

$0 \div 0 = 1$ $0 \div 0 = 6$

$0 \div 0 = 2$ $0 \div 0 = 7$

$0 \div 0 = 3$ $0 \div 0 = 8$

$0 \div 0 = 4$ $0 \div 0 = 9$

Needless to say, we want a certain degree of consistency when we study mathematics. We would like computational results to provide us with consistent answers. Since division by zero has been shown to be impossible, we must disregard the top row of the table as a vehicle for extracting division exercises. In this way we arrive at a total of 90 basic division facts that children should memorize. (See Activities 11.11 through 11.15.)

Basic division facts are usually arranged like multiplication facts. That is, we first consider those facts divisible by 2, 3, 4, and so on. Also, as noted earlier, some writers stress the strategy of relating division to multiplication. Thus, these facts are studied in relation to one another.

$6 \div 2 = \square$ $3 \times 2 = 6$

$6 \div 3 = \square$ $2 \times 3 = 6$

ACTIVITY 11.11

Board Games

Board games can help small groups of children practice division facts. Essentially, a board game has spaces which allow children to move tokens.

This game requires a numbered spinner and a board, which can be constructed easily from tagboard. A set of division fact cards are made for the facts that you want students to practice.

A child draws a card and, if he or she answers it correctly, moves the number of spaces spun on the numbered spinner. An answer key can be provided so that children can consult it if answers are disputed.

ACTIVITY 11.12

Division Squares

Division squares can be made as shown in the diagram below. The large square can be cut up into smaller squares; children are asked to put the squares together so that edges that touch name the same number.

Row 1:
- Square A: top 5; left $10 \div 2$; right $9 \div 3$; bottom $3 \div 1$
- Square B: left 2; center-top $9 \div 3$; right 3; bottom 2; $15 \div 5$
- Square C: $15 \div 5$; $10 \div 2$

Row 2:
- Square: top 3; $12 \div 2$; 6; $2 \div 1$; $12 \div 3$; 4; 3; 6; $18 \div 3$; 5; bottom 10; $15 \div 3$; 2; $20 \div 10$

Row 3:
- Square: top $10 \div 1$; 10; $20 \div 2$; 5; 2; $8 \div 4$; $18 \div 9$; 7; 2; $14 \div 2$; bottom $5 \div 5$; 2; $16 \div 2$; 2

Row 4:
- Square: top 1; $4 \div 2$; 2; $6 \div 3$; 2; 8; 1; $8 \div 4$; $6 \div 6$

**ACTIVITY
11.13**

Math Marks

Math Marks can be used to provide an enjoyable review of all math operations. It can be played with the entire class.

The object of the game is to be the first player to get five marks in a row, either vertically, horizontally, or diagonally. Make the game board below for each student.

15	9	20	1	0	2
6	24	5	24	10	4
11	12	25	36	15	16
6	4	0	10	8	7
20	1	2	0	30	11
18	5	3	7	3	10
1	8	2	18	9	12

Make three number cubes: two cubes with numerals 1 through 6 on them and one cube with numerals 8, 10, 12, 14, 15, and 18 on it. Roll all the cubes and call out the three numbers. Students must use *two* numbers and decide whether to add, subtract, multiply, or divide them (some division exercises cannot be done because they have remainders). Students record their number sentences and make a mark on their game board. The first player to obtain five in a row wins.

**ACTIVITY
11.14**

Computer-Assisted Division

This microcomputer program, written in the BASIC language, can be used to practice division facts.

```
10    PRINT ''DIVISION PRACTICE''
20    PRINT ''ENTER TWO NUMBERS''
30    PRINT ''THEN FIND THE QUOTIENT.''
40    INPUT A,B
```

```
45    PRINT
50    PRINT ''WHAT IS'';A;''/'';B;''=''
60    INPUT X
70    IF X=A/B THEN 100
80    PRINT ''NOT CORECT . . . ANSWER IS'';A/B
90    GOTO 150
100   PRINT ''GOOD . . . CORRECT!''
150   PRINT ''WANT ANOTHER (YES=1, NO=2)''
160   INPUT Y
170   IF Y=1 THEN 20
180   IF Y=2 THEN 200
200   PRINT ''SEE YOU LATER''
210   END
```

ACTIVITY 11.15

Division Track

This is a large-group division practice game.

Make a transparency with the tracks shown below on it. Also, place a pair of tokens at the start positions.

Take a set of division facts that you want students to practice. Separate the class into two teams. Call out a fact and select a student to answer it. If the child is correct, move the token one space. Repeat this procedure with the other team. Alternate play and ask children to record the division sentences that occur.

Checking Division by Multiplication

As children's study of division proceeds, the mathematical meaning of the checking procedure can be developed. Because multiplication and division are inverse operations, elementary students often are required to check division results by multiplication. For instance, $12 \div 4 = 3$ is deemed to be solved correctly because $3 \times 4 = 12$. Why does this customary check work? Elementary school teachers must be able to explain the checking procedure. We can understand why the procedure works by considering the following problem.

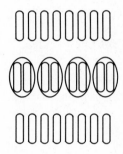

Shown at the left are eight popsicle sticks. We want to solve $8 \div 2 = \square$.

We separate groups of 2 and find that there are four groups of 2. Notice that four groups of 2 can be expressed as 4×2.

Putting the four groups of 2 together yields eight popsicle sticks. Division took our model apart while multiplication reconstructed it.

Again, checking division by multiplication is made possible by an inverse operation relationship, which can be modeled, if necessary, by the strategy developed here.

Summary

This chapter examines the concepts and methods for introducing multiplication and division of whole numbers. Emphasis is placed on strategies that use manipulative material for child involvement or demonstration. The relationship between multiplication and division is shown to be an inverse one. Suggestions for practicing the basic multiplication and division facts are considered. When teaching these operations, especially division, a thorough understanding of the operations is needed before practice at the abstract level is performed.

Discussion Questions

1. Explore and collect activities for using a hand calculator such as the following to enrich the study of multiplication and division.

   A constant for multiplication or division can be developed on the hand calculator. Some calculators require the constant to be entered first whereas others require it to be entered second. For example, punch $8 \div 2 =$ on your hand calculator. You should see a four on the display. Moreover, you have programmed your hand calculator to divide any number by 2. Just enter any number and press the equals button. Here are some examples:

Division Example	Keys Struck
16 ÷ 2	16 =
24 ÷ 2	24 =
40 ÷ 2	40 =

Develop a constant multiplication procedure for your hand calculator.

2. Create two word problems that describe partitive division situations and two more that describe measurement division situations.

3. Research the work of John Napier and learn how to use "Napier's bones" in teaching multiplication.

4. Collect some activities designed to teach students how to estimate products and quotients.

5. Read Robert Kalin's (1983) article, summarize it in a paragraph, and list some of the division facts that are more difficult for children.

6. Construct at least two practice games for reviewing basic division facts. Consult *Ideas from the Arithmetic Teacher,* compiled by George Immerzeel and Bob Wills, available from the National Council of Teachers of Mathematics, 1906 Association Drive, Reston, VA 22091. Other sources may prove helpful as well.

7. Make up a lesson plan for introducing beginning multiplication to children by using Cuisenaire rods.

8. Review a multiplication scope and sequence chart from a textbook publishing company. Be sure that you understand all terms and procedures.

References

Arnsdorff, E. (1972). A game for reviewing basic facts of arithmetic. *Arithmetic Teacher, 19,* pp. 589–590.

Ashlock, R., & Washbow, C. (1978). Games: Practice activities for the basic facts. In Marilyn Suydam (ed.), *Developing computational skills* (pp. 39–50). Reston, Va.: National Council of Teachers of Mathematics.

Bruni, J., & Silverman, H. (1976). The multiplication facts: Once more with meaning. *Arithmetic Teacher, 23,* pp. 402–408.

Davis, E. J. (1978). Suggestions for teaching the basic facts of arithmetic. In Marilyn Suydam (ed.), *Developing computational skills* (pp. 51–60). Reston, Va.: National Council of Teachers of Mathematics.

Grouws, D. A., & Good, Thomas L. (1976). Factors associated with third and fourth grade children's performance in solving multiplication and division sentences. *Journal for Research in Mathematics Education, 3,* pp. 155–171.

Kalin, R. (1983). How students do their division facts. *Arithmetic Teacher, 31*(3), pp. 16–20.

Katterns, B., & Carr, K. (1986). Talking with young children about multiplication. *Arithmetic Teacher, 33,* pp. 18–21.

Laing, R. A., & Meyer, R. A. (1982). Transitional division algorithms. *Arithmetic Teacher, 29,* pp. 10–12.

Lindquist, M., Carpenter, T., Silver, E., & Matthews, W. (1983). The third national assessment: Results and implications for elementary and middle schools. *Arithmetic Teacher, 31,* pp. 14–25.

Richardson, L., Goodman, K., Hartman, N., & LePique, H. (1980). *A mathematical curriculum for early childhood and special education.* New York: Macmillan.

Smith, C. W. (1974). Tiger-bite cards and blank arrays. *Arithmetic Teacher, 20,* pp. 679–682.

Stuart, M., & Bestgen, B. (1982). Productive pieces: Exploring multiplication on the overhead. *Arithmetic Teacher, 29,* pp. 22–23.

Zweng, M. J. (1972). The fourth operation is not fundamental. *Arithmetic Teacher, 16,* pp. 640–642.

CHAPTER 12

Multiplication and Division Algorithms

Objectives

After reading this chapter you will be able to:

1. Model concrete multiplication examples that require algorithmic solutions.

2. Model concrete division examples that require algorithmic solutions.

3. Explain the difference between measurement and partitive division situations.

4. Apply estimation skills to multiplication and division situations.

5. Create and utilize reinforcement materials for practicing multiplication and division.

Introduction

After children develop initial understanding and skill with multiplication and division, mathematics instruction can proceed to more involved algorithms. Children can learn procedures for multiplying and dividing examples such as the following:

$$
\begin{array}{r}
25 \\
\times 16
\end{array}
\qquad
3\overline{)312}
$$

In this chapter we develop techniques for teaching children how to perform multiplication and division of larger-valued numbers. These techniques often involve models and diagrams of real-world situations, which make the operations of multiplication and division more meaningful to students.

Developing Multiplication Algorithms

In this section we consider a variety of multiplication examples (see Activity 12.1) and use concrete models for illustrating the steps in the solution process. The sample sequence for multiplication that appears on page 317 contains specific examples that have been arranged in terms of difficulty; that is, from the simple to the more complex.

ACTIVITY 12.1   Russian Peasant Multiplication

Here is an alternative technique for teaching multiplication. It is called the Russian Peasant Method.

Consider 156 × 85. To calculate the product of 156 × 85, we form two columns. In column A, we start with 156 and successively take *half* of each previous number. Notice that one-half of 39 is 19.5. We *drop* any fractional amount and record the whole number. Again, one-half of 19 is 9.5; however, the whole number, 9, is recorded. We continue until we arrive at 1.

In column B, we start with 85 and successively *double* each number until we reach a number corresponding to 1 in column A. Then, numbers in column B adjacent to *odd* numbers in column A are looped. These numbers are added to obtain the final product. Thus 340 + 680 + 1360 + 10880 = 13,260. This is the product 156 × 85.

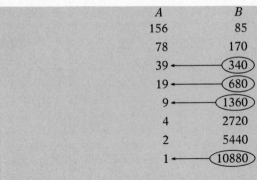

Try this procedure to obtain the product of 136 × 75.

Sample Multiplication Sequence

1. 10
   × 3

2. 20
   × 3

3. 24
   × 2

4. 24
   × 3

5. 211
   × 4

6. 14
   × 12

7. 32
   × 36

8. 734
   × 8

9. 245
   × 67

Let us first consider a concrete model for a number multiplied by 10:

Display 3 tens blocks.

We have shown three groups of 10, or 3 × 10.

Slide the tens blocks together to show 3 × 10 = 30.

Graph-paper models are especially helpful to students working with numbers multiplied by 10. Further, children should manipulate the graph-paper models. In helping them to discover a fast way to get the answer when using paper and pencil, they learn how to generalize results.

Third-grade children should be able to generalize the rules for multiplying numbers by tens and hundreds. Once students have had sufficient experience manipulating concrete objects, they are prepared to multiply numbers by tens using the generalization of placing a zero in the ones place. For example:

$$
\begin{array}{cccc}
10 & 10 & 10 & 10 \\
\times\ 3 & \times\ 4 & \times\ 5 & \times\ 6 \\
\hline
30 & 40 & 50 & 60
\end{array}
$$

After mastering multiplication by tens, other examples can be easily modeled, such as $\begin{array}{r} 24 \\ \times\ 2 \\ \hline \end{array}$. A real-world situation such as the one that follows can be used to illustrate the example. The model also is concrete and can be used for large-group demonstrations.

$$
\begin{array}{r}
24 \\
\times\ 2 \\
\hline
\end{array}
$$

Two children each have 24 stickers. How many stickers do they have combined?

Attach tagboard squares and rectangles with magnetic tape to the chalkboard.

First group of 24.

Second group of 24.

$$
\begin{array}{r}
24 \\
\times\ 2 \\
\hline
8
\end{array}
$$

Ask a child to slide the ones together and record the result.

—Slide ones together.

$$
\begin{array}{r}
24 \\
\times\ 2 \\
\hline
48
\end{array}
$$

Then ask a child to slide the tens together and record the result.

—Slide tens together.

Children should have their own squares and rectangles to model similar exercises at their desks.

Multiplying 1- and 2-Place Numbers

When a 2-place number is multiplied by a 1-place number the computational procedure is performed in the fashion shown in Fig. 12.1 and in the order shown on the next page. This is done in this way because of the *distributive property* of multiplication over addition.

Fig. 12.1

$$2 \times (4 + 20) = (2 \times 4) + (2 \times 20) = 8 + 40 = 48.$$

To demonstrate the distributive property of multiplication over addition we can use models such as the one following, for which we need an overhead projector and round chips of two colors.

⊙ ⊙ ⊙ ⊙ ⊙ ● ● ●
⊙ ⊙ ⊙ ⊙ ⊙ ● ● ●

The first grouping can show either $2 \times (5 + 3)$ or 2 rows of $5 + 3$.

We slide the darker-colored chips to the right so that the design resembles that in the diagram below. Our original figure has thus been altered to show 2 rows of 5 and 2 rows of 3.

⊙ ⊙ ⊙ ⊙ ⊙   ● ● ●
⊙ ⊙ ⊙ ⊙ ⊙   ● ● ●
     (2×5) + (2×3)

Since we did not add or subtract any chips, we can conclude that $2 \times (5 + 3) = (2 \times 5) + (2 \times 3)$.

The distributive property of multiplication is an important concept and should be developed on an individual basis with children if necessary. For students with learning handicaps, it is best to avoid detailed discussions of its significance.

Let us consider another multiplication example, $\begin{array}{r} 15 \\ \times\ 3 \\ \hline \end{array}$, and a concrete model for it.

> There are three boxes of records. Each box contains 15 records. How many records are there?

We need base-10 blocks and an overhead projector to model the situation as follows.

Ask a child to show 3 groups of 15.

$\begin{array}{r} 15 \\ \times\ 3 \\ \hline \end{array}$

Then ask the child to collect ones

$\begin{array}{r} \textcircled{1} \\ 15 \\ \times\ 3 \\ \hline 5 \end{array}$

and then to trade 10 ones for a 10 and to record the results.

Designate in both the model and the numerical recording that the 10 that has been obtained is to be left alone for the moment. It is looped in the diagram.

①
15
× 3
45

Now ask the child to collect the tens, add the regrouped tens, and record the result.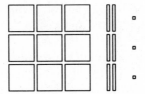

In our example, attention is paid to the regrouped value because the following mistake occurs frequently in this type of multiplication exercise:

①
15
× 3
65

That is, children mistakenly add the looped value and then multiply. Thus, concrete models involving regrouping in multiplication should be developed carefully, explaining clearly each step in the process. Also, graph-paper cutouts are useful in simulating the procedures.

Other materials used for modeling multiplication include the place value pocket chart and the abacus. Consider the following two exercises and the situations used to model them.

321
× 3

Three children work as lifeguards for a month. Each child earns $321. How much did the three children earn together?

Ask a child to collect the ones, then the tens, and finally the hundreds. Thus, there are 9 hundreds, 6 tens, and 3 ones.

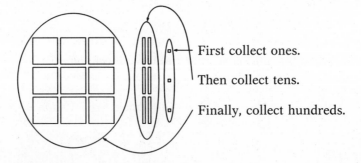

First collect ones.

Then collect tens.

Finally, collect hundreds.

321
× 3
‾‾‾‾
963

The child can then record the results as 963, or $963.

The highest point in Smallville is 424 feet above sea level. The plans for a new building will make it three times as tall as the highest point in the city. What is the height of the new building?

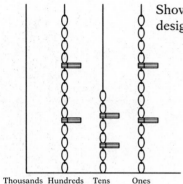

Show three groups of 424 on the abacus. Use clothespins to designate the groups.

Thousands Hundreds   Tens   Ones

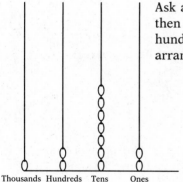

Ask a child to remove the clothespins that separate the groups, and then ask the students to make trades of 10 ones for 1 ten and 10 hundreds for 1 thousand. The beads on the abacus are now arranged to show 1272.

Thousands Hundreds   Tens   Ones

The modeling techniques presented here can be used with individual students, small groups of students, or the entire class. Be sure to incorporate some time for children to work with the materials on their own. Research reviewers Callahan and Glennon (1975) have suggested that at least 50 percent of class time should be devoted to meaningful, developmental work such as that described here, and that sensorimotor teaching strategies and socialization skills should be emphasized in the classroom.

===================== *MATH HISTORY 12.1* =====================

Isaac Greenwood, the first North American to write and publish an arithmetic textbook, used this division process in 1729:

$$
\begin{array}{r}
31 \\
24\overline{)\ 753} \\
-480 \\
\overline{273} \\
-240 \\
\overline{33} \\
-24 \\
\overline{9}
\end{array}
\qquad
\begin{array}{l}
20 \ \text{(twenty-fours)} \\
10 \ \text{(twenty-fours)} \\
\\
\underline{1} \ \text{(twenty-fours)} \\
31 \ \text{(twenty-fours)}
\end{array}
$$

Multiplying Two 2-Place Numbers

Multiplying two 2-place numbers can be concretely modeled. Many elementary textbooks omit a meaningful development of this procedure but elementary school teachers can supplement the textbook by following the strategy outlined here.

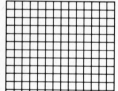

Using tacks, attach graph paper to the bulletin board. The graph paper should have 12 rows of 14 medium-sized squares.

Tell the class, "We have a picture for 12 × 14. Can we count all the squares and find the product? Although counting the squares will give us the product, we can find a better way."

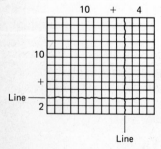

Draw line segments vertically so that 14 = 10 + 4. Likewise, draw a horizontal line segment to show 12 = 10 + 2.

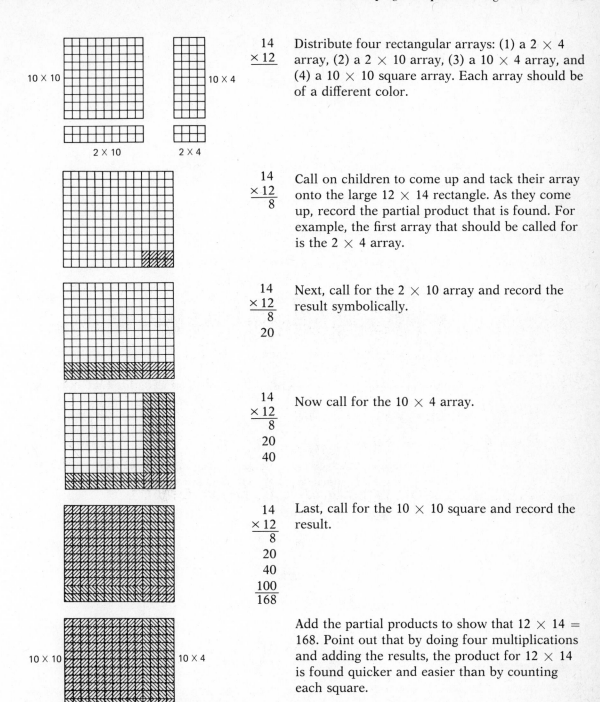

$$\begin{array}{r} 14 \\ \times\,12 \\ \hline \end{array}$$

Distribute four rectangular arrays: (1) a 2 × 4 array, (2) a 2 × 10 array, (3) a 10 × 4 array, and (4) a 10 × 10 square array. Each array should be of a different color.

$$\begin{array}{r} 14 \\ \times\,12 \\ \hline 8 \end{array}$$

Call on children to come up and tack their array onto the large 12 × 14 rectangle. As they come up, record the partial product that is found. For example, the first array that should be called for is the 2 × 4 array.

$$\begin{array}{r} 14 \\ \times\,12 \\ \hline 8 \\ 20 \end{array}$$

Next, call for the 2 × 10 array and record the result symbolically.

$$\begin{array}{r} 14 \\ \times\,12 \\ \hline 8 \\ 20 \\ 40 \end{array}$$

Now call for the 10 × 4 array.

$$\begin{array}{r} 14 \\ \times\,12 \\ \hline 8 \\ 20 \\ 40 \\ 100 \\ \hline 168 \end{array}$$

Last, call for the 10 × 10 square and record the result.

Add the partial products to show that 12 × 14 = 168. Point out that by doing four multiplications and adding the results, the product for 12 × 14 is found quicker and easier than by counting each square.

After a while, the partial products can be condensed to the more conventional approach shown here:

$$
\begin{array}{r}
14 \\
\times\,12 \\
\hline
28 \\
14 \\
\hline
168
\end{array}
$$

Even so, four multiplications are required to solve this exercise. It is important for children to understand the underlying reasons for the computational procedures that they practice.

Sometimes, at the abstract level, examples such as $14 \times 12 = \square$ are solved by considering them as two separate exercises, for example, $14 \times (10 + 2) = (14 \times 10) + (14 \times 2)$.

$$
\begin{array}{rr}
14 & 14 \\
\times\,10 & \times\ \,2 \\
\hline
140 & 28 \quad \text{Add the two results.}
\end{array}
$$

$$168$$

This approach is often used at the intermediate-grade level, prior to practice of computational exercises. It is designed to help children refine their flexibility in viewing numbers. Here children need to recognize that 12 can be written as $10 + 2$. (See Activities 12.2 and 12.3.)

Another strategy for teaching multiplication of larger-valued numbers at the abstract level is to use labeled graph paper in the following manner.

The blocked-in area on the graph paper forces a recording of 10×5 into the appropriate place—the tens place in our diagram.

Hundreds	Tens	Ones
	1	5
	1	6
×		
	9	0
1	5	■
2	4	0

ACTIVITY 12.2   An Application of Multiplication and Division

This is a motivational activity that emphasizes practice of basic addition and division skills. It can be used after students have formally mastered division procedures.

This activity will help you find the day of the week for any month, day, and year since 1752. For example, a person first walked on the moon on July 20, 1969. What day of the week was this?

The following table gives you the numerical values for the months of the year and the centuries.

1725–1799	4	January	1 (0)*	July	0
1800s	2	February	4 (3)*	August	3
1900s	0	March	4	September	6
2000s	6	April	0	October	1
		May	2	November	4
		June	5	December	6

Indicates a leap year.

The next set of procedures is to be followed to obtain the day of the week of the first moon landing.

1. Write the last two digits of the year: 69

2. Divide the result from the first step by 4 (omit the remainder): 17

3. Enter the month code: 0

4. Date of the month: 20

5. Century code: 0

6. Sum of numbers from 1–5: 106

7. Divide the result by 7 (circle the remainder): 15 r1

8. Enter the day for the remainder from the correspondence below.

Sunday	1	Thursday	5
Monday	2	Friday	6
Tuesday	3	Saturday	7
Wednesday	4		

Thus, Sunday was the day of the first lunar walk.

ACTIVITY 12.3 Lattice Method of Multiplication

An alternative algorithm to the traditional multiplication algorithm is the lattice method, first used in Europe in the fifteenth century.

To multiply 84 × 38, we follow these steps.

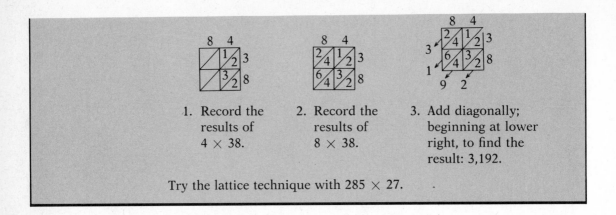

1. Record the results of 4 × 38.

2. Record the results of 8 × 38.

3. Add diagonally; beginning at lower right, to find the result: 3,192.

Try the lattice technique with 285 × 27.

Estimation Strategies for Multiplication

In a technological age, estimating products for multiplication exercises are necessary activities. Hand calculators and microcomputers have reduced the time necessary to do lengthy computational exercises. However, daily-life experiences and the real, if not probable, possibility of technological malfunctions require an ability to estimate products. Let us look at some strategies for estimating products.

Suppose a microcomputer program displays this on the screen:

148 pieces of lumber at $2.50 each, costs a total of $585.50.

Bugs in computer programs occur at times, and students need to recognize this. We could estimate the result by using the distributive property of multiplication over addition in the following manner:

Take 2 × 148 to get 296.
Half of 148 is 74.
The sum of this is about 350.

Thus, the computer program has produced an incorrect result. A detailed look at this result yields the following application of the distributive property.

$$148 \times (2 + 0.50) = (148 \times 2) + (148 \times 0.50)$$

$$= 196 + 74$$

Another estimation strategy is rounding. Consider this situation:

Suppose 385 tickets have been sold for an amateur baseball game at $8 each. How much money has been earned by the amateur baseball team from ticket sales?

385 is about 400.
400 × 8 = 3200.
So, the team made about $3200.

Ample time needs to be allocated for estimation activities. They can be developed throughout the multiplication sequence and provide a worthwhile enrichment of topics. (See Activity 12.4.)

ACTIVITY 12.4   Estimation of Products

There are many different estimating activities available for elementary school students. One classroom strategy is to use a paper bag on which is written an estimation question of the day. Children can drop slips of paper containing their answers into the bag. Here is a sample question that emphasizes a multiplicative procedure:

How many sheets of ordinary notebook paper will you need to write your name 1,000,000 times?

Developing Division Algorithms

In this section we develop techniques for teaching algorithms for division examples. Division is considered to be the most difficult of all the fundamental operations (Laing & Meyer, 1982). To perform division, children need skill in place value concepts, estimation, multiplication, and subtraction. Thus, proficiency with division requires the mastery of several concepts and skills. We can develop these skills by using concrete and semiconcrete material to further children's understanding and retention.

As we begin to develop our techniques for teaching division algorithms, it is helpful to examine a sample sequence of division examples containing some of the major examples used in most elementary school mathematics programs. Some of the examples in the sequence are developed in greater detail with concrete material later in the chapter.

$2\overline{)80}$ Dividing multiples of 10

$2\overline{)48}$ $4\overline{)64}$ $3\overline{)45}$ A 2-place number divided by a 1-place number

$3\overline{)85}$ A 2-place number divided by a 1-place number with a remainder

$6\overline{)126}$ A 3-place number divided by a 1-place number

4)235   A 3-place number divided by a 1-place number with a remainder

3)312   A 3-place dividend with zero difficulty

5)516   A 3-place dividend with zero difficulty and a remainder

7)8792   A 4-place number divided by a 1-place number

8)4589   A 4-place number divided by a 1-place number with a remainder

12)132   32)168   A 3-place number divided by a 2-place number, followed by the same type with remainders

These sample items comprise fundamental division examples that are to be mastered by elementary school students. Most school textbook programs first introduce division examples without remainders. After children have learned to divide exercises such as 6)744, they investigate division of a 3-place number by a 1-place number, which produces a remainder as part of the result.

Modeling Division Examples

Teaching algorithms for division can be done in two ways—a *measurement* or *partitive* approach. Our emphasis here is on the partitive approach because it is more useful in concretely showing the steps of a traditional algorithm such as this:

$$
\begin{array}{r}
31 \\
4{\overline{\smash{\big)}\,124}} \\
\underline{-12} \\
4 \\
\underline{-4} \\
0
\end{array}
$$

Let us consider some of the key examples in the division scope and sequence. To teach 4)48, we can use the following procedures.

Set up four boxes in the front of the room.

We pretend that 48 candy bars are to be distributed equally into four boxes. How many will be in each box? For our modeling purposes, we assume that the candy bars are placed in packages of 10. Thus, we have 4 packages of ten and 8 ones.

Use tens and ones to show 48. Number blocks or proportionally cut-out tagboard may be used.

Call on children to equally distribute the tens among the four boxes.

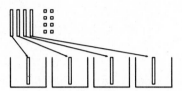

Have other children distribute ones into the boxes. Each box contains 1 ten and 2 ones.

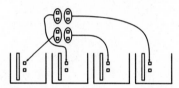

We now repeat this procedure with the recording of the steps of the algorithm, using a similar but slightly more involved exercise. The exercise $3\overline{)45}$ has been chosen because the dividend requires a regrouping from the tens to ones place.

Use 4 tens and 5 ones to show 45.

$$\begin{array}{r} 1 \\ 3\overline{)\,45} \end{array}$$

Separate 3 tens into three groups. There is 1 ten in each group. Record the 1 ten that has been placed in each group.

$$\begin{array}{r} 1 \\ 3\overline{)\,45} \\ -3 \\ \hline 1 \end{array}$$

Multiply 3 × 1 ten and subtract 3 tens. One ten remains to be distributed.

$$\begin{array}{r} 1 \\ 3\overline{)\,45} \\ -3 \\ \hline 1 \end{array}$$

Since we cannot distribute a ten equally to three groups, we exchange a ten for 10 ones, leaving 15 ones. A 5 is brought down to show the exchange.

$$\begin{array}{r} 1 \\ 3\overline{)\,45} \\ -3 \\ \hline 15 \end{array}$$

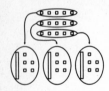

Fifteen ones are distibuted to three groups. We record the distribution of 15 ones. Also, a 5 is placed in the one's place to show that 5 ones have been distributed to each group.

$$
\begin{array}{r}
15 \\
3\,\overline{\smash{)}\,45} \\
-3 \\
\hline
15 \\
-15 \\
\hline
0
\end{array}
$$

The partitive division technique, where we specify the number of sets to be used, is emphasized here to illustrate the concrete model. Of course, students should have tagboard cutouts of hundreds, tens, and ones so that they can actually manipulate and separate objects as they do division exercises at their desks. Remember to link the concrete and semiconcrete images to the actual recording process of the algorithm.

Our next division example is shown in two ways: First as a concrete model using the partitive division approach and then as a measurement approach, which is emphasized as an abstract approach in some current elementary mathematics methods books. A concrete model of $108 \div 4$ using a real-world situation is shown below.

On Halloween 4 children collected 108 pieces of candy. If the candy is to be shared equally, how many pieces will each child receive?

$$4\,\overline{\smash{)}\,108}$$

Ask children if they can equally separate the hundreds piece among 4 boxes. Since they cannot do so, initiate a trade of 10 tens for 1 hundred. The material now looks like this:

$$
\begin{array}{r}
2 \\
4\,\overline{\smash{)}\,108} \\
-8 \\
\hline
2
\end{array}
$$

Two tens have been distributed in each group—8 tens have been shared. Have a child record the numerical result while another makes the distribution of the objects. The concrete material now looks like this:

$$
\begin{array}{r}
2 \\
4\,\overline{\smash{)}\,108} \\
-8 \\
\hline
28
\end{array}
$$

The 8 has been brought down to show a total of 28 ones. Since we cannot share any more tens, we can trade the 2 tens for 20 ones. Thus, the material looks like this:

$$
\begin{array}{r}
27 \\
4{\overline{\smash{)}108}} \\
-8 \\
\hline
28 \\
-28 \\
\hline
0
\end{array}
$$

Have a child separate the 28 pieces into 4 groups. The remaining pieces have been distributed and we record a zero to show this completion. Thus, our model looks like this:

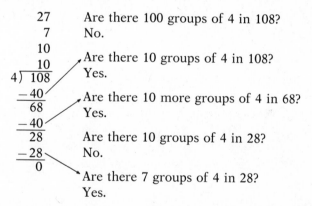

Note that all concrete materials have been distributed.

For best results, children need to use concrete material at their desks to portray the movements of the division process. Also, using pencil and paper, children need to record the results of the computations.

Another possible intermediate technique in the development of the division algorithm is shown by the following measurement division technique, often called a *pyramid algorithm.* This procedure requires minimal knowledge of multiplication facts. Children need only to multiply by tens, hundreds, thousands, and so on.

$$
\begin{array}{r}
27 \\
7 \\
10 \\
10 \\
4{\overline{\smash{)}108}} \\
-40 \\
\hline
68 \\
-40 \\
\hline
28 \\
-28 \\
\hline
0
\end{array}
$$

Are there 100 groups of 4 in 108?
No.

Are there 10 groups of 4 in 108?
Yes.

Are there 10 more groups of 4 in 68?
Yes.

Are there 10 groups of 4 in 28?
No.

Are there 7 groups of 4 in 28?
Yes.

The pyramid procedure is sometimes viewed as a transition to the standard algorithm. However, Kratzer and Willoughby (1973) have reported that children often have difficulty making the transition. Thus, the pyramid procedure is a doubtful technique for bridging the gap between concrete and abstract conceptual steps. Nevertheless, it can be useful with children who have difficulty remembering basic division facts. Thus, it is included here as an alternative for certain children who are unable to remember multiplication and division facts sufficiently for adequate performance of the division algorithm.

Let us use another kind of material to show the partitive division solution to $7{\overline{\smash{)}8799}}$. Maxfield (1974) has shown how play money can be used to illustrate division examples.* We can use play money to show 8799 as we distribute the money into seven equal-sized groups.

*Adapted from Maxfield, M., (1974). Dramatizing division. *Arithmetic Teacher, 20,* pp. 35–38. Used with permission of the National Council of Teachers of Mathematics.

Take 7 children and start passing out money, beginning with the thousands.

$$\begin{array}{r} 12 \\ 7\overline{)8799} \\ -7 \\ \hline 17 \\ -14 \\ \hline \end{array}$$

Each child receives a $1000 bill, and one $1000 bill is left over. We can trade this bill for 10 hundreds, thus giving us 17 hundreds to distribute. We attempt to distribute 17 hundreds to 7 children and find that 14 hundreds have been distributed. Each child has received two $100 bills.

$$\begin{array}{r} 12 \\ 7\overline{)8799} \\ -7 \\ \hline 17 \\ -14 \\ \hline 39 \end{array}$$

Three $100 bills remain that cannot be given to the children. But this can be traded for thirty $10 bills, thus leaving thirty-nine $10 bills for distribution.

$$\begin{array}{r} 125 \\ 7\overline{)8799} \\ -7 \\ \hline 17 \\ -14 \\ \hline 39 \\ -35 \\ \hline 4 \end{array}$$

Each child receives five $10 bills as thirty-five of the thirty-nine bills are distributed. We are unable to share four $10 bills.

$$\begin{array}{r} 1257 \\ 7\overline{)8799} \\ -7 \\ \hline 17 \\ -14 \\ \hline 39 \\ -35 \\ \hline 49 \\ -49 \\ \hline 0 \end{array}$$

Since four $10 bills cannot be distributed among seven students, we trade them for forty $1 bills. We now have 49 ones to give to 7 students. Each student receives 7, and $49 have been distributed, thus completing our task. A zero is recorded to indicate that all the money has been shared. Each child has $1,257.

A troublesome area for some children is a zero difficulty example such as 312 ÷ 3. Sometimes children record an answer such as the following:

$$\begin{array}{r} 14 \\ 3\overline{)312} \end{array}$$

We can use a strategy based on play money to help alleviate this error.

Consider 312 to be shown as:

3 hundreds   [H] [H] [H]

1 ten   [T]

2 ones   [O] [O]

We distribute this money to three people, with each person getting the same amount.

Another situation may be developed in this way:

Suppose three students have sold window ornaments to earn money for the school playground. Each child has earned a bonus for their efforts. We must equally share $312 among these three students.

$$\begin{array}{r} 1 \\ 3\overline{)312} \\ -3 \\ \hline 1 \end{array}$$

Each child receives a $100 bill. Three hundreds have been distributed leaving a $10 bill to be shared. However, we cannot give any children a $10 bill and have an equal sharing. Thus, zero $10 bills are distributed and a zero is recorded in the tens place of the quotient.

$$\begin{array}{r} 104 \\ 3\overline{)312} \\ -3 \\ \hline 12 \\ -12 \\ \hline 0 \end{array}$$

We can, however, trade the $10 bill for 10 ones. Therefore, we pass out 12 ones to three students and each child has $104. The zero at the end of the example shows that we have distributed all of the money.

Zero difficulty division examples need to be carefully developed at the concrete level. Children can use play money to act out division exercises at their desks. Also, creative teaching experiences can be used such as stimulating a business situation. One student might be the company president, another student the banker, and several students the company employees or stockholders. Thus, children can relate zero difficulty division examples, as well as other division exercises, to real-world applications. (See Activities 12.5 and 12.6.)

ACTIVITY 12.5 Analyzing and Correcting Students' Errors

Teachers need to quickly analyze and prescribe corrective work for their students. This activity is designed to help teachers investigate children's work.

Diagnose a child's difficulty with division by analyzing the following solutions to these exercises. Then suggest how you might correct this difficulty.

$$\begin{array}{ccc} 61 & 41 & 53 \\ 4\overline{)424} & 8\overline{)832} & 3\overline{)915} \end{array}$$

More Ways to Diagnose and Correct Students' Errors

ACTIVITY 12.6

> This activity is designed to help you apply the topics of this chapter to the diagnosis and correction of student work.
>
> Find the division procedure that yields the errors in the following division exercises:
>
> $$\begin{array}{c} 211 \\ 6\overline{)346} \end{array} \qquad \begin{array}{c} 234 \\ 2\overline{)168} \end{array} \qquad \begin{array}{c} 114 \\ 4\overline{)371} \end{array}$$

Division with Remainders

Students need to learn that remainders may be dropped, rounded, or represented as fractions or decimals. Most textbook series introduce even division first, followed by a remainder case of the same level of difficulty. For example, children are taught how to solve 28 ÷ 2 and then a remainder case such as 35 ÷ 3 is developed. Both examples, however, exhibit a 2-place dividend and a 1-place divisor.

Generally, remainders are still recorded in the traditional manner shown here:

$$\begin{array}{r} 11 \ r \ 2 \\ 3\overline{)\ 35} \\ -3 \\ \hline 5 \\ -3 \\ \hline 2 \end{array}$$

An innovative way to treat remainders, developed by Connelly and Heddens (1971), emphasizes an application or real-world treatment. For example, suppose three cans of soup cost $1. How much does one can cost? It certainly does not cost 33 r 1¢. Nor does it cost $33\frac{1}{3}$¢. Some real-life situations require a rounding of results. Thus, one can of soup would cost about 34¢. Therefore, one category of real-world applications for remainders involves situations where the remainder is rounded.

Another example of applying remainders to daily life is the following one: Suppose we have 32 boys and girls in a gym class and we want to form teams of three. Obviously we cannot divide 32 by 3 and arrive at an even answer. So, we could choose to have 10 teams of 3 and make the extra two children scorekeepers or referees. In this case, we have dropped the remainder. Our answer to this situation is 10 teams of 3 can be formed from 32 children. Thus, some real-world situations or problems seem to suggest dropping the remainder.

A final example of how to deal with remainders occurs when we consider situations that involve measuring. Suppose we measure 10 meters of fabric and want to form decorations, each decoration to be 3 meters long. We would want to be economical, so each piece would be $3\frac{1}{3}$ meters long. Thus, for measuring situations, yielding remainders as results, fractions, or decimals are used to record results.

Estimation Strategies for Division

Estimation strategies for division can be helpful in two ways: (1) students using the abstract division algorithm can use estimation to help find quotients and (2) application situations can be solved by appropriate use of estimation.

Let us consider these two uses of estimation more closely. For the division example shown below, a student could estimate that 24 could be rounded to 20.

$24\overline{)\,9906}$

$\ \ 4$
$24\overline{)\,9906}$
-96

Since 20 × 4 is 80, a trial quotient of 4 can be tried.

In this case, our trial quotient proved effective. However, an adjustment up or down could be made if this quotient proved to be too large or small. Thus, rounding skills can help students practice division algorithms.

Many current elementary school textbooks emphasize estimation of quotients.

Other examples of estimation in division can be drawn from real-world situations, such as the following. A car costs $15,564.89, including interest on the loan. If 36 monthly payments are scheduled, how much will the owner pay per month? We can estimate the cost by rounding 36 months to 40 months. Also, $15,564.89 can be rounded to $16,000. Thus, $40\overline{)16,000}$ is 400. So, we would estimate the cost to be about $400 per month. Whenever possible, provide real-world examples of estimation for division.

Activity 12.7 offers practice in creating a lesson plan to teach students division, and Activity 12.8 gives a computer program.

ACTIVITY 12.7   Creating a Lesson Plan

Complete the following lesson plan by stating the procedural questions and activities you would use. Also list materials that would be helpful for your lesson.

Objective: To introduce division exercises that emphasize the zero difficulty, such as 3 ÷ 312 and 4 ÷ 424.

Procedure:
Materials:
Evaluation:

ACTIVITY 12.8 Computer Factors

Here is a BASIC computer program that finds all the integer factors of a given number. If you have a microcomputer available, type the program into the computer and see how it works.

```
100    PRINT ''WHAT IS THE NUMBER?''
110    INPUT N
115    PRINT
120    PRINT ''THE FACTORS ARE''
125    PRINT
130    FOR K = 1 TO N
140    LET Q1 = N/K
150    LET Q2 = INT (N/K)
160    IF Q1 = Q2 THEN PRINT K
170    NEXT K
180    END
```

Summary

This chapter presents techniques, models, and examples of multiplication and division algorithms. A sequential approach using concrete models is emphasized. Although textbooks often stress division algorithms at an abstract level, care must be taken by teachers to involve children in concrete, manipulative situations. It is especially important to allow individual children to manipulate objects to gain a thorough understanding of division concepts. Finally, some practice exercises are required to refine and master appropriate multiplication and division skills.

Discussion Questions

1. Diagnose and list some remedial strategies for the errors you find here:

$$
\begin{array}{cccc}
24 & 35 & 16 & 58 \\
\times\,12 & \times\,18 & \times\,11 & \times\,23 \\
\hline
48 & 280 & 16 & 174 \\
24 & 35 & 16 & 116 \\
\hline
72 & 315 & 32 & 290 \\
\end{array}
$$

2. Write a lesson plan for introducing multiplication of 2-place numbers.

3. Develop a concrete model for teaching children 8 × 15. List key questions and draw diagrams to clarify your work.

4. Investigate several current elementary textbook series to determine the techniques used to estimate quotients. Describe the techniques and state your preferred method.

5. On a sheet of squared paper 24 squares wide and 36 squares long, demonstrate that 24 × 36 = 864.

6. Consider the three techniques discussed in this chapter for dealing with division remainders. Write a word problem for each technique.

7. Read Frank Broadbent's (1987) article in *Arithmetic Teacher* on lattice multiplication. Develop several examples of lattice division and share them with your classmates.

8. Explain at least three ways of solving 295 ÷ 35 = □.

References

Ashlock, R. B. (1986). *Error patterns in computation.* Columbus, Ohio: Merrill.

Broadbent, F. (1987). Lattice multiplication and division. *Arithmetic Teacher, 34,* pp. 28–30.

Brueckner, L. J., & Melbye, H. O. (1940). Relative difficulty of types of examples in division with two-figure divisors. *Journal of Educational Research, 33,* pp. 401–414.

Callahan, L. G., & Glennon, V. J. (1975). *Elementary school mathematics: A guide to current research.* Washington, D.C.: Association for Supervision and Curriculum Development.

Connelly, R., & Heddens, J. (1971). "Remainders" that shouldn't remain. *Arithmetic Teacher, 18,* pp. 379–380.

Education Commission of the States. (1983). National assessment of educational progress. *Spring 1983 Newsletter, 11,* pp. 1–2.

Fraser, D. (1980). *Newspaper math.* Palo Alto, Calif.: Dale Seymour Publications.

Hazekamp. D. W. (1978). Teaching multiplication and division algorithms. In M. Suydam (ed.), *Developing computational skills— 1978 yearbook* (pp. 96–128). Reston, Va.: NCTM.

Kratzer, R. O., & Willoughby, M. (1973). Comparison of initial teaching division employing the distributive and Greenwood algorithms with the aid of a manipulative material. *Journal for Research in Mathematics Education, 4,* pp. 197–204.

Laing, R. A., & Meyer, R. A. (1982). Transitional division algorithms. *Arithmetic Teacher, 9,* pp. 10–12.

Maxfield, M. (1974). Dramatizing division. *Arithmetic Teacher, 20,* pp. 35–38.

National Council of Teachers of Mathematics. (1985). *Teacher-made aids for elementary school mathematics: Vol. 2.* Reston, Va.: NCTM.

Suydam, M., & Dessart, D. (1980). Skill learning. In R. Shumway (ed.), *Research in mathematics education* (pp. 207–243). Reston, Va.: NCTM.

CHAPTER 13

Fractions

Objectives

After reading this chapter you will be able to:

1. Model fraction concepts using concrete and semiconcrete materials.

2. Explain prerequisite concepts necessary for effective performance of operations on fractions.

3. Create supplementary learning activities to support the development of fraction number concepts and applications.

4. Explain abstract procedures for performing computations on fractions.

5. Utilize several teacher-made materials for illustrating fraction concepts and applications.

6. Construct several practice activities designed to reinforce concepts and operational understanding of fractions.

Introduction

Rational numbers that can be expressed as fractions, decimals, percents, and ratios are usually emphasized during the intermediate grades. Fractions, still an important part of the elementary school mathematics curriculum, are introduced to children as early as the first or second grade. Needless to say, much experience with concrete objects is necessary to foster a thorough understanding of fraction concepts. This is needed so that a foundation can be built for developing meaningful operations on fractions. For example, research cited in the National Assessment of Educational Progress (1983) describes how 34 percent of the 13-year-olds and 15 percent of the 17-year-olds studied added numerators and denominators for the exercise $\frac{3}{4} + \frac{1}{2} = \square$. These students obtained $\frac{4}{6}$ as an answer. A solid, rich base of understanding prior to the development of operations may help to alleviate this kind of problem.

=== *MATH HISTORY 13.1* ===

The word *fraction* is derived from the Latin word *frangere*, which means "to break."

Beginning Activities and Concepts

Fraction Models

$\frac{1}{4}$

Fig. 13.1

Initially, children need to see fractions represented by concrete objects. Figure 13.1 shows such a technique.

Four tiles of the same shape and size are displayed. One of the four tiles is shaded, thus showing $\frac{1}{4}$. Often, it is helpful to vary the geometric designs that portray fractions. Figure 13.2 shows a circle-shaped paper plate with one of the two equal-sized pieces shaded. Figure 13.3 illustrates a tagboard cutout of a regular hexagon with five of the equal-sized pieces shaded.

$\frac{1}{2}$

Fig. 13.2

A useful method for involving the whole class is to give each child a set of fraction strips. These can be easily constructed from construction paper by cutting out regions to represent fraction values, as indicated in Fig. 13.4. The fraction strips can be placed in envelopes and given to each child in the

$\frac{5}{6}$

Fig. 13.3

the class. The teacher can ask children to display the fraction strip that represents $\frac{1}{6}$. Conversely, one child can hold up a fraction piece and the other children can guess the fraction symbol it represents. Numerous examples using different concrete models, called *continuous models,* are necessary for children to build a firm conception of fractions.

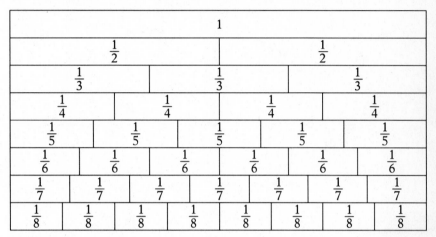

Fig. 13.4

Another type of fraction model is the discrete model. This type of model is used to answer questions such as "Two-thirds of the class brought lunch money. How many students brought lunch money?" The following exercise and diagram are typical of those found in elementary school mathematics textbooks:

Write the fraction for the shaded parts.

        $\frac{3}{5}$

Current elementary school textbooks usually introduce discrete models after continuous models have been developed. Notice the difficulty that can emerge if the following scenario is played out.

A teacher describes to the class that the shaded region in the diagram represents $\frac{1}{2}$ of the circle.

The teacher then explains that the shaded circle represents $\frac{1}{2}$ of the two circles!

Continuous models and discrete models must be taught independently to avoid possible confusion.

Another type of model used to develop the concept of fractions is the number line. Larson (1980) found that less than 20 percent of the seventh graders investigated were able to locate the fraction $\frac{1}{5}$ on the number line shown in Fig. 13.5. Thus, the number line can serve to aid students' understanding of fractional numbers.

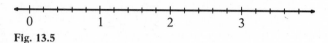

Fig. 13.5

ACTIVITY 13.1   Tic-Tac-Toe Fractions*

Have students complete a tic-tac-toe board by choosing any nine of these fractions:

$\frac{1}{8}$	$\frac{1}{2}$	$\frac{3}{10}$
$\frac{3}{4}$	$\frac{4}{5}$	$\frac{2}{3}$
$\frac{5}{8}$	$\frac{1}{5}$	$\frac{1}{9}$
$\frac{1}{3}$	$\frac{3}{8}$	$\frac{1}{6}$
$\frac{2}{8}$	$\frac{1}{10}$	$\frac{3}{5}$

Make a transparency of the region models pictured on the next page. Randomly point to different regions. Students who have the symbol for the identified region are to make an "X" on their fraction symbol. The first student to obtain three marks in a row, either horizontally, vertically, or diagonally, should announce the result.

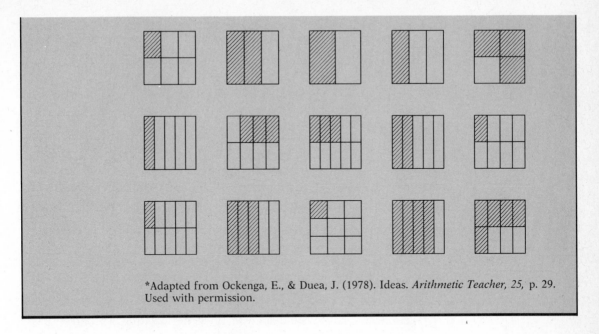

*Adapted from Ockenga, E., & Duea, J. (1978). Ideas. *Arithmetic Teacher, 25,* p. 29. Used with permission.

The Concept of Order

Another beginning fraction concept necessary for children to explore is the *concept of order.* Children need to compare concretely fractions such as $\frac{1}{5}$ and $\frac{1}{3}$ to determine the greater-valued fraction. Again, there are several concrete models available, including the fraction strips described earlier. However, be sure to compare fractions from the same unit base or whole. For example, $\frac{1}{5}$ of 1 million is greater than $\frac{1}{3}$ of 100! Obviously, the unit base that defines the fractions must be the same. Consider the following example.

1			
$\frac{1}{2}$		$\frac{1}{2}$	
$\frac{1}{4}$	$\frac{1}{4}$	$\frac{1}{4}$	$\frac{1}{4}$
$\frac{1}{3}$		$\frac{1}{3}$	$\frac{1}{3}$

Magnetic tape is attached to the back of the pieces shown in the diagram at the left. These can then be displayed on the chalkboard.

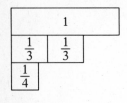

The teacher can show which pieces are to be compared. In our example at the left, $\frac{2}{3}$ is shown being compared to $\frac{1}{4}$. A child can be called on to display $\frac{1}{4}$ and to see that $\frac{2}{3}$ is greater than $\frac{1}{4}$. After numerous experiences, the inequality, or greater than, symbol can be shown: $\frac{2}{3} > \frac{1}{4}$.

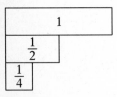

Fig. 13.6

Children can be given fraction pieces to manipulate at their desks to show similar examples. To compare $\frac{1}{4}$ and $\frac{1}{2}$, the pieces in Fig. 13.6 can be manipulated by students. Also, a fraction board can be used to concretely demonstrate order relations among fractions. A rectangular piece of wood, indented to hold wooden fraction pieces, can be constructed as shown in Fig. 13.7. Children observe visual differences in concrete models and eventually can generalize that $\frac{1}{2} > \frac{1}{3} > \frac{1}{4} > \frac{1}{5} > \frac{1}{6} > \frac{1}{7} > \frac{1}{8}$, and so on. For the unit fractions that have been displayed, the generalization is relatively easy. However, for fractions such as $\frac{3}{4}$ and $\frac{2}{7}$, the comparison may not be readily apparent. Again, a concrete device may be used, but in the fifth and sixth grades, it is recommended that an abstract procedure be incorporated.

Fig. 13.7

After numerous concrete experiences, a technique for comparing fractions at the abstract level needs to be developed. Many elementary textbook authors utilize a technique that involves finding common denominators, as shown here:

$$\frac{3}{4} \times \frac{7}{7} = \frac{21}{28}$$

$$\frac{2}{7} \times \frac{4}{4} = \frac{8}{28}$$ Since we have common denominators, we see that $\frac{21}{28} > \frac{8}{28}$.

Thus, $\frac{3}{4} > \frac{2}{7}$.

The development of order relations for fractions is important and needs to evolve from a concrete to an abstract level. At the early elementary school level, most of the development is concrete. However, as children move through the later grades, their abstraction levels increase and provide readiness for abstract experiences. (See Activity 13.1.)

Equivalent Fractions

Equivalent fractions are one of the most important concepts for the development of the operations of addition and subtraction. There are many models used to demonstrate equivalent fractions, including a fraction board. (See also Activities 13.2 through 13.5.) Initially, fractions such as $\frac{1}{2}$, $\frac{2}{4}$, and $\frac{3}{6}$ should be presented. Children can visually compare equivalent fractions by seeing that they represent regions with equal areas. Consider the following problem, which utilizes a fraction board.

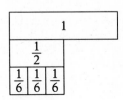

The teacher can choose, for example, the $\frac{1}{2}$ piece, which represents one of the two equal-sized pieces necessary to make up the whole. A child can be called on to find the regions in the fraction board that occupy the same amount of area.

After some exploration, it can be seen that two of the "fourths" pieces can make up one "half" piece. Symbolically, $\frac{1}{2} = \frac{2}{4}$.

Another visual example that can be shown is $\frac{1}{2} = \frac{3}{6}$. Figure 13.8 shows this relationship.

Fig. 13.8

Other materials can be used to show equivalent fractions. For example, a paper-folding activity can illustrate equivalent fractions in a simple, concrete manner.

The teacher gives each student a sheet of paper and asks the class to fold the sheets in half.

Children are told to shade $\frac{1}{2}$ of the region. Next, children can fold the paper again and discover that two of the four regions are shaded.

Folding the paper a third time yields eight regions, four of which are shaded. Children can then see that $\frac{1}{2} = \frac{2}{4} = \frac{4}{8}$.

ACTIVITY 13.2 Trace the Maze

This activity helps children practice the concept of equivalent fractions.

Trace through this maze by entering doors that represent equivalent fractions.

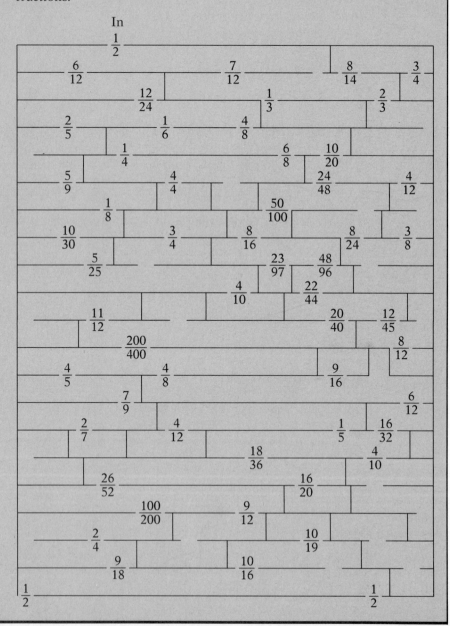

ACTIVITY 13.3   Match the Squares*

This activity helps children to practice the concept of equivalent fractions.

Cut out the squares shown in the diagram. Fit them together so that their edges display the same fractions.

	$\frac{2}{4}$		2		$\frac{7}{10}$		
1		$\frac{12}{36}$	$\frac{2}{10}$		$\frac{1}{8}$	$\frac{3}{7}$	$\frac{2}{3}$
	$\frac{1}{7}$			$\frac{6}{4}$		$\frac{1}{4}$	
			$\frac{5}{3}$		$\frac{2}{14}$		$\frac{2}{6}$
$\frac{4}{24}$		$\frac{8}{10}$		$\frac{4}{4}$ $\frac{2}{16}$	$\frac{10}{16}$ $\frac{2}{4}$		
	$\frac{3}{5}$		$\frac{6}{3}$		$\frac{3}{4}$		
	$\frac{6}{16}$		$\frac{6}{8}$		$\frac{5}{6}$		$1\frac{1}{2}$
$\frac{10}{16}$		$\frac{3}{10}$		$\frac{1}{2}$	$\frac{2}{10}$	$\frac{6}{14}$	$\frac{3}{10}$
	$\frac{4}{12}$				$\frac{7}{10}$		
			$\frac{2}{8}$				$\frac{6}{10}$
$\frac{4}{6}$		$\frac{0}{8}$		$\frac{8}{10}$	0	$\frac{1}{6}$ $\frac{2}{6}$	
	$1\frac{2}{3}$		$\frac{5}{6}$		$\frac{1}{2}$		$\frac{6}{16}$

*Adapted from Immerzel, G., & Wills, B. (1979). *Ideas from the Arithmetic Teacher*, Reston, Va.: NCTM, p. 49. Used with permission.

ACTIVITY 13.4   Match the Popsicle Sticks

This activity is a motivational experience that also helps reinforce the concept of equivalent fractions.

Using popsicle sticks, construct the following pieces.

A	1	2	3	4	5	6	7	8	9
B	2	4	6	8	10	12	14	16	18
C	3	6	9	12	15	18	21	24	27
D	4	8	12	16	20	24	28	32	36
E	5	10	15	20	25	30	35	40	45
F	6	12	18	24	30	36	42	48	
G	7	14	21	28	35	42	49	56	
H	8	16	24	32	40	48	56	64	
I	9	18	27	36	45	54	63	72	

Take any two popsicle sticks and place one over the other, as shown here:

2	4	6	8	10	12	14	16	18
4	8	12	16	20	24	28	32	36

Notice that you have a set of equivalent fractions. Try this with pieces G and I. Do they show equivalent fractions? Try to discover how to add or subtract fractions with these pieces.

ACTIVITY 13.5   Make a Whole*

This game, developed by Joann Rode, helps practice the concept of fractional numbers. It is suggested for use at approximately grade 5*. Children can practice recognition of fractions, equivalent fractions, and to a limited extent, addition of fractions.

The material required for the game is pictured in the diagram below. The sections are made in four different colors and are equally distributed; that is, eight sections representing $\frac{1}{2}$ would have two red, two blue, two green, and two yellow pieces. The area for the "whole" is also prepared in four different colors. The faces of the die are marked with a star and the following fractions: $\frac{1}{2}, \frac{1}{3}, \frac{1}{4}, \frac{1}{6},$ and $\frac{1}{8}$.

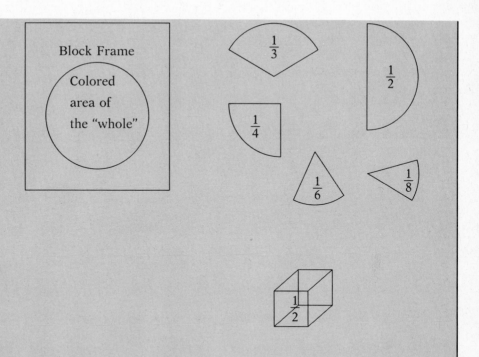

Procedure

The object of the game is to use the fractional sections to construct a multicolored disk—the "whole"—in the black mat frame. The whole may be constructed with any of the colored sections so long as they fit together to make a whole.

Two to eight children can play the game. The color of the area of the whole makes no difference when the game is played in individual competition. If teams are selected, then the whole must be the same color as the color selected by the team of students. The fractional sections are placed in a box, from which they are to be selected by the children as they roll the die, in clockwise order.

The following rules apply to the game:

1. To determine who plays first, each child rolls the die. The child rolling the star or the fraction with the greatest value goes first.

2. At each turn a child must decide whether he or she can use one of the sections represented by the fraction showing on top of the die.

3. If a player cannot use the section, he or she passes.

4. If the player decides to take the section and can use it, it is placed on the child's mat.

5. If the player decides to take a section and cannot use it, his or her next turn is lost.

6. If the player passes up a section that could have been used, he or she loses the next turn.

7. If the star is rolled, the player may choose any section that can be used.

8. The first player to construct a multicolored whole is the winner.

Construction

The pieces described in the following list should be equally divided among four colors.

Mats (8, or 1 for each player)

$\frac{1}{2}$ sections (8)

$\frac{1}{3}$ sections (12)

$\frac{1}{4}$ sections (16)

$\frac{1}{6}$ sections (24)

$\frac{1}{8}$ sections (32)

Die (1)

Tagboard is used to construct the black mat frame and fractional sections. The mats are made by cutting eight 8-inch squares from black tagboard. Disks, 6 inches in diameter, are cut from the center of these squares, and the frames are then glued to other 8-inch squares, two of each of the four colors chosen.

Five disks in each of the four colors are constructed with a diameter of 6 inches. A compass can be used for accuracy. The disks are then divided with the aid of a protractor into sections corresponding to $\frac{1}{2}, \frac{1}{3}, \frac{1}{4}, \frac{1}{6}$, and $\frac{1}{8}$. The central-angle measurements for the five sections are 180°, 120°, 90°, 60°, and 45°, respectively.

The die can be made from a wood cube. Clear varnish or nail polish can be used to laminate the numerals.

*Adapted from Rode, Joann (1971). Make a whole—A game using simple fractions. *Arithmetic Teacher*, 19, pp. 116–118. Used by permission.

Simplifying Fractions

Simplifying fractions can be approached through the use of concrete material. A novel approach developed by Beede (1985), which shows how $\frac{4}{6}$ is transformed into $\frac{2}{3}$, is outlined below.

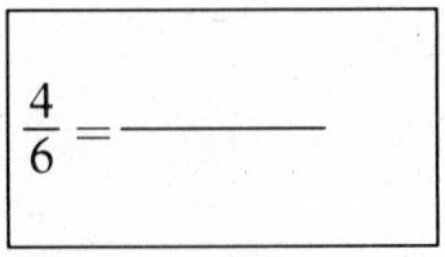

Write a fraction to be renamed on laminated tagboard. The fraction $\frac{4}{6}$ is used here.

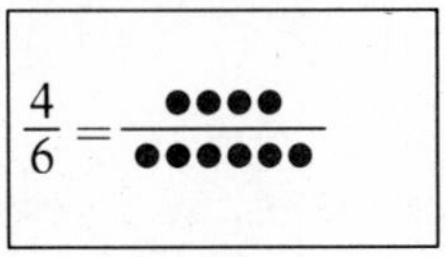

Use chips to express $\frac{4}{6}$. Our example shows four chips in the numerator and six chips in the denominator.

Group the chips representing the numerator and denominator in the largest possible equal-sized groups. Our example shows that groups of 2 can be formed in the numerator and denominator.

Record the result. There are two groups of 2 in the numerator and three groups of 2 in the denominator. Thus, our simplified fraction is $\frac{2}{3}$.

Fraction strips can also be used to demonstrate the process of simplifying fractions (see Fig. 13.9). Sometimes teachers use the term *reducing fractions,* which can be confusing because children think that the "reduced" fraction is smaller. In our example, $\frac{3}{6} = \frac{1}{2}$; that is, the fractions are equal—one is not larger than the other.

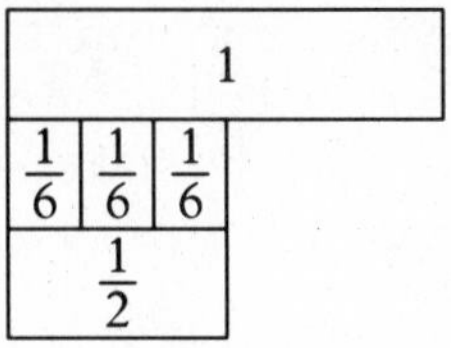

$\frac{3}{6}$ can be traded for $\frac{1}{2}$

Fig. 13.9

Another material that can be used to demonstrate concretely the process of simplifying fractions is a fraction board. Fraction boards can be made of tagboard or wood, as described earlier. Consider the following teacher-child scenario regarding the fraction board method of simplifying fractions.

Teacher: Using our fraction board, locate $\frac{4}{8}$. There are 4 eighths pieces. Can anyone find *one* fraction piece that can cover the 4 eighths pieces?

Child: The $\frac{1}{2}$ piece will cover the 4 eighths pieces.

Teacher's summary: We know that $\frac{4}{8} = \frac{1}{2}$ because we have simplified the picture. Instead of showing 4 eighths pieces, we show 1 of the half pieces. So, $\frac{4}{8} = \frac{1}{2}$. We have reduced the number of pieces yet covered the same amount of area.

This scenario shows how a teacher can use the fraction board to demonstrate the process of simplifying fractions and how children can be led to refine their discoveries of this relationship by manipulating fractional paper strips at their desks.

From Concrete to Abstract Experiences

After concrete, visual experiences, children need to experience abstract ones, such as generating sets of equivalent fractions. An example is shown below.

$$\frac{1}{2}, \frac{2}{4}, \frac{3}{6}, \frac{4}{8}, \frac{5}{10}, \frac{6}{12}, \frac{7}{14}, \cdots$$

At this point children can be shown that multiplying the numerator and denominator by the same number yields an equivalent fraction. A good exercise is to place the first few equivalent fractions and ask students to obtain the rest. For example:

$$\left\{ \frac{1}{3}, \frac{2}{6}, \frac{3}{9}, \underline{\quad}, \underline{\quad}, \underline{\quad}, \underline{\quad}, \underline{\quad} \right\}$$

A technique for simplifying fractions at the abstract level requires the use of the greatest common divisor. Suppose we want to simplify $\frac{6}{8}$. The divisors of 6 can be listed as follows:

$$6 \rightarrow \{1, ②, 3, 6\}$$

For 8 they are the following:

$$8 \rightarrow \{1, ②\, 4 \quad 8\}$$

The greatest common divisor is looped. Thus, we can write $\dfrac{6}{8}$ in the following way:

$$\frac{6}{8} = \frac{2 \times 3}{2 \times 4} = \frac{2}{2} \times \frac{3}{4} = 1 \times \frac{3}{4} = \frac{3}{4}.$$

The greatest common divisor allows us to simplify fractions effectively in a short period of time. Again, a thorough understanding of the concrete process should be developed before the abstract stage is practiced.

Transforming Mixed Numerals to Improper Fractions

Although we could use a fraction board to develop the process of transforming mixed numerals to improper fractions, our example uses common egg cartons. Egg cartons, useful for a variety of purposes, can be used to show such fractional examples as $1\dfrac{1}{2} = \dfrac{3}{2}$.

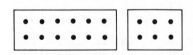 One egg carton and one-half of another show $1\dfrac{1}{2}$.

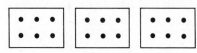 Three half egg cartons show $1\dfrac{1}{2}$.

 Place the three half egg cartons on top of the whole carton and the half carton. Thus, we see that $1\dfrac{1}{2} = \dfrac{3}{2}$.

In summary, the readiness activities presented here utilize fraction strips, fraction boards, egg cartons, and paper-folding to demonstrate fraction concepts. There are other materials that can be used to show fraction concepts; for example, the pie plates that many readers may remember as a model for fractions. Figure 13.10, which shows $\dfrac{1}{4}$, is a pie-shaped model made from a paper plate. All materials should be used by students and demonstrated by the teacher to be effective. Children need to actively manipulate objects in order to extract the meaning of symbols. Similarly, children often need to manipulate a variety of concrete models.

Fig. 13.10

================ *MATH HISTORY 13.2* ================

The practice of writing fractions with the numerator over the denominator appears to have originated with the Hindus, but a dividing line was not in general use prior to the sixteenth century.

Introducing Addition and Subtraction of Fractions

Initially, children begin to work with fractions having the same denominator, such as $\frac{1}{5} + \frac{2}{5}$. Fractional pieces can be used to show that $\frac{1}{5} + \frac{2}{5} = \frac{3}{5}$. Whenever possible, situations drawn from the child's own experience should be incorporated into the lessons. Consider the following problem.

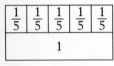

Mary found $\frac{1}{5}$ of the objects on a scavenger hunt. Bob found $\frac{2}{5}$ of the objects. How many of the objects did they find together?

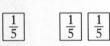

Slide together.

After several experiences moving fraction pieces together, students can be led to the generalization that fractions with like denominators are added by adding the numerator values and placing the result over the denominator. A common error made by students when adding fractions is to add the numerators *and* the denominators:

$$\frac{1}{2} + \frac{1}{6} = \frac{2}{8}.$$

Estimation strategies can help to show students why this answer is incorrect. Since it is reasonable to expect that the answer to this exercise will be greater than $\frac{1}{2}$, we might question the answer of $\frac{2}{8}$, which is less than $\frac{1}{2}$. Thus, estimating the reasonableness of results can be useful in preventing and correcting errors involving addition of fractions.

After children have mastered the task of adding or subtracting two like fractions, the addition and subtraction of unlike fractions can be introduced. Many elementary school textbooks simply instruct students to find the least common denominator without explaining why it is necessary to do so. To develop a rationale for finding the least common denominator, let us consider the example of $\frac{1}{2} + \frac{1}{4}$.

Yellow				1
Orange		Orange		$\frac{1}{2}$
Red	Red	Red	Red	$\frac{1}{4}$

The equivalent fraction pieces can be constructed from colored tagboard. The diagram shows some examples.

Orange $(\frac{1}{2})$	Red $(\frac{1}{4})$

To add $\frac{1}{2} + \frac{1}{4}$, we take the orange piece showing $\frac{1}{2}$ and place it next to the red piece showing $\frac{1}{4}$ (see the diagram to the left). At this point we have an answer but the two different colors make it hard to name the result.

$$\frac{1}{2} + \frac{1}{4} = \frac{3}{4}$$

Orange $(\frac{1}{2})$	Red $(\frac{1}{4})$
Red $(\frac{1}{4})$	Red $(\frac{1}{4})$	Red $(\frac{1}{4})$

$$\frac{1}{4} + \frac{1}{4} + \frac{1}{4} = \frac{3}{4}$$

However, trading the orange piece for two red pieces means we have traded $\frac{1}{2}$ for $\frac{2}{4}$. Thus, the need for a common denominator is established. We need a common denominator because we must have the same-sized pieces when adding fractions. Pieces having the same color helped us to find the common denominator. The answer is now easily named as $\frac{3}{4}$.

After sufficient experience with relatively simple examples at the concrete level, children can learn abstract procedures for adding fractions with unlike denominators. A common procedure for adding or subtracting fractions with unlike denominators is developed by using equivalent fractions. The importance of equivalent fractions cannot be underestimated—a thorough understanding of this concept is vital for success with addition and subtraction of fractions. Often children do not understand the concept well. For example, a British study cited by Driscoll (1985) reported that 40 percent of the 12- and 13-year-olds studied did not understand the concept of equivalent fractions.

A useful readiness activity for finding the least common denominator is the listing of equivalent fractions, described earlier in the section on equivalent fractions. To find the sum of $\frac{1}{5}$ and $\frac{2}{3}$, we would first list fractions equivalent to $\frac{1}{5}$:

$$\frac{1}{5}, \ \frac{2}{10}, \ \left(\frac{3}{15}\right) \ \frac{4}{20}, \ \frac{5}{25}, \ \frac{6}{30}, \ \frac{7}{35}, \ \frac{8}{40} \cdots$$

We would then list fractions equivalent to $\frac{2}{3}$:

$$\frac{2}{3}, \ \frac{4}{6}, \ \frac{6}{9}, \ \frac{8}{12}, \ \boxed{\frac{10}{15}}, \ \frac{12}{18}, \ \frac{14}{21} \ldots$$

By looping the smallest fractions having the same denominator, in our case $\frac{3}{15}$ and $\frac{10}{15}$, the sum of $\frac{1}{5} + \frac{2}{3}$ is shown to be $\frac{13}{15}$. Several current elementary textbooks explain this technique by writing the fractions in the following way:

$$
\begin{array}{r}
\frac{1}{5} = \frac{3}{15} \\
+ \frac{2}{3} = \frac{10}{15} \\
\hline
\frac{13}{15}
\end{array}
$$

Another technique for adding and subtracting fractions involves the use of a number theory concept—the least common multiple. The least common multiple for two numbers can be illustrated by listing the multiples of each number and then looping the least number common to both sets, as shown here:

8:   8, 16, $\boxed{24,}$ 32, 40, 48 . . .
12: 12, $\boxed{24,}$ 36, 48, 60 . . .

When adding two fractions, such as $\frac{1}{6} + \frac{1}{8}$, we can use the least common multiple approach. In fact, the least common multiple for this situation is the desired least common denominator. For example, suppose we want to solve $\frac{1}{6} + \frac{1}{8} = \Box$. First, we would find the least common multiple for 6 and 8.

6:   6, 12, 18, $\boxed{24,}$ 30, 36 . . .
12: 8, 16, $\boxed{24,}$ 32, 40 . . .

The least common multiple serves as the least common denominator for solving $\frac{1}{6} + \frac{1}{8} = \Box$. The completed exercise is shown below.

$$
\begin{array}{r}
\frac{1}{6} = \frac{4}{24} \\
+ \frac{1}{8} = \frac{3}{24} \\
\hline
\frac{7}{24}
\end{array}
$$

Our least common denominator, 24, indicates the denominator of the equivalent fractions that we must form. We can do this by multiplying $\frac{1}{6}$ by 1 in the form of $\frac{4}{4}$. Thus, $\frac{1}{6} \times \frac{4}{4} = \frac{4}{24}$. Also, we can generate an equivalent fraction for $\frac{1}{8}$ having a denominator of 24 by again multiplying by 1. This time the expression is $\frac{3}{3}$. Again,

$\frac{1}{8} \times \frac{3}{3} = \frac{3}{24}$. Since we have the same-sized pieces, we can add the two fractions, yielding $\frac{7}{24}$.

Children in the fourth and fifth grades study addition and subtraction of fractions. During the fifth grade, more emphasis is placed on adding and subtracting mixed numbers. Our remarks for teaching addition of fractions, regarding the use of concrete examples, and the importance of equivalent fractions, are equally applicable for subtraction of fractions. However, there is a slight difference when modeling subtraction examples at the concrete level. Consider the following situation, which we can solve by using concrete materials.

A cat named Tiger is given one can of cat food. Tiger eats $\frac{3}{4}$ of the can for dinner. How much cat food remains?

We can display a region model of 1, or one whole fraction piece. We need to take $\frac{3}{4}$ pieces away. Can we do this with the existing fraction piece? No. Ask the children whether they can exchange the unit piece for 4 fourths.

After doing this, our diagram looks like it does to the left. Have a child remove 3 of the fourths pieces. One-fourth remains. Thus,

$$1 - \frac{3}{4} = \frac{1}{4}.$$

At an abstract level, children draw on the readiness skill of being able to express 1 in many ways. The computation procedure for $1 - \frac{3}{4} = \square$ is shown here:

$$\begin{array}{r} 1 = \frac{4}{4} \\ -\frac{3}{4} \\ \hline \frac{1}{4} \end{array}$$

Another example type often developed in the fifth grade is $1\frac{1}{4} - \frac{1}{2}$. Here we can use tagboard regions with magnetic tape on the back. By doing this, we can use the chalkboard to show a sequence of exchanges. Children can manipulate fraction regions at their desks to parallel the board work. The following problem and diagrams show this concrete, manipulative process.

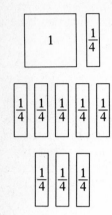

Cathy has $1\frac{1}{4}$ pieces of candy. If she gives Julie $\frac{1}{2}$ piece, how much candy will Cathy have left?

We cannot easily remove a one-half piece from the available concrete material, but we can view $1\frac{1}{4}$ as 5 fourths pieces ($\frac{5}{4}$).

The half piece we wish to remove is the same as 2 fourths pieces ($\frac{2}{4}$). When we remove 2 of the fourths pieces, we are left with 3 fourths pieces.

An abstract computation procedure for the preceding example is shown here:

$$1\frac{1}{4} = \frac{5}{4}$$
$$\frac{1}{2} = \frac{2}{4}$$
$$\overline{\phantom{1\frac{1}{4} =} \frac{3}{4}}$$

In summary, addition and subtraction of fractions, being inverse operations, are usually taught simultaneously. Numerous practice examples should be used to emphasize the concrete and abstract procedures that help children achieve mastery. (See Activities 13.6, 13.7, and 13.8.)

ACTIVITY 13.6 Fraction Baseball

This activity can help children review computational work with fractional numbers.

Construct a baseball diamond design that shows a different fraction at first, second, and third bases. Along the diagonal lines running from home to first base, first to second base, second to third base, and third to home base, write the instructions "add," "subtract," "multiply," and "divide," respectively.

Place the baseball diamond design on the chalkboard. Separate the class into two teams. Make up several cards having fractions on them. Show a child one of the cards. To get to first base, the child must add the fraction to the value at first base. Having done that correctly, another card is displayed. This time the fraction value is subtracted from the value at second base. If the player gets "home" without a mistake, he or she scores a run for the team. A mistake is scored as an out. After three outs, play shifts to the other team. Fractional numerals on the base paths should be changed at the start of each inning.

As is true of many group games, be sure to have each child write down an answer for the exercise given to the batter. This prevents disruption, which often occurs when children have nothing to do.

ACTIVITY 13.7   Fraction Addition

Here is an activity to practice adding fractions.

Materials: Three wooden blocks.

First block $\dfrac{1}{2}$ $\dfrac{3}{3}$ $\dfrac{1}{4}$ $\dfrac{3}{6}$ $\dfrac{1}{8}$ $\dfrac{6}{12}$

Second block $\dfrac{2}{8}$ $\dfrac{3}{4}$ $\dfrac{6}{8}$ $\dfrac{5}{8}$ $\dfrac{6}{12}$ $\dfrac{3}{12}$

Third block $\dfrac{3}{8}$ $\dfrac{5}{8}$ $\dfrac{2}{4}$ $\dfrac{2}{2}$ $\dfrac{7}{8}$ $\dfrac{4}{8}$

Make a game board of tagboard and mark it as shown in the diagram below.

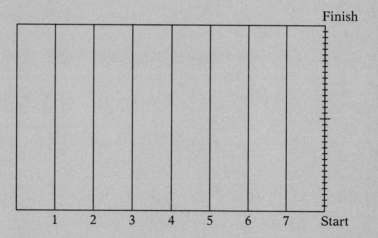

Procedure

Each player chooses a numbered lane on the game board, rolls the blocks, and adds the fractions that turn up. The player moves the correct number of eighths and then awaits his or her next turn. The first player to reach the finish line is the winner of the rally.

ACTIVITY 13.8 Diagnosing Errors

Diagnostic work is an important part of the daily classroom teaching experience. Can you determine the error made by the child who solved these exercises? Can you make some remedial suggestions?

$$5\frac{1}{4} \qquad 6\frac{1}{3}$$
$$-\frac{2}{4} \qquad -2\frac{2}{3}$$
$$5\frac{1}{4} \qquad 4\frac{1}{3}$$

Introducing Multiplication of Fractions

Children exhibit higher achievement on test items dealing with multiplication of fractions than on items dealing with addition and subtraction of fractions. For example, the results of the Third National Assessment of Educational Progress (Lindquist et al., 1983) revealed the following percentage of correct answers for sample subtraction and multiplication items.

$$3\frac{1}{3} - 3\frac{1}{4} \qquad \text{36 percent correct for 13-year-olds}$$

$$\frac{7}{8} \times \frac{5}{3} \qquad \text{60 percent correct for 13-year-olds}$$

An initial example for multiplication of fractions is likely to be that of a whole number multiplied by a fraction, such as $3 \times \frac{1}{2}$. A number line model like the one in Fig. 13.11 can be helpful in illustrating the product.

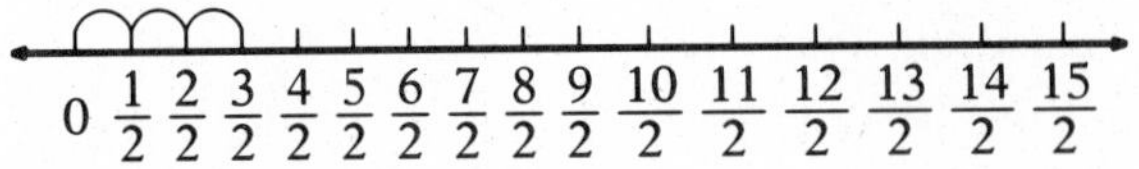

Fig. 13.11

Several examples such as this can help children to discover the following generalization: To multiply a fraction and a whole number, multiply the two numerators and place the product over the product of the two denominators.

$$\frac{3}{1} \times \frac{1}{2} = \frac{3 \times 1}{1 \times 2} = \frac{3}{2}.$$

As children in the fifth and sixth grades progress through multiplication of fractional numbers, they investigate examples such as $\frac{1}{2} \times \frac{1}{6} = \square$. A curious thing happens when the product, $\frac{1}{12}$, is smaller than either of the two factors. Often, elementary teachers will use the word *of* to help children understand the reason for this apparent discrepancy. One-half "of" $\frac{1}{6}$ makes more sense to children and can be explained further by a diagram (see below).

Suppose Billy has a candy bar with six equal parts. He gives Sue one of the parts. Sue then splits the piece into two equal-sized pieces and hands one of the pieces to Bob. Billy asks what part of the original candy bar Bob has received.

A region can be subdivided into sixths. One-sixth is shaded.

One-half of the sixth piece is then shaded. Children can see that the cross-shaded area is $\frac{1}{12}$ of the original region.

The preceding scenario can be acted out with an actual candy bar, many of which have similar proportions to the original example. Children can thus see a relationship to a sometimes abstract process.

Sometimes an overhead projector can be used with transparency overlays to show multiplication of fractional numbers. This technique is shown in the diagrams below.

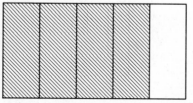

Transparency 1

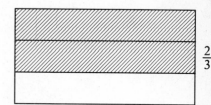

Transparency 2

To show $\frac{2}{3} \times \frac{4}{5}$, place one transparency on top of the other transparency. Two rows of 4 are cross-hatched out of 3 rows of 5 as shown below.

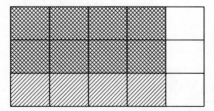

Recalling the array method for demonstrating multiplication of whole numbers yields the following:

$$\frac{2}{3} \times \frac{4}{5} = \frac{2 \times 4}{3 \times 5}.$$

We consider $\frac{2}{3}$ of $\frac{4}{5}$ to be the same as 2 rows of 4 compared to 3 rows of 5. Thus, $\frac{2}{3}$ of $\frac{4}{5}$ is the same as $\frac{8}{15}$.

In summary, multiplication of fractional numbers has widespread applications in daily life. Examples such as those involving changing a cooking recipe of $\frac{2}{3}$ of a cup to $\frac{1}{2}$ of that amount requires multiplication of fractions.

$$\frac{1}{2} \times \frac{2}{3} = \frac{2}{6} \qquad \text{Half of the recipe requirement is } \frac{1}{3} \text{ of a cup.}$$

$$= \frac{1}{3}.$$

Children need to sense how mathematics relates to daily life experiences and to appropriately apply computational skills (see Activity 13.9).

ACTIVITY 13.9 Fractional Magic Square

$3\frac{1}{2}$	0	$2\frac{1}{2}$
1	2	3
$1\frac{1}{2}$	4	$\frac{1}{2}$

Using the fractional magic square shown at the left, try multiplying each number by $\frac{1}{3}$ to see if each row, column, and diagonal yield the same sum. Then try dividing each number by $\frac{1}{4}$ to see if another magic square is found.

Introducing Division of Fractions

Division of fractional numbers, perhaps not as immediately useful as the other three operations, is important for children to learn. For some special education curriculums that emphasize "survival" skills in daily life, this topic could be omitted.

For many students, a cursory, rote rendition of a rule called *invert and multiply* is presented. All too often this method results in a lack of retention and application of the division process for fractions. Our approach here is to provide a meaningful, concrete method for initial examples that require division of fractions for their solution.

A concrete approach for dividing fractions can be developed by first considering the idea of related multiplication examples for division of whole numbers. Reviewing, we know that $6 \div 2 = \square$ can be written as $\square \times 2 = 6$. These number sentences are equivalent because they yield the same numerical answer. When we study division of fractions, we can apply this principle. For example, consider the following situation and teaching scenario.

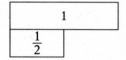

Suppose we have a half piece of candy. How many fourths pieces do we have?

We can solve this by solving the number sentence $\frac{1}{2} \div \frac{1}{4} = \square$. Let us look at this by asking a related question: How many $\frac{1}{4}$ pieces will make up $\frac{1}{2}$?

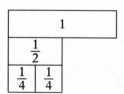

A child can be called on to fit the $\frac{1}{4}$ pieces together to form the region labeled with the fraction $\frac{1}{2}$. Two of the $\frac{1}{4}$ pieces take up the same area as the $\frac{1}{2}$ piece. So, $\frac{1}{2} \div \frac{1}{4} = 2$.

Another example that can be used is $\frac{1}{2} \div \frac{1}{6}$. Initially, examples should be selected that yield simple results. That is, the pieces fit without any further modifications. An example such as $\frac{7}{8} \div \frac{1}{5}$ would not be a good beginning example. As we start to develop division of fractional numbers we are attempting to encourage meaning and understanding. Discovery, intuition, and exploration are to be emphasized rather than rote computational procedures. Let us look at another example, $\frac{1}{4} \div \frac{1}{8} = \square$, to show a visual model and the related multiplication form.

Change $\frac{1}{4} \div \frac{1}{8} = \square$ to $\square \times \frac{1}{8} = \frac{1}{4}$.

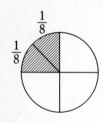

Now we ask how many groups of $\frac{1}{8}$ will make up $\frac{1}{4}$.

Two $\frac{1}{8}$ pieces can be placed over one $\frac{1}{4}$ piece; thus, $\frac{1}{4} \div \frac{1}{8} = 2$.

After several examples in which children explore with concrete materials, we might list some of our results in order to develop a pattern for making a generalization.

$$\frac{1}{2} \div \frac{1}{4} = 2$$

$$\frac{1}{2} \div \frac{1}{6} = 3$$

$$\frac{1}{4} \div \frac{1}{8} = 2$$

Suppose we invert, or as it is sometimes described, take the reciprocal of the divisor and multiply. We obtain the following results:

$$\frac{1}{2} \times \frac{4}{1} = 2$$

$$\frac{1}{2} \times \frac{6}{1} = 3$$

$$\frac{1}{4} \times \frac{8}{1} = 2$$

Children can then discover the principle of inverting and multiplying.

There is also a more abstract way of demonstrating why the procedure of inverting and multiplying works. For many children, the explanation that follows is delayed until sixth or seventh grade. For many special education students, it should be omitted entirely.

Fractions are mathematically considered to be members of the set of rational numbers. This set is defined as follows: $\left\{ \frac{a}{b} \mid a \text{ and } b \text{ are integers and } b \neq 0 \right\}$. The previous mathematical symbolism is saying that a rational number can be expressed as the ratio of two integers where the denominator cannot be zero. Notice that fractions such as $\frac{-2}{3}$, not studied until the seventh or eighth grade, are also considered in this definition. Our purpose, through the elementary years, is to develop an understanding of positive-valued fractional numbers. (See Activities 13.10 and 13.11.)

The rational numbers contain two properties of interest when validating the invert and multiply procedure. First, there is a multiplicative identity, 1. This means any fraction multiplied by 1 yields the original fraction as a product. For example, $\frac{2}{3} \times 1 = 1 \times \frac{2}{3} = \frac{2}{3}$. A second property inherent in the rational number system is the existence of a multiplicative inverse, sometimes called the *reciprocal*. Specifically, the multiplicative inverse of $\frac{3}{4}$ is $\frac{4}{3}$ because $\frac{3}{4} \times \frac{4}{3} = 1$. A number multiplied by its multiplicative inverse yields the multiplicative identity as a result. We can use these two properties to establish the reason why the invert and multiply procedure works. The strategy is explained below for $\frac{2}{3} \div \frac{4}{5}$.

$\dfrac{\frac{2}{3}}{\frac{4}{5}}$

We can write the division of fractions in the way shown at the left. This form is sometimes called a *complex fraction*.

$\dfrac{\frac{2}{3} \times \frac{5}{4}}{\frac{4}{5} \times \frac{5}{4}}$

We want to simplify this somewhat cumbersome expression, so we select the multiplicative inverse of the denominator $(\frac{5}{4})$. This is multiplied to both the numerator and denominator of the original fractions.

$\dfrac{\frac{2}{3} \times \frac{5}{4}}{1}$

Notice that multiplying the numerator and the denominator by $\frac{5}{4}$ means we have multiplied by 1. We now have $\frac{2}{3} \times \frac{5}{4}$, which yields $\frac{10}{12}$, which equals $\frac{5}{6}$ as our result.

ACTIVITY 13.10

Using 4 Threes

This activity can be used as a culminating activity at the conclusion of a unit on fractions. It is a problem-solving task.

Use exactly 4 threes to express each number from 1 through 10. You can use the operations of addition, subtraction, multiplication, and division. The first two exercises have been done for you.

$1 = \frac{3}{3} + (3 - 3)$ $6 = \underline{\hspace{2cm}}$

$2 = \frac{3}{3} + \frac{3}{3}$ $7 = \underline{\hspace{2cm}}$

$$3 = \underline{\hspace{2cm}} \qquad 8 = \underline{\hspace{2cm}}$$

$$4 = \underline{\hspace{2cm}} \qquad 9 = \underline{\hspace{2cm}}$$

$$5 = \underline{\hspace{2cm}} \qquad 10 = \underline{\hspace{2cm}}$$

**ACTIVITY
13.11**

Fractional Time

This problem-solving activity promotes the concept of fractions.

If your doctor gives you three pills and tells you to take one every half hour, how long will the pills last?

Summary

This chapter presents various methods and materials for developing fractions with elementary school children. Emphasis is placed on developing conceptual understanding through manipulation of concrete material. Also, activities to supplement the textbook are provided.

Discussion Questions

1. Prepare a lesson plan for introducing fractions to a first-grade class.
2. Investigate the materials available from commercial suppliers for teaching fractions. Consult several educational supplier catalogs (see Appendix B).
3. Discuss the role of division of fractions in a curriculum serving special education students.
4. Consider the importance of microcomputers, hand calculators, and the metric system in today's society. Recognizing these influences, evaluate the curriculum emphasis that should be placed on fractions and decimals.
5. Construct a concrete learning aid for teaching fractional concepts. Share your materials with your fellow students.

6. Prepare a report on the history of fractions. Consult mathematics history books and relevant journal articles to help you organize your presentation.

7. List some microcomputer software programs available for helping children understand and develop skill with fractions (see Appendix C).

8. Construct five word problems that utilize fractional concepts.

References

Beede, R. (1985). Dot method for renaming fractions. *Arithmetic Teacher, 33,* pp. 44, 45.

Driscoll, M. J. (1985). *Research within reach: Elementary school mathematics.* Reston, Va.: NCTM.

Kennedy, L. (1984). *Guiding children's learning of mathematics.* Belmont, Calif.: Wadsworth.

Larson, C. N. (1980). Locating proper fractions on number lines: Effect of length and equivalence. *School Science and Mathematics, 80,* pp. 423–428.

Lindquist, M., Carpenter, T., Silver, E., & Matthews, W. (1983). The third national assessment results and implications for elementary and middle schools. *Arithmetic Teacher, 31,* pp. 14–25.

National Council of Teachers of Mathematics. (1978). *Developing computational skills.* Reston, Va.: NCTM.

National Council of Teachers of Mathematics. (1979). *Ideas from the arithmetic teacher: Grades 4–6.* Reston, Va.: NCTM.

Ockenga, E., & Duea, J. (1978). Ideas. *Arithmetic Teacher, 25,* pp. 28–32.

Rode, J. (1971). Make a whole—A game using simple fractions. *Arithmetic Teacher, 19,* pp. 116–118.

Seymour, D. (1981). *Developing skills in estimation.* Palo Alto, Calif.: Dale Seymour Publications.

Smith, D. E., & Ginsburg, J. (1972). *Numbers and numerals.* Reston, Va.: NCTM.

CHAPTER 14

Decimal Numeration and Operations

Objectives

After reading this chapter you will be able to:

1. Identify concrete and semiconcrete teaching strategies designed to develop understanding of decimal numeration.

2. Construct models for teaching decimal concepts and operations.

3. Recognize the value of decimal understanding prior to the development of operations.

4. Explain in a meaningful manner fundamental decimal computational procedures.

5. Create activities designed to supplement a textbook unit on decimal numeration.

6. Explain fundamental concepts of exponential and scientific notation.

Introduction

Decimals, another way of representing rational numbers, are commonly developed in the fifth and sixth grades. Although some innovative school mathematics curricula have introduced decimal notation prior to fractions, most elementary textbooks and school mathematics programs favor a sequence that develops fractions before decimals. In today's highly complex, technological world, a thorough understanding of decimal notation is vital. Hand calculators, microcomputers, and increasing use of the metric system of measurement all require a complete understanding of decimal numeration. Thus, in many ways, decimal numeration is perhaps more important than fractional number understanding in today's computer-oriented world.

Although computational procedures for decimals are important, estimation and conceptual skills are often necessary for functioning in the world of daily life. This area needs to be developed through the curriculum for decimal numeration. Research by the National Assessment of Educational Progress (Lindquist et al., 1983) has shown that children need to develop more effective methods for estimating decimal operation results. Only 21 percent of the 13-year-olds tested were able to correctly estimate the product of $3.04 \times 5.3 = \Box$ (Lindquist et al., 1983). Thus, as we emphasize concrete and semiconcrete images to develop decimal understanding of concepts and operations, a parallel concern needs to be the appropriate use of estimation skills for real-world applications. Furthermore, a review of the fourth NAEP assessment (Kouba et al., 1988) indicated that middle school students are lacking in conceptual knowledge about decimals.

=== *MATH HISTORY 14.1* ===

The first book ever published on decimal fractions was written by Simon Stevin and published in 1585.

Beginning Decimal Concepts

Initially, children need concrete and semiconcrete experience with decimal numeration. Centimeter-sized graph paper or number blocks, preferably scored to indicate tenths and hundredths, can be used. In effect, we are developing a new notation and image association. This is shown in the diagram below.

1 —   A unit piece

.1 —   A tenth, since 10 of these make up the whole

.01 — ▫   A hundredth, since 100 of these make up the whole

Beginning decimal experiences should pair decimal symbols with appropriate models. Children can be given graph paper cutouts of decimal regions and asked to display appropriate models for decimal symbols. For example, a teacher can ask to see a model for 2.3 (read as "two and three tenths," not "two point three"). Children can then display the semiconcrete image, as shown in Fig. 14.1.

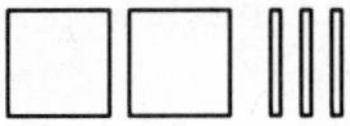

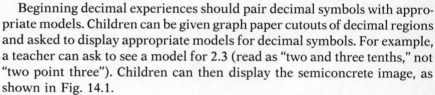

Fig. 14.1

Perhaps a word on our decimal models is in order. Although number blocks and graph-paper models have been used to develop operations for whole numbers, time has gone by so that these same models, appropriately defined, should not cause confusion to children. Decimal numeration is usually developed at least two grade levels after introductory work with whole numbers has been completed.

As we develop initial understanding of decimal numeration for tenths and hundredths, a number line can be used to supplement our modeling technique. Figure 14.2 shows a number line that identifies decimals as distances from a zero point or origin. Children can locate .2 and .5 on the number line. Figure 14.3 illustrates the use of the number line to show .3.

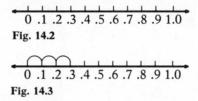

Fig. 14.2

Fig. 14.3

Developing meaning for tenths and hundredths requires more time than some elementary curriculums provide. For example, Zarrojewski (1983) found that fourth-, fifth-, and sixth-grade students were able to understand tenths and hundredths but unable to understand questions pertaining to mixed tenths and hundredths. One of the questions that children had difficulty with was the following:

Which one does not mean .52?
52 hundredths
5 hundredths, 2 hundredths
5 tenths, 2 hundredths

=============== *MATH HISTORY 14.2* ===============

Although there is some disagreement about the introduction of the decimal point, considerable credit is given to John Napier, who, in 1617, recommended the use of a period or a comma as the separator of units and tenths.

Ordering Decimals

Comparing decimals such as .3 and .5 can be performed in a concrete fashion. Simply take decimal strips made of tagboard and then compare .3 and .5. A child can place 3 tenths pieces next to 5 tenths pieces and determine that the 5 tenths pieces take up more area. Thus, .5 > .3. Figure 14.4 shows this comparison. Notice that we need to refer to the same whole region for the comparison to have meaning.

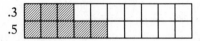

Fig. 14.4

Hundredths can be compared by placing two regions, each having 100 squares, next to each other. Figure 14.5 shows a comparison of .25 and .13.

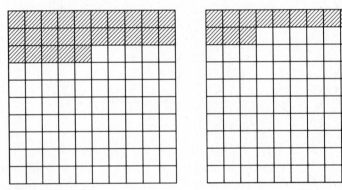

Fig. 14.5

The regions shown can be easily made into overhead projector transparencies. The display of a model for .25 and .13 shows clearly that more hundredth squares are shaded for .25 than for .13. Children thus observe a visual, semiconcrete model rather than hear an abstract comparison. Sometimes money is used as a model for decimals. When comparing the size of .82 and .03, we would refer to the fact that 82 cents is greater than 3 cents. Although money is a natural model for many decimal concepts, the region approach is initially preferred because of its proportional visual qualities.

Many elementary textbook series attempt to teach children thinking strategies for comparing decimals at an abstract stage (see Activities 14.1 and 14.2). For example, suppose we need to compare 46.873 and 46.526. Children are taught to compare in the following way:

46.873   46.526
Tens and ones are the same for both numbers.
Look at the tenths place; since 8 > 5, it follows that 46.873 > 46.526.

ACTIVITY 14.1   Trace a Path of Decimals

This activity helps students to practice decimal order relations.

Trace a path of decimals by entering cells that have a value greater than .4.

5.2	.048	5 hundredths	.2596	.35
.3987	4 hundred 56 thousandths	.58	.03	.1
8 thousandths	1 tenth	0.518	2 hundredths	.25
.01	5 tenths	4.236	.31	8 thousandths
.008	.03	4 thousand 249 ten thousandths	.45871	8.236

ACTIVITY 14.2   Number Accordion

Decimal place value can be reinforced by using this activity.

Make up a number accordion for decimals (see the diagram below). Refer to Activity 4.3 for exact instructions.

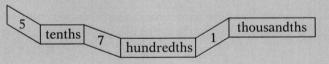

=============== *MATH HISTORY 14.3* ===============

Writers in the sixteenth and seventeenth centuries wrote decimal expressions for 5.912 in the following ways:

5/912
5^{912}
5,912

Equivalent Decimals

Another readiness skill for working with operations on decimals is the understanding of equivalent decimals. For example, .2 = .20 = .200 are equivalent decimals. Teachers can introduce this in a semiconcrete fashion by making overlay transparencies for an overhead projector. Figure 14.6a and b show that .2 = .20. Figure 14.6a has two of the ten equal-sized regions shaded, thus showing .2. Figure 14.6b is then placed over Fig. 14.6a so that the overhead projector displays the visual image shown in Fig. 14.7. Now 20 of the 100 squares are shaded so .20 is shown. Children can be asked some of these questions: How many rows did we shade on the first transparency? What decimal did we show? How many squares are shaded when we put the two transparencies over one another? What decimal is shown? Since we did not place any more shading on the transparencies, what can we conclude?

Discovery lessons using semiconcrete material can help children to understand equivalent decimals (see Activities 14.3 and 14.4). After a while, a generalization for constructing equivalent decimals may be developed. That is, we can generate equivalent decimals by annexing a zero in the place to the right of the decimal numeral. For example, .3 = .30 = .300 = .3000.

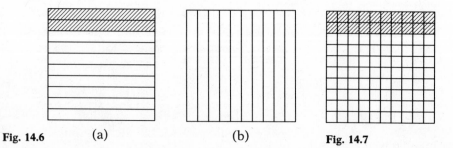

Fig. 14.6   (a)   (b)   Fig. 14.7

ACTIVITY 14.3 Creative Decimal Models

This activity is helpful in relating art and mathematics.

Take a piece of graph paper with 100 squares on it. Show .56 or .23 with the most creative shading of the individual squares that you can think of. Using color, shade the squares and make up some interesting mosaics.

ACTIVITY 14.4 Tic-Tac-Toe Decimals

.8	.71	.6
.1	.53	.77
.24	.3	.41

This activity is designed to practice order relations of decimals.

1. Play by placing an X on a decimal.
2. You win if you get three Xs in a row that are in order (lesser to greater or greater to smaller).

Reading Decimals

It is important that children develop an understanding of decimal place value in order to properly read decimal numerals. In a recent study conducted by the National Assessment of Educational Progress (Lindquist, et al., 1983), only 37 percent of the 13-year-olds tested were able to correctly read .0042 as "forty-two ten thousandths." Often, elementary school textbooks develop a diagram such as that shown in Fig. 14.8 to help children read decimal numerals.

6	3	5	6	7	.	4	8	9	3	2
Ten thousands	Thousands	Hundreds	Tens	Ones		Tenths	Hundredths	Thousandths	Ten thousandths	Hundred thousandths

Fig. 14.8

Thousands	Hundreds	Tens	Ones		Tenths	Hundredths	Thousandths
6	3	5	6	.	8	7	2

Fig. 14.9

Another technique for helping children read decimal numerals is to point out that decimal numerals are symmetric about the ones place, as illustrated in Fig. 14.9.

Notice that one place to the left of the ones place is tens; one place to the right of the ones place is ten*ths.* Likewise, two places to the left of the ones place is hundred place; two places to the right of the ones place is hundred*ths* place. Thus, if a child understands place value for numbers greater than 1, all he or she has to do is count the appropriate places to the right of the ones place and attach a "th" to the corresponding place value term identified on the left side of the ones place.

A hand calculator can be a valuable aid in helping children read decimal numerals. A teacher can orally name a decimal numeral such as "three hundred and fifty-six thousandths." Children can punch the keys of a hand calculator to display a decimal numeral; in this case, .356 will appear on the screen. The children are then asked to replace the 5 on the display with a zero. To do this, a child must see that the 5 occupies the hundredths place and must subtract .05, thus yielding .306. This activity helps children transcribe oral descriptions of decimal numerals to written form. Also, decimal place value is reinforced. (See Activity 14.5.)

Decimal place value can also be expressed in expanded notation form. For example, 256.687 can be expressed as

$$(2 \times 100) + (5 \times 10) + 6 + (6 \times .1) + (8 \times .01) + (7 \times .001).$$

Although this particular form is often not used until the sixth or seventh grade, some children can increase their understanding of decimal numeration by writing decimal numerals in expanded form.

ACTIVITY 14.5 Reading Decimals with a Calculator

This activity helps to reinforce the reading of decimal numbers.

Use a hand-held calculator and have students punch in decimal numerals for the following oral or written decimal numbers. If the translation from oral to numeric form is correct, then turning the hand calculator upside down will yield a word.

1. Eight hundredths
2. Ninety-three hundredths
3. Seven thousand, seven hundred, thirty-four ten thousandths
4. One hundred forty thousandths
5. Seven hundred fifteen thousandths

Transforming Decimal Numbers to Common Fractions

Since decimals and fractions are both representations of rational numbers, children in the fifth and sixth grades need to convert decimal numbers to fractions. Decimals can be expressed as fractions having a denominator that is a multiple of 10. Following are some examples of this equivalence.

$$.1 = \frac{1}{10}$$

$$.2 = \frac{2}{10}$$

$$.01 = \frac{1}{100}$$

$$.001 = \frac{1}{1000}$$

$$.0001 = \frac{1}{10000}$$

Transforming Fractions to Decimals

Another activity emphasized in elementary mathematics curriculums is the task of transforming fractions to decimals. Some textbook series have children generate equivalent fractions having a denominator with multiples of 10. Then the appropriate decimal numeral is written. This technique is shown below.

$$\frac{1}{5} \times \frac{2}{2} = \frac{2}{10} = .2$$

Another common method for changing fractions into decimals is to divide the numerator by the denominator. This can be shown in a meaningful way by observing the following teaching scenario.

Today we will change $\frac{1}{4}$ into a decimal. Since a fraction symbol can mean division of the numerator by the denominator, we can divide 1 by 4. Let's take a $1 bill and share it equally among 4 students. Remember, since we are using decimal notation, we will use denominations of 1 dollar, dimes, and pennies to preserve a multiple of tens relationship. There are no quarters in our bank!

Children, can we give each of 4 students a dollar? No. So, we know that each child will get less than 1 dollar. We will record, just as we do with money, to the *right* of the decimal point.

Can we trade the 1 dollar for 10 dimes? Yes. Let's distribute the 10 dimes to 4 children. Each child has 2 dimes. I have passed out 8 dimes leaving 2. We can make a trade of the 2 dimes for 20 pennies. This amount can be shared among 4 students with each student getting 5 pennies. How much does each student have? Two dimes and 5 pennies.

The preceding teaching scenario shows how a meaningful approach for changing fractions to decimals can be established by using a partitive division process.

It is significant for elementary school teachers to understand that fractions converted to decimals can be of two forms. The resulting decimals may be terminating or nonterminating (repeating).

Terminating	Repeating
$\frac{1}{5} = .2$	$\frac{1}{3} = .33\overline{3}$
$\frac{1}{4} = .25$	$\frac{2}{3} = .66\overline{6}$
$\frac{1}{20} = .05$	$\frac{1}{7} = .\overline{142857}$
$\frac{1}{8} = .125$	$\frac{1}{6} = .16\overline{6}$
$\frac{3}{10} = .3$	$\frac{2}{9} = .22\overline{2}$

Notice that the numerals of the decimal that repeat are indicated by a raised line segment. On closer inspection of the fractions that generate repeating decimals, we note that the prime factors are always multiples of 2 or 5. Remember, a prime number is only divisible by itself and one. Thus, 2, 3, 5, 7, 11, 13, 17, 19 are some examples of prime numbers. The factorizations of the terminating decimals are shown below.

$$\frac{1}{5} \qquad\qquad \frac{1}{5}$$

$$\frac{1}{2 \times 2} \qquad\qquad \frac{1}{4}$$

$$\frac{1}{2 \times 2 \times 5} \qquad\qquad \frac{1}{20}$$

$$\frac{1}{2 \times 2 \times 2} \qquad\qquad \frac{1}{8}$$

$$\frac{3}{2 \times 5} \qquad\qquad \frac{3}{10}$$

Any other prime number appearing in the factorization of the denominator will indicate that the resulting decimal will be one that repeats. Teachers who want to quickly check a child's work can use this principle to aid their observations. Also, a discovery exercise can be developed for use with children. The outlined form is shown below.

Change the following fractions to decimals.

$$\frac{1}{2} = \square \qquad\qquad \frac{5}{6} = \square$$

$$\frac{3}{8} = \square \qquad\qquad \frac{1}{4} = \square$$

$$\frac{1}{7} = \square \qquad\qquad \frac{2}{5} = \square$$

$$\frac{3}{4} = \square \qquad\qquad \frac{1}{11} = \square$$

$$\frac{2}{9} = \square \qquad\qquad \frac{4}{9} = \square$$

$$\frac{1}{8} = \square \qquad\qquad \frac{1}{20} = \square$$

Identify each decimal that repeats and each decimal that terminates. Now, factor all of the denominators into prime factors. When you have done this, see if you can discover a relationship between the factorization of the denominators and the type of decimal numeral obtained.

Addition and Subtraction of Decimal Numbers

Addition and subtraction of decimal numbers, being inverse operations, are usually developed in close proximity in most elementary mathematics textbook series. At the onset, concrete and semiconcrete models are developed for adding tenths and hundredths. Children can be given tagboard regions to model addition of tenths. This is shown below for .3 + .4 = □.

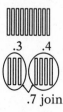

Thus, after concretely manipulating decimal regions, children can obtain sums for examples such as .3 + .4 = .7.

Another model, this one semiconcrete, is a decimal number line. For an example, let us consider .5 + .6 = □ (see Fig. 14.10). The addend of .5 is shown, followed by .6. The resulting movements on the number line show the sum to be 1.1.

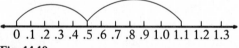

Fig. 14.10

A final model for adding tenths is to use our money system. We can think of .4 as 4 dimes and .8 as 8 dimes. Thus, .4 + .8 can be thought of as 12 dimes with a trade of 10 dimes for $1, yielding a solution of 1.2.

$$\begin{array}{r} .4 \\ +.8 \\ \hline 1.2 \end{array}$$

Although our money system is a good model for decimal operations, caution should be employed when using this material. Money is not a visually proportional material. You cannot fit together or arrange 10 dimes to see 1 dollar. The equivalence of 10 dimes and 1 dollar is a completely abstract process. Thus, for many children, the region model should be used first; after understanding is reached, then money models can be effectively employed.

Modeling addition of decimals having hundredth place value can be performed by using graph paper having 100 squares. Children can be given graph paper and asked to model an example such as .25 + .43. Children can shade 25 squares, followed by 43 squares. As Fig. 14.11 shows, we find that 68 squares out of 100 have been shaded. So, .25 + .43 = .68.

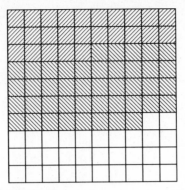

Fig. 14.11

For examples involving regrouping, such as $1.4 + .7 = \square$, a region model that shows units and tenths is best employed. Similar to place value blocks for numbers greater than 1, these blocks are redefined to express decimal values.

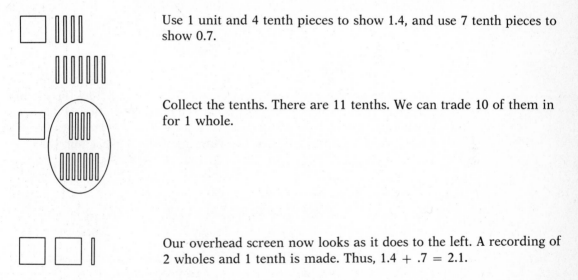

Use 1 unit and 4 tenth pieces to show 1.4, and use 7 tenth pieces to show 0.7.

Collect the tenths. There are 11 tenths. We can trade 10 of them in for 1 whole.

Our overhead screen now looks as it does to the left. A recording of 2 wholes and 1 tenth is made. Thus, $1.4 + .7 = 2.1$.

An example such as $1.43 + 2.81 = \square$ can be modeled using several materials. We will select a region model and follow that with a model based on our money system. Sometimes teachers will place magnetic tape on the back of the pieces to show the actions of the operation on the chalkboard. Children can be called on to manipulate the material and record the computational results.

Situation: Bob ran 1.43 kilometers and his brother Jim ran 2.81 kilometers. How much did they run in all?

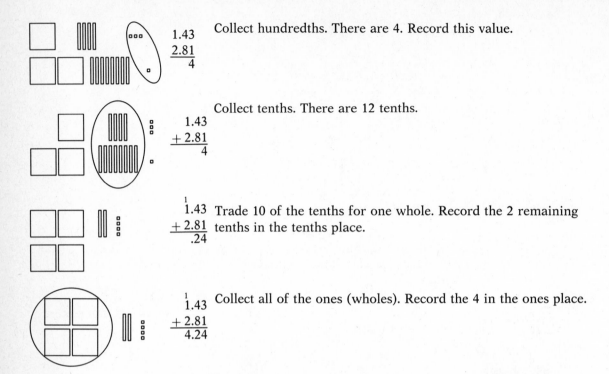

1.43
2.81
—
4

Collect hundredths. There are 4. Record this value.

1.43
+ 2.81
——
4

Collect tenths. There are 12 tenths.

¹
1.43
+ 2.81
——
.24

Trade 10 of the tenths for one whole. Record the 2 remaining tenths in the tenths place.

¹
1.43
+ 2.81
——
4.24

Collect all of the ones (wholes). Record the 4 in the ones place.

We have already mentioned that money is a useful model for decimal concepts. Here, we use money as a tool for modeling addition of decimals. We can think of a decimal numeral such as 2.47 as a representation of 2 dollars, 4 dimes, and 7 pennies. Consider the following teaching situation.

> Bill made $2.47 and $1.95 for his work at home this week. How much did he make in all?

2.47
+ 1.95
——

A teacher can display the following monetary amounts: 2 dollars, 4 dimes, and 7 pennies. Also, 1 dollar, 9 dimes, and 5 pennies.

2.47
+ 1.95
——
2

The cents can be collected (12) by a child and then traded for 1 dime and 2 pennies. Another child can record the result.

2.47
+ 1.95
——
4.42

Next, the dimes can be collected (14) and traded for 1 dollar and 4 dimes. Again, a recording can be made. Finally, the 4 dollars can be collected and the numerical result recorded.

In summary, graph paper, region models, money, and an emphasis on socially significant situations can be presented when developing beginning decimal operations.

Subtraction of decimals can be approached by using the same materials as addition. Consider an example such as 1.5 − .7 = □. Children can be given graph paper regions to act out the solution steps.

> Mary bought 1.5 meters of yarn. She used .7 meters for an athletic award she was making. How many meters of yarn are left?

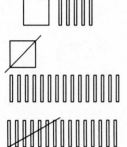

Can we remove 7 tenths from this region model? No.

We can trade a whole region for 10 tenth pieces, leaving 15 tenths.

Removing 7 tenths results in 8 tenths left. Thus, 1.5 − .7 = .8.

Notice that for subtraction of decimals, as with subtraction of whole numbers, we do not show the subtrahend of the amount to be removed. Although there are other ways to model subtraction, particularly a comparison technique that allows for a modeling of a subtrahend, most elementary school textbook authors and journal contributors favor the approach used here.

Estimating computational results should be performed throughout a unit on addition and subtraction of decimals. A common error that children make when adding decimals is illustrated by the following example.

$$\begin{array}{r} 4.526 \\ +\,5.813 \\ \hline 9.1339 \end{array}$$

Here, a child has forgotten to regroup. Estimation can help children see that .526 is about one-half; similarly, .813 is greater than one-half. Thus, their sum must be greater than 1. We can estimate that 9 + 1 = 10 and recognize that the sum of 4.526 + 5.813 should be greater than 10.

For subtraction, a common error is shown below; here, the lesser value is subtracted from the greater value regardless of where it occurs:

$$\begin{array}{r} 2.5 \\ -\ .9 \\ \hline 2.4 \end{array}$$

Again, estimation skills can help direct us toward a correct answer. The subtrahend, .9, can be rounded to 1. Therefore, 2.5 − 1 = 1.5. So, we expect an answer of about 1.5 for this exercise.

Another example of how estimation aids computation occurs when a column of numbers is added. Often, a hand calculator is used to perform the computation (see Activity 14.6). Nevertheless, estimation can help us to check the result and ensure a correct answer. A rounding strategy is most helpful, as the following example shows.

3.8571	Rounded to 4
5.1321	Rounded to 5
3.2131	Rounded to 3
+7.6592	Rounded to 8
	Estimated sum is 20

A final point on adding and subtracting decimals occurs when we consider adding a group of numbers such as .51 + .324 + .1. We usually line up the decimal points as shown below and then add.

.51	.51	= .510
.324	.324	= .324
+.1	.1	= .100

Notice that lining up the decimal points serves as a means of adding the place values. For example, we add tenths to tenths, hundredths to hundredths, and thousandths to thousandths. In effect, we create equivalent decimals as shown in the right column of the preceding equations. For example, .1 or one-tenth is equivalent to .100 or one hundred thousandth. (See Activity 14.7.)

ACTIVITY 14.6 Magic Square

Integrating a hand calculator into a unit on decimals is a valuable experience for students. This activity is an example of how a hand calculator can be used to help students look for patterns and verify hypotheses.

Use a hand calculator to determine if the following square is a magic square.

4.85	4.91	5.3	5.24
5.06	5.27	4.88	5.09
5.21	5.00	5.15	4.94
5.18	5.12	4.97	5.03

Add 5.8 to each number. Do you have a magic square?

ACTIVITY 14.7   Trace a Path

This enrichment activity helps students to practice addition of decimals.

Trace a path through the maze below so that the sum of all the decimal numerals for your path is 1.00.

Start

.3	.5	.89	.3	.7
.91	.1	.6	.83	.41
.6	.3	.25	.31	.33
.4	.1	.61	.22	.91
.5	.2	.39	.12	.8
.83	.714	.62	.5	.01

End

Multiplication of Decimal Numbers

Beginning decimal multiplication examples such as $2 \times .3 = \square$ can be modeled by using decimal pieces.

A teacher can give students decimal pieces. Children show 2 groups of .3. Bring these together to show 6 tenths.

Another vehicle for developing understanding for multiplication of decimals is the number line. In Fig. 14.12, $3 \times .4 = \square$ is modeled as 3 groups of .4.

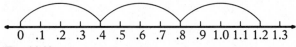

0 .1 .2 .3 .4 .5 .6 .7 .8 .9 1.0 1.1 1.2 1.3

Fig. 14.12

Examples such as $.4 \times .3$ can be modeled in a manner similar to that of fractions. Overhead transparencies can be constructed. Also, region models of tenths made from tagboard can explain examples of this type. The example that follows shows how to construct an overhead projector transparency for the multiplication of two decimals.

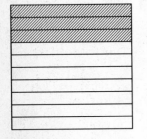

Take a transparency divided into tenths. Shade 3 tenths. Consider .4 × .3 to mean 4 tenths of 3 tenths.

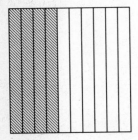

Make another transparency which has 4 tenths shaded in a vertical manner.

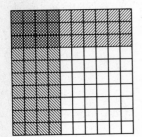

Placing one transparency over another results in the following image: 12 hundreds are cross-hatched; thus, .4 × .3 = .12. In effect, we are showing .4 *of* .3.

A clever adaptation of this model would be to color the 3 tenths blue and the 4 tenths yellow. The overlap or intersection would then be green. Mixing primary colors can be a novel way to develop decimal multiplication.

The same activity can be performed by students at their desks. They can be given graph paper and instructions to show similar examples of multiplication of decimals. After several examples, we would generalize the location of the placement of the decimal point. In our example, an explanation elicited from students might be, "You multiply tenths times tenths to get hundredths."

Another way of helping students to understand a generalization for the placement of the decimal point when multiplying decimals is to write the decimals as fractions.

1.58 × .5 = ☐

$$1.58 = 1\frac{58}{100} = \frac{158}{100}$$

$$.5 = \frac{5}{10}$$

Thus, $\frac{158}{100} \times \frac{5}{10} = \frac{790}{1000} = .790.$

The result of 1.58 × .5, solved by expressing the decimals as fractions, is then converted back to a decimal numeral, .790. A generalization developed after several examples might be the following: To locate the decimal point when multiplying decimals, for each numeral count the number of decimal places to the right of the decimal point, and then find the sum of the decimal places and use it to place the decimal point of the product. (See Activity 14.8 for a way to practice this technique.)

Multipling by 10, 100, and a 1000 is another important skill for developing understanding of multiplication of decimals. This can be shown by using tagboard regions, as shown in Fig. 14.13. In this way, 10 groups of 2 tenths, 10 × .2, is shown to be 2. As other examples are developed, a pattern will emerge: to multiply a decimal by 10, simply move the decimal point one place to the right.

10 × .2

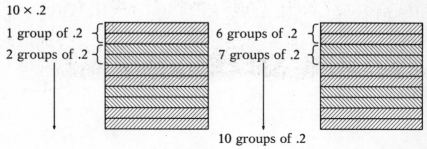

1 group of .2
2 groups of .2

6 groups of .2
7 groups of .2

10 groups of .2

Fig. 14.13

10 × .2 = 2

10 × .3 = 3

10 × .4 = 4

10 × .5 = 5

10 × .6 = 6

Multiplying a decimal number by 100 follows a similar pattern:

$100 \times .25 = 25$

$100 \times .36 = 36$

$100 \times .02 = 2$

$100 \times .43 = 43$

$100 \times 2.5 = 250$

Here the pattern is to place the decimal numeral two places to the right of the original number. In general, multiplying a decimal number by a multiple of 10 requires a placement of the decimal point the same number of places to the right of the original point as there are zeros in the multiple of 10. For example, a placement of one place occurs when multiplying 10, two places when multiplying by 100, three places when multiplying by 1000, and so on.

Estimating decimal products is commonly developed in current fifth- and sixth-grade textbook series. A rounding strategy seems most appropriate, especially when estimating products of decimals before using a hand calculator to perform the actual computation.

$$\begin{array}{r} 2.87 \\ \times\, 5.32 \\ \hline \end{array}$$ Rounded to 3
Rounded to 5
Product estimate is 15

ACTIVITY 14.8   Spinning Decimals*

This activity promotes practice in adding and multiplying decimals.

For this game you need two spinners, two sheets of paper, and two pencils. The spinners should look like this:

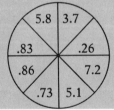
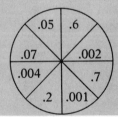

> ### Rules
>
> 1. Players alternate play. For a given turn, spin both spinners at once.
>
> 2. Multiply the two decimal numbers.
>
> 3. Add the same numbers.
>
> 4. Your score for that round is the sum of the digit in the tenths place of the product (step 2) and the digit in the tenths place of the sum (step 3).
>
> 5. Keep a running score. Play five rounds. The winner is the player whose total score is the largest.
>
> *Adapted from Bright, G., & Harvey, J. (1982). Using games to teach fraction concepts and skills. In Silvey, L., & Smart, J. (eds.), *Mathematics for the middle grades*. Reston, Va.: NCTM, pp. 205–216. Used with permission.

Division of Decimal Numbers

Dividing a decimal by a whole number can be explored, initially, by using concrete material. Consider the following example, which uses region models and partitive division for its solution:

$$4\overline{)12.48}$$

A diagram of 12 unit or whole pieces, 4 tenth pieces, and 8 hundredth pieces is shown below, and a realistic situation for this example is developed.

A total of 12.48 kilograms of ice cream is to be shared by four baseball teams. How many kilograms of ice cream will each team get?

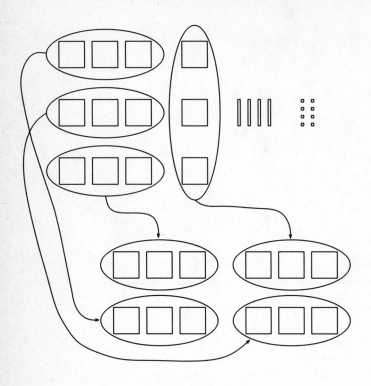

Students can record the distribution of 3 whole pieces into 4 groups.

$$3$$
$$4\overline{)12.48}$$
$$\underline{-12}$$
$$4$$

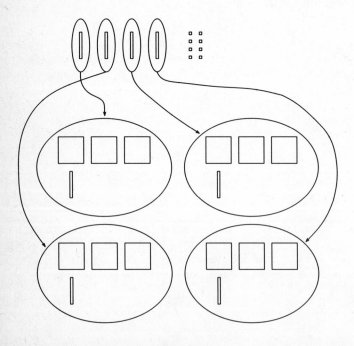

Next, we distribute the tenths and have students record the result.

$$3.1$$
$$4\overline{)12.48}$$
$$\underline{-12}$$
$$4$$
$$\underline{-4}$$
$$8$$

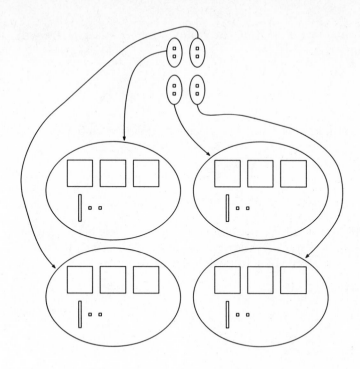

Finally, the
remaining
hundredths are
distributed and the
result recorded.

$$
\begin{array}{r}
3.12 \\
4\overline{)\,12.48} \\
-12 \\
\hline
4 \\
-4 \\
\hline
8 \\
-8 \\
\hline
0
\end{array}
$$

Thus, each baseball team will get 3.12 kilograms of ice cream.

Again, a partitive division process where objects are separated into a predetermined number of groups is preferred for showing division of decimals.

Although regions could be used to show a division that requires placement of a zero in the dividend, we use money to show an alternative way of modeling.

$$4\overline{)\,7.4}$$

Suppose that you are given 7 dollars and 4 dimes. This money must be shared equally by four friends. How much will each person receive?

$$
\begin{array}{r}
1. \\
4\overline{)\,7.4} \\
-4 \\
\hline
3
\end{array}
$$

First we share as many dollars as we can, equally distributed among the four friends. Each person receives 1 dollar and 4 are distributed, leaving 3 dollars.

$$
\begin{array}{r}
1.8 \\
4\overline{)\,7.4} \\
-4 \\
\hline
34 \\
-32 \\
\hline
2
\end{array}
$$

Since we cannot distribute 3 dollars equally, we will trade them for 30 dimes; thus, 34 dimes are left for sharing. We can give 8 dimes to 4 people, leaving 2 dimes.

$$\begin{array}{r} 1.8 \\ 4\overline{)7.4} \\ \underline{-4} \\ 34 \\ \underline{-32} \\ 20 \end{array}$$

Since we cannot equally distribute 2 dimes among 4 people, we will trade them for 20 pennies.

$$\begin{array}{r} 1.85 \\ 4\overline{)7.4} \\ \underline{-4} \\ 34 \\ \underline{-32} \\ 20 \\ \underline{-20} \\ 0 \end{array}$$

The 20 pennies are distributed to 4 people, leaving each person with 5 pennies. All 20 pennies have been distributed and each friend has 1 dollar, 8 dimes, and 5 pennies.

Dividing by 10, 100, and 1000 is another fundamental topic in the elementary mathematics curriculum. Patterns are helpful in observing the placement of the decimal point as the following examples show.

$$123.89 \div 10 = 12.389$$

$$12.389 \div 10 = 1.2389$$

$$1.2389 \div 10 = .12389$$

When dividing a decimal number by 10, the decimal point is moved one place to the left in the numeral. Similarly, when dividing by 100, the decimal point is moved two places to the left. For decimal numbers divided by 1000, the decimal point is moved three places to the left.

Our final example for dividing decimal numbers considers a case in which the divisor is a decimal, but before doing the example we need a brief review.

$$\frac{2}{1} = \frac{20}{10} = \frac{200}{100} = 2.$$

Equivalent fractions can be generated by multiplying both numerator and denominator by the same number. When we write a fraction, we can consider this to mean an indicated division. We use this technique to solve the following decimal exercise.

A fishing boat brought back 14.7 kilograms of sponges. If the average weight of each sponge was 0.07 kilograms, how many sponges were found?

$$\frac{14.7}{.07} \times \frac{100}{100} = \frac{1470}{7} = 210.$$

$$\begin{array}{r} 210. \\ .07\overline{)14.70.} \\ \underline{-1470} \\ 0 \end{array}$$

So, when we move the decimal point in the divisor and dividend, we are really multiplying both numbers by a multiple of 10. Children need to see a meaningful explanation of why the decimal point is moved when dividing decimal numbers (see Activity 14.9). Research has shown that children retain for a longer period of time computational rules that are developed from a meaningful, understandable approach. (Glennon & Callahan, 1968).

ACTIVITY 14.9 Math Rummy

This card game can relate fractions and decimals.

The game is played with a deck of 52 cards. Two, three, or four players can play the game. To make the cards, make a list of 13 different values, each of which has four equivalent forms. Some samples are shown here:

$$\frac{1}{2}, .50, \frac{8}{16}, .5$$

$$\frac{1}{5}, .20, .2, \text{two-tenths}$$

The object of the game is for a player to lay all of his or her cards on the table. Each player is dealt seven cards. The top card is placed faceup and forms the discard pile.

The player to the left of the dealer plays first. He or she may either pick up the top card on the discard pile or draw the top card from the pack. The player then discards a card of choice and the play goes to the next player.

Play continues until one player has accumulated three cards of equivalent value. Then that player may lay them faceup on the table. The player who draws the fourth equivalent value of a set that has been played may lay the single card faceup. When the pack disappears, the discard pile is turned over and becomes the pack.

The first player to have all of his or her cards faceup on the table, except for a possible discard, is the winner of that hand. Players receive five points for each card they have on the table and are deducted five points for each card still in their hands. The first player to reach a score of 100 is the winner.

Estimating Decimal Quotients

A valuable skill that needs to be developed when introducing decimal division is the estimation of quotients. We consider two strategies here—the rounding strategy and that of estimating a sensible answer. A rounding strategy is shown in the following example.

$$4.2\overline{)15.6}$$

The divisor (4.2) can be rounded to 4.
The dividend (15.6) can be rounded to 16.
Thus, $16 \div 4 = 4$, so we expect the quotient for $15.6 \div 4.2$ to be about 4.

Estimating a sensible answer is most helpful when solving word problems involving decimal numbers.

Laura paid $285.45 for paint. If each can of paint was $12.36, how many cans of paint did she buy? Which of the answers below indicates the most sensible result?

1. 23   2. 230   3. 2.3

Exercises such as these can be developed throughout a unit on decimals (see Activities 14.10 and 14.11). Most current elementary mathematics textbook series develop estimation topics such as rounding and reasonableness of results.

ACTIVITY 14.10

Calculator-Assisted Estimation

This activity integrates the hand calculator with estimation experiences.

Take 20 seconds to estimate answers to these real-world problems. Then check your results with a hand calculator. Were you a good estimator?

1. A candleholder made of silver weighs 2.13 kilograms. If silver is worth $8.86 a kilogram, how much is the candleholder worth?

2. One pair of socks costs $3.25. Can you buy six pairs with $15?

3. Gasoline costs $1.14 a gallon. If you buy 12.3 gallons, how much will you pay?

4. There are 14,876 people at a football game. Each person paid $4.25 for a ticket. How much money was collected?

ACTIVITY 14.11   Estimating to Find the Problem

Loop the exercises that yield the correct answers. You must estimate here. No pencils are allowed, but you may use a hand calculator to check your work.

Exercises			Answers
3.8 × 4.1	20.82 − 12.31	5.31 + 8.3	15.58
18.36 ÷ 5.21	12.6 ÷ 3	5.32 − 1.48	4.2
4.9 + 3.2 + 8.6	22.83 − 6.28	14.55 − 2.9	11.65
18.32 + 6.18	13.35 + 7.1	18.5 + 3	20.45

Make up several more examples.

Exponential and Scientific Notation

Powers of ten, also referred to as *exponential notation,* are often introduced at the middle school level (grades 6–8). Consider the following patterns.

$$10 = 10 = 10^1$$

$$.1 = .1 = 10^{-1}$$

$$10 \times 10 = 100 = 10^2$$

$$.1 \times .1 = .01 = 10^{-2}$$

$$10 \times 10 \times 10 = 1000 = 10^3$$

$$.1 \times .1 \times .1 = .001 = 10^{-3}$$

$$10 \times 10 \times 10 \times 10 = 10000 = 10^4$$

$$.1 \times .1 \times .1 \times .1 = .0001 = 10^{-4}$$

When using powers of ten, sometimes called exponential notation, a base (in our examples, 10) and an exponent can be identified. The exponent tells us how many times the base is to be multiplied. For example, $10^2 = 10 \times 10$; thus, the base of ten is used as a multiplier two times. For 10^3, the base of ten is used as a multiplier three times.

When dealing with negative exponents, a fundamental law of exponents is used, as shown below.

$$10^{-1} = \frac{1}{10^1}$$

$$10^{-2} = \frac{1}{10^2}$$

$$10^{-3} = \frac{1}{10^3}$$

Therefore, 10^{-2} is an expression for $\dfrac{1}{10^2} = \dfrac{1}{100}$ or hundredths place. Likewise, $10^{-3} = \dfrac{1}{10^3} = \dfrac{1}{1000}$, and is seen to be an expression for thousandths place.

Using expanded notation and powers of ten helps us to write a decimal number such as 218.953 in the following way:

$$(2 \times 10^2) + (1 \times 10^1) + (8 \times 1) + (9 \times 10^{-1}) + (5 \times 10^{-2}) + (3 \times 10^{-3})$$

Scientific notation allows us to write large or small numbers in a compact and efficient manner. It is often considered an enrichment topic at the elementary school level and given more attention at the seventh- and eighth-grade levels.

Consider the following example.

900,000 can be written as 9×10^5 in scientific notation. When a number greater than 1 is written in scientific notation, we move the decimal point to the left.

9.00000

9×10^5

Move the decimal point five places to the left to make a number between 1 and 10. The number of places that we have moved the decimal serves as the exponent of 10.

Another example for a number greater than 1 is shown here:

5.86000000

$586,000,000 = 5.86 \times 10^8$

We move the decimal point eight places to the left to form a number between 1 and 10 (5.86) from 586,000,000.

For numbers greater than zero but less than one, a similar approach is used. But here we must move the decimal point to the right to form a number between 1 and 10. Consider the following example.

0.00003 can be written in scientific notation as: 3×10^{-5}.

00003,

$3 \times 10^{-5} = .00003$

We move the decimal point five places to the right to form a number in scientific notation between 1 and 10. Since our original number was less than 1, we have a negative exponent.

Another example shows how numbers less than 1 but greater than zero can be written in scientific notation. Once again, the exponent of 10 will be negative because the original number is less than 1.

.0045

.004.5 Exponent is $^{-}3$

$4.5 \times 10^{-3} = .0045$

Scientific notation has wide applications in many fields of science. For example, Earth is 150,000,000 kilometers from the sun. In scientific notation, this is 1.5×10^8 kilometers.

Summary

This chapter develops the key topics involved in a unit on decimal numbers. Concrete and semiconcrete models are emphasized with particular reference to region graph paper and money models. Throughout the chapter a learning hierarchy of decimal concepts and operations is developed. Activities designed to enrich and supplement textbook examples are provided. Also, because decimal numeration concepts and operations can be taught independently of fractions, reference to fraction numbers is limited. Our modeling techniques emphasizes decimal numeration models.

Discussion Questions

1. Draw diagrams to show $5.46 + 1.39 = \square$. List key questions and procedures in the process.

2. Draw diagrams to show $2.31 - .58 = \square$. Again, list key questions and procedures in the process.

3. Write a lesson plan for teaching an introductory lesson on decimal multiplication.

4. Create four word problems in solving decimal numbers.

5. Construct at least two of the games or activities developed in this chapter.

6. Research some of the catalogs available from suppliers of educational materials and find some microcomputer software that introduces or reviews decimal concepts and operations (see Appendixes B and C).

7. Read the article by Reys (1985) and prepare a set of mental computation exercises pertaining to decimal numeration.

8. Prepare a bulletin board display showing the importance of decimals in our technologically oriented society. Consider the influences of the metric system, hand calculators, and microcomputers.

References

Bright, G. W., & Harvey, J. G. (1982). Using games to teach fraction concepts and skills. In L. Silvey and J. Smart (eds.), *Mathematics for the middle grades (5–9)*, pp. 205–216. Reston, Va.: NCTM.

Driscoll, M. J. (1985). *Research within reach: Elementary school mathematics.* Reston, Va.: NCTM.

Glennon, V. J., & Callahan, L. G. (1968). *A guide to current research: Elementary school mathematics.* Washington, D.C.: Association for Supervision and Curriculum Development.

Grossnickle, F. E., Reckzeh, J., Perry, L. M., & Ganoe, N. S. (1983). *Discovering meanings in elementary school mathematics.* New York: Holt, Rinehart & Winston.

Jacobson, M. H. (1983). Teaching rational numbers—Intermediate grades. *Arithmetic Teacher, 31,* pp. 40–42.

Kouba, V., Brown, C., Carpenter, T., Lindquist, M., Silver, E., & Swafford, J. (1988). Results of the fourth NAEP assessment of mathematics: Number, operations, and word problems. *Arithmetic Teacher, 35,* pp. 14–19.

Lindquist, M. M., Carpenter, T. P., Silver, E. A., & Matthews, W. (1983). The third national mathematics assessment: Results and implications for elementary and middle school. *Arithmetic Teacher, 31,* pp. 14–19.

National Council of Teachers of Mathematics. (1983). *The agenda in action.* Reston, Va.: NCTM.

Reys, R. (1985). Estimation. *Arithmetic Teacher, 32,* pp. 37–41.

Underhill, B. (1981). *Teaching elementary school mathematics.* Columbus, Ohio: Merrill.

Yeager, D. C. (1985). *Decimal story problems.* Palo Alto, Calif.: Creative Publications.

Zawojewski, J. (1983). Initial decimal concepts: Are they really so easy? *Arithmetic Teacher, 30,* pp. 52–56.

CHAPTER 15

Ratio, Proportion, and Percent

Objectives

After reading this chapter you will be able to:

1. Introduce initial ratio and proportion experiences to children.

2. Develop meaningful visual models for introducing the concept of percent.

3. Explain the use of ratio and proportion when solving percentage problems.

4. Construct learning games designed to develop skill with percent concepts.

5. Use estimation strategies to help calculate everyday uses of percents.

Introduction

Rational numbers can be expressed as fractions, decimals, and percents. A rational number is one that can be expressed in the form $\frac{a}{b}$ where a and b are integers and b is not equal to zero. The application of rational numbers as percents is often taught in grades 6–8.

The concept of percent is used throughout our culture and especially in personal and business matters, such as home and auto loans, test scores, statistics, and department store sales. Even though a knowledge of percents is required for effective functioning in our culture, there is evidence that the concept is not understood well by many students. Evidence from a recent study (NAEP, 1983) shows that only 14 percent of the 13-year-olds tested were able to correctly answer the following item:

> A store is offering a 15-percent discount on fishing rods. What is the amount a customer will save on a rod regularly priced at $25?

In view of this finding, more time should be devoted to teaching percents and more meaningful models should be provided in the instruction. However, before we consider the methods for teaching percents, we need first to examine the readiness concepts of ratio and proportion.

=== *MATH HISTORY 15.1* ===

In 1481, Giorgio Chiarino, an Italian writer, used "XX per C." to mean 20 percent. The use of percentages was well established by the fifteenth century.

Introducing the Concepts of Ratio and Proportion

A *ratio,* usually expressed as a fraction, compares two quantities. Some common examples of ratios include miles per hour, meters per second, words per minute, and cost per pound. For example, to express as a ratio "five pencils for 86 cents," we would write the fraction $\frac{5}{86}$, thus indicating the comparison.

A concrete example of a ratio situation can be shown by placing two sets of chips as shown below.

4 black chips   ● ● ● ●

8 white chips   ○ ○ ○ ○ ○ ○ ○ ○

Thus, $\frac{4}{8}$, a fraction, shows the comparison of black chips to white chips.

Sometimes, a good teaching strategy is to describe a ratio using one number, such as "It rains *half* of the days of the year in Caribou, Maine." Children are then asked to identify which quantities are being compared (Usisken & Bell, 1984).

A *proportion* exists when there are two equal ratios. Numerous examples of proportions can be found in everyday situations. For example, often nature photographers take pictures so that the sky occupies about one-third of the area of the photo and the ground about two-thirds. Consider the example in Fig. 15.1 of a photo with a 3-inch height and an enlargement with a 6-inch height.

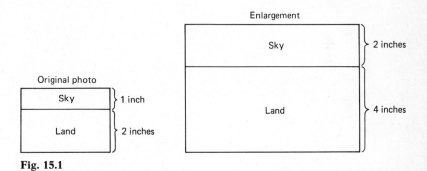

Fig. 15.1

In the original photograph, the area of the sky is $\frac{1}{3}$ of the total area; in the enlargement it is $\frac{2}{6}$. A proportion for this relationship is $\frac{1}{3} = \frac{2}{6}$.

Other examples of proportions can be found in scale drawings and maps. See, for example, Fig. 15.2.

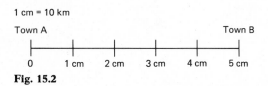

Fig. 15.2

Suppose that town A is 5 cm from town B, as in the figure. Since 1 cm represents 10 km, we know that town A is 50 km from town B. A more abstract mathematical statement for this proportion is shown below.

$$\frac{1 \text{ cm} \longrightarrow 1}{10 \text{ km} \longrightarrow 10} = \frac{5 \longleftarrow 5 \text{ cm}}{x \longleftarrow x \text{ km}}$$

Proportions have an interesting quality—the cross products are equal:

$$\frac{1}{2} \bowtie \frac{2}{4}$$

$$1 \times 4 = 2 \times 2$$
$$4 = 4$$

Thus, if we have a proportion with an unknown value, we can cross-multiply to help us find the unknown.

$$\frac{3}{8} = \frac{n}{16}$$

$$3 \times 16 = 8 \times n$$

$$48 = 8 \times n$$

$$\frac{48}{8} = \frac{8}{8} \times n$$

$$6 = 1 \times n$$

$$6 = n$$

Obviously, we could simply look at this example and find the value. However, in many cases, when the unknown value turns out to be a decimal or fraction, this procedure helps to identify the unknown.

Ratios and proportions are valuable mathematical concepts, independent of the study of percents. Nevertheless, our focus here is on one particular adaptation that helps children understand the concept of percent.

================= *MATH HISTORY 15.2* =================

The symbol for percent (%) first appeared in an Italian manuscript dated 1425.

Introducing the Concept of Percent

Percent, derived from the Latin, means "per hundred." The following problem demonstrates why we need to use percents.

The Indian Hills school district sold raffle tickets to obtain money for school sports equipment. The following graph shows each school's predetermined goal and the actual funds collected from the sale of the raffle tickets. Each block represents $5.

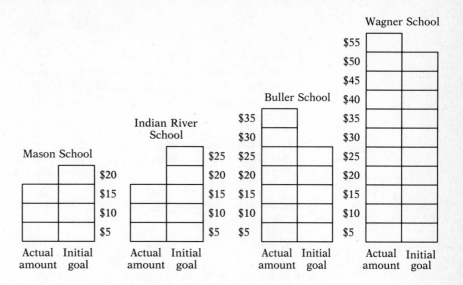

How can we determine which school performed the best? By "best," we can only mean the school that most nearly met its initial goal. Since each school had a different goal, comparison is difficult. Also, one school may have had certain advantages over the others of which we are not aware, such as being larger than the other schools and able to sell raffle tickets to a greater proportion of the community. Thus, our limited information makes comparison difficult. However, let us examine the following table, which lists the information we do have—ratios that show the amounts earned in the numerators and the initial goals in the denominators:

	$\dfrac{A}{}$	$\dfrac{B}{}$	$\dfrac{C}{}$
Mason School	$\dfrac{15}{20}$	$\dfrac{75}{100}$	75%
Indian River School	$\dfrac{15}{25}$	$\dfrac{60}{100}$	60%
Buller School	$\dfrac{35}{25}$	$\dfrac{140}{100}$	140%
Wagner School	$\dfrac{55}{50}$	$\dfrac{110}{100}$	110%

Notice that column A does not tell us which school did the "best" because the initial goals are different. However, in column B, where equivalent fractions with 100 as the denominator are shown, we can more readily compare each school's performance. It is clear that the Buller School overachieved its goal, earning 140 percent of its targeted amount, followed by the

Wagner (110 percent), Mason (75 percent), and Indian River (60 percent) schools.

The preceding example shows how the use of percent helps us to compare quantities that are at first unclear. By transforming nonequivalent ratios into equivalent ratios with denominators of 100, we can easily make comparisons. Consider also the following example.

County A	*County B*
Of 125 people in the county, 45 voted for Malcolm Smith as governor.	Of 521 people in the county, 178 voted for Malcolm Smith as governor.

We can compare the two counties' voting preferences by using percents.

County A	*County B*
36 percent voted for Smith	34 percent voted for Smith

Thus, the voting preferences in the two counties were rather close.

The words *percent* and *percentage* are often confused. Suppose a store has discounted certain items by 33 percent. The rate or *percent* is 33; the actual dollar amount of quantity that is found is the *percentage*. (See Activity 15.1.)

ACTIVITY 15.1   Misleading Uses of Percents

Percents are often used in daily life, and sometimes in misleading ways. Children at the middle school level need to become aware of the consumer issues related to percent.

Suppose a television advertiser made this statement for a toothpaste company: "People who use our toothpaste have 40 percent fewer cavities than people who use competing brands."

Criticize this statement by identifying the misleading nature of the advertisement.

Patterns are also helpful in determining percent as a ratio. For example, suppose we want to develop the meaning of percent by finding the percent of *a*s in the word *Manhattan*. A table can help us approximate the percent as a special ratio with a denominator of 100.

Number of Words	Number of a's	Number of Letters	Ratio
1 Manhattan	3	9	$\frac{3}{9}$
2 Manhattans	6	18	$\frac{6}{18}$

3	Manhattans	9	27	$\dfrac{9}{27}$
10	Manhattans	30	90	$\dfrac{30}{90}$
11	Manhattans	33	99	$\dfrac{33}{99}$
12	Manhattans	36	108	$\dfrac{36}{108}$

We observe that $\dfrac{33}{99}$ occurs when we have 11 of the words *Manhattan*. Thirty-three letter a's compared to 99 letters give us approximately 33 percent.

Patterns such as the preceding one can help children obtain a comprehensive meaning of percent as a special ratio with a denominator of 100.

Consider this a final example, designed to show children how to illustrate the concept of percent using graph paper made of 100 small squares. Figure 15.3 shows two examples of graph-paper models for percent. In Fig. 15.3a, 8 of the 100 squares are shaded. Thus, $\dfrac{8}{100}$ is 8 percent. In Fig. 15.3b, 25 of the 100 squares are shaded. Thus, $\dfrac{25}{100}$ is 25 percent.

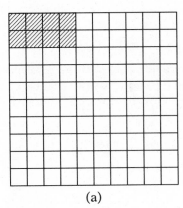 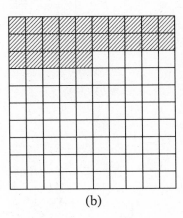

(a)   (b)

Fig. 15.3

Using Ratios to Solve Percent Problems

Solving problems dealing with percent can be performed rather easily by the use of ratio and proportion. Consider the following situation.

On Tuesday, the fourth-grade class brought pets into class. There were 25 students in the class and 16 pets. What percent of the class brought pets?

We know that if there were 100 students in class, $\frac{n}{100}$ would tell us the percent of the class that brought pets. A ratio for the 16 pets compared to the class of 25 is $\frac{16}{25}$.

Thus, $\frac{16}{25} = \frac{n}{100}$. In effect, we take our original ratio and assume that we can construct an equivalent ratio based on 100. Let us do this:

$$\frac{16}{25} \times \frac{4}{4} = \frac{64}{100}.$$

Thus, 64 percent of the class brought pets.

A more comprehensive way of doing this is to set up the proportions and solve them as shown below.

$$\frac{16}{25} = \frac{n}{100}$$
$$1600 = 25n \qquad \text{Cross multiply!}$$

$$\frac{1600}{25} = \frac{25n}{25} \qquad \text{Divide both sides of the equation by 25.}$$

$$64 = n \qquad \text{Thus, } \frac{64}{100} \text{ indicates 64 percent.}$$

Many elementary school textbooks teach a rote, mechanical procedure to solve this type of percent question. To find what percent 16 is of 25, children are instructed to do the following. (Notice that a proportional procedure is shown alongside.)

Conventional Textbook Procedure	*Ratio and Proportion Procedure*
To find what percent 16 is of 25, we perform the following operations.	$\dfrac{16}{25} = \dfrac{n}{100}$
Divide 16 by 25: .64	$16 \times 100 = 25 \times n$
Multiply by 100: 64	Cross multiply: $1600 = 25n$
16 is 64% of 25	$\dfrac{1600}{25} = \dfrac{25}{25}n$
	$64 = n$

Two other percent situations that can be solved by proportions are shown below together with their conventional textbook approaches.

A student scored 92% on a test. If there were 35 items, how many did the student answer correctly?

Conventional Textbook Procedure	*Ratio and Proportion Procedure*
92% = .92	92% means that if there were 100 items, 92 would be correct.
	$\frac{92}{100}$
.92 × 35 = 32.20 $\doteq$ 32	
Thus, 32 correct responses.	

Since there were 35 items, the student must have made n correct responses. Thus,

$$\frac{92}{100} = \frac{n}{35}$$

$$100n = 3220$$

$$n = \frac{3220}{100}$$

$$n = \frac{3220}{100} = 32.2 \text{ correct}$$

Rounded off, the student obtained 32 correct responses.

Mary Murphy scored 55 points in a basketball tournament. If she scored 35% of her team's total points, how many points did her team score?

Conventional Textbook Procedure	*Ratio and Proportion Procedure*
Mary scored 35% of n.	$\frac{55}{n}$ represents the ratio of Mary's points to the total points scored.
	$\frac{35}{100}$ represents Mary's ratio of points to a "pretend" 100-point score.
.35 × n = 55	
$\frac{.35}{.35} \times n = \frac{55}{.35}$	$\frac{55}{n} = \frac{35}{100}$
$n = \frac{55}{.35}$	$35n = 5500$
$n = 157$	$n = \frac{5500}{35} = 157$

So, there were 157 points scored in the tournament. Notice that we have rounded off a slight decimal remainder.

Activities 15.2, 15.3, and 15.4 are designed to help reinforce your understanding of the ratio and proportion technique for solving percent problems.

ACTIVITY 15.2   Percent by Ratio and Proportion

> Use ratio and proportion to find 25 percent of 130.

ACTIVITY 15.3   An Application of Percent

> Suppose an item in a department store has been marked down from $145 to $95. Use ratio and proportions to find the percent of reduction.

ACTIVITY 15.4   Another Application of Percent

> Suppose a baseball team won 75 percent of their games. If they won 35 games, how many games did they play? Use a ratio and proportion method to solve this percent situation.

Applications of Percent—Estimation Strategies

We use percents often in our daily life. When we go to a restaurant to eat, we have to figure a tip. Estimation is most helpful here.

> To estimate a 15 percent tip, take 10 percent of the bill and add half of that. Ten percent of $25.86 is about $2.60. One-half of that is $1.30. Thus, the tip is $3.90.

Notice that 10 percent can be thought of as $\frac{1}{10}$ to help us perform our calculation. Another way to estimate the tip, assuming that the sales tax is about 5 percent, is to triple the tax.

Estimating the purchase cost of an item that has been reduced in a department store sale is another application of percent. Consider the following situation.

> A sport coat retailing at $139.99 has been reduced by 33 percent. How much will the coat cost?

An estimation of the coat's cost might follow these steps:

1. Round the coat's cost to $140.

2. Consider 33 percent to be about one-third.

3. One-third of $140 is about $45. Thus, the coat will cost about $95.

Awareness of relationships among percents is also helpful to know. For example, $a\%$ of b gives the same result as $b\%$ of a. Specifically, if we are asked to find 24 percent of 50, we can find 50 percent of 24, which is 12. Check to see that 24 percent of 50 is indeed 12! Other examples of relationships for percents can be found in Glatzer (1984). (See Activities 15.5 and 15.6.)

ACTIVITY 15.5   Calculator Percents

Hand calculators can be used to explore a wide range of percent problems.

If your calculator has a percent button, you can use it to calculate sales tax. Suppose you want to find 7 percent of $4.95. First, *estimate* $\frac{7}{100}$ of $5.00 to be about $.35. On your calculator, push 4.95 × 7%.

Ordinarily, pushing the percent button displays the product. On some calculators, you may need to push the equals button. Use a hand calculator to find some other percentages.

ACTIVITY 15.6   Rummy Card Game

This activity can help children to practice important relationships among fractions, decimals, and percents.

Make a rummy card game of equivalent fractions, decimals, and percents. Fifty-two cards should be made with sets of four equivalent fractions, decimals, and percents. The rules of the game are the same as the rules established for Activity 14.9. Some sample equivalent sets are shown below.

$\frac{1}{4}$ .25   25% $\frac{25}{100}$

$\frac{1}{5}$ 20% $\frac{20}{100}$ .20

Relationships Among Fractions, Decimals, and Percents

Rational numbers can be expressed as fractions, decimals, and percents. It is necessary that children be acquainted with this relationship. In fact, research reviewed by Callahan and Hiebert (1987) suggests that children ineffectively relate decimal symbols to fractional symbols. Thus, emphasis on relating fractions, decimals, and percents needs to be considered. A table like the one that follows can illustrate the relationship of fractions, decimals, and percents.

$\frac{1}{10}$	.1	10%
$\frac{1}{4}$	.25	25%
$\frac{1}{2}$	.5	50%
$\frac{3}{4}$	.75	75%
1	1.0	100%

Also, for many children at the middle school level, practice changing fractions to decimals and percents is provided. (See Activities 15.7 and 15.8.)

ACTIVITY 15.7   Concentration

This activity helps children practice the relationships among fractions, decimals, and percents.

A game of concentration can be easily constructed by making 24 cards having 12 pairs of matching answers. The cards can be placed face down on a table and played as a concentration game. Some sample pairs are shown below.

90%	.9
25% of 100	25
33%	$\frac{1}{3}$

ACTIVITY 15.8   Computer Assisted Interest Calculation

This program may be useful to gifted middle school children interested in application of percent concepts.

```
100   REM INTEREST
```

```
110     PRINT ''ENTER THE AMOUNT OF PRINCIPAL''
120     PRINT ''AND THE INTEREST RATE PER YEAR.''
130     PRINT ''I WILL SHOW HOW YOUR MONEY GROWS.''
140     PRINT: PRINT
150     PRINT ''PRINCIPAL'';
155     INPUT P
160     PRINT ''INTEREST RATE'';
170     INPUT R
180     PRINT ''NUMBER OF YEARS''
190     INPUT Y
200     FOR N = 1 TO Y
210     PRINT: PRINT
220     LET A = P * (1 + R/100)^N
230     PRINT ''YEAR='';  N
240     PRINT ''AMOUNT='';  A
250     NEXT N
260     END
```

Summary

This chapter develops the concepts of ratio, proportion, and percent. Emphasis is placed on meaningful models and visualizations. Ratio and proportion are used as the bases for solving problems related to percents. Finally, estimation of real-world situations is considered.

Discussion Questions

1. Collect several newspaper and magazine examples of the use of percent in daily life. Cut out several examples and create a bulletin board that depicts the use of percents in our society.

2. Make at least one of the activities or games mentioned in this chapter. Use the activity with elementary school students.

3. Investigate the unitary analysis procedure for teaching percents. One source is Riedesal (1985). Compare the approach to the method used in this text.

4. Develop a list of historical uses of percent. Refer to Roman as well as medieval times to compile your list of examples.

5. Discuss the prerequisite knowledge needed for children to study the concept of percent.

6. Define these terms, which are encountered in the study of percents: *base, rate, percent, percentage.*

7. Collect newspaper samples of the use of percent in sports and make up three word problems dealing with sports and percents.

8. Make up a math bingo game for percents. Cards with decimal and percent equivalents can be made. A student can call out percent or decimal numbers. If a student has an equivalent decimal or percent, then he or she may cover the value. The first person to get five in a row is the winner. A sample card is shown below.

50%	.25	.30	12%	.06
.52	28%	.05	.71%	125%
2%	.91	.01	75%	.95
8%	.03	.09	.68	100%
.86	92%	18%	59%	.58

References

Callahan, L., & Hiebert, J. (1987). Research report—Decimal fractions. *Arithmetic Teacher, 34,* p. 22.

Dollins, A. (1981). How I teach it: Percent. *Arithmetic Teacher, 29,* p. 37.

Driscoll, M. J. (1985). *Research within reach: Elementary school mathematics.* Reston, Va.: National Council of Teachers of Mathematics.

Glatzer, D. J. (1984). Teaching percentage: Ideas and suggestions. *Arithmetic Teacher, 31,* pp. 24–26.

Grossnickle, F., Reckzeh, J., Perry, L., & Ganoe, N. (1983). *Discovering meanings in elementary school mathematics.* New York: Holt, Rinehart & Winston.

Lindquist, M., Carpenter, T., Silver, E., & Matthews, W. (1983). The third national mathematics assessment: Results and implications for elementary and middle schools. *Arithmetic Teacher, 31,* pp. 14–25.

National Council of Teachers of Mathematics. (1982). *Ideas from the Arithmetic Teacher.* Reston, Va.: NCTM.

Riedesal, C. A. (1985). *Teaching elementary school mathematics.* Englewood Cliffs, N.J.: Prentice-Hall.

Teahan, T. (1979). How I learned to do percents. *Arithmetic Teacher, 27,* pp. 16–18.

Usisken, Z., & Bell, M. (1984). Ten often ignored applications of rational-number concepts. *Arithmetic Teacher, 31,* pp. 48–50.

CHAPTER 16

Special Topics: Integers and Number Theory

Objectives

After reading this chapter you will be able to:

1. Develop number-line models that help children understand the concept of integers.

2. Demonstrate introductory operations on integers by using a variety of manipulative aids.

3. Explain the difference between prime and composite numbers.

4. Develop the greatest common factor and least common multiple using prime factorization.

5. Identify several common divisibility tests for whole numbers.

Introduction

In this chapter we consider two special topics developed in the elementary school years: integers and number theory. Some mathematics curriculums emphasize these later, often in grades 7 and 8.

Integers

The set of integers consists of the following set of numbers: { . . . $^-4$, $^-3$, $^-2$, $^-1$, 0, $^+1$, $^+2$, $^+3$, $^+4$ . . . }. In effect, we extend the set of whole numbers to include their negative values, which are sometimes called their *additive inverses*. An *integer* involves magnitude and direction. For example, the number line in Fig. 16.1 shows how $^-5$ can be located by first noting the direction (positive or negative) and then the magnitude.

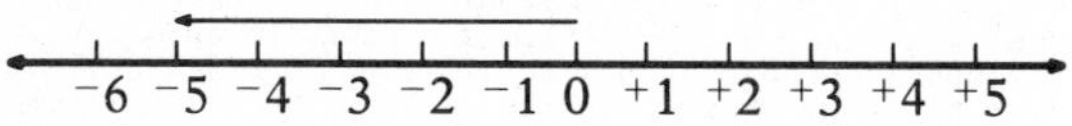

Fig. 16.1

Children need experience seeing how integers are used in daily life. We speak of a football player losing 10 yards in a passing attempt. Temperatures are recorded in negative degrees. In certain games such as pinochle, negative scores are possible. In some buildings, we can travel several floors below ground, thus illustrating negative integers. Ordering integers can be illustrated by making a large thermometer model out of tagboard. Children can discover that warmer temperatures are associated with higher integer values and colder temperatures with lower integer values.

Properties of Integers

Integers contain the same properties as whole numbers; that is, for addition and multiplication, we have closure (e.g., any two integers added together yield an integer). Also, a commutative property exists, which means that for any two integers the order of addition or multiplication does not affect the sum or product. The additive identity is 0, while the multiplicative identity is 1. Also, the associative property, such as $a \times (b \times c) = (a \times b) \times c$ and $a + (b + c) = (a + b) + c$, is present. The distributive property, or $a \times (b + c) = (a \times b) + (a \times c)$, is also true for any three integers.

A property unique to the system of integers is the *additive inverse* property. This property is not present in the whole-number system. For every integer there is an additive inverse. For example, $^+2 + {}^-2 = 0$; thus, the additive inverse of $^+2$ is $^-2$. Also, the additive inverse of $^-2$ is $^+2$. Another example will suffice to make our point: $^+5$ and $^-5$ are additive inverses because $^-5 + {}^+5 = 0$.

At the seventh- and eighth-grade levels, the structure of integers is sometimes presented. Also, for gifted elementary school students, integers can be an appropriate topic for enrichment.

Addition and Subtraction of Integers

Several models are available for illustrating addition and subtraction of integers. Two models—the number line and the charged particle—are considered here. (See also Activities 16.1 and 16.2.)

ACTIVITY 16.1 ## Integer Nomograph

This integer nomograph can be used to motivate the study of the addition of integers. Simply take a ruler and connect the two integers that you want to add. The middle line segment displays the sum. Our example shows $^+1 + {}^-4 = {}^-3$.

ACTIVITY 16.2   Name Positive 4

This activity can help children practice adding integers in a creative way.

In two minutes, name as many sums of integers that yield positive 4 as you can. You may loop pairs of integers that are next to each other, either horizontally, vertically, or diagonally.

$^-4 + 8$	$^-3$	7	$^-2$	4	$^-7$	5	$^-1$	9	$^-4$	7
1	$^-8$	2	$^-4$	5	$^-5$	1	$^-7$	6	$^-4$	8	$^-5$
$^-9$	2	$^-5$	7	$^-3$	8	$^-8$	2	$^-3$	6	$^-5$	4
5	$^-1$	2	$^-4$	4	$^-6$	5	$^-4$	9	$^-1$	4	$^-7$
$^-7$	6	$^-1$	8	$^-3$	2	$^-1$	4	$^-3$	6	$^-7$	3
3	$^-2$	8	$^-5 + 7$	$^-9$	4	$^-3$	7	$^-2$	5	$^-5$
$^-8$	6	$^-4$	3	$^-7$	2	$^-9$	6	$^-2$	1	$^-8$	5
2	$^-4$	6	$^-2$	5	$^-1$	7	$^-5$	5	$^-6$	9	$^-3$
$^-6$	9	$^-2$	8	$^-1$	7	$^-2$	3	$^-3$	9	$^-1$	6
4	$^-3$	2	$^-9$	7	$^-3$	6	$^-5$	7	$^-8$	3	$^-2$

Addition of Integers. Consider the following example in which $^+5 + {}^+2 = {}^+7$ is shown on the *number line*. Here we use the "positive" sign $(+)$ to move to the right, whereas the "negative" sign $(-)$ indicates a movement to the left.

We again can use a number line to show $^-4 + {}^-3 = {}^-7$. In this case, we make a leftward movement of 4 units, followed by another leftward movement of 3 units.

To show $^-5 + {}^+2 = {}^-3$ on a number line, we first move 5 units to the left because of the negative sign. Then, from that point, we move 2 units to the right, ending at negative 3.

Another medium for modeling integer operations is the *charged particle model.* A charged particle model is simple to make. Simply cut out pieces of paper with plus and minus signs on them. Then attach magnetic tape to the back of the paper. This will allow for the pieces to be placed on the chalkboard. The diagrams below show this procedure.

Positive and negative pieces put together yield a charge of zero. Construct positive and negative pieces as semicircles so that when fit together they will look like zero.

Again, when a positive and a negative piece are joined, the result is zero. The diagram to the left contains four such combinations. The charge for the entire diagram is still zero (think of $0 + 0 + 0 + 0$).

Since three positive charges are isolated, the charge for this diagram is positive 3. Simply place a specified number of positive or negative charges to make the diagram have any predetermined positive or negative charge.

When using the charged particle model to show an integer addition exercise such as $^+5 + {}^-2 = \square$, first make a neutral diagram of zero. Next, introduce the first addend, $^+5$, by placing five positive pieces onto the diagram.

Next, introduce the second addend, $^-2$, by placing two negative pieces on the diagram.

Combine as many positive and negative pieces as you can.

The uncombined pieces represent the sum of the addition exercise. For our example, there are three positive charges that have been isolated. Thus, $^+5 + {}^-2 = {}^-3$. Remember, start with a neutral diagram, show the first addend in terms of the number of charged pieces, and then do the same for the second addend. Combine as many pieces as you can. The resulting uncombined pieces represent your answer or sum to the addition exercise.*

Subtraction of Integers.   Subtraction of integers can also be treated using the number line and charged particle models. First, it is necessary to review a subtraction sentence such as $^-5 - {}^+2 = \square$, which can be rewritten in related addition forms as $^+2 + \square = {}^-5$. This style of interpretation is

*From Battista, M. T. (1983). A complete model for operations on integers. *Arithmetic Teacher, 30,* pp. 26–30. Adapted with permission.

used for our number line example (see Fig. 16.2). In the figure we show the first addend as positive 2. In what direction do we need to go to end up at negative 5? The movement is left (or negative). Thus, we move 7 units to the left, ending at $^-5$. Thus, $^-5 - {}^+2 = {}^-7$.

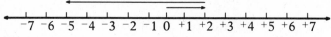

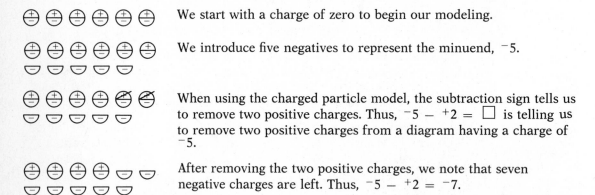

Fig. 16.2

Here $^-5 - {}^+2$ is modeled using the charged particle model.

We start with a charge of zero to begin our modeling.

We introduce five negatives to represent the minuend, $^-5$.

When using the charged particle model, the subtraction sign tells us to remove two positive charges. Thus, $^-5 - {}^+2 = \square$ is telling us to remove two positive charges from a diagram having a charge of $^-5$.

After removing the two positive charges, we note that seven negative charges are left. Thus, $^-5 - {}^+2 = {}^-7$.

In general, when using the charged particle model for subtraction of integers we (1) start with a neutral diagram, a charge of zero; (2) introduce the minuend value onto the diagram as a number of positive or negative pieces; (3) remove a specified number of positive or negative charges as determined by the subtraction sign; (4) determine the resulting charge of the diagram, which represents the solution to the subtraction example.

Let us consider another example, again using the charged particle model.

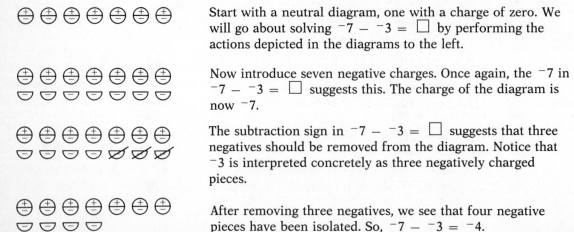

Start with a neutral diagram, one with a charge of zero. We will go about solving $^-7 - {}^-3 = \square$ by performing the actions depicted in the diagrams to the left.

Now introduce seven negative charges. Once again, the $^-7$ in $^-7 - {}^-3 = \square$ suggests this. The charge of the diagram is now $^-7$.

The subtraction sign in $^-7 - {}^-3 = \square$ suggests that three negatives should be removed from the diagram. Notice that $^-3$ is interpreted concretely as three negatively charged pieces.

After removing three negatives, we see that four negative pieces have been isolated. So, $^-7 - {}^-3 = {}^-4$.

Addition and subtraction of integers, or inverse operations, can be modeled carefully using our two methods. Much work needs to be done at the developmental level to ensure that understanding takes place. Only after this can "rules" such as "two negatives make a positive" be applied. Also, note that in our work we distinguish between the sign of the operation and the sign of the number. The number sentence $^-6 - {}^+5 = \square$ means that we subtract positive 5 from negative 6.

Multiplication and Division of Integers

Since multiplication and division are inverse operations, we treat only multiplication situations. The generalizations made regarding signs for multiplication are equally applicable to division. We view two cases—the situations in which factors have opposite signs and those in which the signs are both negative. Several models are shown.

Multiplying a Positive and a Negative Integer. We can use the number line to show two groups of $^-3$ (see Fig. 16.3). This movement shows the product to be $^-6$. Thus, $^+2 \times {}^-3 = {}^-6$.

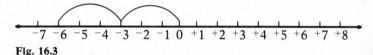

Fig. 16.3

When the factor on the left side is negative, as in $^-3 \times {}^+4 = {}^-12$, a number line model is ineffective because it is impossible to model negative three groups of 4 on the number line. Teachers need to structure their examples to enhance the number line's effectiveness as a meaningful model. Remember that $^+4 \times {}^-2$ means 4 *groups* of $^-2$.

For examples such as $^-4 \times {}^+3 = \square$, the charged particle model is effective. As stated earlier, the charged particle model can be used effectively with any of the operations on integers (Battista, 1983). For the specific example of $^-4 \times {}^+3 = {}^-12$, we can use the following procedure.

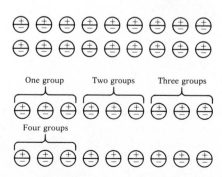

Show a neutral field. Be sure to have enough neutral combinations on the diagram, in this case 15 to 20.

Now we show how to interpret the charged particle model for $^-4 \times {}^+3 = \square$. The first factor, $^-4$, offers two ideas. As in ordinary multiplication, the 4 suggests four groups. The negative sign tells us to *remove;* thus, we will remove four groups. The second factor also suggests two ideas. Since we have a positive 3, we remove groups of three positives. Thus, we remove four groups of three positives from the diagram.

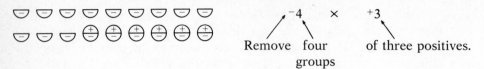

Remove four groups of three positives.

We now view the diagram and note that after the removal of four groups of three positives, 12 negative charges are isolated. Thus, $^-4 \times {}^+3 = {}^-12$.

In general, when using the charged particle model for multiplication, the sign of the first factor tells us whether to place down or take away a certain number of groups of negative or positive charges. The second factor indicates the elements of the group, a specified number of positive or negative pieces. For example, a slightly different exercise such as $^+4 \times {}^-3 = \square$ would tell us to *place down* four groups of three negative pieces.

Multiplying Two Negative Integers.   The product of two negative integers can be shown in several ways. One method is to use patterns, and an example of this is shown below.

$^-3 \times {}^+4 = {}^-12$	Increase of $^+3$
$^-3 \times {}^+3 = {}^-9$	Increase of $^+3$
$^-3 \times {}^+2 = {}^-6$	Increase of $^+3$
$^-3 \times {}^+1 = {}^-3$	Increase of $^+3$
$^-3 \times 0 = 0$	Increase of $^+3$
$^-3 \times {}^-1 = {}^+3$	

We build on the fact that students are able to multiply a positive and a negative integer. A pattern emerges in which each product is three more than its predecessor. Continuing this pattern yields the conclusion that $^-3 \times {}^-1 = {}^+3$.

Another method of showing that the product of two negative integers is positive is the now familiar charged particle model. Let us use this model to solve $^-3 \times {}^-2 = \square$.

We start with a neutral diagram.

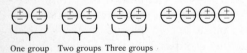

One group   Two groups   Three groups

We interpret $^-3 \times {}^-2$ to mean that we *remove* three groups of two negative charges from the diagram. In review, the first factor, $^-3$, implies the *removal* of three groups. The second factor, $^-2$, suggests that each of the three groups has two negative charges.

⊕⊕⊕⊕⊕⊕⊖⊖⊖⊖   The diagram now contains six isolated positive charges. Thus, as a result of this modeling technique, $^-3 \times {}^-2 = {}^+6$.

After several experiences with the charged particle model or the pattern list, students are ready for a generalization such as "the product of two negative integers is a positive integer." Practice activities at the abstract level are then implemented (see Activity 16.3).

ACTIVITY 16.3   Story Problems

This activity is a story problem that applies the system of integers.

An elevator started at the fourteenth floor, descended 7 floors, rose 3 floors, rose 2 floors, and dropped 13 floors. What floor is the elevator on?

Write another story problem involving integers suitable for use with middle school children.

Number Theory

Special topics in number theory are often found in elementary school mathematics textbooks. Here we consider the fundamental concepts of prime and composite numbers, develop procedures for finding the greatest common divisor and least common multiple of two numbers, and discuss tests of divisibility.

Prime and Composite Numbers

Prime Numbers.   *Prime numbers* are those numbers of the counting number system that can be factored only by themselves and 1. Examples of prime numbers are 2, 3, 5, and 7. The number 1 is not to be considered a prime number.

A useful activity for prime numbers is based on the following experiment. Children are given square shapes and asked to form as many rectangular arrangements as possible, and then they record the number of arrangements on a chart. A sample chart is shown in Fig. 16.4 and some examples of arrangements are shown in Fig. 16.5.

Our partially completed chart now looks like the one in Fig. 16.6. Do you notice anything about the number of rectangular arrangements for the prime numbers? They have only two rectangular arrangements. Try completing the table to validate this thought.

Composite Numbers.   Counting numbers that are not prime numbers are called *composite numbers.* Examples of composite numbers are 6, 12,

Number of Squares	2	3	4	5	6	7	8	9	10	11	12	13
Number of Rectangular Arrangements												

Fig. 16.4

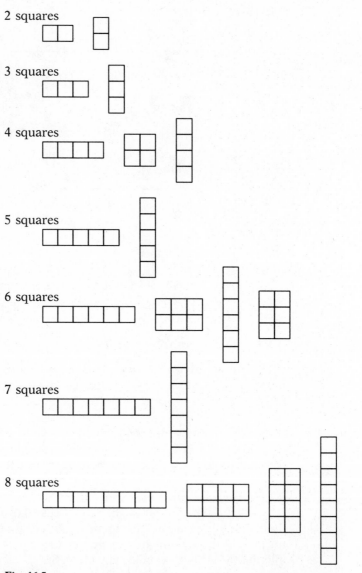

Fig. 16.5

Number of Squares	2	3	4	5	6	7	8	9	10	11	12	13
Number of Rectangular Arrangements	2	2	3	2	4	2	4	3	4	2		

Fig. 16.6

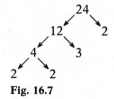

Fig. 16.7

and 15. Each composite number can be uniquely factored in terms of prime numbers (see Activity 16.4). Figure 16.7 can help to perform this factorization. Thus, $24 = 2 \times 2 \times 2 \times 3$. Writing this in exponential notation yields $24 = 2^3 \times 3$.

The following is another technique for factoring a composite number into prime factors.

$$\begin{array}{r|r} 2 & 36 \\ 2 & 18 \\ 3 & 9 \\ \hline & 3 \end{array}$$

Start with the least prime. Continue dividing until the next higher prime is needed as a divisor. Keep going until you reach a prime number as your last quotient. Thus, $36 = 2 \times 2 \times 3 \times 3$, or $36 = 2^2 \times 3^2$.

ACTIVITY 16.4 Factoring Composite Numbers

This activity helps elementary students to practice factoring composite numbers into prime numbers.

Use prime factorization to trace a path of prime factors that yields 840. Explore making one of these paths with a fellow college student.

5	3	10
6	7	2
11	2	4

840

Sieve of Eratosthenes. Eratosthenes was a Greek astronomer-geographer of the third century B.C. He developed a system for separating prime and composite numbers from a set of consecutive counting numbers. Intermediate-grade children often investigate this procedure.

Here is how we can identify the prime numbers from 1 to 100.

1. Start with a hundreds chart.

2. Two is the smallest prime. Cross out all the multiples of 2 with a red pen.

3. Since 3 is the next prime number, cross out all the multiples of 3. This time use a green pen.
4. Five is the next prime, so cross out any multiples of 5 with a blue pen.
5. Seven is a prime number—the smallest multiple of 7 remaining is 49. Using a yellow pen, cross out the multiples of 7.
6. Eleven is the next prime, and its multiples—22, 33, 44, 55, 66, 77, 88, 99—are crossed out.

1	②	③	~~4~~	⑤	~~6~~	⑦	~~8~~	~~9~~	~~10~~
⑪	~~12~~	⑬	~~14~~	~~15~~	~~16~~	⑰	~~18~~	⑲	~~20~~
~~21~~	~~22~~	㉓	~~24~~	~~25~~	~~26~~	~~27~~	~~28~~	㉙	~~30~~
㉛	~~32~~	~~33~~	~~34~~	~~35~~	~~36~~	㊲	~~38~~	~~39~~	~~40~~
㊶	~~42~~	㊸	~~44~~	~~45~~	~~46~~	㊼	~~48~~	~~49~~	~~50~~
~~51~~	~~52~~	(53)	~~54~~	~~55~~	~~56~~	~~57~~	~~58~~	(59)	~~60~~
(61)	~~62~~	~~63~~	~~64~~	~~65~~	~~66~~	(67)	~~68~~	~~69~~	~~70~~
(71)	~~72~~	(73)	~~74~~	~~75~~	~~76~~	~~77~~	~~78~~	(79)	~~80~~
~~81~~	~~82~~	(83)	~~84~~	~~85~~	~~86~~	~~87~~	~~88~~	(89)	~~90~~
(91)	~~92~~	~~93~~	~~94~~	~~95~~	~~96~~	(97)	~~98~~	~~99~~	~~100~~

Since all the multiples of 11 have already been crossed out, we do not need to try any higher prime numbers. Also, a number having several colored slashes has several factors and is, thus, a composite number. So, a listing of prime numbers from 2 to 100 is the following:

2, 3, 5, 7, 11, 13, 17, 19, 23, 29, 31, 37, 41, 43, 47, 53, 59, 61, 67, 71, 73, 79, 83, 89, 97

Other patterns may be gleaned from the preceding figure. For example, 3 and 5, 5 and 7, and 11 and 13, among others, are called *twin primes* because there is only one composite number between them. (See Activity 16.5.)

ACTIVITY 16.5 Problem Solving

This is a problem-solving activity that can be explored by gifted elementary school students.

What integers in the set {7, 17, 27, 37, 47, . . .} can be written as the sum of two primes?

Finding the Greatest Common Factor by Using Prime Numbers

The greatest common factor is discussed in detail in Chapter 13 on fractional numbers. Although the procedure described there is preferred, the greatest common factor can be found by a method involving prime numbers.

Suppose we want to find the greatest common factor for 18 and 48. A procedure involving prime factorization is shown in Fig. 16.8. The greatest common factor for 18 and 48 is 2×3, or 6.

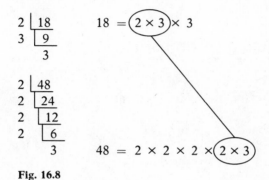

Fig. 16.8

Finding the Least Common Multiple by Prime Factorization

As with the greatest common factor, the least common multiple is described in Chapter 13. Sometimes a technique involving prime factorization is used to find the least common multiple.

To find the least common multiple (LCM) for two numbers such as 40 and 28, we would use the procedure outlined in Fig. 16.9. We would need to inspect the prime factorizations as follows.

$$
\begin{array}{r|r}
2 & 40 \\
2 & 20 \\
2 & 10 \\
& 5
\end{array}
\qquad 40 = 2 \times 2 \times 2 \times 5
$$

$$
\begin{array}{r|r}
2 & 28 \\
2 & 14 \\
& 7
\end{array}
\qquad 28 = 2 \times 2 \times 7
$$

Fig. 16.9

$2 \times 2 \times 2$ Two appears as a factor three times in 40. Thus, to construct a multiple of 40, 2 must be used three times.

$2 \times 2 \times 2 \times 5$
$2 \times 2 \times 2 \times 5 \times 7$ Similarly, 5 must be used to have a multiple of 40. Since we also want a multiple of 28, we want to have two factors of 2. But we already have these in our construction of a multiple of 40.

We also need a factor of 7 to complete our construction of a multiple of 40 and a multiple of 28.

Thus, the LCM of 28 and 40 = 2 × 2 × 2 × 5 × 7

For adding fractional numbers, the least common multiple procedure shown in Chapter 13 is preferred. However, at times a special topic enrichment such as this is shown in elementary school curriculums. (See Activities 16.6 through 16.9.)

ACTIVITY 16.6   Goldbach's Conjecture

This activity is designed as an enrichment activity for culminating a middle school unit on prime and composite numbers.

Goldbach's conjecture (1742 A.D.) stated that "Every even number greater than 2 may be expressed as the sum of two prime numbers." Some examples are shown below.

$$4 = 2 + 2$$

$$6 = 3 + 3$$

$$8 = 5 + 3$$

$$10 = 5 + 5$$

Show that Goldbach's conjecture is valid for every even number from 12 to 50.

ACTIVITY 16.7   Triangular Numbers

Number theory has historical origins. This enrichment activity is developed to enhance middle school students' perspectives.

Triangular numbers were known by the ancient Greeks.

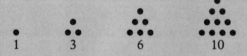

1   3   6   10

Can you find the next three triangular numbers? Draw a diagram to show them.

ACTIVITY 16.8 Number Curiosities

Number theory often involves what can be called number curiosities. This activity promotes problem-solving behavior as well as a search for number relationships.

A number is perfect if it is the sum of its divisors, with the exception of the number itself. For example, $6 = 2 + 3 + 1$ is a perfect number. Can you find another perfect number less than 30?

ACTIVITY 16.9 Number Tricks

This motivational activity for prime numbers can be easily developed.

Take six 3×5 note cards and write prime numbers on them as shown below.

| 2 | 3 | 5 | 7 | 11 | 13 |

Shuffle the cards and hand them to a child. Have the child select any two cards. Then have the child state the product of the numbers on the cards. Suppose the child says 77. Since each of the cards has a prime number on it, the product can be factored in only one way. Factor the product into prime numbers, in this case 7 and 11. You announce to the child that he or she is holding a card with a 7 on it, and one with an 11 on it.

Try this activity with a friend. Notice, again, that we are attempting to motivate the study of prime factorization through this number trick.

Tests of Divisibility

It is often helpful to enrich the study of elementary school mathematics by studying divisibility tests. When we say that a number is divisible by a given number, we mean that the quotient has no remainders. Many of these divisibility tests can be shown through concrete material. Also, since the divisibility rule for 7 is more involved than simply dividing the number, we suggest not using it for practical application.

Divisibility by 2   Any even number can be divided by 2. For example, 9856 is divisible by 2.

Divisibility by 3

To determine whether a number is divisible by 3, add the sum of the digits. If the sum is divisible by 3, then so is the original number. For example, 35,823 is divisible by 3 because $3 + 5 + 8 + 2 + 3 = 21$. 21 is, of course, divisible by 3.

Divisibility by 4

To determine whether a number is divisible by 4, check the number indicated by tens and ones. If it is divisible by 4, then the original number is as well. 15*48* is divisible by 4 because 48 is divisible by 4.

Divisibility by 5

Any whole number that ends in 0 or 5 is divisible by 5. For example, 4385 and 4380 are divisible by 5.

Divisibility by 6

Any even number that is divisible by 3 is divisible by 6. 354 is an example of a number divisible by 6.

Divisibility by 7

One divisibility test for 7 is this: multiply the digit in the ones place by 2. Subtract the product from the number named by the remaining digits. If the difference is divisible by 7, then the entire number is divisible by 7. For example, consider 5236.
$6 \times 2 = 12$
$523 - 12 = 511$
511 is divisible by 7.
   Once again, this divisibility test has more motivational than practical value.

Divisibility by 8

A whole number is divisible by 8 if the number defined by the digits from hundreds to ones is divisible by 8. For example, 27,*624* is divisible by 8 because the italicized value 624 is divisible by 8.

Divisibility by 9

A whole number is divisible by 9 if the sum of the digits is divisible by 9. For example, 35,847 is divisible by 9 because $3 + 5 + 8 + 4 + 7 = 27$ is divisible by 9.

Summary

This chapter is devoted to two supplementary topics in the elementary school mathematics curriculum. The study of integers and topics in number theory are often developed in the middle school grades (grades 6–8). This chapter considers introductory concepts, activities, and skills related to integers and number theory.

Discussion Questions

1. Use a number line model to show $^-5 - {}^-8 = \square$.
2. Use the charged particle model to illustrate $^-4 - {}^-1 = \square$.
3. Using the charged particle model, show $^-3 \times {}^-6 = \square$.
4. Factor 64 as a product of prime numbers.
5. Use the divisibility tests described in this chapter to determine whether 3286 is divisible by 2, 3, 4, 5, 6, 7, 8, and 9.
6. Read Ian Beattie's article (1986) and develop an activity for concretely demonstrating the least common multiple of two numbers.
7. After reviewing Activity 16.1, make a nomograph out of tagboard. Laminate it so that students can use it at a learning center.
8. Make charged particle models. Take magnetic tape, construction paper, and glue. Cut out some positive and negative pieces from the construction paper. Make about 20 positive models and 20 negative models by gluing the magnetic tape to the pieces. You can put these on a chalkboard to demonstrate various integer operations.

References

Battista, M. T. (1983). A complete model for operations on integers. *Arithmetic Teacher, 30,* pp. 26–30.

Beattie, I. D. (1986). Building understanding with blocks. *Arithmetic Teacher, 34,* pp. 5–11.

Hohfeld, J. (1981). An induction approach to prime factors. *Arithmetic Teacher, 28,* pp. 28–29.

National Council of Teachers of Mathematics. (1970). *Experiences in mathematical discovery—Positive and negative numbers.* Washington, D.C.: NCTM.

National Council of Teachers of Mathematics. (1968). *More topics in mathematics for elementary school teachers* (Thirtieth Yearbook). Washington, D.C.: NCTM.

Peterson, J. A., & Hashisaki, J. (1967). *Theory of arithmetic.* New York: Wiley.

Peterson, J. C. (1972). Fourteen different strategies for multiplication of integers, or why $(-1)(-1) = (+1)$. *Arithmetic Teacher, 19*(5), pp. 396–403.

Werner, M. (1973). The case for a more universal number line model of subtraction. *Arithmetic Teacher, 20*(1), pp. 61–64.

CHAPTER 17

Probability, Statistics, and Graphs

Objectives

After reading this chapter you will be able to:

1. Introduce beginning probability experiments to elementary school children.

2. Explain the differences between theoretical and experimental probability.

3. Construct line and bar graphs.

4. Interpret line, bar, circle, and coordinate graphs.

5. Create problems that ask children to collect and interpret data.

6. Construct learning activities for developing the topics of probability, statistics, and graphs with elementary school children.

Introduction

In this chapter we develop beginning ideas of probability and statistics. Constructing and interpreting graphs, valuable mathematical tools in today's society, also are considered. Many curriculum groups, writing in journals of the National Council of Teachers of Mathematics, have advocated teaching probability in the elementary school mathematics curriculum. Also, researchers such as Piaget and Inhelder (1975) have outlined carefully the stages of probabilistic thinking in young children. For example, children at age 7 or 8 made unstable predictions and were unable to understand the concept of randomness. As children matured (ages 11 or 12), they were increasingly able to collect data, make predictions, and understand probability as an expressed mathematical ratio.

Probability instruction at the elementary school level needs to be experimental in nature. Research by Hirt (1977), Schroeder (1983), and Armstrong (1975) strongly supports the use of experiments to teach probability, so this approach is emphasized in this chapter.

===================== *MATH HISTORY 17.1* =====================

Blaise Pascal and Pierre de Fermat, seventeenth-century mathematicians, are considered to be the founders of probability. Pascal worked on probability ideas to help a gambler friend. Fermat, a magistrate by occupation, was only a part-time mathematician who, nevertheless, made major contributions to mathematical thought.

Probability

Primary-Grade Instruction

With the exception of death and taxes, most events in our lives are associated with some element of chance. At the elementary school level, most probability experiences should be intuitive, involving experiments with real objects. At the primary-grade level, terms like *impossible, certain, less likely,* and *more likely* can be developed. For example, children can be asked whether it is likely that it will rain sometime during the year or that they will grow in height 1 meter within a year. Numerous situations, which can be described by varying degrees of chance, can be developed informally at this level.

Primary school children also should perform activities designed to informally develop the concept of probability, such as the following.
Take 15 red blocks and 5 blue blocks. Place them in a paper bag and shake the bag. Select a child to draw a block from the bag.

Also have children record their guesses of the color block they expect to be drawn from the bag. After a block has been drawn from and then replaced in the bag, children should record the result. Repeat this activity at least 10 times. A sample tally sheet for one child is shown below.

Guess	Actual Drawing
Blue	Red
Red	Red
Red	Blue
Blue	Red
Red	Red

While discussing individual results, children can be led to the conclusion that drawing a red block is the most likely event because there are more red blocks than blue ones. Also, the results of the entire class may be pooled to confirm the hypothesis that a red block is most likely to be drawn.

Spinner games are also useful for experimenting with probability concepts at the primary-grade level. One such game is shown below.

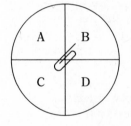

Make a circular playing board with a paper-clip spinner in the center, as shown to the left. Spin, and record the letter that is found. Record the results. Repeat this 50 times.

Children can compare their results. Also, discussion can be developed regarding the procedure used for spinning the spinner. Valuable experience in tabulating and recording information is also a significant part of this activity. After the activity is played and the results recorded, the teacher can elicit predictions from children regarding the likelihood of obtaining a given letter. Questions can be asked such as "What letter is most likely to appear?" and "Are all four letters equally likely to be found?"

Intermediate-Grade Instruction

At the intermediate-grade level, probability can be developed as a ratio. That is, we can conceive of the probability of an event occurring as the following ratio:

$$\frac{\text{Number of possible success outcomes}}{\text{Number of possible outcomes}}$$

For example, since a coin has only two sides, heads or tails, we can expect that in two coin flips one head would appear. Thus, the probability of a coin flip producing heads is $\frac{1}{2}$. Likewise, 50 flips, theoretically, would yield 25 heads or $\frac{25}{50}$. In real experiments, however, this theoretical probability is usually not seen unless we observe a great number of trials. Factors can affect the experimental probability that we obtain (e.g., coins have uneven sides, or we might flip them in an unsystematic fashion). Thus, experimental probability results often do not equal the theoretical ratio.

Current mathematics textbooks at the fifth- and sixth-grade levels emphasize both *theoretical probability* and *experimental probability*. Some examples of these types of probability follow.

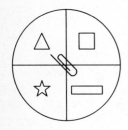

Suppose we use a spinner game with four different designs, as shown in the diagram to the left. Since we have four equal-sized regions in the circle, we can expect the *theoretical probability* of spinning any one design, such as a square, in 4 spins to be $\frac{1}{4}$. In 8 spins, we would expect 2 squares, or a probability of $\frac{2}{8}$.

However, the actual spinning of the circle may yield only one square in eight spins. This is called the *experimental probability*. For the most part, experimental probability experiences are to be emphasized in the later elementary school years.

The following example is a probability activity that also emphasizes an experimental approach.

First flip	Heads	
Second flip		Tails
Third flip	Heads	

Take a coin and flip it 50 times. Chart the number of heads obtained by using a table like the one shown to the left.

Suppose we obtained 30 heads for the 50 flips. The fraction $\frac{30}{50}$ would represent the *experimental* probability. If we pooled the class results of 300 flips, we might find that $\frac{152}{300}$ more closely approximates the *theoretical* value of $\frac{150}{300}$. Note that for some children a discussion of the experimental probability is sufficient. Also, notice that as we increase the number of trials, the experimental probability approaches the theoretical probability.

Probability notation is sometimes developed in the intermediate grades. The probability of obtaining a head in a coin flip is symbolized by Pr(H) $= \frac{1}{2}$. Similarly, the probability of obtaining a tail is symbolized by Pr(T) $= \frac{1}{2}$. Probability values range from 0 to 1. Impossible occurrences or events are given a probability of 0, while certain events are given a probability of 1. For example, the probability of finding a three-headed college professor at your college is 0! On the other hand, the probability that you will brush your teeth at least once a week is 1.

A final probability example shows how we can integrate probability experiments with graphing.

> Suppose we have two number cubes with the numbers 1, 2, 3, 4, 5, and 6 marked on the faces of both cubes. We can challenge the class by saying that when the cubes are rolled the teacher wins if a sum of 5, 6, 7, 8, or 9 is obtained. The class wins if a sum of 2, 3, 4, 10, 11, or 12 is obtained. Have children roll the cubes several times to determine whether the teacher or the class is more likely to win.

To follow up this activity, ask students to list the possible combinations of sums as shown below.

Sum		*Combination*
2 → 1 + 1		1 combination
3 → 2 + 1; 1 + 2		2 combinations
4 → 2 + 2; 3 + 1; 1 + 3		3 combinations
5 → 4 + 1; 1 + 4; 2 + 3; 3 + 2		4 combinations
6 → 3 + 3; 4 + 2; 2 + 4; 1 + 5; 5 + 1		5 combinations
7 → 6 + 1; 1 + 6; 5 + 2; 2 + 5; 3 + 4; 4 + 3		6 combinations
8 → 2 + 6; 6 + 2; 3 + 5; 5 + 3; 4 + 4		5 combinations
9 → 3 + 6; 6 + 3; 4 + 5; 5 + 4		4 combinations
10 → 4 + 6; 6 + 4; 5 + 5		3 combinations
11 → 6 + 5; 5 + 6		2 combinations
12 → 6 + 6		1 combination

A bar graph can now illustrate our results (see Fig. 17.1).

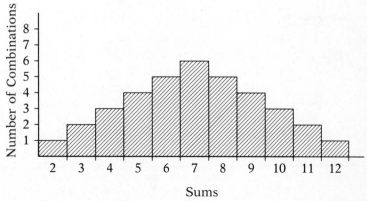

Fig. 17.1

Notice that there are 36 possible combinations of sums. Sums of 5, 6, 7, 8, and 9 have 24 possibilities. Thus, although the teacher has given the children one more sum, the probability is $\frac{24}{36}$ in favor of the teacher's gamble!

The preceding activity involves experimentation, probability, and graphing, topics that contribute greatly to the development of mathematical thinking. (See Activities 17.1, 17.2, and 17.3.)

ACTIVITY 17.1 Find the Most Common Letter

This activity helps students find the most frequently used letters in the alphabet.

A	H	O	U
B	I	P	V
C	J	Q	W
D	K	R	X
E	L	S	Y
F	M	T	Z
G	N		

Choose 100 words on randomly selected pages from a book. Tally the frequency of each letter of the alphabet. After finding the most frequently used letter, compare your results to those of your fellow students. Then combine your results with the entire class and inspect the results.

ACTIVITY 17.2 Favorite Numbers*

Ask children to write down the numbers 1, 2, 3, and 4. Then ask them to loop their favorite number. Draw a bar graph to display the results.

Survey results show that most people prefer the number 3. Try repeating this experiment with other classes to obtain a large sample. Then observe the results by drawing a bar graph.

*Adapted from Burns, M. (1983). Put some probability in your classroom. *Arithmetic Teacher. 30*, pp. 21–22. Used with permission.

ACTIVITY 17.3 Computer-Assisted Probability Calculations

Here is a computer program that can, among other things, calculate the probability that two students in your class have the same birthday (month and day).

```
5     REM DUPLICATION PROBABILITIES
10    HOME
20    PRINT
35    PRINT ''NUMBER OF CHOICES'': INPUT N
40    PRINT ''NUMBER OF PEOPLE'': INPUT M
45    PRINT
50    PRINT ''PROBABILITY OF''
60    PRINT ''AT LEAST ONE''
65    PRINT ''DUPLICATION''
70    PRINT: PRINT
80    P = 1
90    FOR A = 1  TO M + 1
100   P = P * (N - A + 1)/N
110   D = 1 - P
120   PRINT A,D
130   NEXT A
140   END
```

A sample run shows:

```
NUMBER OF CHOICES 365
NUMBER OF PEOPLE 30
30  0.70631627
```

Thus, in a class of 30 students, the likelihood of two students having the same birthday is 70 percent!

Pascal's Triangle

Blaise Pascal, a seventeenth century mathematician, developed an arrangement of numbers called *Pascal's triangle.* The pattern shows that a number in any row can be found by adding the numbers in the two adjacent places in the row above the given number (see Fig. 17.2). Examples have been looped in the figure. Can you continue the pattern for the next row and complete the pattern in row 8?

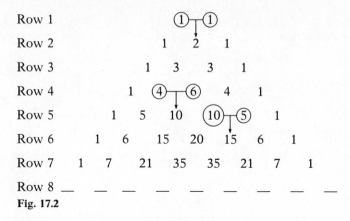

Fig. 17.2

Pascal's triangle has numerous applications in teaching elementary probability. For example, suppose we flipped a coin three times. The possibilities of obtaining heads (H) and tails (T) are shown below.

HHH	TTH
HHT	THH
HTT	HTH
TTT	THT

We have eight possibilities when flipping a coin three times. The probability of obtaining three heads is $\frac{1}{8}$. The third row of Pascal's triangle shows the number of ways that these combinations can occur.

1	3	3	1
One way for three heads to occur	Three ways for two heads and a tail to occur	Three ways for one head and two tails to occur	One way for three tails to occur
HHH	HHT	HTT	TTT
	HTH	THT	
	THH	TTH	

Thus, Pascal's triangle can help us evaluate the possible combinations for events that have two options or outcomes, such as coin flipping. If we want to determine the possible combinations for four coin flips, we would look at row 4 of Pascal's triangle; for five coin flips, we would look at row 5; and so on (see Fig. 17.2).

Another probability problem that shows the use of Pascal's triangle is birth order. For example, what is the probability of having two females in two births? The second row of Pascal's triangle shows us that there are four possibilities for two births. Two female births would occur once out of four possibilities. So, the probability is $\frac{1}{4}$:

1	2	1
Two males	One male, one female	Two females

When you observe the numerals that comprise the triangle, you can discover that Pascal's triangle has numerous patterns independent of probability applications. Can you find some of these patterns? (See Activity 17.4.)

ACTIVITY 17.4   Simulation Game

The diagrams below show a simulation game based on Pascal's triangle.

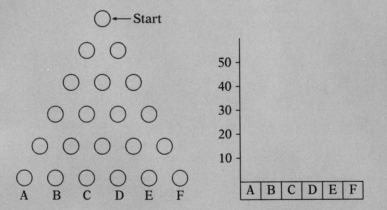

Take a token and place it in the start position on the first diagram. Flip a coin. If it is heads, move the token down and to the *right.* If it is tails, move it down and to the *left.* Repeat this procedure until you arrive at one of the circles labeled A, B, C, D, E, or F. Repeat this 100 times—other students may also do this to get more data. Then record the frequency of each letter's occurrence on the graph. Which letters do you predict to be the most frequent?

Statistics

Statistical topics confront us every day. In newspapers we read about batting averages in baseball, inflation rates, and current enrollments at local colleges. In our society, statistics support political positions of competitors for public office. Box-office statistics help us determine our choices for movies and other entertainment options. At the elementary school level, statistics, and its closely related sibling, probability, are often thought of as enrichment topics. Nevertheless, many intermediate-grade students can benefit by experiences with statistical topics.

In effect, statistics involve collecting, organizing, and interpreting data. Data can be collected about a wide range of topics that interest children—their birthdays, hobbies, and favorite cars, television shows, and rock groups. Predictions, informal at this stage, can be made on the basis of collected data.

Let us take an example to illustrate how we can collect data for a question of interest to students. Suppose we want to determine the most common favorite food of sixth graders. We can poll the class and draw up a list of tentative favorite foods. An imaginary list is shown below.

Pizza
Spaghetti
Hamburgers
Ice cream
Tacos

Next, we would tally a vote of students' preferences as shown here. The frequency of each vote is given to the right of the food items.

Pizza											
Spaghetti					
Hamburgers								
Ice cream								
Tacos				

A bar graph like the one shown in Fig. 17.3 can help us organize the results. Inspecting the graph shows us that pizza is the favorite choice among students, with tacos being the least favorite. After the data are collected and organized, the stage of interpretation is reached. To interpret the data, we could ask questions such as "Would other sixth-grade classes exhibit similar results?" and "Can we make a prediction of the most likely favorite foods?" More data can be gathered to help validate the predictions that students make.

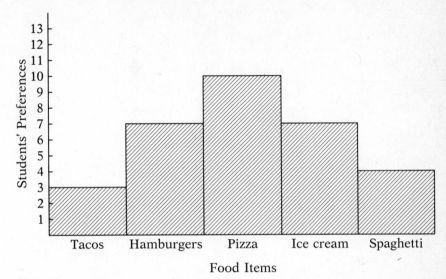

Fig. 17.3

Another common method of displaying statistical information is by way of the *histogram*. For example, a simple histogram can be made to display the results of data collected on the height measurements of students.* First, we would arrange the data from smallest to largest in terms of height, as shown in the following table.

**Height Data for a
Sixth-Grade Class**

110 cm	151 cm
112 cm	152 cm
126 cm	154 cm
126 cm	155 cm
132 cm	156 cm
134 cm	157 cm
135 cm	159 cm
138 cm	162 cm
142 cm	163 cm
143 cm	170 cm
144 cm	175 cm
145 cm	
146 cm	
148 cm	
149 cm	

*Adapted from Klitz, R., & Hofneister, J. (1979). Statistics in the middle school. *Arithmetic Teacher, 26,* pp. 35–36. Used with permission.

Next, we notice that the first two digits of each number in the grouped data are the following: 11, 12, 13, 14, 15, 16, 17. For example, *11*0 and *11*2 have 11 as the first two digits. Also, 151, 152, 154, 155, 156, 157, and 159 all have *15* as the first two digits. We would then list these in order as shown below.

11
12
13
14
15
16
17

Further, we note that in the original data, there are two numbers in the decade from 110 to 120. These are 11*0* and 11*2*. Thus, we place the 0 and 2 side by side next to the 11, as shown here in our partially constructed histogram:

1102
12
13
14
15
16
17

Let us do another example. The decade from 150 to 160 has seven numbers. The units digits are alongside of 15 as shown in our partially completed histogram.

1102
12
13
14
151245679
16
17

In effect, we are showing the frequencies of each grouped set of data by annexing the ones-place digits of that decade. The completed listing is shown here and on the next page:

1102
1266

132458
142345689
151245679
1623
1705

If we turn this listing of frequencies horizontally, we have a histogram that shows the frequencies of each decade of height measurement results (see below).

1102 1266 132458 142345689 151245679 1623 1705

A visual inspection of this numerical display shows that the most frequent heights lie between 140 and 160 centimeters.

Sometimes, *measures of central tendency,* often called *averages,* are developed with elementary school children. The most commonly taught average is the *mean.* To develop this concretely, let us consider another height measurement example. Suppose we take two children and use a strip of paper to measure each of their heights (see Fig. 17.4a).

Next, we tape the two paper strips end to end (see Fig. 17.4b).

Then we fold this long strip into two equal-sized pieces (see Fig. 17.4c)

We now place this piece against a meter stick and measure its length. This gives us the mean height. For three children, we would use three strips folded into three equal parts; for four children, four strips folded into four equal parts; and so on.

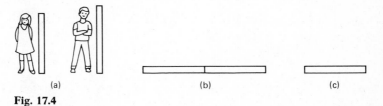

    (a)   (b)   (c)

Fig. 17.4

Calculating the mean for a collection of data can be easily incorporated into a hand calculator activity. Suppose we collected the following data on the amount of pocket change of each child and found the following amounts.

23¢	26¢	35¢
45¢	56¢	36¢
82¢	85¢	26¢
95¢	43¢	45¢
17¢	26¢	27¢
18¢	26¢	54¢

To find the mean, we would add all the numbers in the group and divide by the number of group members:

$$\frac{765}{18} = 42.5$$

Rounding the mean to 42 means the "average" student has 42¢ in pocket change.

The *mode*, another measure of central tendency, is the most frequent number obtained in a collection of data. For our example with children's pocket money, the most frequent amount was 26¢, occurring four times. Thus, the mode for our data is 26.

The *median* is, at times, a more reliable measure of average than the mode, especially when an extreme score, either high or low, is present in the collection of data. Let us consider an example that illustrates how we can obtain a median score from an odd number of scores. Suppose a school has the following numbers of students at various grade levels:

Kindergarten	24
First grade	32
Second grade	22
Third grade	31
Fourth grade	27
Fifth grade	30
Sixth grade	23

First, we would arrange the number of students in order.

32
31
30
27
24
23
22

The median, 27, is the middle number in this set of numbers. If we had an even number of values, we would, again, arrange them in numerical order. This time, however, the two middle values would be averaged to find the median.

The concept of a sample is an important statistical idea. For example, if we want to know the average height of American women, we obviously cannot measure the height of every woman in the United States. However, we can select a sample of a smaller number of women to represent the female population. Their heights can be measured and we can make a prediction of the height of the entire population of American women. The term *random sample* refers to a sample in which each person or thing has an equally likely possibility of being selected. Activity 17.5 shows how we can develop the idea of a random sample with elementary school children.

In summary, an introduction to statistics at the elementary school level helps children raise questions, collect and organize data, and make informal conclusions and predictions. Activities 17.6, 17.7, and 17.8 can be used to introduce students to the concept of statistics.

ACTIVITY 17.5 Predicting Proportions*

Take 400 popsicle sticks. Mark 100 of them with a red star, 200 with a blue star, and 100 with a white star. Mix them up and place them in a covered box. Tell the children that there are 400 popsicle sticks in the box and that some have red stars, others blue stars, and still others white stars. The students are to determine approximately how many sticks are red, blue, and white. Rather than simply reaching in and counting them, the children should draw a lesser amount, say 100, and make a chart (see below) to see if they can predict the overall proportion of red-, blue-, and white-starred sticks.

100 Sticks

Red star	_____
Blue star	_____
White star	_____

Try this initial drawing of 100 sticks, then use a proportion to try to predict how many of each color are found in the entire group of 400.

*Adapted from Shryock, J. (1981). Sampling and popsicle sticks. In Shulte, A., & Smart, J. (eds.), *Teaching statistics and probability*. Reston, Va.: NCTM, pp. 45–48. Used with permission.

ACTIVITY 17.6   Collecting Data

Collect data on the following question: How long does it take you to write your name 20 times? Use your data to help you estimate how long it would take you to write your name 1 million times.

Make up some claims such as "Johnny can write his name 1 million times in 20 minutes." Then use students' data to determine whether they can justify such assertions. Try an activity like this with intermediate-grade children.

ACTIVITY 17.7   Statistical Mistakes

Sometimes statistics can yield erroneous information. In the 1948 presidential election, the Gallup Poll predicted that Harry Truman would finish a distant second to Thomas Dewey. Evidently the sample and the method were incorrect, because Truman won an overwhelming victory, capturing 303 electoral votes to Dewey's 189.

See if you can analyze and criticize the following television commercial claim: "Research shows that Top Flight aspirin relieves pain 25 percent faster than competing brands."

ACTIVITY 17.8   Computer-Assisted Statistical Calculations

Here is a computer program for calculating the mean of a set of numbers. A microcomputer program such as this, written for an Atari computer, can be useful in a statistics unit.

```
100    REM AVERAGE
110    PRINT ''AVERAGE''
120    POKE 82,12
130    PRINT: PRINT
140    PRINT ''I WILL COMPUTE''
150    PRINT ''THE MEAN FOR A SET''
160    PRINT ''OF NUMBERS''
170    PRINT: PRINT
180    PRINT: PRINT
190    PRINT ''HOW MANY NUMBERS'': INPUT X
200    M = 0
210    FOR T = 1 TO X
220    PRINT: PRINT
```

```
230   PRINT ''NUMBER'': INPUT Y
240   M = M + Y
250   NEXT T
260   PRINT: PRINT
270   PRINT ''TOTAL'': PRINT ''MEAN''
280   PRINT M, M/X
```

With minor adaptations, this program can be used with any microcomputer using the BASIC language.

Graphs

One of the most important and sometimes neglected aspects of the elementary mathematics curriculum is the topic of graphing. This section examines several kinds of graphs, including bar, circle, and line graphs as well as coordinate graphing procedures.

Bar Graphs

Bar graphs, sometimes called *histograms,* are convenient devices for organizing and displaying statistical data. Earlier in the chapter we used bar graphs to display frequencies of responses (look back to Figs. 17.1 and 17.3). In effect, graphs allow us to view a picture of the relationship among data.

For example, suppose that we collected information on the amount of money obtained by several schools during a fund-raising drive. The bar graph in Fig. 17.5 summarizes our results. At a glance we can see that Jones and Muir schools collected the most money. In contrast, the Preston and Brown schools collected the least amount of money.

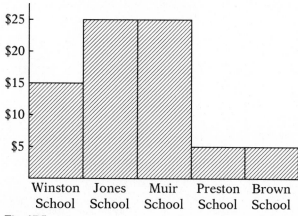

Fig. 17.5

When constructing bar graphs, we need to consider several things. First, bar graphs are most suitable for discrete data; that is, distinct, separate, and discontinuous data. For example, suppose we want to picture the number of freshmen, sophomores, juniors, and seniors at a university. Since freshmen, sophomores, juniors, and seniors are distinctly different categories, a bar graph might be drawn. Second, as we draw a bar graph, we need to be sure that all the bars are the same width. Also, the categories to be compared are placed on the horizontal axis and the frequencies on the vertical axis. Finally, the scale used for the frequency of units should not be compressed or extended, and zero must be the starting unit. In short, the area of the bar should be proportional to its frequency.

Line Graphs

Line graphs, in contrast to bar graphs, are more suitable for continuous data. Change over time is one example of data that a line graph can describe accurately. When drawing line graphs, a major consideration is to select a proper scale. The scale must accommodate the collected data, account for the variance between the greatest and least values to be graphed, and provide a fine degree of accuracy. In some ways, a line graph can be thought of as being formed from a bar graph by taking the bars off and connecting the center point of each bar.

When constructing a line graph, the time variable is placed on the horizontal axis. The numerical change is plotted on the vertical axis. Suppose we want to graph the temperature outdoors over a 12-hour period. The 12 hours of the day would form the equal intervals along the horizontal axis. The changes in temperature, expressed in degrees Celsius, would constitute the vertical axis of the graph. Figure 17.6 shows the constructed line graph of temperature variation over the course of a 12-hour period.

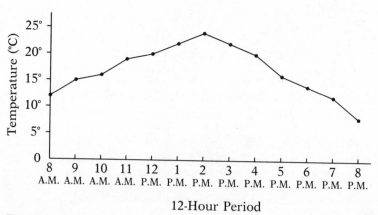

Fig. 17.6

Looking at both the horizontal and vertical scales, we see that the highest temperature of 23°C was reached at 2 P.M.

Circle Graphs

Circle graphs are often used with percents. The sectors of a circle graph refer to percentages of the data being studied. The following table shows how to construct a circle graph depicting the essential expenditures from a family budget.

Family Budget Expenditures

	Money Spent	*Percent of Budget*	*Measure of Sector*
Housing	$ 246.00	30%	30% of 360° = 108°
Food and clothing	164.00	20	20% of 360° = 72°
Savings	123.00	15	15% of 360° = 54°
Entertainment	205.00	25	25% of 360° = 90°
Gifts	82.00	10	10% of 360° = 36°
Total	$ 820.00	100%	

We can use the degree measurements by placing a protractor at the center of a circle and marking off the appropriate angle measurements. The completed circle graph is shown in Fig. 17.7.

Fig. 17.7

Circle graphs are rather easy to read. However, their construction requires students to understand percents, angular measure, and how to use a protractor to measure angles. For these reasons, elementary school students are usually taught to interpret rather than construct circle graphs.

Coordinate Graphs

Coordinate graphs are described by sets of ordered pairs. For example (6, 2) means to move 6 units to the right and 2 units up on a rectangular grid. Figure 17.8 shows the location from the origin of several sets of points.

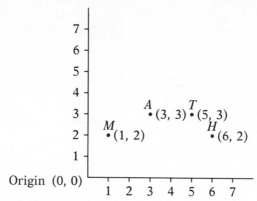

Fig. 17.8

We often use two references when describing a location; for example, we say "Meet me at the corner of Elm and Maple." In effect, coordinate graphing systems are refinements of a common way of describing points on a plane.

At the fifth- and sixth-grade levels, emphasis is placed on locating points by moving horizontally and then vertically (see Activities 17.9, 17.10, and 17.11). A useful device for concretely developing the idea of coordinate graphs can be made with a pegboard, golf tees, and rubber bands. The diagram and description below show how this can be done.

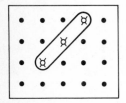

Place golf tees on appropriate points, such as (2, 2), (3, 3) or (4, 4). These points have been marked by Xs in the diagram. Next, take a rubber band and connect the golf tees. The resulting image shows the likeness of a straight line.

=== *MATH HISTORY 17.2* ===

Rene Descartes, a seventeenth-century mathematician, is credited with the development of coordinate graphing systems. It has been written that, while lying in bed, he observed a fly walking on the ceiling and found that he could describe the fly's position by using two directions, a right and left distance from a corner. Thus, the idea of the ordered pair was born.

ACTIVITY 17.9 Monte Carlo Simulation

Monte Carlo simulation can be an enjoyable activity at the intermediate school level, particularly for gifted students. Suppose we have the following problem:

Each box of a brand of cereal contains one of six stickers of a favorite animal. How many boxes of cereal must be purchased before it is likely that all six stickers can be obtained?

Monte Carlo simulation works this way. Put the names of the six animals on note cards and put the cards into a box. Have the students draw a card, write the name of the animal, and replace the card. Continue until all six cards have been drawn. Students should record how many drawings they made to get all six cards. Repeat the entire procedure 25 times to find the mean number of cereal boxes purchased. A hand calculator can be used to calculate the mean.

ACTIVITY 17.10

Graphing Stock Market Fluctuations

A stock market activity can be an interesting way of developing line graphs.

Children can select a stock from the listing in the daily newspaper. They can chart the stock's daily closing price and then draw a line graph to show the price changes. At the end of 1 week, results can be compared. Numerous questions can be asked, such as "Who made the most money?" or "How did the class fare as a group?" Using a hand calculator, the average or mean price of the stock at the end of the week can be compared to the mean price at the beginning of the week. The graph below shows a fictitious stock and its price changes.

Monday	$25.25
Tuesday	$26.75
Wednesday	$24.50
Thursday	$24.75
Friday	$30.00

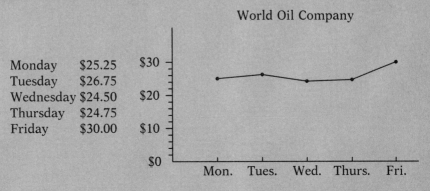

World Oil Company

ACTIVITY
17.11   Find the Graph's Message

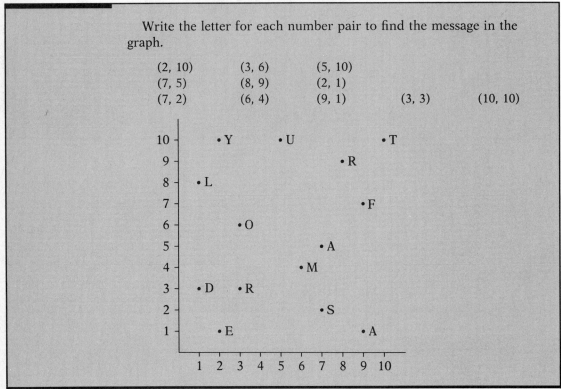

Write the letter for each number pair to find the message in the graph.

(2, 10)	(3, 6)	(5, 10)
(7, 5)	(8, 9)	(2, 1)
(7, 2)	(6, 4)	(9, 1) (3, 3) (10, 10)

Summary

This chapter develops the fundamental ideas of probability, statistics, and graphing. The emphasis on these topics is informal and experimental in nature. Particular emphasis needs to be placed on integrating graphical topics within the elementary school mathematics curriculum. Graphs are widely used in business, industry, and everyday applications. Probability and statistics concepts, although less widely developed in elementary school programs, are important as well. Enrichment or gifted programs certainly can emphasize these topics. However, informal introduction of selected topics, such as collecting data and making predictions on the basis of data, are experiences that should be afforded to all elementary school children.

Discussion Questions

1. Study the newspapers for a week. What surveys are reported? What kind of information is given in each survey? What are the strengths and weaknesses of each survey?

2. Develop a lesson plan for introducing a beginning probability experience to intermediate-grade students.

3. Read Huff (1954) and find four interesting misuses of statistics that might be enjoyable for gifted middle school students to consider.

4. Investigate several elementary textbook series (see Appendix B) to determine the extent to which probability and statistics are developed at the intermediate-grade level.

5. Collect examples from advertising that show misleading claims for endorsements.

6. Suppose that the mean age of the people attending a picnic at a park was 17. Does this mean that most of the people attending the picnic were teenagers?

7. Collect a set of graphs from newspapers and magazines. Construct a bulletin board display of the ways that graphs are used in daily life.

8. Find journal articles from the *Arithmetic Teacher* that describe ways to teach probability and statistics to elementary school children. Share your findings with other students in your class.

References

Armstrong, P. W. (1975). *The ability of fifth and sixth graders to learn selected topics in probability.* Unpublished Ph.D. dissertation, The University of Oklahoma.

Bohan, H., & Moreland, E. J. (1981). Developing some statistical concepts in the elementary school. In A. Shulte & J. Smart (eds.), *Teaching statistics and probability* (pp. 60–63). Reston, Va.: NCTM.

Burns, M. (1983). Put some probability in your classroom. *Arithmetic Teacher, 26,* pp. 21–22.

Choate, S. A. (1979). Activity in applying probability ideas. *Arithmetic Teacher, 26,* pp. 40–42.

Enman, V. (1979). Probability in the intermediate grades. *Arithmetic Teacher, 26,* pp. 38–39.

Hirt, H. (1977). Probability. *Mathematics Teaching, 80,* pp. 6–8.

Horak, V. M., & Willis, J. H. (1976). Collecting and displaying the data around us. *Arithmetic Teacher, 23,* pp. 34–35.

Huff, D. (1954). *How to lie with statistics.* New York: Norton.

Johnson, E. M. (1982). Bar graphs for first graders. *Arithmetic Teacher, 29,* pp. 30–31.

Jones, G. (1979). A case for probability. *Arithmetic Teacher, 26,* pp. 37, 57.

Keely, M. (1986). Elementary school activity: Graphing the stock market. *Arithmetic Teacher, 7,* pp. 17–20.

Nibbelink, W. (1982). Graphing for any grade. *Arithmetic Teacher, 30,* pp. 28–31.

Pereira-Mendoza, L. (1981). Using dice: From place value to probability. *Arithmetic Teacher, 28,* pp. 10–11.

Piaget, J., & Inhelder, B. (1975). *The origin of the idea of chance in children.* New York: Norton.

Schroeder, T. L. (1983). *An assessment of elementary school students' development and application of probability concepts while playing and discussing two strategy games on a microcomputer.* Unpublished Ph.D. dissertation, Indiana University.

Shulte, A. P. (1979). A case for statistics. *Arithmetic Teacher, 26,* p. 24.

Souviney, R. J. (1970). Probability and statistics. *Learning, 5,* pp. 51–52.

Watkins, A. E. (1981). Monte Carlo simulation: Probability the easy way. In A. Shulte & J. Smart (eds.), *Teaching statistics and probability* (pp. 203–209). Reston, Va.: NCTM.

Woodward, E. (1983). A second-grade probability and graphing lesson. *Arithmetic Teacher, 26,* pp. 23–24.

CHAPTER 18

Measurement

Objectives

After reading this chapter you will be able to:

1. Identify fundamental metric system units that children in elementary schools need to master.

2. Identify fundamental customary units that elementary school children need to understand.

3. Create learning activities that help children experiment with metric system units.

4. Examine the structure of the metric system and relate it to everyday environmental references.

5. Create learning activities designed to reinforce customary measurement units.

Introduction

Measurement experiences are an important component of the elementary school mathematics curriculum. Starting at the kindergarten level, children are comparing the lengths of pencils, the weight of stones, and the volume of pitchers and drinking glasses. In Chapter 3, suggested activities for initial measuring experiences are provided. To review, much of the early work with measurement involves direct comparison of lengths, weights, and volumes. Standard units of measure are gradually introduced. At first, arbitrary units, such as hand lengths, are used to develop the idea of repetitively using a unit. Convenient objects such as desk tops or chalkboards can be measured by repeatedly placing an arbitrary unit along the length. Informal experiences, often in a play atmosphere, characterize beginning measurement experiences of children.

As we develop a systematic measurement program for children in the elementary school, we must first consider what it means to measure. Performing a measurement task involves several assumptions. First, we decide on an attribute that we desire to measure. This may be the height of a person, a duration of time, or the weight of an object. Next, we must decide on a unit of measure, perhaps a centimeter, a second, or a gram may be the selected unit. Units that are commonly agreed on by members of a society are called *standard units.* After selecting a standard unit, we determine a measure, how many of the standard units are used to describe the attribute we are measuring. Thus, a *measurement* involves a standard unit as well as a measure; that is, how many standard units describe the attribute. For example, when we say a building is 150 feet high, we are saying the standard *unit* is feet. Also, the *measure,* how many units describe the building's height, is 150.

As children develop increasing skill with measurement, precision is gradually introduced. Smaller and smaller units are used to give more precise measurement results. Since all measurements involve some degree of error, we attempt to reduce error of measurement by using smaller, more refined units of measure. A linear measurement made in $\frac{1}{4}$ inches has an error of measurement of $\frac{1}{8}$ inch. A linear measurement made in $\frac{1}{16}$ of an inch has an error of measurement of $\frac{1}{32}$ of an inch. In general, the measurement unit selected has an error of measurement one-half the size of the selected measurement unit.

Accuracy of a measurement refers to the degree of error in a measurement. The less error, the more accurate our measurement. Generally, more precise units, more refined instruments, and greater skill in using measurement instruments, contribute to increasing accuracy of measurement. However, it is important to avoid rushing accuracy and precision of measurement. Children need to explore, estimate, and intuitively develop experience with measurement. Perhaps in the fifth and sixth grades we can emphasize precision and accuracy in socially important measurement situations. Even so, a list of 15 items to measure to the nearest $\frac{1}{16}$ of an inch or nearest millimeter is hardly the way to encourage children to use measurement in their daily life. It is better to treat two or three examples of measurement in a precise and accurate manner than to provide meaningless, repetitive experiences.

Measurement, always having some degree of error, is always approximate. Thus, when teaching measurement to children, estimation experiences need to play a big part in the curriculum. Reys and Reys (1986) cited research evidence that indicates mental computation and estimation are used in more than 80 percent of all real-world, problem-solving situations outside the classroom. Certainly, if we examine our daily lives, we note that we estimate whether the volume of our car will fit into a parking space. We estimate distances, cooking measurements, and liquid measurements every day. An interesting historical note on estimation is found in the record of Columbus' 1492 journey to discover the New World. Columbus used estimation to observe the height of the foam produced by his ship as it moved through the ocean. He was able to estimate the distance of the trip by using this estimate of his ship's speed. Remarkably, modern oceanographers have found that Columbus' rather unique form of estimation was within 5 percent of the total trip distance. Truly, a magnificent feat of estimation. Thus, estimation activities need to be an integral part of children's measurement experience. Only then can precision and accuracy of measurement be meaningfully investigated.

=========== *MATH HISTORY 18.1* ===========

A simple decimal system of measurement for both science and commerce was first proposed in 1670 by Gabriel Mouton of France. A century later, the idea for such a system was transformed into the French metric system.

A Brief History of Measurement

We need to investigate briefly several historical cultures in order to become more aware of the contributions that have been made to our present measurement systems. This history reveals a rather surprising sophistication as well as a gradual increase in standardization.

Early systems of measurement were found on clay tablets excavated from Babylonian civilization. Some of these clay tablets date as far back as 2100 B.C. Babylonian measurement was intimately related to the practical needs of an agricultural economy. Thus, the Babylonians were familiar with the general rules for calculating the area of a rectangle, the areas of right and isosceles triangles, and the volumes of cubes and prisms. These calculation procedures were most likely used to calculate land areas and granary volumes. Further, we credit the Babylonians with our current use of 60 seconds in a minute. Astronomical calculations by the Babylonians yielded a year having 365 days, 6 hours, and 11 minutes, a calculation within three minutes of the modern calculation!

Egyptian mathematics, although not as advanced as Babylonian, also made contributions to measurement and geometry. For example, the great pyramid of Gizeh, erected about 2900 B.C., required great measurement and engineering skill. This structure covers 13 acres and contains 2 million stone blocks, averaging 2.5 tons in weight, very carefully fitted together. It has been reported that the sides of the square base involve a relative error of less than 1/14,000 and that the relative error in the right angles at the corners is less than 1/27,000. This great engineering marvel was accomplished by an army of 100,000 laborers working for a period of 30 years.

The Greeks, developers of geometry, were also interested in measurement. Areas of geometric figures such as triangles, rectangles, and squares were well known to the Greeks. Deductive logic was used to validate theorems regarding geometric figures. Numerous discoveries in geometry and measurement were made by the Greeks. For example, Erathosthenes (230 B.C.), using only the shadows formed by sticks, calculated the circumference of the earth to within a few percent of the current value. The Greeks synthesized and further elaborated on the discoveries of Babylonia and Egypt. Advances in measurement, astronomy, and mathematics abounded in Greek culture.

During the Middle Ages, measurement units were often defined in terms of parts of the human body. For example, a fathom was considered to be the distance between the tips of fingers when both arms are outstretched. Similarly, a human foot served as the standard for that unit of length. The Romans under Julius Caesar had introduced to England the mile as 1000 double paces. Thus, medieval England used the Roman definitions of the mile. Needless to say, the wide variety of standard units during the medieval period produced rather haphazard measurement systems.

During the later medieval period, crude attempts at standardization continued. Perhaps one of the first attempts at standardizing the yard occurred during the reign of Henry I of England (1068–1135). Henry decreed that the yard should be defined as the length of his outstretched arm (nose to tip of fingers or thumb). Also, during the medieval era, English kings defined an inch to be three barley corns laid end to end.

In Colonial America, a system of measurements was inherited from England. Terms such as *inch, yard, pound,* and *foot* were all transported to the colonies. In the 1790s, the French developed the metric system. Enlightened leaders such as Thomas Jefferson gave serious thought to adopting the metric system in the United States.

Today, we live in a complex measurement world. Standards are defined with increasing precision. For example, a meter is defined to be 1,650,763.73 wavelengths of the red-orange line of Krypton 86. Although precise standards are abundant in today's world, care must be taken when selecting the most appropriate mix of customary units and metric system units for elementary school students to investigate. Further, children at the elementary school level need to explore informally important measurement units. Thus, estimation activities of lengths, capacities, and weight are emphasized in this chapter.

=========== *MATH HISTORY 18.2* ===========

In 1900, the Chinese had two different units called a *mile*—an uphill mile and a downhill mile. The uphill mile was the shorter of the two.

=========== *MATH HISTORY 18.3* ===========

Libra, the Latin word for *pound,* was abbreviated *lb.* England is given credit for adopting this Roman term for weight.

Development of the Metric System

The metric system of measurement originated in France during the 1790s. In 1799, the standard units for length and mass (weight) were developed. Initially, the *meter* was defined to be one-ten millionth of the distance from the equator to the North Pole along the meridian from Dunkirk, France.

Discussion on whether to adopt the metric system of measurement began rather early in our nation's history. Thomas Jefferson, secretary of state in 1790, proposed a decimal system of measurement that would integrate the bewildering assortment of measurement units used at that time. For example, in 1800, the term *pound* applied to 391 different weights and the term *foot* applied to 282 different lengths. In 1821, John Quincy Adams commissioned a study to investigate the adoption of the metric system in this country. By an act of Congress on July 28, 1866, the metric system of measure became legal in the United States. At various points during the twentieth century, governmental groups debated the adoption of the metric system in the United States. In 1975, President Ford signed a bill creating a metric system board to oversee voluntary changeover to the metric system in this country. Today, the metric system board has been abolished.

So, just where are we today with the metric system? Governmental legislation has not been forthcoming in initiating change to the system. However, business and industry have been leaders in initiating change. Since the United States is the only major industrial country in the world that has not adopted the metric system, it is in the best interest of American business to change to metric measurement in order to remain competitive in global markets. Coca-Cola, Pepsi-Cola, Ford Motor Company, and General Motors are just a few of the many companies that have changed to metric measurements in order to attain a more effective stance in international markets.

Today, schools are teaching children metric measurements and, at the same time, also teaching customary units such as the inch and pound. It is necessary that children be equipped to deal with a bilingual world where metric and customary units are both used. Thus, elementary school teachers need to prepare lessons that develop the fundamental units of the customary system as well as the metric system.

Metric System Units.   Today, the refinement and development of the metric system has resulted in an agreeable, unified system of metric measure. This system is called the *International System of Units,* commonly called *SI.* This system is used internationally and involves measurement of length (meter), time (seconds), electric current (ampere), and luminous intensity (candela), among others. The seven basic units in the SI system are shown in Table 18.1.

Table 18.1 Basic Units of the SI System

Measurement	Standard Unit	Symbol
Length	Meter	m
Time	Second	s
Mass	Kilogram	kg
Electric current	Ampere	A
Amount of substance	Mole	mol
Temperature	Kelvin	K
Luminous intensity	Candela	cd

The *meter* is the basic unit for length. Since metric system units are related by multiples of 10, all other length units can be derived easily from the meter. The most common length units are shown in Table 18.2.

Table 18.2 Most Common Length Units

Length Unit	Relationship to Meter	Symbol
Kilometer	1000 meters	km
Hectometer	100 meters	hm
Dekameter	10 meters	dam
Meter		m
Decimeter	.1 meter	dm
Centimeter	.01 meter	cm
Millimeter	.001 meter	mm

A *kilogram* is a basic SI unit designed to measure mass, the amount of matter of a substance. The amount of matter is independent of a gravitational system. Therefore, we have the same amount of matter on the earth or on the moon. However, our weight on the moon is less than our weight on the earth. Thus, our weight changes when a gravity force changes. Fortunately, the mass and weight values are nearly the same on the Earth. So, elementary school teachers and students can use the more common term *weight* and avoid the less familiar descriptor, *mass.*

Table 18.3 shows the fundamental weight units used in the metric system. Notice the use of the metric system prefixes. Also, note we have provided symbols only for the more commonly used weight units. The prefixes used in the metric system exhibit an interesting pattern. Kilo always represents 1000 of a given unit; hecto, 100 units; deka, 10 units; deci, .1 unit; centi, .01 unit; and milli, .001 unit. Once we determine a base unit for length, weight (mass), or liquid capacity, all the related units may be found by placing appropriate prefixes in front of the base unit. This pattern, based on powers of 10, allows us to list quickly key metric units.

Table 18.3 Fundamental Units of Weight

Weight (Mass) Unit	Relationship of Units	Symbol
Kilogram	1000 grams	kg
Hectogram	100 grams	
Dekagram	10 grams	
Gram		g
Decigram	.1 gram	
Centigram	.01 gram	cg
Milligram	.001 gram	mg

The *liter,* serving as a base unit for liquid capacity, can be derived from the fundamental SI units. It has been defined to be the volume of one kilogram of pure water under specified conditions. An approximate equality to the liter can be found by filling with water a cube having sides 10 centimeters long. Most often, we use the liter and milliliter in business and industry.

To illustrate the powers-of-10 relationship of the units for liquid capacity and volume, Table 18.4 is presented. Notice again that symbols are provided only for the more common units.

Table 18.4 Relationship of the Units for Liquid Capacity and Volume

Liquid Capacity Unit	Relationship to Base Unit	Symbol
Kiloliter	1000 liters	
Hectoliter	100 liters	
Dekaliter	10 liters	
Liter		L
Deciliter	.1 liter	
Centiliter	.01 liter	
Milliliter	.001 liter	mL

This brief overview provides us with a view of the structure of the metric system. Activity 18.1 offers a way to familiarize yourself with metric terms. Volume, measured in terms of cubic centimeters and cubic meters, as well as temperature, measured in Celsius, are investigated later in the chapter.

Finally, some texts and journals write numbers such as 1,256 as 1 256. The space is used instead of a comma because of the international appeal of the metric system. Many European countries use a comma as a decimal point; thus, to avoid ambiguity in international metric reporting, a space is used in numerals instead of a comma. We use the comma to separate thousands, hundred thousands, and so on because many elementary textbook series still do this. However, if readers encounter 2 587 469 instead of 2,587,469, they should not panic. These expressions mean the same thing, and the former writing is simply a result of international metric usage.

ACTIVITY 18.1 Metric Proverbs

Take these common sayings and revise them using metric terms.

1. There was a crooked man and he walked a crooked _____ .

2. An _____ of prevention is worth a _____ of cure.

3. Hundred _____ dash.

4. Penny wise and _____ foolish.

Make up some more sayings that can be converted to metric usage.

Guidelines for Teaching Measurement to Children

Providing measurement experiences for children requires elementary school teachers to follow several guidelines.

1. Children need "hands-on" measurement experience. Metric system units and customary units can be developed through a wide variety of laboratory experiences. Children need to use rulers, graduated cylinders, and scales as they explore both customary and metric system units.

2. Metric system and customary units need to be taught independently of each other. Conversions from one system to another should be avoided. Most textbook series follow this guideline by introducing metric system and customary units at different points in the school year.

3. Children need to estimate and "think" within a given system. For example, Lindquist (1987) has described several useful strategies when estimating measurements:

    a. *Using references*—If a student has an image of a 6-foot-tall person, then this knowledge can be used to help estimate heights such as of a doorway. Similarly, an image of a centimeter as the width of a paper clip can help a student estimate the length of a chewing gum package.

    b. *Chunking*—When estimating the height of a room, we can break the task into component parts. For example, we could estimate the distance from the floor to the window, the length of the window, and the distance from the window to the ceiling.

    c. *Unitizing*—Suppose we were to measure the length of a field. We could break the field up into eight equal parts and estimate the length of each part.

The practical nature of estimating measurements demands that we incorporate this approach throughout our teaching of measurement. References are particularly helpful; that is, children can use convenient household objects like paper clips or nickels to refer to metric system units. As you read through this chapter, you should note the many examples of metric system units related to real-world estimates.

Metric Measurement Experiences

Primary-Grade Students (K–3)

Children in the primary grades should estimate and then measure such common items as the length of the chalkboard, the height of a small bush, and their own height. A rather enjoyable activity is to give children pieces of string and have them use it to measure the width of their smiles. After the smile length has been marked off on the string, the string can be placed against a metric ruler to find its length. Data can be recorded and the student with the largest smile can be identified. Children can also use string to measure the diameter of tree trunks, their head size, as well as their bicep size. In short, children at the primary level need to measure all sorts of common objects, thus gaining a familiarity with fundamental metric units. Also, ruler marking should be kept to a minimum. A ruler marked off in centimeters is appropriate for children in the primary grades. Figure 18.1 shows such a ruler. It is useful for children to estimate metric length units by using common references. For example, a centimeter is the approximate width of the distance between a paper clip's metal fasteners, a millimeter is the thickness of a dime, a meter is the approximate distance from the chalkboard to the floor.

Fig. 18.1

During the primary grades, weight experiences for gram and kilogram are provided. Convenient references for weight (mass) units are a paper clip, which weighs 1 gram; a nickel, which weighs 5 grams; and a coffee can filled with coffee, which weighs about 1 kilogram. Children can use a balance scale to determine the weight, in grams, of common household objects such as a comb or a pencil.

Teachers can bring sample food items from the local supermarket to show children how metric weight measurements are used in daily life. Cereal boxes, soup cans, and laundry detergents all have metric weight measurements on the containers. These and other items from a simulated shopping trip can be used as a basis for a class discussion.

During the primary school years, we emphasize liter and, to a lesser degree, milliliter, as liquid capacity measures. For illustrating liters, an easily constructed model can be made by taking a half-gallon milk container and measuring up $9\frac{1}{2}$ centimeters from the bottom. Cut the milk carton at that place. You now have a model for a liter container! Using a model such as this, children can fill drinking glasses, soda pop bottles, and other containers with water. Then, they can pour the water into the liter model and estimate the metric liquid capacity. Remember, initial experiences with metric units need not be precise. We can say that a soda pop bottle holds less than one-half liter of water. There is no need to state a specific amount such as 238 milliliters. More precise measurement recordings can be made at the intermediate level.

Celsius temperature readings also can be performed at the primary level.

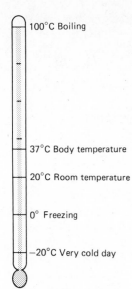

100°C Boiling

37°C Body temperature

20°C Room temperature

0° Freezing

−20°C Very cold day

Fig. 18.2

At first, children should see a modified thermometer that shows key markings, as shown in Fig. 18.2.

Later, as children are accustomed to reading higher numerical values, a Celsius thermometer can be used with all the temperature markings. Discussion can be held in an incidental manner. The following questions may be asked: What is the temperature today? What is the temperature of your body? When does water freeze? Another activity that children can perform is to list the high temperature for each day of the school week. Again, the central point is to have children relate measurements to their daily life.

In summary, fundamental metric units need to be experienced by having primary children perform measurements. (See Activities 18.2 and 18.3.) Children should learn the names of these units, but the symbols for them should be delayed until the intermediate grades.

ACTIVITY 18.2   Outdoor Mathematics

The outdoors can provide a nice experience for children to practice measuring. Children can find leaves and group them into categories less than 5 centimeters and more than 5 centimeters. Rocks less than a kilogram can be located. Twigs shorter than 50 centimeters can be found. Children can make estimates of these measurements and then actually test them.

ACTIVITY 18.3   Spin a Meter

This activity can be played with two primary-aged children. As shown in the diagram below, you need a meter stick, a spinner, and a set of Cuisenaire rods. Also, each child is given a centimeter-sized ruler.

7 8
6   1
5   2
4 3

1 meter
(Represents one meter.)

Children are to take turns spinning the spinner. After reading the numeral, a child uses the centimeter ruler to locate a rod the same length as the identified number. After doing this, the rod is placed on one side of the meter stick. The other child repeats this procedure and places the rod on the other side of the meter stick. Play alternates until one player reaches the end of the meter stick.

Intermediate-Grade Students (4–6)

During the latter elementary years, increasing precision of measurement is developed. Children perform length measurements of meters, centimeters, millimeters, and kilometers. Volume and liquid capacity are measured by using graduated cylinders to measure liters and milliliters. Grams and kilograms are measured by balance scales and bathroom scales. For some children, the structure of the metric system in terms of the prefixes used to generate units as multiples of 10 is studied. All children need to measure objects; however, some children who have special needs will not benefit by an introduction to the relationship among units. Their instructional time will be best served by measuring and mastering several basic, widely used metric units. Finally, symbols need to be developed only for the more important metric units.

Table 18.5 presents metric system units for length, weight (mass), liquid capacity, and temperature. An asterisk denotes the more important units. Mastery of these units would constitute a minimum competency for children exiting the elementary school. (See Activities 18.4 through 18.7.)

Table 18.5 Metric System Units

	Unit	Relationship	Real-World References
Length	*Kilometer	1000 meters	km—about 2 laps around a college track
	Hectometer	100 meters	
	Dekameter	10 meters	
	*Meter		m—distance from chalkboard to floor
	Decimeter	.1 meter	dm—about the width of your hand
	Centimeter	.01 meter	cm—about the thickness of your small fingertip

Table 18.5 Metric System Units (*Continued*)

	Unit	Relationship	Real-World References
	*Millimeter	.001 meter	mm—about the thickness of a dime
Weight (mass)	*Kilogram	1000 grams	kg—about the size of a 2-pound coffee can
	Hectogram	100 grams	
	Dekagram	10 grams	
	*Gram		g—weight of a paper clip
	Decigram	.1 gram	
	Centigram	.01 gram	
	*Milligram	.001 gram	mg—used for measuring prescription drugs and vitamins
Liquid capacity (volume)	Kiloliter	1000 liters	
	Hectoliter	100 liters	
	Dekaliter	10 liters	
	*Liter		L—a little larger than a quart
	Deciliter	.1 liter	
	Centiliter	.01 liter	
	*Milliliter	.001 liter	mL—about the amount of water that would fill a box with dimensions 1cm × 1cm × 1cm
Temperature	100°C	Boiling water	
	37°C	Body temperature	
	20°C	Room temperature	
	0°C	Freezing	

ACTIVITY 18.4 Metric Weights of Common Items

This activity can help children to estimate the weight of common objects. Similarly, it can be used by adults to gain familiarity with key metric system measurements.

Estimate the weight of these common objects. Record your results in both grams and kilograms. How good an estimator were you?

	Estimated Weight	Actual Weight
Iron	_____	_____
Hammer	_____	_____
Shoe	_____	_____
Dictionary	_____	_____
Purse	_____	_____
Package of chewing gum	_____	_____
Ring	_____	_____

ACTIVITY 18.5 Metric Volumes of Common Items

This activity helps children and adults to gain firsthand experience with metric system measurements.

Using graduated cylinders and beakers, determine the liquid capacity of the following items. Be sure to estimate and then actually measure the amount.

	Estimated Volume	Actual Volume
Coffee cup	_____	_____
Drinking glass	_____	_____
Soup bowl	_____	_____
Soda pop bottle	_____	_____
Paper cup	_____	_____

ACTIVITY 18.6 Metric Measurements of Height

To gain necessary reference information regarding metric system lengths, you can measure your height in meters and centimeters. Record your measurements. Now guess two classmates' heights. How accurate were you?

ACTIVITY 18.7 Metric Measurements of Weight

Experience with metric weights is the intention of this activity. Also, developing the idea of a reference unit to aid estimation is considered.

Weigh yourself on a metric calibrated bathroom scale. Record your weight in kilograms and grams. Use your personal data to guess the weight of several willing classmates.

Conversions Within the Metric System

Some basic conversions within the metric system can be developed in grades 6–8. These are shown below with specific examples.

Representation of
.25 of another
1-meter stick

Representation of 1-meter stick

Length: 125 cm = 1.25 m

This can be demonstrated by placing a meter stick and .25 of another stick together. This represents 1.25 m

We can also count out 125 centimeters on these two meter sticks and arrive at the same points. So, 125 cm = 1.25 m. Move the decimal point two places to the left to change from centimeters to meters.

Weight: Using the tables provided earlier in this chapter, we determine that 1000 g = 1 kg. So, 2,456 g = 2.456 kg. Just move the decimal point three places to the left to convert from grams to kilograms. Conversely, changing from kilograms to grams requires us to move the decimal point to the right. For example, 2.53 kg is equal to 2,530 g.

Liquid capacity: Referring to the tables in this chapter, we determine that 1000 mL = 1 L. So, 3542 mL = 3.542 L. Just move the decimal point three places to the left to convert from milliliters to liters. Also, to change from liters to milliliters, move the decimal point three places to the right. For example, 3.568 L is equal to 3568 mL.

So far, we have developed the more important conversions within the metric system. A more systematic approach, which helps students convert many more metric units, is shown in Fig. 18.3. Each step in the figure represents a linear unit, from millimeter to kilometer. Similarly, each step represents a power of 10. When changing from a large unit to a smaller unit, we need more of the smaller units. Thus, when converting from meters to centimeters, we take two steps down the staircase, meaning we multiply the number of meters by 10 × 10, or 100. Conversely, when changing from meters to hectometers, we are changing from a smaller unit to a larger one. Moving two steps up the ladder requires us to divide the number of meters by 10 × 10, or 100.

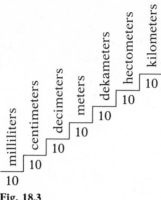

Fig. 18.3

Let us consider a specific example. Suppose we have a measurement of 2,565 centimeters that we wish to convert to dekameters. Using Fig. 18.3, we determine that three steps upward will bring us to the dekameter level. Since we are changing from a smaller unit to a larger unit, we divide by 10 × 10 × 10, or 1,000. Recalling that division of decimals by multiples of 10 can be performed easily by moving the decimal point, we move the decimal point three places to the left and obtain 2.565 dekameters for our result.

Conversions within the metric system require a good understanding of decimals, particularly multiplying and dividing by powers of 10. Assuming this, we can convert easily within the metric system by simply moving the decimal point to the left or right depending on whether we are dividing or multiplying.

Instruction on metric units needs to be individualized. For some children, the structure of the metric system, meaning its multiples-of-10 relationship, can be developed by investigating all of the units listed in the preceding table. However, for many children at the elementary school level, a "survival" course in metric measurement is more important. Fundamental units for length such as kilometer, meter, centimeter, and millimeter are used in everyday life. Likewise gram, kilogram, and milligram are encountered. We speak of milliliters and liters for liquid-capacity measurements. Estimates of Celsius temperature based on everyday experiences are also fundamental. These are the most important experiences for many children to have. Science, business, and industry and everyday commercial life require an educated citizen capable of interpreting fundamental metric language. Estimation rather than preciseness should be emphasized at the elementary school level. However, some children who are capable with mathematics can profit from a study of the base-10 structure of the metric system.

During the later elementary school years, the relationship among length, weight, and volume measurements can be developed. This should be done with appropriate models as shown below.

A cubic centimeter is a cube with each of its sides being 1 cm in length. It will hold 1 mL of water. At room temperature and at sea level, the milliliter of water will weigh 1 g. Visualizing this cube will model three metric units—the centimeter, gram, and milliliter.

A cubic decimeter (10cm × 10cm × 10cm) will hold 1 L of water and, again, at sea level and room temperature, a liter of water will weigh 1 kg. Visualizing this cube will yield three models for metric units—the decimeter, liter, and kilogram.

Although perimeter, area, and volume are developed extensively in Chapter 19, a brief review that focuses on metric units is presented here.

Perimeter

Perimeter, or the distance around a geometric figure, is measured with length units. Figure 18.4 shows the perimeter for a rectangle. Centimeter-sized graph paper can be used for children to trace geometric figures and then count the length units around the figure.

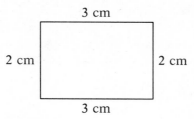

Fig. 18.4

Area

Since the concept of *area* is developed in Chapter 19, one example will serve to illustrate this point.

The rectangle shown in Fig. 18.5 can be covered with four rows of six square centimeters. The area is found by multiplying 4 × 6 = 24. Thus, the area of the rectangle is 24 square centimeters. Children can use graph paper to draw and discover the area of various geometric shapes. Again, it is important to keep this informal. Delay formulas for finding the area of squares, rectangles, and triangles until children have a good understanding of the concept of covering with a square unit.

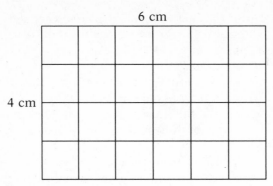

Fig. 18.5

Another area unit considered in the latter stages of the elementary school is the square meter. This is used for finding larger areas such as the school parking lot. In fact, a useful experience is to actually measure and calculate the area of the school parking lot or playground. (See Activity 18.8.)

ACTIVITY 18.8 Estimating the Area of Irregular-Shaped Objects

Take centimeter-sized graph paper and estimate how many square centimeters your hand occupies. Then trace the surface area of your hand, count the squares, and find the area of your hand. Repeat this activity with leaves, feet, and other irregular-shaped objects. Compare your results with those of your classmates.

Volume

Volume for solids usually requires the use of cubic centimeters or cubic meters. Children need to fill solids with cubic centimeters to gain an understanding of volume formulas.

An example for a rectangular prism is shown in Fig. 18.6. Children can fill this solid with cubic centimeters. They can discover that 70 cubic centimeters will fill the prism. Several experiences such as this can yield the volume formula $V = l \times w \times h$. Specifically, in this case $V = 2 \times 5 \times 7 = 70$ cubic centimeters. Note that we could have used the symbol cm^3 for cubic centimeters. Also, note that the dimensions of the prism are scaled representations, not exact lengths.

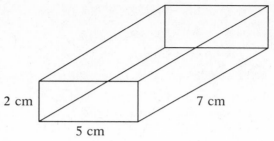

2 cm   7 cm

5 cm

Fig. 18.6

Customary Units of Measurement

Terms such as *inch, foot, yard,* and *mile* are still a part of the elementary mathematics curriculum. Although elementary textbooks teach the metric system of measurement, there is still a need for children to be familiar with customary system (sometimes called the English system). We live, today, in a bilingual world where important units of the metric system and customary systems exist side by side. Although conversions between the two systems should be avoided, we still need to have students learn important units of each system.

Length

At the primary-grade level, children begin to explore length units such as inches and feet. They can find, for example, the height of a friend in terms of feet. Estimating lengths such as the distance across the teacher's desk can be checked by using a standard ruler (see Activities 18.9 and 18.10). Results for estimates can be recorded and shared with classmates.

ACTIVITY 18.9   Measurement Scavenger Hunt

This activity can be used to promote practice with customary measurements at the primary-grade level.

Students can explore their environment and find objects of various lengths. They can validate their estimates by actually measuring the objects with an inch ruler.

1. Find an object less than 10 inches long. _____

2. Find an object more than 1 foot long. _____

3. Find an object more than 1 yard long. _____

4. Find an object of 1 to 2 feet in length. _____

5. Find an object more than 18 inches long. _____

6. Find an object longer than 2 feet. _____

7. Find an object of 2 to 4 feet in length. _____

ACTIVITY 18.10

Personal Data—Customary Units

This activity is designed to help students practice measuring with customary units. Also, students can discover a pattern that emerges from an examination of the data.

Measure your height and armspread in inches. Record your results on the following chart. Also, record the results obtained by other members of the class. Do you see a pattern?

Height	*Armspread*

Early measurement estimates are checked by using simplified rulers to measure inches and feet. Use the classroom environment as a resource for measuring lengths of desk tops, window sills, and floor tiles, among others. As children begin to use rulers, the simplified version shown in Fig. 18.7 should be used. A ruler such as this does not have too many markings, which can distract a young child's attention.

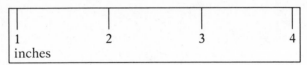

Fig. 18.7

Many of our adult assumptions about using rulers need to be set aside when teaching young children to measure. Research by Piaget (1960), Hiebert (1984), and others suggests that children need to be taught how to place a ruler end to end when measuring. Also, children need to measure objects that are arranged in vertical, horizontal, and diagonal positions. All too often, elementary mathematics textbooks provide linear measurement experiences with objects that are placed in only one position, a horizontal position.

By the end of the third grade, children are selecting the most appropriate measurement units for a given situation from these units: inches, feet, yards, and miles. By the end of the sixth grade, children have increased the precision of measurement to include measurements to $\frac{1}{16}$ of an inch. Also, conversion among units is expected to be mastered. For example, 4 feet 7 inches can be expressed as 55 inches. The following list shows the common relationships among linear units.

> 12 inches (in) = 1 foot (ft)
> 3 feet (ft) = 1 yard (yd)
> 36 inches (in) = 1 yard (yd)
> 5,280 feet (ft) = 1 mile (mi)
> 1,760 yards (yd) = 1 mile (mi)

Units of Capacity

During the primary years, children investigate cups, pints, quarts, and gallons. Again, measurement experiences need to emphasize a hands-on approach, where children are pouring pints into quart containers, quarts into gallon containers, and so on (see Activity 18.11). By the end of the third grade, we expect children to know the relationship among cups, pints, quarts, and gallons. As we progress through the elementary grades, we extend the capacity units to include tablespoons (tbsp), fluid ounces (oz), and half gallons. The following list shows the key units for capacity and some of the relationships among units.

> 2 tablespoons (tbsp) = 1 fluid ounce (fl oz)
> 8 fluid ounces (fl oz) = 1 cup (c)
> 2 cups (c) = 1 pint (pt)

2 pints (pt) = 1 quart (qt)

2 quarts (qt) = 1 half gallon ($\frac{1}{2}$ gal)

4 quarts (qt) = 1 gallon (gal)

A useful teaching aid that helps children to relate some of the various units is shown in Fig. 18.8. A bulletin board can be constructed around the theme of a gallon robot. This robot has 4 quarts leading into the main section of the body. Also, 2 pints lead into the quart extremity, and 2 cups into the pint extremity. Thus, several unit equivalences are demonstrated. For example, we can see that 4 quarts comprise 1 gallon, 8 pints make up 1 gallon, and 16 cups are equivalent to 1 gallon.

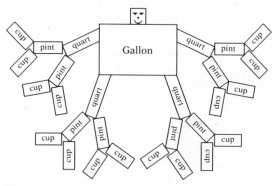

Fig. 18.8

Estimating Liquid Capacities of Common Objects

This activity helps children to estimate and measure the liquid capacity of common household objects. At the primary level, children can gain experience with customary liquid-capacity units by estimating and then comparing their estimates to actual measurements of the object's liquid capacity.

You will need to collect some common household containers for this activity.

1. Estimate how many pints a water pitcher holds. _____

2. Estimate how many quarts of water a bucket holds. _____

3. Estimate how many quarts of water a cider jug holds. _____

4. Estimate how many cups of water a soda pop bottle holds. _____

5. Estimate how many cups of water will fill a paint can. _____

6. Estimate how many pints of water will fill a flower watering pail. _____

7. Estimate how many gallons will fill a bathtub. _____

Weight

By the end of the sixth grade, children should have ample experience measuring objects using ounces and pounds as weights. Also, relationships among ounces, pounds, and tons are provided. (See Activities 18.12, 18.13, and 18.14.) Students need to be able to select the appropriate unit for a given situation. For example, often elementary textbooks have children completing such conversions as 3 lb = ☐ oz. Also, symbols for ounce, pound, and ton are to be mastered. Relationship among units are shown in the following list.

16 ounces (oz) = 1 pound (lb)
2000 pounds (lb) = 1 ton (T)

ACTIVITY 18.12

Estimating the Weight of Common Objects

This activity is designed to promote the ability to estimate common weights of household objects.

Children can guess the weight of common materials and then test their hunches by weighing the objects with either a balance or a bathroom scale.

1. Estimate how many ounces your math textbook weighs. _____

2. Estimate how many pounds the tallest boy in the class weighs. _____

3. Estimate how many ounces a baseball glove weighs. _____

4. Estimate how many pounds five books weigh. _____

5. Estimate how many ounces a box of candy weighs. _____

ACTIVITY
18.13
Personal Data

This activity helps children to relate customary units to their own bodies.

A data sheet can be filled out by each student. Practice in measuring is linked to personal knowledge. When appropriate, comparisons of heights and weights may be performed.

Name _____

Height ____ feet ____ inches

Weight ____ pounds

Reach ____ inches

Length of shoe ____ inches

Chest ____ inches

Waist ____ inches

ACTIVITY
18.14
Concentration

Here is a card game that you can play to practice measurement units at the intermediate-grade level. This is a variation of the familiar concentration game.

The cards are placed face down and then turned over. When a match is found, the cards are kept. The person with the most cards is the winner. Here are some sample cards.

foot	12 inches
quart	2 pints
4 quarts	gallon
16 ounces	1 pound
36 inches	1 yard
5280 feet	1 mile
boiling water	212°F
freezing water	32°F
3 feet	1 yard

Temperature

Fahrenheit temperatures are still in use today. Thus, as children mature through the elementary school, experience reading a Fahrenheit thermometer needs to be provided (see Activity 18.15).

Figure 18.9 shows a Fahrenheit thermometer and some important temperature readings. You can easily make a classroom model of a thermometer such as this by taking a piece of tagboard and cutting it into a large rectangle. Next, label temperature degrees from ⁻32°F to 212°F. At the top and bottom of the rectangle, cut a narrow slit as shown in the figure. Then take a piece of ribbon and color half of it red and the other half white. Insert the ribbon into the slits so that the back of the rectangle shows the red portion and the front side shows the white section. To illustrate temperature readings, gradually pull the ribbon near the bottom slit. This will pull the red portion of the ribbon to the front section of the thermometer and will conveniently illustrate various temperatures.

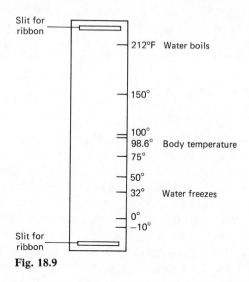

Fig. 18.9

ACTIVITY 18.15

Measurement Stories

This activity helps promote a coordination between language arts and mathematics. Students are to read and then correct the measurement errors in this story. At the sixth-grade level, students might create their own error-filled measurement stories and then see if their classmates can correct them.

We went to the beach the other day. It was 30°F, so we decided to get a cool drink. I got a 10-gallon glass of lemonade and an inch-long hotdog. My friend, who is overweight, weighs 175 ounces. So he ate only a 10-pound hamburger. We drove back home at 100 miles per hour and arrived in just a few minutes. The total trip was 350 miles long.

Perimeter, Area, and Volume

Concepts of perimeter, area, and volume are discussed at some length in Chapter 19. Current elementary school textbooks include examples of perimeter, area, and volume calculations for metric as well as customary units. Thus, included here are some brief examples of experiences common to several elementary textbook series. (Note that all of the figures in this section are scaled representations of the actual lengths.)

Figure 18.10 shows the sample perimeter of a rectangle. Again, area is found by covering a geometric figure with a prescribed square unit such as square feet or square yards. There are 12 square feet that cover the rectangle in Fig. 18.11. Thus, the area is 12 square feet.

The volume of solids such as the rectangular prism shown in Fig. 18.12 can be found by filling the solid with cubes of a prescribed size such as cubic feet or cubic inches. The volume of the rectangular prism in the figure is 24 cubic feet because 24 cubic feet can be placed inside the solid. The volume can also be found by multiplying the length, width and heights. $V = 2 \times 3 \times 4 = 24$. Thus, the volume is calculated to be 24 cubic feet.

Whenever possible, try to have children estimate volumes, perimeters, and areas. Take children outside to measure perimeters and areas of playgrounds, parking lots, doorways, window sills, and other convenient objects. In short, attempt to relate measurement experiences to daily life. All too often, elementary textbooks contain two or three pages of dry, lifeless measurement experiences. We need to broaden the horizons of children by showing them how mathematics relates to their environment. We can also add interest by using a computer, as Activity 18.16 offers.

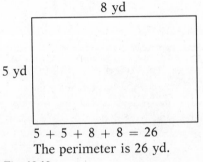

5 + 5 + 8 + 8 = 26
The perimeter is 26 yd.

Fig. 18.10

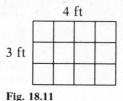

Fig. 18.11

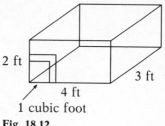

2 ft

4 ft

3 ft

1 cubic foot

Fig. 18.12

ACTIVITY
18.16

BASIC Program for Finding the Perimeter and Area of a Rectangle

```
10    REM THIS PROGRAM IS DESIGNED TO CALCULATE
20    REM THE PERIMETER AND AREA OF A RECTANGLE
30    PRINT ''THIS PROGRAM FINDS PERIMETER''
40    PRINT ''AND AREA OF RECTANGLES''
50    PRINT ''YOU ENTER THE LENGTH''
60    PRINT ''AND WIDTH''
70    PRINT ''WHAT IS THE LENGTH?''
80    INPUT L
90    PRINT ''WHAT IS THE WIDTH?''
100   INPUT W
110   A = L * W
120   P = 2 * L + 2 * W
130   PRINT ''THE AREA OF THE RECTANGLE'', A
140   PRINT ''THE PERIMETER OF THE RECTANGLE'', P
150   END
```

Sample Lesson Plan

The following lesson plan shows how we can creatively use the outdoors as a resource for creatively teaching about customary units.

> *Objective:* To reinforce the measurement units of feet and yards.
> *Materials:* Inch rulers and yardsticks. Each child should bring an old shoe.
> *Procedures:* Review the meaning of inch, foot, and yard.

Emphasize that we make choices regarding the selection of a measurement unit. Inches are used for smaller objects, feet for larger objects such as the length of a house. Yards are used to measure longer lengths such as the length of a football field.

Explain to children that the game "shoe launch" is played as follows:

1. Children place their old, untied shoe on their dominant foot. They kick it off their foot as far as they can.
2. Children measure the distance that the shoe traveled and record the length in inches and feet.

A follow-up discussion is held to compare measurements.

Evaluation: A time estimate of 20 minutes for this lesson is reasonable. Since children have paper and pencil, each child records the results of their classmates. They are, thus, kept active and disruptions are kept to a minimum. Also, children respond well to this lesson.

The next outdoor lesson will find out how many children are able to stand in a square meter.

Summary

In Chapter 3, beginning experiences with measurement are developed. In this chapter, an extension and refinement of measurement experiences for children is explained. A discussion of assumptions regarding the nature of measurement is followed by an explanation of metric system units and corresponding teaching activities. Following this, customary units are discussed and, again, teaching activities developed.

More attention is paid to the development of metric system units than customary units because it is possible that many readers are less familiar with these units than with customary units such as feet and inches. It seems that customary units, at the time of this writing, have maintained their dominance in American life. However, metric system units are taught in many elementary school programs. Teachers, therefore, need to be competent with metric system units. Similarly, examples of metric system units such as temperature reports in degrees Celsius are often observed in daily life. Therefore, children need to have competence with selected metric units.

For both customary and metric systems, the emphasis is on estimating and measuring objects. Measurement experience, whatever the system, must be an active process. Children need to measure and apply this valuable skill to daily life.

Discussion Questions

1. Consider a customary unit measurement such as 3 yards or 8 feet. Examine the facts and operations needed to convert this measurement to inches. Contrast this conversion with a change of 2.53 meters to 253 centimeters. Which conversion is easier?

2. Examine current elementary school textbooks to determine how metric and customary system units are developed.

3. Outline plans for developing a metric system learning center in your classroom.

4. Find some current educational catalogs and list some measurement devices that you would purchase for a classroom measurement experience (see Appendix B).

5. Write to the National Assessment of Educational Progress for recent research on children's measurement capabilities.

6. Write to the American National Metric Council or the U.S. Metric Association for up-to-date metric information. The addresses are the following: U.S. Metric Association, 10245 Andasal Avenue, Northridge, CA 91325; American National Metric Council, 625 Massachusetts Avenue NW, Washington, DC 20036.

7. Create some file-folder activities, card games, and visual aids for teaching customary and metric units.

References

Bitter, G. G., Mikesell, J. L., & Maurdeff, K. (1976). *Activities handbook for teaching the metric system.* Boston: Allyn & Bacon.

Bowles, R. D. (1971). Get ready for the metric system. *Instructor, 81,* pp. 61–70.

Gilbert, T., & Gilbert, M. (1973). *Thinking metric.* New York: Wiley.

Harrison, W. (1987). What lies behind measurement? *Arithmetic Teacher, 34,* pp. 19–21.

Helgren, F. (1973). Schools are going metric. *Arithmetic Teacher, 21,* pp. 265–267.

Hiebert, J. (1984). Why do some children have trouble learning measurement concepts? *Arithmetic Teacher, 31,* pp. 19–24.

Lindquist, M. M. (1987). Estimation and mental computation—Measurement. *Arithmetic Teacher, 34,* pp. 16–17.

Lindquist, M. M., & Dana, M. E. (1976). Let's do it—The neglected decimeter. *Arithmetic Teacher, 24,* pp. 3, 11–17.

National Council of Teachers of Mathematics. (1974). *A metric handbook.* Reston, Va.: NCTM.

National Council of Teachers of Mathematics. (1976). *Measurement in school mathematics.* Reston, Va.: NCTM.

Piaget, J., Inhelder, B., & Szeminska, A. (1960). *The child's conception of geometry.* New York: Basic Books.

Reys, R., & Reys, B. (1986). Mental computation and computational estimation: Their time has come. *Arithmetic Teacher, 33,* pp. 4–5.

Viets, L. (1973). Experiences for metric missionaries. *Arithmetic Teacher, 20,* pp. 269–273.

West, T. A. (1972). The case for metric units. *School Science and Mathematics, 72,* pp. 600–602.

CHAPTER 19

Geometry

Objectives

After reading this chapter you will be able to:

1. Develop activities for teaching informal geometric concepts to primary-grade children.

2. Construct teaching activities to help children identify lines, line segments, rays, and angles.

3. List fundamental properties of various polygons.

4. Experiment informally with concepts related to congruence.

5. Explain how motion geometry may be used to develop congruence of triangles.

6. Teach informally perimeter and area formulas of fundamental geometric figures.

7. Create activities for introducing the fundamental properties of solids.

8. Explain several activities and materials useful for teaching geometric topics to children.

Introduction

Geometry is generally defined as the study of shapes in space. The word *geometry* is derived from the Greek and means "earth measure." The importance of geometry in the elementary school curriculum has increased in recent years; however, research has indicated a need for greater emphasis on certain geometric topics. For example, the results of the Third National Assessment of Educational Progress (Lindquist et al., 1983) indicate that elementary school children are proficient in recognizing geometric shapes such as squares, rectangles, and circles. On the other hand, topics in metric geometry such as finding the area of a selected geometric figure are not well understood. In this study, over one-half of the 13-year-olds were unable to calculate the area of a rectangle when given the dimensions.

Thus, it seems clear that children need many experiences manipulating materials and exploring the perimeter and area of geometric figures prior to using formulas for calculation. Children need to discover geometric properties intuitively. Emphasis needs to be placed on real-world models (e.g., seeing triangular shapes in the environment). Strict definitions and formulas need to be delayed until children have a firm grasp of underlying concepts.

Early Geometric Experiences

Children live in a three-dimensional world, so their first experiences likely will be with three-dimensional models. Chapter 3, which discusses the foundations of beginning mathematics, emphasizes the need for topological concepts (e.g., inside and outside, open and closed) before considering Euclidean geometric ideas (e.g., squares and circles).

As we look at kindergarten mathematics curriculums, we see that children initially investigate boxes and cans and compare sizes and shapes of these and other geometric solids. At the intermediate level of the elementary school mathematics curriculum, these examples are named, respectively, as rectangular prisms and cylinders. At the kindergarten level, balls of various sizes are identified and classified as different from cans and boxes. Later we formalize language and call balls *spheres.* Figure 19.1 shows how the terminology evolves from an informal to a formal level.

Attention is also paid to recognizing squares, circles, rectangles, and triangles. These two-dimensional figures are part of Euclidean geometry, named after the famous Greek mathematician who developed geometric ideas that have lasted for over 2000 years. Classification—sensing similarities and differences—becomes important as well. Children are often given

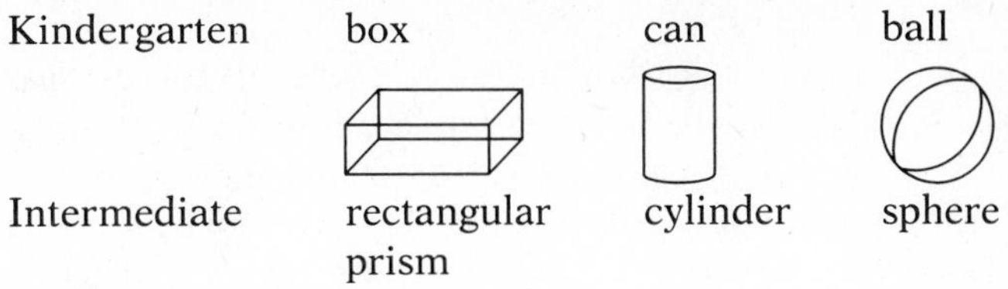

Kindergarten   box   can   ball

Intermediate   rectangular   cylinder   sphere
                    prism

Fig. 19.1

a set of geometric figures and asked to find the shape that does not belong, as shown in Fig. 19.2.

In Fig. 19.2, the triangle does not belong in the set because it is the only shape with three sides. Often, beginning mathematics students use commercial textbooks or printed handouts for these types of activities. It is much better to have tagboard cutouts of geometric shapes such as triangles, circles, squares, and rectangles so that children can handle and move these figures themselves (see Activity 19.1).

Fig. 19.2

ACTIVITY 19.1   Constructing Geometric Shapes

This activity relates mathematics to the construction of geometric shapes.

Take tagboard and have children cut out squares, circles, rectangles, and triangles. Then have them tape the shapes together to form images of people.

Patterns, discussed in detail in Chapter 3, form an integral part of beginning geometric experiences. Children are often asked to find the pattern and place the appropriate geometric shape so that the pattern is extended. An example of this is seen in Fig. 19.3.

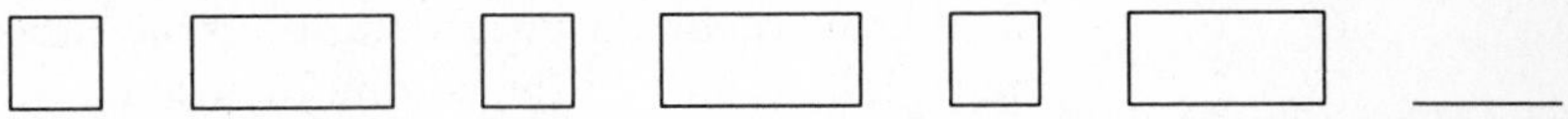

Fig. 19.3

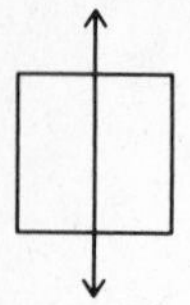

Fig. 19.4

The study of symmetry is often found in current first-grade texts as well. Symmetric shapes can be folded along a horizontal or vertical line (see Activity 19.2). For example, a line drawn through the midpoint of one of the sides of a square allows a fold to occur, which results in a perfect correspondence of points (see Fig. 19.4). Many examples from nature such as leaves and flowers can also exhibit symmetric designs.

ACTIVITY 19.2   Exploring Symmetric Designs

Children can explore symmetric designs in a variety of ways. Have them fold a paper in half, then draw a design. Cut the design out, and open the folded paper. This yields a symmetric design. See if you can make a heart-shaped design.

Fig. 19.5

In summary, children need to see fundamental geometric shapes from different points of view. Children tend to force geometric representations into standard textbook illustrations. For example, identifying the altitude (height) of triangle B in Fig. 19.5 probably would be harder than doing the same for triangle A because triangle A is pictured in standard textbook form. Therefore, at the primary-grade level, teachers should help children to see squares and other geometric shapes in a variety of ways. Teachers need to have students rotate triangles, squares, and rectangles to see that the shapes are still called by the same names.

Introducing Geometric Concepts

Points, Lines, and Planes

Line segment *XY*

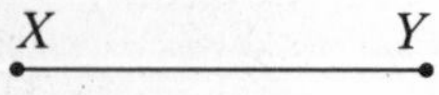

As early as the fourth grade, children begin to systematically study points, lines, and planes. Treatment of these topics is informal at first; gradually, symbols and abstractions are introduced. For example, a point is informally developed as a pencil dot on a piece of paper. Also, children are often asked to draw a line segment between two points, as shown in Fig. 19.6.

Fig. 19.6

Similarly, vocabulary and definitions have their place in the intermediate grades. Table 19.1 lists the commonly used terms, definitions, and symbols of popular elementary mathematics textbooks. These geometric terms should be identified through actual drawing experiences (see Activity 19.3). Not until the fifth and sixth grades are symbols such as $\overline{AB}$ for line segment *AB* introduced.

Table 19.1 Geometric Terms Commonly Used in Textbooks

Geometric Term	Symbol	Description
Point	•	A point is represented by a pencil dot.
Line	←——→	A line goes on forever in both directions. A line is named by two of its points.
Line segment	•——•	A line segment consists of two end points and all the points between them.
Ray	•——→	A ray has one end point. It goes on forever in one direction only.
Plane	▱	A plane is an infinite flat surface.
Parallel lines	←——→ ←——→	Parallel lines are two lines in the same plane that do not intersect.
Intersecting lines	✕	Intersecting lines cross at a point.
Perpendicular lines	✛	Perpendicular lines intersect at right angles.

ACTIVITY 19.3   Geometric Problem Solving

This activity can be used as an enrichment activity for sixth-grade students.

Two lines intersect in at most one point.

Three lines intersect in at most three points.

Complete the table below. Draw diagrams and look for a pattern in the numbers to help you complete the table. Study the differences in the bottom row of the table.

Number of lines	2	3	4	5	6	7	8
Maximum number of intersections	1	3					

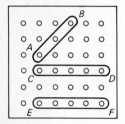

Fig. 19.7

A geoboard can be a nice vehicle for developing many geometric ideas (see Fig. 19.7). Commercial geoboards can be used to show line segments, intersecting lines, angles, and many other geometric ideas. Rubber bands can be attached to the protruding points to show a particular concept. Figure 19.7 shows $\overline{AB}$ (line segment AB) and $\overline{CD} \parallel \overline{EF}$ (parallel line segments).

The geoboard is an excellent medium for allowing children to manipulate and illustrate geometric concepts. Commercial suppliers sell geoboards that children can use at their desks as well as transparent geoboards, which can be placed on an overhead projector for large group presentations.

Angles

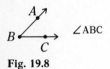

Fig. 19.8

An *angle* is defined as a figure that consists of two noncollinear rays originating from a common end point called a *vertex*. Figure 19.8 shows an angle and its label. Note that the term *degree* is developed in the fifth and sixth grades. This allows us to measure angles with a protractor (see Fig. 19.9).

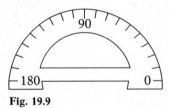

Fig. 19.9

Children need to discover that angles are classified into three main categories: right angles, acute angles, and obtuse angles.

A *right angle* measures 90°.

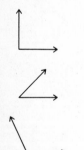

An *acute angle* has a measurement greater than 0° and less than 90°. Our example shows an angle of 45°.

An *obtuse angle* has a measurement of greater than 90° and less than 180°. Our example shows an angle of 115°.

Generally, children at the fifth- and sixth-grade levels should learn to draw and measure numerous angles (see Activities 19.4 and 19.5). Also, outdoor walks can sharpen perception of angles seen in the environment. For example, corners illustrate right angles and windows illustrate acute or obtuse angles. Thus, children can describe the angle images that they observe in the natural environment.

ACTIVITY 19.4   Identifying Angles and Lines

This activity helps children to practice finding various angles and lines.

The following point values are used:

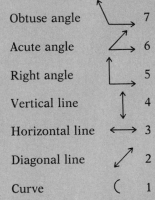

Obtuse angle   7

Acute angle   6

Right angle   5

Vertical line   4

Horizontal line   3

Diagonal line   2

Curve   1

Have children print their name and then determine the point values of their name, as shown below.

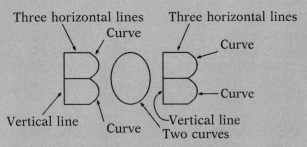

Three horizontal lines   Three horizontal lines
Curve   Curve
Curve
Vertical line   Curve   Vertical line
Two curves

The total value for "Bob" is 32.

ACTIVITY 19.5   Make a Clinometer

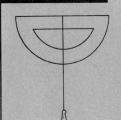

Another way to have children measure angles is to make a clinometer.

Take a protractor and turn it upside down. Attach a string with a weight at the end, as shown in the diagram to the left.

A clinometer can be used to measure angles of elevation or depression. For example, suppose we want students to measure the angle of elevation of a hill. Have a child stand at the bottom of the hill while another child stands at the top of the hill (see the diagram below). The children should be the same height.

The child at the bottom of the hill should line up a sighting of the child at the top of the hill by following the line at the top of the clinometer. The diagram to the left shows this. Notice the weight swings from the 90° mark. The degree of movement indicates the approximate angle of elevation of the hill.

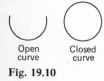

Open and Closed Curves

Open curve   Closed curve

Fig. 19.10

Current elementary school textbooks informally develop an understanding of open and closed curves. By using examples like those in Fig. 19.10, children gain some understanding of open and closed paths or curves at the primary level. These topological concepts appear early in the developmental stages of children.

Current elementary school textbooks have activities similar to the following:

Color inside each closed curve.

However current elementary textbook series do not systematically investigate open and closed curves beyond a preliminary introduction. Further work such as the determination of simple versus convex curves may be appropriate for enrichment. Readers interested in learning more about curves are referred to the National Council of Teachers of Mathematics (1969).

Polygons

During the intermediate grades, children begin to systematically study the qualities of polygons. The typical fourth-grade text defines a *polygon* as a shape made up of three or more line segments. The sides of a polygon form a closed figure that does not cross itself.

Triangles.   Polygons with three sides are called *triangles.* Children can use rulers and protractors to discover three types of triangles as follows.

Equilateral triangles—all the sides are the same length and each angle is 60°.

Isosceles triangles—two sides have the same length. The angles opposite these sides also have the same degree measure.

Scalene triangles—none of the sides have the same length. None of the angles have the same degree measure.

Right triangles have a right angle.

Children need to actually measure length and angles of triangles to validate their classification. Whenever possible, concrete models should be used to illustrate geometric figures. For example, straws can be fit together to show various geometric figures such as squares, triangles, and rectangles.

Quadrilaterals.   *Quadrilaterals* are polygons comprised of four line segments. A *parallelogram* is a quadrilateral that has the opposite sides parallel. A particular type of parallelogram is the rectangle, which has four right angles. Continuing, a square is a rectangle with four congruent (same-length measurement) sides. Finally, a rhombus is a parallelogram with four congruent sides. Figure 19.11 shows this classification arrangement. Included there as well is a trapezoid, which is a quadrilateral with one pair of parallel sides.

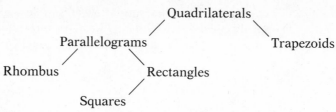

Fig. 19.11

Additional Guidelines for Teaching Polygons.   The preceding classification scheme for polygons is meant to be a guideline for readers. Most sixth-grade mathematics textbooks provide this information, but it is not expected that children will memorize the definitions. Instead, emphasis is placed on recognizing visual pictures of these figures (see Activities 19.6 and 19.7). For example, teachers may draw several geometric figures and ask children to identify each one. Also, many interesting projects can be related to quadrilaterals. Using tagboard and a coat hanger, children can make mobiles to illustrate geometric shapes. Finally, children can use a camera to photograph quadrilateral shapes found in nature. If the elementary teacher is apprehensive about children using a 35 mm camera, then the teacher can shoot the images that children select. After the film is developed, the class can make a bulletin board display of geometric images.

Some elementary mathematics curricula extend the meaning of polygons to those with five through ten sides. For convenience sake, Table 19.2 shows all of the polygons that elementary school pupils may encounter.

Table 19.2 Polygons

Polygon	Number of Sides	Drawing
Triangle	3	
Quadrilateral	4	
Pentagon	5	
Hexagon	6	
Octagon	8	
Decagon	10	

ACTIVITY 19.6   Sum of the Angles of a Triangle

This activity helps to establish the fact that the angles of a triangle total 180°.

Draw several triangles. Pick a triangle and measure each of its angles. Record the total number of degrees. Repeat this procedure with the rest of the triangles.

For fifth- and sixth-grade pupils, this is the preferred way to establish the fact that there are 180° in a triangle.

ACTIVITY 19.7   A Hands-on Method for Showing That a Triangle Has 180°

Another excellent way to develop the idea that there are 180° in a triangle is the following.

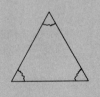

Draw a large triangle on a sheet of paper. Tear off the angles. Then fit them together.

Place a protractor so as to measure the resulting angle that has been formed. The angle measure will be 180°.

In summary, as children in the second and third grades investigate polygons, the initial emphasis is placed on visual recognition. Later in the elementary school program, classifications are made on the basis of relationships between sides and angles.

Circles

The study of circles begins in the primary grades. Children observe circular shapes in nature as well as in the classroom. As children are observing circular shapes, relationships such as inside and outside are developed. Later we call them the *exterior* and *interior* of a circle (see Fig. 19.12).

It is important that teachers use correct vocabulary when developing recognition of circles. A circular disk, shown in Fig. 19.13, is a circular *shape*, not a circle. A *circle* is a set of points, each point being a fixed distance from a center point. A circle model is shown in Fig. 19.14. Notice that the

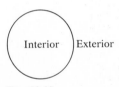

Fig. 19.12

Fig. 19.13

Fig. 19.14

visual image of a circle in Fig. 19.14 does not have its interior shaded as in Fig. 19.13. In the later elementary school years, when students study the properties of circles, difficulties emerge if students think of a circle as comprised of a boundary and an interior. Therefore, primary-grade students should, by all means, study circular shapes, but when the teacher draws a representation of a circle, care should be taken to make a proper description. (See Activity 19.8.)

ACTIVITY 19.8 A Circle Problem

Here is a problem-solving activity that relates to circles.

Separate a circle into two parts that have the same *area* but do *not* have the same *shape.*

During the intermediate grades, particularly at the sixth-grade level, various properties of a circle are developed including the following.

$$d = 2r$$

A *radius (r)* is a line segment from the center of the circle to a point on the circle itself.

A *diameter (d)* is a line segment from one point on the circle, through the center, to another point on the circle, as shown in the diagram. Notice that the diameter (d) is equal to $2r$.

The *circumference (c)* of a circle is the distance around the outside of the circle. Children can use string wrapped around a circle to measure its circumference.

During the middle school years (grades 6–8), children study a formula for finding the circumference of a circle. The value of pi (π) is usually stated to children without further explanation. Actually, π is an estimate of the ratio of a circle's circumference to its diameter. Children can measure several circular shapes and record the circumference and diameter of each. Further, using a hand calculator, children can discover that dividing the circumference by the diameter will always be close to 3.14. No matter what size circle is used, the ratio of circumference to diameter (π) will approximate 3.14. Mathematicians call π an irrational number because the decimal expansion of π does not terminate or repeat in a pattern. Since $\frac{c}{d} = \pi$, we can obtain a formula for the circumference by multiplying both sides of the equation by d. Thus, $c = \pi \times d$ is a formula for finding the circumference of a circle.

=========== *MATH HISTORY 19.1* ===========

Archimedes (287–212 BC) calculated the value of π to be 3.14. Electronic computers have calculated the value of π to over 500,000 decimal places.

Further Study of Solids

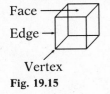

Face
Edge
Vertex
Fig. 19.15

During the intermediate-grade level, solids are studied in a more formal manner. For example, a box is now called a *cube* (see Fig. 19.15). The face is one of the sides. A cube has six faces. A vertex point occurs where two edges meet. In general, we speak of solids as having faces, edges, and vertices. Also, a rectangular box is now called a *rectangular prism* and a can is now called a *cylinder*. Figure 19.16 shows some of the solids that are identified at the sixth-grade level.

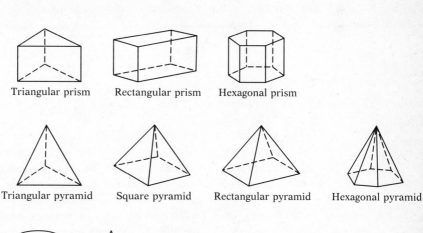

Triangular prism   Rectangular prism   Hexagonal prism

Triangular pyramid   Square pyramid   Rectangular pyramid   Hexagonal pyramid

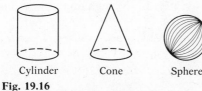

Cylinder   Cone   Sphere
Fig. 19.16

Most of the work with solids deals with identification (see Activity 19.9). A common activity is to bring everyday items to class and have students name the solids in question. For example, students can name the geometric names for such common household objects as an ice cream cone, a drinking glass, and a box of cereal (*cone, cylinder,* and *rectangular prism,* respectively).

ACTIVITY 19.9 A Discovery About Solids

A good enrichment activity for solids is to consider a relationship among the faces, edges, and vertices. A cube has 6 faces, 8 vertices, and 12 edges. Let us consider other solids by referring again to Fig. 19.16. We will complete the following table by listing the number of faces, vertices, and edges for the solids listed in Fig. 19.16.

Figure	Number of Faces	Number of Edges	Number of Vertices
Cube	6	12	8
Triangular pyramid	4	6	4
Hexagonal pyramid			
Rectangular prism			
Triangular prism			
Hexagonal prism			
Square pyramid			

Can you see a relationship among the faces, edges, and vertices?

Introducing the Concept of Congruence

The concept of congruence is taught through the intermediate grades. Many readers may remember their own high school geometry classes in which they "proved" two triangles congruent. At the elementary school level, the concept of congruence is treated intuitively. *Congruence* means that two geometric figures have the same shape and their corresponding measurements are equal. Thus, children need to measure angles, line segments, and polygons as one way of establishing congruence. Also, children can slide, flip, and rotate geometric figures to validate that they "fit together." These intuitive, informal procedures are advised when developing congruence ideas with elementary children.

Angles

Let us start with *congruent angles.* Consider Fig. 19.17, which shows two angles.

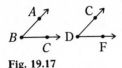

Fig. 19.17

∠*ABC* and ∠*CDF* are congruent because they have the same measure of 45°. Children can use a protractor to determine whether two angles are congruent.

Line Segments

For congruent *line segments,* a similar approach is advised. Two line segments are congruent if they have the same length. Children can use centimeter rulers to find that two line segments are congruent by measuring them. Some mathematics textbook series use a compass to construct congruent line segments, as shown below.

To construct a congruent line segment, open the compass so that the point is on *C* and the pencil tip is on *D.*

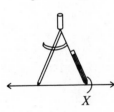

Keep the setting the same length and mark an *X* on the line with the pencil tip of the compass.

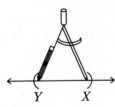

Repeat the procedure by reversing the compass and marking point *Y* with the pencil tip. Thus, $\overline{YX}$ is now congruent to $\overline{CD}$.

Polygons

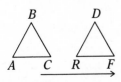

Fig. 19.18

When congruence of *polygons* is considered, most often triangles, it is best to have tagboard models for children to manipulate themselves. Essentially, congruence means the same size and shape. Children can move two triangles such as those shown in Fig. 19.18 to see that they fit. That is, students can slide triangle *ABC* so that it rests on triangle *RDF.* Note that the slide arrow is used in the figure to show the direction and distance of the slide.

This motion, called a *slide* or *translation,* is helpful for informally showing that two triangles are congruent. More formally, two triangles are said to be congruent when all corresponding sides and angles are congruent. Thus, six pairs of corresponding sides and angles are said to be congruent. For the example in Fig. 19.18, the following congruencies exist.

$\overline{AB}$ and $\overline{RD}$ are equal in measure.
$\overline{BC}$ and $\overline{DF}$ are equal in measure.
$\overline{AC}$ and $\overline{RF}$ are equal in measure.
$\angle A$ and $\angle R$ are equal in measure.
$\angle B$ and $\angle D$ are equal in measure.
$\angle C$ and $\angle F$ are equal in measure.

Children can measure each pair of sides and each pair of angles to investigate whether two triangles are congruent.

Considering that the images may not be lined up horizontally on a plane surface, we have a second type of movement for establishing two triangles to be congruent. This is a *flip motion.* Figure 19.19 demonstrates this motion for establishing the congruence of triangles. In the figure, triangle *ABC* can be ℓ flipped about line ℓ to show that triangle *ABC* is congruent to triangle *DEF.* Triangle *DEF* is said to be a flip image of triangle *ABC.*

A final motion that can be used to establish that two triangles are congruent is a *rotation* or *turn.* For triangles *ABC* and *DEF* in Fig. 19.20, a rotation or turn is used to establish that the two triangles are congruent. The curved arrow in Fig. 19.20 shows the amount and direction of the turn about the point *C.* In effect, each point on triangle *ABC* is rotated 90° and slid to its image point on triangle *DEF.*

Rotations or turns are rarely used in elementary school mathematics. However, the three motions of flips, slides, and turns are encountered during middle school mathematics enrichment programs. Flip motions lead naturally to the idea of line symmetry. Some examples of line symmetry are shown below.

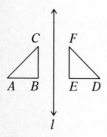

Fig. 19.19

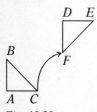

Fig. 19.20

Flip about line *l*

Flip about the diagonal

A mira is a useful device for exploring concepts related to symmetry. When the mira is placed on a piece of paper beside a figure, an image of the figure is seen in a mirror. With a pencil, the child can trace the image on paper that is placed to the opposite side of the original figure on the mira. Mira math materials are available through Creative Publications (see Appendix B).

As children study congruence, they need to move and manipulate geometric shapes and measure the sides and angles of polygons (see Activities 19.10, 19.11, and 19.12). Motion geometry usually is used as an enrichment device, particularly with gifted students. However, all children can benefit from the concrete experience of sliding polygons together or finding flip images related to lines of symmetry.

ACTIVITY 19.10

Symmetrical Lines

This activity can help children find lines of symmetry for geometric figures.

Draw two lines of symmetry for this square. Remember that you should be able to fold the figure along the line of symmetry to obtain two congruent figures. Repeat the activity for the following shapes. Equilateral triangle

Rectangle

Circle

ACTIVITY 19.11

Tangrams

Tangrams are a useful material for developing spatial relationships.

The seven figures in the diagram below can be put together to form a large number of geometric shapes. Squares, rectangles, parallelograms, and rhombi are only a few of the many geometric shapes that can be shown with tangrams.

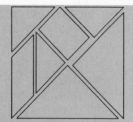

Use the seven tangram pieces to show a rectangle. Then try to make a parallelogram.

ACTIVITY
19.12

Geometric Shadows

A creative way to study images of geometric shapes is to investigate shadows.

Cut out these shapes: square, rectangle, equilateral triangle, and right triangle. Use tagboard so that you can hold these shapes firmly.

Go outside and hold each shape so that the sun casts an image of the shape on the ground.

Now rotate the shape and see what other images you can form. For example, can you take the square and show the image of a rectangle. Of a rhombus? Record your results for each shape.

The Development of Perimeter and Area

It is not until age 11 or 12 (fifth or sixth grade) that most children are capable of formally calculating the area of a rectangle. Even so, perimeter and area development need to be concrete and intuitive before abstract formulas are applied.

During the primary grades, children are asked to determine which of two geometric figures is largest or which has a greater distance around it. Area is calculated concretely by simply counting the number of tiles needed to cover a geometric region. For example, elementary texts at the third-grade level show activities such as this:

Count the tiles to find the area of this geometric figure.

Perimeter

At the fifth- and sixth-grade levels, children systematically study perimeter. Most experience with finding the perimeter of geometric figures is done with squares and rectangles (see Activity 19.13). The following teaching strategy may be used to develop a formula for finding the perimeter of a rectangle.

Measure the perimeter of the following rectangles and record the results in a table.

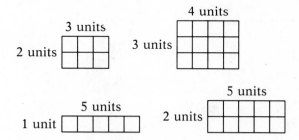

Children can count the units to measure the dimensions of each rectangle. The results of the exploration are shown in the following table.

Length	Width	Perimeter
3	2	$10 = (2 \times 3) + (2 \times 2)$
4	3	$14 = (2 \times 4) + (2 \times 3)$
4	1	$10 = (2 \times 4) + (2 \times 1)$
5	2	$14 = (2 \times 5) + (2 \times 2)$

After numerous experiences using rectangles drawn on graph paper and measuring the distances around the figures, children can be led to generalize the idea that the perimeter of rectangle can be found by the following formula: $P = 2\ell + 2w$. Teachers can raise several questions such as the following:

1. Are the two length measurements of a rectangle the same?
2. Are the two width measurements the same?
3. What is the value of the length measurement when it is doubled?
4. What is the value of the width measurement when it is doubled?
5. Suppose we add these two numbers. Do we get the value of perimeter?
6. Suppose we let ℓ stand for any length measurement. Is 2ℓ the value for the length when it has been doubled?
7. Supposed we let w stand for any width measurement. Is $2w$ the value for the width when it has been doubled?

8. Is $P = 2\ell + 2w$ a suitable formula for finding the value of the perimeter of a rectangle?

For squares and other geometric figures, the same inductive procedure can be used prior to the development of perimeter formulas. Most elementary textbooks today develop metric geometry ideas with customary (inches and feet) as well as metric system measurements (centimeters and meters).

ACTIVITY 19.13

Perimeter Problems

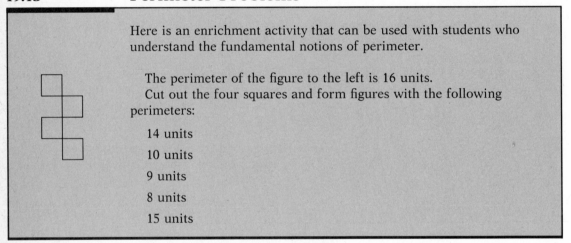

Here is an enrichment activity that can be used with students who understand the fundamental notions of perimeter.

The perimeter of the figure to the left is 16 units.
Cut out the four squares and form figures with the following perimeters:

14 units

10 units

9 units

8 units

15 units

Area of Squares and Rectangles

Area involves covering a geometric region with a square unit. We speak of square miles, square feet, square centimeters, and square meters, among others, when we talk about area. Elementary school students need to cover many squares and rectangles with square tiles before they apply formulas for calculation. One activity is to cut out square units, perhaps square centimeters, and to place a larger square on the floor. Children can place square tiles on the large square until it has been covered completely.

After several experiences covering various squares with selected square units, children are ready to record their results in tabular form (see below) and make the generalization that the area of a square is given by the formula $A = s^2$.

Side Length	Area
4 units	16 square units
3 units	9 square units
2 units	4 square units
6 units	36 square units
S	s^2

Continuing, the area of a rectangle needs to be developed intuitively. Some teachers use graph paper as a material for children to use. Children can shade in squares and determine the area of various-sized rectangles. Also, a geoboard (see Fig. 19.7) can be used to help children find the area of various rectangles. After several experiences, children can be led to find the area formula for rectangles. The following scenario shows how an elementary school teacher might lead the class to this discovery.

Teacher: Today we have a table summarizing our work with the area of a rectangle. Can anyone find a quick way of using the length and width measurements to obtain the area?

Length	Width	Area
4 cm	3 cm	12 cm²
2 cm	2 cm	8 cm²
5 cm	3 cm	15 cm²
8 cm	4 cm	32 cm²
5 cm	1 cm	5 cm²

Eventually, a student discovers that the length and width can be multiplied to obtain the area. However, the teacher might further refine the student's discovery by suggesting that if l stands for any length value and w stands for any width value, then what general formula would yield the area of a given rectangle? After pausing for a while, a student might offer $A = l \times w$ as a reasonable formula. To provide closure to the lesson, the teacher could have students practice finding the area of selected rectangles by using the area formula.

Area of Parallelograms

Graph paper can be an effective vehicle for developing the area of a parallelogram.

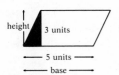

Each child can be given a sheet of graph paper and asked to draw a parallelogram. The teacher can develop the idea that the base is 5 units and the height is 3 units, as shown in the diagram.

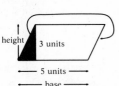

Children can use scissors and cut the triangle along the dotted line shown in the diagram. It can then be placed along the opposite end of the parallelogram.

Thus, we now have a rectangle whose base is 5 units and height 3 units. The area formula for a rectangle tells us the area is 15 square units ($A = b \times h$).

Children can explore this finding by drawing other parallelograms and using scissors to construct rectangles. After understanding has been developed, application can be practiced by using the parallelogram area formula to solve real-world problems. One such problem is shown below.

A field shaped as a parallelogram has a base of 100 m and a height of 85 m. How many square meters of area are contained in the field?

Area of Triangles

There are several materials that are useful for developing the area of a triangle with children. One of these is to give each child tracing paper and have them perform the following activity.

Two congruent equilateral triangles are drawn. We start with an equilateral triangle that has a base of 3 units and height or altitude of 2 units.

Children are instructed to make two tracings of this triangle. Suppose we wish to find the area of *one* of the triangles shown in the diagram.

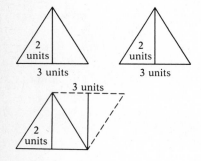

Children are directed to cut out the two triangles. Next, they fit them together to form a parallelogram. The area of this parallelogram is given by the formula $A = b \times h$. In this case, the area $A = 2 \times 3 = 6$ square units. But, in effect, we have doubled the area of the original triangles. So, the area of one of them is given by the formula $A = \dfrac{1}{2} (b \times h)$.

The preceding activity can be repeated with right triangles and scalene triangles. After completing the activities, children are led to the generalization that the area of a triangle is given by the formula $A = \dfrac{1}{2} (b \times h)$.

Area of Circles

Finding the area of a circle is usually delayed until the seventh- or eighth-grade level. However, at times, gifted elementary students investigate an informal procedure for finding the area of a circle. The following activity is suggested as an informal approach. It is assumed here that children already know that the circumference of a circle is given by the formulas $C = \pi \times d$ and $C = 2\pi r$.

Make a ditto sheet containing a large circle and draw in numerous radii to form several regions that approximate triangular regions (see the diagram). Have the students cut the circle in half along any diameter.

Next, children should cut along the radii up to the circle, being careful not to cut through the circumference of the circle. This yields two cutout strips, as shown in the diagram.

   Top half of radii cut

   Bottom half of radii cut

The strips should be put together to form a "parallelogram," the "base" of which is one-half of the circumference of $2\pi r$. The "height" of the "parallelogram" is r. Thus, the area of this parallelogram is $\pi r \times r = \pi r^2$. Since we approximated the area of the original circle, its area is πr^2. Thus, the most common area formula for a circle is $A = \pi r^2$.

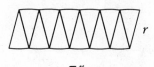

Surface Areas

Sometimes fifth and sixth graders investigate the surface area of a rectangular prism. A teacher can bring to class a box to use as a model of a rectangular prism (see Fig. 19.21). Note that there are six faces on the rectangular prism. To find the surface area of this rectangular prism, children need to find the area of each face. Since we have six rectangles on the faces, the following calculations yield the desired result. Note also that the six faces, all rectangles, can be labeled A through F as is done here.

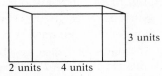

2 units   4 units

3 units

Fig. 19.21

Area of face A = 2 × 3 =   6 square units

Area of face B = 2 × 4 =   8 square units

Area of face C = 3 × 4 = 12 square units

Area of face D = 2 × 3 =   6 square units

Area of face E = 3 × 4 = 12 square units

Area of face F = 2 × 4 =   8 square units

Total surface area: 52 square units

See Activity 19.14.

**ACTIVITY
19.14**

Geometric Visualizations

This enrichment activity can be used with gifted intermediate-grade students.

Do the two patterns pictured below fold into a box without a top?

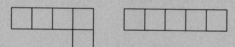

Draw as many patterns of five squares as you can that will fold into boxes without tops. If necessary, use scissors to cut the patterns out and actually fold the pattern.

Volume of Solids

Volume studies are undertaken during the later elementary school years. For able sixth graders, an investigation of the volume of a rectangular prism may be developed on an intuitive basis. Children should use cubes, perhaps cubic centimeters, to fill various rectangular prisms. After sufficient experience, a formula for finding the volume may be developed.

Suppose we have the rectangular prism shown in Fig. 19.22. Children can start filling one layer of this prism using a cubic unit shown in Fig. 19.23. Ten cubic units fill one layer of this prism. This fact can be found by multiplying 2 × 5 (length value times width value). Children can see that 40 cubic

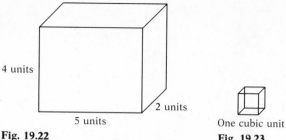

4 units

2 units

5 units

Fig. 19.22

One cubic unit

Fig. 19.23

units fill the prism, which can be found by multiplying the layers, 4, by the number of cubic units in each layer, 10.

After several examples, children can generalize the concept that the volume of a rectangular prism is given by $V = l \times w \times h$. (See Activities 19.15 and 19.16.)

ACTIVITY 19.15

Spatial Relationships

This geometric activity uses toothpicks to form various geometric shapes. Thinking about spatial relationships is an important mathematical skill.

1. With 9 toothpicks, make the figure to the left.

    a. Remove 2 toothpicks and leave 3 triangles.

    b. Remove 3 toothpicks and leave 1 triangle.

    c. Remove 2 toothpicks and leave 2 triangles.

2. Use 17 toothpicks to construct the figure to the left.

    a. Remove 5 toothpicks and leave 3 squares.

ACTIVITY 19.16

Computer Graphics

This computer program, written in the BASIC language for the Apple computer, creates a geometric design of a Christmas tree. Programs can be created to show many artistic, geometric forms.

```
100    GR: HOME: COLOR = 4
110    FOR X = 5 TO 16
120    REM DRAW TREE
```

```
130    Y = -1.5 * X + 25
140    PLOT X,Y
150    NEXT X
160    FOR X = 16 TO 28
170    Y = 1.5 * X - 24
180    PLOT X,Y
190    NEXT X
200    REM DRAW TRUNK
210    HLIN 5,27 AT 18
220    VLIN 18,24 AT 15
230    VLIN 18,24 AT 16
240    VLIN 18,24 AT 17
250    REM DRAW LIGHTS
260    COLOR = 1: PLOT 10,15
270    COLOR = 1: PLOT 20,12
280    COLOR = 9: PLOT 15,10
290    COLOR = 9: PLOT 26,16
300    COLOR = 13: PLOT 16,16
310    REM DRAW STAR ON TOP
320    COLOR = 15
330    HLIN 15,17 AT 1
340    VLIN 0,2 AT 16
345    END
```

Summary

This chapter traces geometric ideas from the kindergarten to the middle school level. Essential concepts of two-dimensional and three-dimensional geometric figures are developed. Because of the importance of perimeter and area development of polygons, this topic is stressed here as well as in Chapter 18.

Discussion Questions

1. Locate any third-grade elementary textbook series and list the important geometric concepts it develops. Discuss with your class members how you would teach some of these topics. For one topic, describe the materials and procedures by listing at least five questions that you would use to introduce the lesson.

2. Create a lesson plan for introducing acute, obtuse, and right angles to children. State an objective, describe the materials to be used, list your procedures, and give some criteria for evaluating your lesson.

3. Develop a ten-item true/false test that measures sixth-grade geometric topics.

4. Which of the following figures can be traced without lifting your pencil or retracing an entire line segment?

Draw some figures that are traceable and some others that are not. Can you discover a pattern that enables you to discover quickly whether or not a figure is traceable?

5. Read the article by Renshaw (1986). Use the ideas presented there to make a middle school bulletin board display on symmetry.

6. Research the use of the LOGO computer language with children. Your sources can include library books and sample programming guides available through Creative Publications (see Appendix C). Develop some sample programs and use them with primary-aged children.

7. Toothpick puzzles can be interesting enrichment activities for the upper elementary grades. Here is one for you to try.

Move the smallest number of toothpicks to get the dot outside of the toothpick "glass." The glass should still be the same shape.

8. After consulting Arnsdorf (1978), compile a list of activities for a geometry unit taught outdoors.

References

Arnsdorf, E. (1978). Orienteering: New ideas for outdoor mathematics. *Arithmetic Teacher, 25,* pp. 14–17.

Bernstein, R., & Barson, A. (1975). Decoding student names, or if Alan is 42, then Robyn must be 82. *Arithmetic Teacher, 23,* p. 591.

Bright, G., & Harvey, J. (1988). Learning and fun with geometry games. *Arithmetic Teacher, 35,* pp. 22–26.

Burger, W. F. (1985). Geometry. *Arithmetic Teacher, 33,* pp. 52–55.

Cangelose, J. S. (1985). A "fair" way to discover circles. *Arithmetic Teacher, 33,* pp. 11–13.

Horak, W., & Horak, V. (1983). Geometry is right here. *Instructor, 24,* pp. 76–78.

Hart, K. (1984). Which comes first—length, area or volume? *Arithmetic Teacher, 32,* pp. 16–18, 27.

Lindquist, M., Carpenter, T., Silver, E., & Matthews, W. (1983). The third national assessment: Results and implications for elementary and middle school mathematics. *Arithmetic Teacher, 31,* pp. 14–25.

Mansfield, H. (1985). Projective geometry in the elementary school. *Arithmetic Teacher, 33,* pp. 15–19.

National Council of Teachers of Mathematics. (1969). *More topics in mathematics: Thirtieth yearbook of the National Council of Teachers of Mathematics.* Washington, D.C.: NCTM.

Renshaw, B. (1986). Symmetry the trademark way. *Arithmetic Teacher, 34,* pp. 6–13.

Shaw, J. M. (1983). Exploring perimeter and area using centimeter squared paper. *Arithmetic Teacher, 31,* pp. 4–11.

Thompson, C. S., & Van de Walle, J. (1985). Patterns and geometry with logo. *Arithmetic Teacher, 33,* pp. 6–13.

APPENDIX A

Mathematics Exams

Iowa Test of Basic Skills, Forms 7 and 8
Multilevel Edition: 9–14
Grades 3–7; mathematics skills—concepts, problems, and computation.
Riverside Publishing Co.
8420 Bryn Mawr Avenue
Chicago, Ill. 60631

Mathematics Test: Elementary Level
Grades 4–9; criterion-referenced; 7 tests; number and numeration, addition and
    subtraction with whole numbers, multiplication and division with whole
    numbers, operations with fractions, multiplication and division with frac-
    tions, measurement, graphs, geometry, operations with decimals.
McGraw-Hill School Division
Box 25308
Oklahoma City, Okla. 73125

Peabody Mathematics Readiness Test
Grades k–1; number, containment, size, shape, configuration, drawing test.
480 Meyer Road
P.O. Box 1056
Bensenville, Ill. 60106

California Achievement Tests: Mathematics, Form C
Grades 3–6; computation, concepts, and applications.
Del Monte Research Park
Monterey, Calif. 93940

Mathematics Anxiety Rating Scale
Grades 7–12; college and adult.
Rocky Mountain Behavioral Science Institute, Inc.
P.O. Box 1066
Fort Collins, Colo. 80522

Kraner Preschool Math Inventory
Ages 3–6; criterion-referenced test measures quantitative concepts acquisition
    and a norm-referenced subtest (Math/Screen) derived from KPMI mea-
    sures mathematics language development.
Teaching Resources Corporation
50 Pond Park Road
Bingham, Mass. 02043

Diagnosis: An Instructional Aid: Mathematics, Levels A and B
Grades K–3, 3–8; Survey tests—provide quick survey of broad areas of mathe-
    matical understandings and skills in numbers, addition, subtraction, story
    problems, geometry and measurement, multiplication and division;
    probes—designed to pinpoint student weaknesses.
Science Research Associates, Inc.
155 N. Wacker Drive
Chicago, Ill. 60606

Watson-Glaser Critical Thinking Appraisal
Grades 9–12; inference, recognition of assumptions, deduction, interpretation,
    evaluation of arguments.
The Psychological Corp.
757 Third Avenue
New York, N.Y. 10017

Stanford Diagnostic Mathematics Test
Grades 1.5–6.5; number system and numeration, computation, applications.
The Psychological Corp.
757 Third Avenue
New York, N.Y. 10017

Stanford Early School Achievement Test
Grades 1–1.8; environment, mathematics, letters and sounds, aural comprehen-
    sion, word reading, sentence reading.
The Psychological Corp.
757 Third Avenue
New York, N.Y. 10017

Metropolitan Achievement Tests: Mathematics Instructional Test
Grades K.5–6.9; numeration, geometry and measurement, operations and prob-
    lem solving (whole numbers), laws and properties, operations (fractions
    and decimals), graphs and statistics.

The Psychological Corp.
757 Third Avenue
New York, N.Y. 10017

Key Math Diagnostic Arithmetic Test
Preschool–grade 6; originally developed for testing educable mentally retarded
    children, items require almost no reading or writing ability. Content—nu-
    meration, fractions, geometry and symbols, operations and applications.
American Guidance Service
Publishers' Building
Circle Pines, Minn. 55014

Mathematics Material Suppliers

Activity Resources Co.
P.O. Box 4875
Hayward, Calif. 94540

American Home Economics Association
2010 Massachusetts Avenue, NW
Washington, D.C. 20036

Brooks/Cole
Ralston Park
Belmont, Calif. 91002

California State Department of Education
P.O. Box 271
Sacramento, Calif. 95802

Coronet Films
65 E. South Water Street
Chicago, Ill. 60601

Creative Publications
P.O. Box 10328
Palo Alto, Calif. 91303

Cuisenaire Company of America, Inc.
12 Church Street
New Rochelle, N.Y. 10805

Educat
P.O. Box 2891
Clinton, Iowa 52735

Eike International, Inc.
27882 Camino Capistrano
Laguna Niguel, Calif. 92677

Encyclopedia Britannica Educational Corp.
425 N. Michigan Avenue
Chicago, Ill. 60011

Enrich
3437 Alma Street
Palo Alto, Calif. 94300

Follett Publishing Co.
4300 W. Ferdinand Street
Chicago, Ill. 60624

Harcourt, Brace, Jovanovich
Orlando, Fla. 32887

Holt, Rinehart & Winston, Inc.
111 Fifth Avenue
New York, N.Y. 10003

Houghton Mifflin Co.
One Beacon Street
Boston, Mass. 02107

LaPine Scientific Co.
6001 S. Knox Avenue
Chicago, Ill. 60620

Little, Brown & Co., Inc.
34 Beacon Street
Boston, Mass. 02100

Macmillan Publishing Co.
866 Third Avenue
New York, N.Y. 10022

McGraw-Hill School Division
Box 25308
Oklahoma City, Okla. 73125

Charles E. Merrill Publishing Co.
1300 Alum Creek Drive
Columbus, Ohio 43210

Michigan Council of Teachers of Mathematics
2165 E. Maple Road
Birmingham, Mich. 48000

Milliken Publishing Co.
1100 Research Boulevard
St. Louis, Mo. 63132

Milton Bradley Company
Educational Division
Dept. AT–N
Springfield, Mass. 01101

National Council of Teachers of Mathematics
1906 Association Drive
Reston, Va. 22091

Phi Delta Kappa
Eighth and Union Streets
Box 789
Bloomington, Ind. 47401

Prentice-Hall Learning Systems
P.O. Box 47X
Englewood Cliffs, N.J. 07632

Prindle Webber & Schmidt
20 Newbury Street
Boston, Mass. 02116

Rand McNally Publishing Co.
Box 7600
Chicago, Ill. 60680

Random House
201 E. 50th Street
New York, N.Y. 10022

Science Research Associates
259 E. Erie Street
Chicago, Ill. 60611

Scott Foresman Co.
855 California Avenue
Palo Alto, Calif. 94304

John Wiley & Sons, Inc.
605 Third Avenue
New York, N.Y. 10016

Computer Software Publishers and Distributors

Active Learning Systems Inc.
5365-J Ave. Encinas, Suite J
Carlsbad, Calif. 92008
1-800-423-0818

Advanced Ideas
2902 San Pablo Ave.
Berkeley, Calif. 94702
415-526-9100

American Educational Computer Inc.
7506 N. Broadway, Suite 505
Oklahoma City, Okla. 73116
405-840-6031

Aquarius Instructional
P.O. Box 128
Indian Rocks Beach, Fla. 34635-0128
1-800-338-2644
in Fla. 813-595-7890

Berta-Max Inc.
3420 Stone Way N
P.O. Box 31849
Seattle, Wash. 98103
206-547-4056

Britannica Software
345 Fourth St.
San Francisco, Calif. 94117
1-800-572-2272

Broderbund Software Inc.
17 Paul Drive
San Rafael, Calif. 94903-2101
1-800-527-6263
415-492-3500

C&C Software
5713 Kentford Circle
Wichita, Kan. 67220
316-683-6056

Classroom Consortia Media Inc.
#1 Edgewater Plaza, Suite 209
Staten Island, N.Y. 10305
1-800-237-1113
718-447-6777

Continental Press
520 E. Bainbridge St.
Elizabethtown, Pa. 17022
1-800-233-0759
1-800-847-0656

Davidson & Associates Inc.
3135 Kashiwa St.
Torrance, Calif. 90505
1-800-556-6164
213-534-4070

DC Heath School Division
125 Spring Street
Lexington, Mass. 02173
1-800-334-3284
617-862-6650

Decision Development Corp.
2680 Bishop Drive, Suite 122
San Ramon, Calif. 94583
415-830-8896

Didatech Software Ltd.
3812 William St.
Burnaby, BC V5C 3H9
604-299-4435

DLM
1 DLM Park
Allen, Tex. 75002
1-800-527-4747
in Texas 1-800-442-4711
214-248-6300

E. David & Associates
22 Russett Lane
Storrs, Conn. 06268
203-429-1785

Educational Activities, Inc.
PO Box 392
Freeport, N.Y. 11520
1-800-645-3739
516-223-4666

Educational Publishing Concepts, Inc.
P.O. Box 715, 6N426 Riverside Dr.
St. Charles, Ill. 60174
1-800-323-9459

EduSoft
P.O. Box 2560
Berkeley, Calif. 94702
1-800-edusoft
in Calif. 415-548-2304

E.M.E. Corporation
P.O. Box 2805
Danbury, Conn. 06813-2805
1-800-345-2050
203-798-2050

First Byte
2845 Temple Ave.
Long Beach, Calif. 90806
1-800-523-8070

Focus Media Inc.
839 Stewart Ave.
Garden City, N.Y. 11530
1-800-645-8989
516-794-8900

Gamco Industries Inc.
P.O. Box 1911
Big Spring, Tex. 79721
1-800-351-1404

Hartley Courseware Inc.
133 Bridge St.
Dimondale, Mich. 48821
1-800-247-1380

Houghton Mifflin Company
Educational Software Division
P.O. Box 683
Hanover, N.H. 03755
603-448-3838

HRM Software
175 Tompkins Ave.
Pleasantville, N.Y. 10570
1-800-431-2050
914-769-7496

IBM
PC Software Department
One Culver Road
Dayton, N.J. 08810
1-800-IBM-2468

K-12 MicroMedia Publishing
6 Arrow Rd.
Ramsey, N.J. 07446
1-800-922-0401
201-825-8888

Krell Software
Flowerfield #7
St. James, N.Y. 11780
1-800-245-7355
516-584-7900

LCSI
1000 Roche Blvd.
Vaudreuil, Quebec J7V 6B3
1-800-321-5646

The Learning Company
6493 Kaiser Drive
Fremont, Calif. 94555
1-800-852-2255
415-792-2101

Looking Glass Learning Products Inc.
865 Busse Highway
Park Ridge, Ill. 60068
312-698-0290

MECC
3490 Lexington Ave. North
St. Paul, Minn. 55126
1-800-228-3504
612-481-3500

Media Materials Inc.
2936 Remington Ave.
Baltimore, Md. 21211
1-800-638-1010
in Md 301-235-1700

Micro Power & Light Co.
12810 Hillcrest Road, #120
Dallas, Tex. 75230
214-239-6620

Milliken Publishing Co.
1100 Research Blvd.
St. Louis, Mo. 63132
1-800-643-0008

MindPlay
100 Conifer Hill Drive, Suite 301
Danvers, Mass. 01923
1-800-221-7911

Mindscape Inc.
3444 Dundee Rd.
Northbrook, Ill. 60015
1-800-221-9884
312-480-7667

Orange Cherry Software
P.O. Box 390 Westchester Ave.
Pound Ridge, N.Y. 10576
1-800-672-6002
914-764-4104

Queue Inc.
562 Boston Ave.
Bridgeport, Conn. 06610
1-800-232-2224
203-335-0906

Random House Media
201 East 50th St.
New York, N.Y. 10022
1-800-638-6460 x5000
in Md. 1-800-492-0872
212-572-2433

Scholastic Software
730 Broadway
New York, N.Y. 10003
212-505-3000

Scott, Foresman & Company
1900 E. Lake Ave.
Glenview, Ill. 60025
312-729-3000

Society For Visual Education Inc.
1345 W. Diversey Parkway
Chicago, Ill. 60614
1-800-621-1900
in Ill. 312-525-1500

Softwriters Development Corp.
4718 Hartford Road
Baltimore, Md. 21214
1-800-451-5726
301-426-4460

Spinnaker Software
One Kendall Square
Cambridge, Mass. 02139
1-800-826-0706
617-494-1200

Springboard
7808 Creekridge Circle
Minneapolis, Minn. 55435
612-944-3915

Sunburst Communications
39 Washington Ave.
Pleasantville, N.Y. 10570
1-800-431-1934
914-769-5030

Tom Snyder Productions
90 Sherman St.
Cambridge, Mass. 02140
1-800-342-0236

Unicorn Software Company
2950 E. Flamingo Road, Suite B
Las Vegas, Nev. 89121
702-737-8862

Weekly Reader Software
Optimum Resource Inc.
10 Station Place
Norfolk, Conn. 06058
1-800-327-1473
203-542-5553

Word Associates Inc.
3226 Robincrest Drive
Northbrook, Ill. 60062
312-291-1101

WordPerfect Corporation
1555 North Technology Way
Orem, Utah 84057
1-800-321-4566

APPENDIX D

Sample Children's Books

Abisch, R. (1968). *Do you know what time it is?* Englewood Cliffs, N.J.: Prentice-Hall.

Anno, M. (1977). *Anno's counting book.* New York: Crowell.

Anno, M. (1979). *The king's flower.* New York: Collins.

Bayley, N. (1977). *One old Oxford.* New York: Atheneum.

Bishop, C., & Wiese, K. (1938). *Five Chinese brothers.* New York: Howard McCann.

Branley, F. (1976). *How little and how much: A book about scales.* New York: Crowell.

Cleary, B. (1968). *Ramona the pest.* New York: Morrow.

Dennis, R. J. (1971). *Fractions are parts of things.* New York: Crowell.

Elkin, B. (1957). *Six foolish fishermen.* Chicago: Children's Press.

Enskey, M. (1973). *Three sides and the round one.* Chicago: Children's Press.

Fey, J. T. (1971). *Long, short, high, low, thin, wide.* New York: Crowell.

Ford, H. W. (1965). *Dr. Frick and his fractions.* New York: Holt, Rinehart and Winston.

Froman, R. (1971). *Bigger and smaller.* New York: Crowell.

Heide, F. P., & Van Clief, S. W. (1968). *How big am I?* Chicago: Follett.

Hoban, T. (1970). *A bargain for Frances.* New York: Harper & Row.

Hoban, T. (1972). *Push-pull, empty-full.* New York: Macmillan.

Hoban, T. (1974). *Arthur's honey bear.* New York: Harper & Row.

Hoban, T. (1974). *Circles, triangles, and squares.* New York: Macmillan.

Kellogg, S. (1976). *Much bigger than Martin.* New York: Dial Press.

Kent, J. (1973). *Jack Kent's twelve days of Christmas* New York: Scholastic Books.

Kessler, E., & Kessler, L. (1966) *Are you square?* New York: Doubleday.

Mack, S. (1974). *10 bears in my bed.* New York: Pantheon.

Maestro, G. (1974). *One more and one less.* New York: Crown.

Mendoza, G. (1971). *The scarecrow clock.* New York: Holt, Rinehart and Winston.

Reiss, J. J. (1974). *Shapes.* Scarsdale, N.Y.: Bradbury.

Sendak, M. (1962). *One was Johnny.* New York: Harper & Row.

Sitomer, M., & Sitomer, H. (1976). *How did numbers begin?* New York: Crowell.

Spier, P. (1972). *Fast-slow, high-low.* New York: Doubleday.

Trivett, J. (1975). *Building tables in tables. A book about multiplication.* New York: Crowell.

Viorst, J. (1978). *Alexander, who used to be rich last Sunday.* New York: Atheneum.

Watson, J. (1977). *Disney's numbers are fun.* New York: Golden Press.

Index

Abacus, 96, 98, 99, 180, 233, 244, 320, 321
Abstract level, 9–10, 156, 344
Acceleration strategies, for gifted students, 151
Accountability, 37
Achievement tests, 49–50
Active learning, 10
Acute angle, 492
Adams, John Quincy, 461
Addends, missing, in conceptual problems, 141
Addition
  checklist for, 48–49
  of decimals, 380–385
  of fractions, 354–357, 359
  of integers, 417–419
  multiplication and, 288
  repeated addition technique, 170, 290
Addition, beginning, 196–204
  basic facts of, 214
  basic properties of, 212, 213
  counting and, 196
  inverse operation relationship of subtraction and, 211–212
  materials and strategies for, 200–204
  organization/memorization of basic facts, 214–217, 220–225
  set theory in, 197–198
  in vertical/horizontal formats, 212
Addition algorithm, 230–241
  estimation strategies for, 238–241

  with nonregrouping, 230, 231–234
  with regrouping, 235–238
  sequential approach to, 230–231
  verbal (number word) approach to, 232
Additive inverse property of integers, 416
Agenda for Action (NCTM), 8, 256
Aiken, Howard H., 12, 180
Aiken, L. R., 112
Algorithms, 230–254, 316–336
  addition. *See* Addition algorithm
  defined, 230
  demonstrating with hand calculator, 169–170
  division. *See* Division algorithm
  low-stress, 243
  multiplication. *See* Multiplication algorithm
  subtraction. *See* Subtraction algorithm
Al-Khowarizmi, 230
American Association on Mental Deficiency (AAMD), 130
Ames, L. B., 72
Analytical test, 50
Angles, 492–494
  categories of, 492
  congruent, 501
  measuring, 492–494
Anton, W. D., 113
Apraxia, 138

Archimedes, 499
Area
    of circles, 508–509
    customary measurement of, 482, 484
    with hand calculator, 176
    metric measurement of, 473–474
    of parallelograms, 507–508
    of rectangle, 507
    of square, 506
    surface, 509–510
    of triangles, 508
Armstrong, P. W., 434
Arnsdorff, E., 305
Array model of multiplication, 290, 302–303
Ashlock, R., 302
Assessment, 45–54. *See also* National Assessment of Educational Progress (NAEP)
    achievement tests in, 49–50
    of attitudes toward mathematics, 52–53
    checklist for, 48–49
    diagnostic tests in, 50–51, 234
    interpreting results of, 45–46
    interviews in, 47–48
    during lesson, 47
    of mathematics anxiety, 114
    for special education, 128–129
    standardized tests in, 52
Associative property
    of addition, 213
    of integers, 416
    of multiplication, 295
Assumptions, hidden, 15
Attention span, increasing, 132–133
Attitude toward mathematics. *See also* Mathematics anxiety
    female, 14–15, 112
    measurement of, 52–53
Attribute classification skill, 61, 62
Auditory counting, 66
Auditory perception problems, 136–137
Averages, 445–447
Averaging effect, 269
Avoidance behavior, and mathematics anxiety, 118

Babbage, Charles, 180
Babylonians
    measurement system of, 460
    numeration of, 87–88
    time concept of, 73
Back-to-basics movement, 6–8
Backup activities, 37, 38
Banker's Game, The, 94–95
Baratta-Lorton, M., 63
Bar graph, 442–445, 449–450

Barnett, J., 281
BASIC programs, 12–13, 180, 221, 309–310, 336, 484, 511–512
    for gifted students, 160–161
    sample, 188–189
Battista, M. T., 419
Beansticks, 244
Beberman, Max, 6
Becker, J. R., 112
Bedell, J., 113
Beede, R., 351
Beginning mathematics. *See* Mathematics, beginning; Mathematics, preformal
Behavior modification, 134
Bell work, 41
Benner, C. V., 91
Bestgen, B., 290
Betweenness, 79–80
Bingo, math, 303, 412
Bley, N., 233
Board games, for division facts, 308
Branca, N., 256
Breathing exercise, for mathematics anxiety, 120–121
Bright, G., 389
Brophy, J., 37
Brown, Joseph, 207
Brownell, William, 4–5, 221, 257
Bruner, Jerome, 21–23, 24
Buddy system, 43
Bulletin board
    in classroom management, 40–41, 66
    measurement on, 478
Bundling activities, 96
Burns, M., 37
Burton, G. M., 61, 63
Buxton, Jedediah, 174
Byrket, D. R., 90

Calendar, identifying patterns on, 241
Callahan, L. G., 50, 321, 393, 410
Calculator. *See* Hand calculators
Capacity measurement. *See* Liquid capacity units
Cardinal numbers, 65, 70–71
Carpenter, T. P., 249
Carr, K., 288
Castaneda, A. M., 63
Cautiousness, excessive, and mathematics anxiety, 115–116
Celsius temperature, 466–467, 469, 472
Central tendency, measures of, 445–447
Challenge Math, 184
Charged particle model of integers addition, 419

multiplication, 421–423
subtraction, 420
Checklist of concepts, in assessment
    process, 48–49
Chiarino, Giorgio, 400
Child-centered curriculum, 4
Chip-trading activities, 94–95
Circle
  area of, 508–509
  circumference of, 498–499
  diameter of, 498
  exterior/interior relationships of,
    497–498
  radius of, 498
Circle graph, 451
Circular shape, 497, 498
Circumference of circle, 498–499
Classification, 22, 60–62
Classroom management, 29–54. *See also*
    Assessment; Lesson plan
  effective, 30–31
  planning for, 31–32
  sexual bias in, 14–15, 112–113
  strategies for, 40–45
Clements, D. H., 185
Clinometer, making, 493–494
Clithero, D., 160
Clocks
  digital, 73
  reading, 72–73
Closure, 213, 416
Colburn, Warren, 3–4
Collection games, 93–95
Color-coded diagram, 233
Commutative property
  of addition, 15, 213
  of integers, 416
  of multiplication, 295
Comparison model of subtraction,
    205–206
Compensation strategy, 239, 249, 250
Competition, and mathematics anxiety,
    116, 119
Complex fraction, 365
Composite numbers, 425–426
Compulsive behavior, and mathematics
    anxiety, 118
Computers. *See also* Microcomputers
  defined, 181
  history of, 180–181
Concentration game
  addition/subtraction, 223
  fractions/decimals/percent, 410
  measurement, 480
Concept of order, 343–344
Conceptual problems, 140–141
Concrete level, 9–10
Concrete operations stage, 19
Conditions of Learning, The (Gagne), 23

Congruence, concept of, 500–504
Connectionism theory, 4
Connelly, R., 334
Conservation of quantity, 19–20
Consumer-related problems, with hand
    calculator, 176–177
Continuous models, 341
Cooking applications of measurement,
    78
Coordinate graph, 451–454
Copeland, Richard, 20, 61, 71
Corrective teaching, 13
Counting. *See also* Numeration
  addition and, 196
  practicing, 69
  rational, 65–67
  refinements of, 86–87
Counting persons, 98
Cousins, Norman, 122
Cox, Elbert Francis, 258
Cox, L. S., 50
Creative imagery, for mathematics
    anxiety, 121
Creative Publications, 503
Creativity, measures of, 148–149
Creativity activity, 146, 148
Cube, 499
Cuisenaire rods, 67, 68, 467
  addition, 201
  division, 298
  subtraction, 208
Cuneiform, 87–88
Cup, 477
Curves, open and closed, 494–495
Customary units of measurement, 465,
    475–484
  area, 482, 484
  length, 475–477
  liquid capacity, 477–479
  perimeter, 482, 484
  temperature, 481
  volume, 482
  weight, 479–480
Cylinder, 499, 500

Data collection, 173–174, 442
Davis, E. J., 305
Davis, G., 142
Decimal equivalents, 12–13
Decimals, 370–397
  addition/subtraction of, 380–385
  beginning concepts of, 370–379
  conversion to fractions, 377
  division of, 389–395
  equivalent, 374–375
  in exponential notation, 395–396
  fractions converted to, 377–379
  in measurement system, 459, 461
  multiplication of, 385–389

Decimals (*Continued*)
    ordering, 372–374
    reading, 375–377
    relationship with fractions and
        percent, 410–411
    in scientific notation, 396–397
Decomposition method of subtraction,
    242, 243
Deductive ability, 156
Degree, 492
Dependency characteristic, and
    mathematics anxiety, 116
Descartes, René, 452
Dessart, D. J., 93, 196, 242
Developmentally handicapped (DH),
    130
Developmental stages, 18–21
Diagnostic approach, 4
Diagnostic teaching strategies, 13, 108,
    248, 333, 334, 360
Diagnostic tests, constructing, 50–51
Diagram making, 266–267
Diameter of circle, 498
Diet, and hyperactivity, 133–134
Digits, 91
Diophantus, 199
Discrete models, 341–342
Distractibility, control of, 130–132
Distributive property
    integers, 416
    multiplication, 318–319, 327
Divergent thinking, 146
Divisibility tests, 429–430
Division
    conceptual problems with, 141
    of decimals, 389–395
    of fractions, 362–366
    with hand calculator, 169
    subtraction and, 288
Division, introductory, 295–301, 306–311
    basic facts of, 306–307
    checking by multiplication, 310–311
    impossibility of division by zero, 307
    measurement technique in, 296, 297,
        331
    memorization of basic facts, 308–310
    number line model in, 299
    partitive technique of, 296–297
    relating to multiplication, 297–298,
        307
    repeated subtraction method of, 299
    terminology and symbolism in,
        289–301
Division algorithm, 327–336
    diagnosing errors in, 333–334
    estimation strategies for, 335
    with hand calculator, 169
    partitive technique of, 328–332
    pyramid, 331
        with remainders, 334–335
        sample sequence for, 327–328
        zero difficulty examples, 332–333
Division squares, 308
Division track game, 370
DLM Teaching Resources, 137
Dominance test, 70
Domino cards, matching, 222–223
Dot cards, 209
Downie, D., 113
Doyle, W., 40
Dunlap, W. P., 53
Driscoll, M. J., 355
Dürer, Albrecht, 196

Educable mentally retarded (EMR),
    130
Education for All Handicapped Children
    Act, 128
Education of the Handicapped Act
    Amendments, 128
Egyptians
    measurement system of, 460
    numeration of, 88, 89
Enactive level, 21
English measurement system, 460, 461.
    See also Customary units of
    measurement
ENIAC computer, 180
Enrichment strategies, for gifted
    students, 151
Envelope
    addition/subtraction, 210–211
    computer, 203
Equal-addition method of subtraction,
    242–243
Equal sign (=), 200
EQUALS program, 113
Equation loop, 250
Equilateral triangle, 495
Eratosthenes, 256, 460
    Sieve of, 425–426
Ernest, J., 149
Estimation
    as addition strategy, 238–241
    characteristics of good estimators,
        238–239
    of decimal operation results, 370,
        383–384, 388, 394–395
    of decimal quotients, 394
    as division strategy, 335
    with hand calculator, 175–177,
        394–395
    in measurement, 459, 465, 476,
        478–479
    with microcomputers, 11–12
    as multiplication strategy, 326–327
    in percent, 408–409
    in problem solving, 278–279

of reasonableness of results, 249–250, 354, 383
strategies for development of, 87, 104–107, 219–220
as subtraction strategy, 249–252
Evaluation
of lesson, 38–39, 40
of student performance. *See* Assessment
Even numbers, 86
Examples and counterexamples, 37
Experimental probability, 436
Explorer Metros, 184
Exponential notation, 99, 395–396
EZ-LOGO, 190

Factoring composite numbers, 423
Factory, The, 158, 159
Fact Track, 184
Fahrenheit temperature, 481
Fathom, 460
Fear of failure, and mathematics anxiety, 116
Feingold, Benjamin, 134
Fennema, E., 112
Fermat, Pierre de, 434
Fine motor problems, 138–139
First Lessons in Arithmetic (Colburn), 3–4
Fishing game, 100–101
Flip motion, 502
Folsom, M., 199
Foot, 460, 461, 475, 477
Formal operations stage, 19–21
4004 microprocessor, 181
Fraction baseball, 358–359
Fraction board, 345, 351–352
Fractions, 340–367
addition/subtraction of, 354–359
beginning activities and concepts in, 340–353
concept of order, 343–344
concrete models of, 340–341, 351–353
conversion to decimals, 377–379
decimal equivalents for, 12–13
decimals converted to, 377
diagnosing errors in, 360
discrete models of, 341–342
division of, 362–366
equivalent, 344–350, 392
multiplication of, 360–362
number line, 342, 360
problem-solving activities with, 365–366
relationship with decimals and percent, 410–411
simplifying, 351–353
Fraction strips, 351
Friesen, C. D., 238

Front loading, 240
Fuller, Thomas, 174

Gagne, Robert, 23, 24
Gallimard, J. E., 289
Gallon, 477
Gallup poll, 30
Gauss, Karl Freidrich, 265, 271
Generalizations, 270–271
with hand calculator, 170–172
Geoboard, 63, 492, 507
Geometric shapes
constructing, 489, 496, 511
shadows as, 504
Geometry, 488–513
angles in, 492–494
area development in, 504, 506–510
in beginning mathematics program, 78–80, 488–490
circles in, 497–499
congruence concept in, 500–504
curves in, 494–495
defined, 488
perimeter development in, 504, 505–506
points/lines/planes in, 490–492, 493
polygons in, 495–497, 501–504
solids in, 499–500
terminology of, 490, 491
topics for emphasis in, 488
and topology, 79–80
from visual/spatial viewpoint, 13–14
volume studies in, 510–511
Gertrude's Secrets, 185
Gesell, A., 72
Get to the Point, 184
Gibb, E. G., 63
Gifted students, 16, 142–162
characteristics of, 143–147
goals for, 153
microcomputer use by, 159–162
program options for, 151–153
selection criteria for, 148–151
teacher attitudes toward, 149–150, 151
and teacher resources, 150–151
teaching strategies for, 153–159
as underachievers, 142–143
Ginsburg, H. P., 196
Glennon, V. J., 93, 321, 393
Gnagney, W. J., 42, 43
Good, T. L., 37, 301
Graph paper
color-coded, 233
models, 104, 317, 322–324, 380
Graphs/graphing, 449–454
bar, 442–445, 449–450
circle, 451
coordinate, 451–454
histograms, 443–445, 449

Graphs/graphing (*Continued*)
  line, 450–451
  probability, 437, 438
  in problem solving, 263–264
  of stock market fluctuations, 453
Greater sum game, 240
Greater than (>), 67, 141
Greatest common divisor, 352–353
Greatest common factor, 427
Greeks, measurement system of, 460
Greenes, C., 143, 144–145
Greenwood, Isaac, 322
Gregory, J. W., 52
Grossman, H., 130
Grouping
  estimation and, 105
  nonstandard, 103–104
Group motivation, 43
Grouws, D. A., 37, 301
Guessing, systematic, 36, 248, 272
Guided discovery approach, 21–22

Hall, G. Stanley, 4
Hamacheck, D., 2
Hand calculators, 10–11, 156, 166–179
  availability of, 166
  estimation with, 240, 251–252
  instructional strategies for, 169–179,
    210
  pattern finding with, 266
  percent with, 409
  in problem solving, 283
  pros and cons of usage, 166–167
  reading decimals with, 376–377
  in reading practice, 100
  selection criteria for, 168
Handicapped students, mainstreaming,
    17, 46, 47, 128–142
  adapting to needs of, 141–142
  attention control in, 132–133
  auditory perception problems and,
    136–137
  conceptual problems and, 140–141
  distraction reduction in, 130–132
  fine motor problems and, 138–139
  hyperactivity and, 133–135
  impulsivity control in, 135–136
  legislative guarantees for, 128
  with mild mental retardation, 130
  reading problems and, 139–140
  resistance to change and, 140
  with specific learning disability (SLD),
    129
  visual perception problems and,
    137–138
Hanger and clothespins
  addition, 201
  subtraction, 209
Hangman, systematic guessing in, 248

Hartman, R. R., 149
Harvey, B., 160
Harvey, J., 389
Heddens, James W., 48, 334
Hembree, R., 166
Hershberger, J., 143, 153
Hiebert, J., 74, 410, 477
Hieroglyphics, 88, 89
Hindu-Arabic system, 91, 92
Hindu Pyramid Puzzle, 157
Hirt, H., 434
Histograms, 443–445, 449
Hofneister, J., 443
Hollerith, Herman, 180
Holtan, B., 279
Hostility, and mathematics anxiety,
    118
Houlihan, D. M., 196
How Children Learn Mathematics
    (Copeland), 20
How to Teach Arithmetic (Brown), 207
Humor, for mathematics anxiety, 122
Hundreds board, 100
Hutchings, Barton, 243
Hypatia, 14
Hyperactivity
  defined, 133
  diet intervention for, 133–134
  environmental intervention for,
    134–135
  medication for, 134

Iconic level, 21
Identity element
  addition, 213
  multiplication, 295
Ilg, F., 72
Immerzel, G., 347
Impulsivity, control of, 135–136
Inch, 460, 475, 477
Independent Drill Mastery Tapes, 137
Individual Education Plan (IEP),
    128–129
Inhelder, B., 61, 434
Integers, 416–423
  addition of, 417–419
  multiplication of, 421–423
  nomograph, 417
  ordering, 416
  properties of, 416
  subtraction of, 419–421
Integrated circuit, 181
Intel Corporation, 181
Intelligence tests, 148
International Business Machine
    Company (IBM), 180
International system of units (SI). *See*
    Metric system
Intersecting lines, 491

Interview, in assessment procedure, 47–48
Invert and multiply rule, 363, 364
Iowa Test of Basic Skills, 148
IQ, of gifted students, 148
Isosceles triangle, 495

James, William, 4
Jarret, J., 238
Jefferson, Thomas, 461
Johns Hopkins University, 148
Johnson, M. L., 143
Judd, Wallace, 100

Kagan, J., 17
Kalin, R., 298
Kaseberg, A., 113
Katterns, B., 288
Key Math Diagnostic Arithmetic Test, 51
Kilogram, 463
Kindergarten. *See* Mathematics, beginning; Mathematics, preformal
Kindergarten competencies, 58–59
King's Rule, The, 159
Klitz, R., 443
Knifong, J. D., 279
Kouba, V., 257, 281, 370
K-P Diet, 134
Kramer, T., 216
Kratzer, R. O., 331
Kreinberg, N., 113
Krug, D. A., 216
Krutetski, V. A., 143
Kurtz, V. R., 58

Laing, R. A., 295, 327
Laotse, 82
Larson, C. N., 342
Lattice method of multiplication, 325–326
Learning Company, 185
Learning theories
Bruner, 21–23
Gagne, 23
integration of, 24–25
Piaget, 17–21
Skinner, 24, 25
Least common denominator, 354–356
Least common multiple, 356–357
by prime factorization, 427–428
Leblanc, J., 261
Lectures, 10
Leibniz, Gottfried, 289
Length, conservation of, 20
Length units
arbitrary, 75–76
customary, 475–477
metric, 463, 465–466, 468, 470, 471–472, 473
Leonardo of Pisa, 91
Lerner, J. W., 138
Lesson plan, 32–40
components of, 32
for division algorithms, 335–336
evaluation of, 38–39, 40
materials for, 36
objectives in, 33, 34, 39
procedures in, 36–38, 39
sample, 39–40
Less than (<), 67, 141
Liber Abaci, 91
Lindquist, M. M., 257, 288, 360, 370, 465, 488
Linear measurement. *See* Length units
Line graphs, 450–451
Lines, 490–491, 493
Line segments, 490, 491
congruent, 501
Line symmetry, 502, 503
Liquid capacity units
in beginning mathematics, 77–78
customary, 477–479
metric, 464, 466, 469, 470, 471, 473
Liter, 463, 466
LOGO programs, 81, 180
for gifted students, 159–160
sample, 189–191
Lo Shu magic square, 196

McDonald, M., 52
McKillip, W. D., 49
McLeish, J., 10
Magic squares
constructing, 203–204
defined, 196
fractional, 362
with hand calculator, 178, 384
Magnet schools, for gifted, 152
Mainframe computers, 181
Mainstreaming. *See* Handicapped students, mainstreaming
Mark I, 180
Martin, R. P., 115
Mass. *See* Weight (mass) units
Materials, lesson, 36
Math calendar, 43, 44
Math center, 30–31
Mathematical patterns, 159
Mathematics, basic skills in, 7–8
Mathematics, beginning, 58–62. *See also* Mathematics, preformal
computer usage in, 81
geometric tasks in, 78–80, 488–490
and kindergarten competencies, 58–59
measurement tasks in, 74–78
money concepts in, 73–74

Mathematics (*Continued*)
  number concepts in, 64–65
  numeral formation in, 69–70
  order relations in, 67–73
  ordinal numbers in, 70–71
  place-value concept in, 93–95
  rational counting in, 65–67
  time concepts in, 71–73
Mathematics, preformal, 59–60
  classification in, 60–62
  patterns in, 63
  seriation in, 62–63
  vocabulary terms in, 63–64
Mathematics achievement
  evaluation of. *See* Assessment
  and sexual/racial bias, 14, 112
Mathematics anxiety, 14, 111–126
  characteristics of, 115–118
  coping strategy for, 119–124
  measuring, 113–115
  physical symptoms of, 112
  sexual/racial bias and, 112–113
Mathematics day, 42
Mathematics instruction, 2–25. *See also*
    specific topics
  back-to-basics movement in, 6–8
  beginning. *See* Mathematics,
    beginning; Mathematics,
    preformal
  classroom management in. *See*
    Classroom management; Lesson
    plan
  current trends in, 8–17
  effective, 2–3
  of exceptional students. *See* Gifted
    students; Handicapped students,
    mainstreaming
  historical trends in, 3–5
  learning theories for. *See* Learning
    theories
  in "new math" era, 6
Mathematics resource room, 152
Mathematics structure, 15. *See also*
    Integers; Numbers
Math joke, 21, 24, 170
Math marks game, 309
Math rummy, 393
Matthews, W., 249
Maxfield, M., 331
Mayan numeration, 90
Maze, 137–138, 346, 385
Mean, 445–446
Meaningful instruction, 4–5
Measure, 458
Measurement, 458–485. *See also*
    Customary units of measurement;
    Metric system
  accuracy and precision in, 458–459
  assumptions of, 458

  in beginning mathematics, 74–78
  computer program for, 484
  cooking application of, 78
  estimation in, 459, 465, 476, 478–479
  history of, 459–461
  outdoor experiences with, 467, 483
  teaching guidelines for, 465
Measurement approach to order
    relations, 67
Measurement division, 296, 297, 331
Meconi, L. J., 113
Median, 446–447
Medication, and hyperactivity, 134
Megatrends (Naisbitt), 7
Mental-discipline approach, 4
Merwin, J. C., 49
Meter, 461, 462
  square, 474
Metric system, 461–474
  adoption of, 461–462
  area, 473–474
  conversion within, 471–474
  intermediate-grade instruction of,
    468–471
  and international usage, 464
  kindergarten instruction of, 75–76
  length, 463, 465–466, 468, 470,
    471–472, 473
  liquid capacity, 464, 466, 469, 470,
    471, 473
  origins of, 461
  perimeter, 473
  primary-grade instruction of,
    465–468
  temperature, 466–467, 469, 472
  units of, 75, 462–464
  volume, 464, 474
  weight (mass), 463, 466, 469–470, 471
Meyer, J., 115
Meyer, R. A., 295, 327
Microchip, 181
Microcomputers, 179–192. *See also*
    BASIC programs; LOGO programs
  access to, 11
  addition practice on, 221
  in beginning mathematics, 81
  decimal equivalents on, 12–13
  division on, 309–310, 336
  and estimation, 11–12
  geometry on, 511–512
  with gifted students, 159–162
  influence on mathematics, 11
  literacy courses, 11
  measurement on, 484
  number sequencing on, 102–103
  percent on, 410–411
  probability calculations on, 439
  software evaluation for, 185–188
  statistical calculations on, 448–449

strategies for use of, 41, 183–185
terminology of, 181–183
Mildly handicapped, 129–130
Mild mental retardation, 130
Mile, 75, 460, 461, 475, 477
Million, 232
Minnesota Educational Computing
  Consortium, 184, 185, 190
Minus sign, 4
Mira math materials, 502–503
Mode, 446
Model, constructing, 274–275
Money
  coin value relationships of, 73–74
  modeling decimals with, 380, 382
  modeling place value with, 96
  trading concept of, 74
Monte Carlo simulation, 452–453
More Teasers by Tobbs, 185
Moser, H. E., 221
Motivation
  group, 43
  with hand calculator, 177–179
  measures of, 149
  tone setting, 41
Motor problems, fine, 138–139
Mouton, Gabriel, 459
Moyer, J. C., 46
Moyer, M., 46
Multiplication
  addition and, 288
  of decimals, 169, 385–389
  division and, 297–298, 307,
    310–311
  of fractions, 360–362
  with hand calculator, 169, 170,
    171–172
  of integers, 421–423
  properties of, 295, 318–319
Multiplication, introductory, 288–295,
    302–306
  array model of, 290
  basic facts of, 301
  finger, 293
  memorization of basic facts, 302–306
  number balance in, 290, 291
  number line in, 290
  relating division to, 297–298, 307
  repeated addition model of, 290
  set model of, 289–290
  situation cards in, 291–292
  terminology and symbolism of, 289,
    293–294
Multiplication algorithm, 316–327
  estimation strategies of, 326–327
  with hand calculator, 169, 170, 171
  lattice method of, 325–326
  1- and 2-place numbers in, 318–322
  Russian Peasant Method of, 316–317

sample sequence of, 316, 317–318
two 2-place numbers in, 322–326
Multiplicative inverse, 365

Naisbitt, John, 7, 256
Napier, John, 371
National Advisory Committee on
  Mathematics Education
  (NACOME), 6
National Assessment of Educational
  Progress (NAEP), 15, 257, 281,
  288, 340, 360, 370, 375, 400, 488
National Council of Supervisors of
  Mathematics (NCSM), 7–8, 256
National Council of Teachers of
  Mathematics (NCTM), 3, 8, 11, 14,
  166, 180, 191, 256, 434, 495
*New and Complete System of Arithmetic,
  A* (Pike), 3
"New Math," 6
Nomograph, integer, 417
Nonproportional materials, 96–97, 98–99
Non-regrouping
  addition, 230, 231–234
  subtraction, 241, 243–244
Number accordian
  decimal, 374
  place value, 101–102
Number balance
  addition, 202
  multiplication, 290–291
  subtraction, 208–209
Number blocks, 233
Number cards, 225
Number concepts, 64–65, 86
Number curiosities, 429
Number family approach, 219
Number line
  addition, 202
  decimal, 371, 380, 385
  division, 299
  fraction, 342, 360
  integer, 416, 418, 420, 421
  multiplication, 290
  subtraction, 207–208
  walking, 86
Number March, The, 135
Number pattern, 231
Numbers. *See also* Integers
  cardinal, 65, 70–71
  composite, 425–426
  comprehension, 65
  divisible, 429–430
  greater-valued, 100, 107–108
  grouping, 103–104
  vs numerals, 87
  odd and even, 86
  order relations of, 67–69
  ordinal, 70–71

Numbers (*Continued*)
  prime, 425–426
  rational, 340, 364–365, 370, 400
  sequencing, 102–103
Number sentence, problem solving with,
    278
Number theory, 356, 423–430
Number tricks, 156, 429
Numerals
  formation of, 69–70
  vs numbers, 87
  reading, 99–101
Numeration, 86–108. *See also* Counting;
    Place value
  extending, 99–103
  Hindu-Arabic system of, 91, 92
  history of, 87–90
  place-value concept of, 91–92
  refinements of, 103–108

Objectives, lesson plan, 33, 34, 39
Obtuse angle, 492
Odd numbers, 86
One, 237
One-to-one correspondence, 64–65, 141
Operant behavior, 24
Order relations, 67–73
Ordinal numbers, 70–71
Oregon Trail, 185
Oughtred, William, 289
Ounce, 477, 479

Palindromes, 179, 238
Palmer, Hap, 135
Papert, Seymour, 190
Parallel line, 491
Parallelogram, 495, 496
  area of, 507–508
Parental involvement, as classroom
    strategy, 43
Parental rejection, and mathematics
    anxiety, 116–117
Partitive division, 296–297, 328–332
Pascal, Blaise, 166, 180, 434, 439
Pascal's triangle, 439–441
Patterns, determination of, 63, 264–266,
    489
Pelletier, K. R., 119
Percent, 400, 402–411
  circle graph of, 451
  in comparison of quantities, 402–404
  as estimation strategy, 408–409
  misleading uses of, 404
  patterns in determining, 404–405
  vs percentage, 404
  ratio and proportion in, 405–408
  relationship with fractions and
    decimals, 410–411
Percentage, 404

Perimeter
  customary measurement of, 482, 484
  metric measurement of, 473
  of rectangle, 505–506
Perpendicular line, 491
Personal data, measurement of, 476, 480
Peterson, P. L., 112
Phillips, B. N., 115
Physical exercise
  for hyperactivity, 135
  for mathematics anxiety, 123
Piaget, Jean, 10, 17–21, 24, 61, 64, 66,
    71, 77, 434, 477
Picture writing, 88, 89
Pike, Nicholas, 3
Place value, 67, 88, 90
  base-10, 95–97
  decimal, 374, 375–376, 384
  defined, 91–92
  diagnosing errors in, 108
  games for teaching, 100–103
  with nonproportional materials, 98–99
  with nonstandard groupings, 103–104
  with proportional *vs* nonproportional
    materials, 96–97
  in readiness technique, 93–95
  and regrouping in addition, 235
  research on, 93
Place-value card game, 101
Place-value pocket chart, 98, 320
Planes, 490–491
Plus sign (+), 4, 200
Pocket chart, 66
Point, 490–491
Polya, George, problem solving method
    of, 259–261
Polygons, 495–497
  area and perimeter of, 505–509
  congruent, 501, 504
Positive reinforcement, 24
Pound, 461, 479
Powers of ten, 395–396
Practice work, success rates for, 37
Praise, effective use of, 42
Predictions, 442, 447–448
Preformal mathematics. *See*
    Mathematics, preformal
Preoperational stage, 18–19
Price, estimating, 106–107
Primary Math/Prereading, 184
Prime factorization, 427–428
Prime numbers, 425–426
Private schools, gifted programs in,
    152
Probability, 434–441
  computer-assisted, 439
  experimental and theoretical, 436
  founders of, 434
  and graphing, 437, 438

intermediate-grade instruction of, 435–438
notation, 437–438
Pascal's triangle and, 439–441
primary-grade instruction of, 434–435
Problem of the Week, 41, 281
Problem solving, 11, 256–285
change of perspective in, 276–277
characteristics of good problem solvers, 258
classroom environment for, 257–258
vs computational exercises, 256
creating word problems for, 281, 283
current trends in, 8–9
diagram making in, 266–267
estimation in, 278–279
geometric, 274, 491
graph making, 263–264
in groups, 281
with hand calculator, 172–174, 283
identifying wanted and given information, 277–278
and job market, 256
microcomputer simulation programs for, 184–185
model making in, 274–275
of multistep word problems, 281–282
nontraditional, 9
with number sentence, 278
pattern finding in, 264–266
planning in, 9
Polya's model for, 259–261
reading comprehension in, 279–281
several solution possibilities in, 275–276
systematic guessing in, 272
table making in, 262–263, 264
working backward in, 273–274
working simpler problems in, 268–271
Proper subset, 197
Proportion, 401–402
Proportional materials, 96–97
Protractor, 492, 493, 495, 497
Public Law, 94–142, 128
Pull-out programs, for gifted students, 152
Punch and check cards, 305
Pyramid algorithm, division of, 331

Quadrilaterals, 495, 496
Questioning, 36–37, 257
Quotients, decimal, estimation of, 394

Radius of circle, 498
Random access memory (RAM), 183
Random sample, 447
Rathmell, E. C., 215
Ratio, 400–413
Rational counting, 65–67

Rational numbers, 340, 364–365, 400
Ray, 491
Rea, R. E., 58, 70, 78, 80
Reading problems, 139–140
Reasonableness of results, estimating, 249–250, 354
Reciprocal, 365
Rectangle, 495, 496
perimeter of, 505–506
Rectangular prism, 499, 500
area of, 509–510
volume of, 482, 510–511
Region model, 381–382
Regrouping
in addition, 235–238
in multiplication, 320
in subtraction, 242–243, 244–249
Reis, S. M., 148, 149
Related multiplication sentences, 300
Relaxation exercises, for mathematics anxiety, 121
Remainders, division, 334–335
Renzulli, J. S., 148, 149
Resistance to change, 140
Resource people, 42
Reys, B., 459
Reys, R. E., 58, 70, 78, 80, 239, 459
Rhombus, 495, 496
Riddles, 122–123
Right angle, 492
Right triangle, 495
Rigidity, 140
Rimm, S., 142
Robinson, Edith, 79, 80
Rode, Joann, 348
Romans
measurement system of, 460, 461
numeration of, 88, 89, 90
Rotation, 502
Rounding, 240, 249, 250, 326, 384, 388
Rowe, M. B., 257
Rulers, 75, 76, 466, 476–477
Rules, classroom, 40
Rummy card game, 393, 409
Russian Peasant Method of multiplication, 316–317

Sample, statistical, 447
Scale for Rating Behavioral Characteristics of Superior Students, 149
Scalene triangle, 495
Scavenger hunt, measurement, 475–476
Schoen, H. L., 48, 238
Scholastic Aptitude Test (SAT), 6, 148
Schroeder, T. L., 434
Science Research Associates, 184
Scientific notation, 396–397
Scott Resources, 94–95

Seboket, Severus, 91
Self-esteem, and mathematics anxiety, 118
Sells, L., 118
Semiconcrete level, 9–10
Seriation, 62–63
Sets
    addition, 198
    defined, 197
    multiplication, 289–290
    and subset, 197
    subtraction, 206
    union and intersection of, 198
Sexigisimal system, 88
Sexual stereotyping, 14, 112–113
Seymour, D., 250
Shape classification, 62
Sherrill, J. M., 242
Shryock, J., 447
Silver, E. A., 249
Similarities exercise, 147
SI System. See Metric system
Situation cards, multiplication, 291–292
Skinner, B. F., 24, 25
Slide (translation), 502
Smith, C. W., 298
Smith, H. L., 148, 149
Software, evaluation of, 185–188
Sovchik, R. J., 113
Sowder, L., 281
Spatial relationships exercise, for gifted students, 147
Special-class approach, to gifted students, 152
Special education
    assessment for, 128–129
    standards for, 130
Special schools, for gifted students, 152
Specific learning disability (SLD), 129
Speed, in mathematics, 116, 119
Speer, W., 48
Speilberger, C. D., 113
Spinner games
    decimal, 388–389
    measurement, 467–468
    probability, 435, 436
Square units, 506
Standardized tests, 52
Standard units, 458
Stanley, J. C., 148
Statistics, 442–449
    averages in, 445–447
    computer-assisted calculations, 448–449
    and data collection, 442
    erroneous, 448
    graphing, 442–445
    predictions from, 442, 447–448
    sample in, 447
Steiner, E., 113

Stern, Catherine, 67
Stern counting board, 67, 68
Stevin, Simon, 370
Stuart, M., 290
Subsets, 197
Subtraction
    division and, 288
    of decimals, 382–385
    of fractions, 357–359
    with hand calculator, 169
    of integers, 419–421
    repeated subtraction method, 299
    symbol for, 199
Subtraction, beginning, 196, 205–226
    basic facts of, 217
    basic properties of, 212–213
    comparison model of, 205–206
    inverse-operation relationship of addition and, 211–212
    materials and strategies for, 207–211
    missing addend model of, 206
    organization/memorization of basic facts, 217–219, 220–225
    set concepts in, 197–198, 206
    take-away model in, 205, 206–207
    in vertical/horizontal formats, 212
Subtraction algorithm, 241–252
    decomposition method of, 242, 243
    diagnosing errors in, 248
    equal-addition method of, 242
    estimation strategies in, 249–252
    with hand calculator, 169
    with nonregrouping, 241, 243–244
    with regrouping, 242–243, 244–249
    sequential approach to, 241–242
    verbal (number word) approach to, 249
Sunburst Communications, 158, 159, 184, 185
Sunshine subtraction, 211
Surface area, 509–510
Suydam, M. N., 93, 166, 196, 206, 221, 238, 242, 258
Swenson, E., 91
Symbolic level, 21, 22
Symmetry, 14, 490
    line, 502, 503

Table making, 262–263, 264
Tablespoon, 477
Take-away model of subtraction, 205, 206–207
Tangrams, 503–504
Task perseverance, measures of, 149
Teacher expectations, 149
Teasers by Tobbs, 159, 185
Temperature reading
    Celsius, 466–467, 469, 472
    Fahrenheit, 481
    in kindergarten, 78

Tests
  achievement, 49–50
  administration of, 119
  standardized, 52
Theoretical probability, 436
Thompson, C., 87
Thorndike, E. L., 4
Thornton, C. A., 233
Tic-tac-toe
  decimal, 375
  fraction, 342–343
  multiplication, 306
  problem-solving, 282–283
"Tiger bite" cards, 298
Time concepts
  clock reading, 72–73
  and digital clock, 73
  of duration, 72
  Piagetian research on, 71–72
Ton, 479
Toothpick shapes, 511
Topology, 79–80
Torrance Test of Creative Thinking, 149
Trading games, 74, 93–94
Transistors, 181
Translation (slide), 502
Trapezoid, 495, 496
Triangle
  area of, 508
  congruent, 501–502
  demonstrating 180°, 497
  types of, 495
Turns, 502
Tutorial programs, microcomputer, 184
Twin primes, 426
Two, 237

Unifix cubes, 200–201
Unit of measure, 458
University of Illinois Committee on
    School Mathematics, 6
Urbatsch, T. D., 238

Van de Walle, J., 87
Verbal approach, 232, 249
Vertex, 492, 499
Visual perception problems, 137–138
Vocabulary, development of, 63–64
Volume
  in beginning mathematics, 77–78
  metric measurement of, 464, 474
  of solids, 482, 510–511
Vox, K., 281

Washbow, C., 302
Weight (mass) units
  in beginning mathematics, 76–77
  customary, 479–480
  metric, 463, 466, 469–470, 471
Wheatley, G., 143, 153
Widman, Johannes, 4
Willoughby, M., 331
Wills, B., 347
Wills, H., 246
"Wipe Out," 100
WISC-R, 148
Women, and mathematics, 14–15,
    112–113
Working-backward strategy, 273–274
Workjobs (Baratta-Lorton), 63
Workjobs II (Baratta-Lorton), 63
Worksheets, creative, 139

Yard, 460, 461, 475, 477

Zarrojewski, J., 371
Zero, 88, 90, 92
  identity of, 213
  illustrating, 67, 141
  impossibility of division by,
    306–307
  number concept of, 67, 86
  origins of, 25
Zielsche, Shirley, 101
Zweng, M. J., 278